A VOYAGE WITH HITCHCOCK

A VOYAGE WITH HITCHCOCK

MURRAY POMERANCE

Cover image of Joan Barry and Percy Marmont in *Rich and Strange* (Alfred Hitchcock, British International Pictures, 1931). Digital frame enlargement.

Published by State University of New York Press, Albany

© 2021 State University of New York

All rights reserved

Printed in the United States of America

No part of this book may be used or reproduced in any manner whatsoever without written permission. No part of this book may be stored in a retrieval system or transmitted in any form or by any means including electronic, electrostatic, magnetic tape, mechanical, photocopying, recording, or otherwise without the prior permission in writing of the publisher.

For information, contact State University of New York Press, Albany, NY
www.sunypress.edu

Library of Congress Cataloging-in-Publication Data

Names: Pomerance, Murray, 1946- author.
Title: A voyage with Hitchcock / Murray Pomerance.
Description: Albany : State University of New York, [2021] | Includes bibliographical references and index.
Identifiers: LCCN 2021016721 (print) | LCCN 2021016722 (ebook) | ISBN 9781438485256 (hardcover) | ISBN 9781438485263 (ebook) | ISBN 9781438485249 (pbk)
Subjects: LCSH: Hitchcock, Alfred, 1899-1980—Criticism and interpretation. | Travel in motion pictures. | Thrillers (Motion pictures)—History and criticism.
Classification: LCC PN1998.3.H58 P67 2021 (print) | LCC PN1998.3.H58 (ebook) | DDC 791.4302/33092—dc23
LC record available at https://lccn.loc.gov/2021016721
LC ebook record available at https://lccn.loc.gov/2021016722

10 9 8 7 6 5 4 3 2 1

to
NELLIE

I've been abroad, and it's not good.

—George V

CONTENTS

Acknowledgments, ix

Introduction: Where We Go from Here, 3

1. Whither Thou Goest: *Psycho*, Metamorphosis, Mother, 8
2. "God made the country": Remember *The 39 Steps*, 68
3. "Where do you come from?": Hitchcock's Winged Victory, 108
4. Say Nice Things or *Dial M for Murder*, 154
5. *Rich and Strange*: To the End of the World and Back Again, 222
6. Legal Tender: *Suspicion*, Passion, Perplexity, 258

Notes, 325

Works Cited, 339

Index, 349

ACKNOWLEDGMENTS

For a project about voyaging one makes a voyage, and the beginning of this one was a long time ago. I am grateful to many generous souls now lost: the late Kenneth Boulding (Ann Arbor), the late Dennis Brisset (Buffalo), the late Henry Bumstead (San Marino), the late Herbert Coleman (Los Angeles), the late Guy Davenport (Lexington), the late "Doc" Erickson (Los Angeles), the late Edgar Z. Friedenberg (Buffalo), the late Erving Goffman (Philadelphia), the late Martin Gold (Plymouth, Michigan), the late Assheton Gorton (Montgomery, Wales), the late Max Lerner (New York), the late Paul Gary Levy (Hamilton), the late Talcott Parsons (Cambridge), the late Victor Perkins (Coventry), the late Rabbi Stuart Rosenberg (Toronto), the late Rabbi Eugene Weiner (Hamilton; New York), the late Norman Lloyd (Los Angeles) . . .

. . . and to many colleagues and friends who, thriving upon cinema as I feel I do, nourished this book, each in a unique way: Merle Benjamin (Toronto), Adam Brown (Toronto), Dan Cazzola (Santa Monica), Alex Clayton (Bristol), Tom and Verena Andermatt Conley (Cambridge), Gary Michael Dault (Hamilton), David Edelberg, M.D. (Chicago), Blake Fitzpatrick (Toronto), Jay Glickman (Albuquerque), Gayatri Gorton (Montgomery), Elliott Gould (Los Angeles), Tom Gunning (Chicago), Barbara Hall (Los Angeles), Tom Hemingway (Coventry), Christopher Husted (Los Angeles), Jason Jacobs (Brisbane), Steven Jacobs (Ghent), Ann Kaplan (New York), Mark Kermode (Hampshire), Andrew Klevan (Oxford), Bill Krohn (Long Beach), James Lawson (Vancouver), Matthew Leggatt (Verwood), Gillian Leslie (Edinburgh), Dario Llinares (Brighton), John Long (Buffalo), Douglas and Catherine McFarland (San Francisco), Stephen Miller (Manhattan), Jerry Mosher (Long Beach), Stephen Rebello

(Pasadena), Jenny Romero (Los Angeles), Bill Rothman (Miami), Fay Thompson (Los Angeles), Peter Treherne (London), Daniel Varndell (Southampton), Christina Wilkins (Winchester). Various forms of assistance came by way of institutions: Susan Halpert at Houghton Library, Harvard, Louise Hilton at the Margaret Herrick Library (Beverly Hills), staff at the McElroy Octagon House (San Francisco), and staff at The Winchester Book Shop (Winchester).

My colleagues and friends at SUNY Press have been their usual sprightly, amicable, talented, and very considerate selves. I thank Michael Campochiaro, Ryan Morris, James Peltz, Eric Schramm, and Aimee Harrison. And as we see in all the films examined here, no voyage is truly wonderful without the very best companionship, in my case that of Nellie Perret and Ariel Pomerance who always find the best star to navigate by.

A VOYAGE WITH HITCHCOCK

INTRODUCTION

WHERE WE GO FROM HERE

"Our voyage was very prosperous," Jonathan Swift writes in *Gulliver's Travels*, "but I shall not trouble the reader with a journal of it." Trouble? Well, reader, you weren't there. Here, to trouble with pleasure, I hope, is not a journal but a series of meditations, not even about the specifics of voyages along which Hitchcock escorts us so much as about his penchant for making narrative a voyage, and his even stronger penchant for putting his characters to voyages they sometimes recognize and sometimes do not. Journeys from placidity, from surety, from complacency, from stability, from the enforced orders of the civilized. Voyages away from silence, from indication, from certainty, from the past. Voyages of discovery, of embarrassment, of terror, of delirium. And voyages to . . . ? To further doubt, to further uncertainties? To illuminations? To the trouble of illuminations that are accompanied—as illuminations must be—by shadows.

Alfred Hitchcock knew what T. S. Eliot knew when he wrote that iconic line, "We shall not cease from exploration." He knew it young and he knew it old, he knew it framing a scene and he knew it effecting transitions forward and summoning recollections from the past. Those who have treated themselves to serious consideration of his films have repeatedly been stunned by the variety and magnitude and number of explorations he invokes and shares. While it is fair enough to claim that all his films—for that matter all films—are types of exploration, there are in truth some particular films where the problem of the voyage, call it moving forward, is articulated with express contrast and deeply affecting light. There is no claim to be made that the six films I write about in the following pages are *the* Hitchcockian voyage pieces. Only that each of them nobly, brilliantly, and with great evocation brings a voyage into our consciousness. That they are metaphors through which we can come to a new understanding of the voyage and its meaningfulness, and a new understanding, one hopes, of Hitchcock.

The analyses here work through: *Psycho*, a voyage into mystery, doubling, innocence, justice, horror, and ... and supremely, mystery, mystery, mystery. No one understands *Psycho*, one tries in vain to cut all the way into it and see the way the blood flows. In opening it, my sensibility finds repetitions, one after another, and the chapter tries to convey the tonal quality of repetition deeply implicit in the film. And the eerie quality of repetition talked about. *The 39 Steps*, a voyage about a voyager, trapped by circumstances that would never have befallen him had he stayed home, wherever home is, but that now hurl him forward into confrontation with the elements, with distrustful strangers, with nefarious agents, and with a culture he can only take as alien. Here is a film of loneliness and sadness, bleakness and exposure, and the chapter works to recreate that atmosphere as well as to reach for an understanding of what a secret might be. *The Birds*, about a young woman piqued by attraction and following her sensibilities by chasing a young lawyer to the California seaside where a cataclysm is on the verge of happening. Is she the cause of the cataclysm? Is he? Is anyone? And do the legion birds, who constitute the chaos, speak of it, plan it, intend it? Bird flying here, bird flying now, then later, then spontaneously, then after a warning, bird flying, bird dispersing; the chapter is written, as Gromek in *Torn Curtain* says, "strickly fer da boids." *Dial M for Murder*, stringing us along as accomplices to a cagey husband's almost perfect plan to get his wife's money. A voyage with echoes, a voyage in the present and the past simultaneously, and a voyage into the London middle class, but a voyage made with words more than movement. *Rich and Strange*, bringing the promise of freedom and the taste of promise, exit from a routine choreography, the exoticism of the self, all of which arrive through invocations of the East. Here, an analysis couched in mysteries, as such voyages were for western Europeans in the 1930s. And lastly *Suspicion*, a sweet waif's odyssey into terror, and a bizarre man of whom we may voyage toward faulty perceptions. In writing about this I wanted to touch on the tender strings of doubt. All six are well-known films, *Rich and Strange* least of them and

Psycho definitively most. In every case the analysis here takes us on a voyage that departs from the quay of accepted readings, heads out to sea, and does not exactly return. There are other Hitchcock films expressly invoking travel, such as *The Lady Vanishes* and *The Trouble with Harry* and *The Man Who Knew Too Much*,[1] but in order to suggest its contours and tastes one need not sketch the complete universe.

The voyage is central to both contemporary culture and cinema, the telltale art of modernity. Not only is cinema inherently traveling, frame to frame, scene to scene, but one participates in the experience of watching by way of a personal odyssey, a leaving behind of what is familiar and customary and an openness to encountering the strange and wonderful. This is one very good reason for going into a film with as little detailed knowledge as possible, so that the film can, itself, do the work of introduction and solicitation. The culture is obsessed with travel, movement, voyaging. Of the *Fortune* 500, all are principally devoted to the movement of goods, services, information, ideas, representations, reflections. But this is not to suggest that in the six films examined here there is nothing but voyaging, for surely there is a great deal more. The voyage is a metaphor for carrying us across the empty gulf of pure confrontation, a path toward reception.

Regarding Hitchcock's stories: it is sometimes regarded as a healthy challenge to take the Hitchcockian plot, in all its turns and twists, with the greatest seriousness, but in these chapters my principal regard is for the relationship between events and aesthetic context, the story's voyage into form. Hitchcock was a master of cinematic form, which goes far beyond contriving an elegant frame composition—always the case here—to include such elements as preparations, nuances, foreground-background relations, play with realism, rhythmic pattern, and tickling reiteration, not to mention reverberations, color nuances, manifestations of size, alarming choreographies, and twistings of time. The reader might consider it useful to watch each film before reading the relevant chapter, only so that the screen visions—as discreet from the narrative events—will be fresh in mind. Or, on another itinerary, to read each chapter as an analogue to the film, something of a stand-in. The text reaches to express details of the image.

There is a tradition of scholarship and analysis within which this writing stands. The close reading of V. F. Perkins asks for open-hearted and perceptually extensive attention to film in its details and its passages. The philosophy of Stanley Cavell asks for a fully devoted relation of perception to the perceiver's true experience. The aesthetic analysis of Abraham Kaplan asks for acceptance of the critical moment as ongoingly balanced by the creative one: in short, to attend not only to what is said by a piece but also to the challenges involved in making it. The criticism of Bill Krohn is a model of background analysis, most specifically of script versions and technical adaptations. The considerations of William Rothman extend themselves broadly over the space of each film he examines, demonstrating boldly how a discussion will suffer if it is curtailed too abruptly, how every movement of the film is essential. And there is ongoing reference here to a series of considerations of the filmic moment, as opposed to the lonely shot. I would openly disclaim any attempt to be definitive about these six films, hoping instead that my observations might tickle the reader into wanting further contact with Hitchcock by way of his work. Many of those who actually did have contact with him, who were involved in making at his side, have given me guidance along the way.

No voyage takes the voyager everywhere in a territory, no voyager discovers the universe. In this voyage, which these pages intend to incite, the voyaging reader will most happily avoid assuming I have a predilection for making a complete, total, and uncompromising map of the pictures of Alfred Hitchcock. For instance, with any film there are certain moments I choose to dwell upon and others I may seem to casually neglect, but the intent, I humbly affirm, is to make the dwelt-upon moments richer and more seductive, not to skip over what is essential. To put this another way: there is so very much in any Hitchcock film it is quite impossible not to skip over something, just as, crossing the great ocean, one can count only so many waves....

Each chapter here is a kind of voyage.

This volume is intended as a follower of two others. *An Eye for Hitchcock* (Rutgers University Press, 2004) dealt with *North by Northwest, I Confess, Marnie, Torn Curtain, Spellbound,* and *Vertigo. A Dream of Hitchcock* (SUNY, 2018) addressed *Strangers on a Train, Rear Window, Saboteur, Rebecca, To Catch a Thief,* and *Family Plot*. The structures of all three volumes are identical and make the same kinds of assumptions about this filmmaker's brilliant intent as marriageable with the reader's committed love. In the books so far, quite evidently, some quite provocative and wonderful films have been left to the side, and in apology I can say only that there must be a time for exploration and a time to cease from exploration with every project, and with every breath. The culminating volume of this Hitchcock Quartet, *A Silence from Hitchcock*, is on the drawing board. Hitchcock is a very great force. And he will repay our eyes.

London, Los Angeles, Toronto
June 2021

CHAPTER ONE

WHITHER THOU GOEST

Psycho, Metamorphosis, Mother

> Man, when we first see him configured in art, is a whole
> body. His fate is in his running legs and versatile hands,
> in his sexual organs and in his kinship to animals.
>
> —Guy Davenport, *Objects on a Table*

THE WATER RUNS

Poor, poor, not-so-poor, poverty-stricken Marion Crane.

Her sanctum of purification is broken, her *shadirvan* become an abattoir, her privacy invaded and shocked. The blood-letting efficient and wholesale. The carcass draped over the edge of a bathtub, exactly where diligent Norman will soon almost miss—almost, almost—a tiny dark drop when, to protect Mother, he mops up. Diligent Norman, loving Norman, O, mother! "Mother, mother! Blood, blood!" Yes, Mother and blood together. Mother's blood, the blood of innocence lost, the blood conveyor of nutrition, the blood of birth, the blood of engorgements. "Kill the beast! Cut his throat! Spill his blood!" (Golding 140).

"The aristocrat eats Nature," Jean-Paul Sartre writes,

and the product in whose form he consumes it should smell a little of entrails or urine; it is good that wool retain a musty smell of grease, that honey have a slight taste of wax, that the pearl be not quite round. Strong and vague odors, the taste of cooked blood, the exquisite imperfection of forms, the blurred discreetness of colors, are the best guarantees of authenticity. (361)

Yes: Kill-Drink. The waters of death. For real. Guaranteed authentic.

Permit an immediate interruption in the name of progress, for "Sometimes you have to go a long way out of your way in order to come back a short distance correctly" (Albee, *The Zoo Story*). In September 1960, when for the first time crowdfuls of people who had lined up for hours entered theaters and saw *Psycho*, they did not know that a death, a bloody death, would occur so brutally and so soon—soon, as it certainly felt—after the film began. More: they could not possibly have expected that the very famous Hollywood star, whose name was on the marquee—"and Janet Leigh," a teaser if ever there was one—might appear and disappear in a breath (Hollywood had not yet entered the age of the throwaway cameo). While Hitchcock had taken care to engineer a landmark exhibitors' agreement, ensuring that once projection began no one, but no one, would be admitted, nevertheless audiences—certainly the audience that contained me—knew only that the theater was clamping down, not who was behind the move, or why. A cold shock for the viewer, then, was the warm shock for poor, poor, not-so-poor, poverty-stricken Marion Crane.

Before she steps into the shower—*that* shower—(and I will return to it: we all return to it)—before she takes the decisive step across the threshold, she sloughs off her garment in the telltale unforgiving bedroom light (in Norman's direct line of vision, because he has become the second 1960 version of Peeping Tom who once lurked in Coventry[1]) and sits in her robe to check her finances, scribbling, thinking, gazing, thinking, thinking, thinking . . . then moves herself into the cloister tossing the scribbled note into the toilet, and flushes the toilet, and lets her robe fall, and turns on the water . . . to irrigate the Land of the Fisher King:

> He looked around him from that stand
> But saw no more than sky and land.
> He cried, "what have I come to see?
> Stupidity and trickery! (De Troyes, vv. 3037–40)[2]

Nothing so very peculiar here, perhaps, except that, now the showering having begun, as part of the viewer's cinematic experience of this, Alfred Hitchcock's admittedly most famous film, a certain oddness does inhere in the sound of water running:

> Water, water, every where,
> And all the boards did shrink;
> Water, water, every where,
> Nor any drop to drink.
> (Samuel Taylor Coleridge, "The Rime of the Ancient Mariner"
>   [1834])

The water, the boundless water, running and running and running into our ears, when nothing else is going on for us to apprehend. Running water, a sound of nature or of human foibles, a brook or a leak. Running to bless and enrich Marion, water from a font, in this rather cramped bathroom, and originating in what might well be a pool in the furthest faraway.[3] (Where does Marion's shower water come from?) Nothing else engaging, not *for us*, at least; and normatively so, since a person cleaning her body has for others only an objective value, and marginal value at that. Marion is not *actually*, though she may be metaphorically, washing a stain. She is just doing what anybody and everybody does in the tedious everydayness of life, and in privacy, and on her own. It's the end of a long day; clean up. The water tickles and rings, we hear it and hear it, cannot avoid hearing it, as though with some interest. We hear it more than she seems to: oddly in this so tidily visual a composition she seems very much *not to hear*. Is the running water a constant, ineffable reminder of where we are and what is happening there? A reminder permitting, even urging us to say, *This is but a perfunctory moment.*

For us at Norman's peephole a great deal was going on, of course: a good show (generically, originally). Norman used a hole in the wall and we have a screen. Query: if in some even vague way the rudimentary peephole is vaginal, and we are peeking, are we looking in or looking out? If the latter, perhaps we want to be born.

Certainly, in the little sequence of Marion's preparing to be nude, we are confused in stance and status. Who are we, at any rate, that we should be seeing this? Not that we shirked the chance to avail ourselves of so sweet a view. Looking forward with the inner eye to presentation of the naked nude. This isn't one of our familiars, not quite yet; nor is she even a stranger we have spied upon regularly. She is the Marion we saw Norman meet only moments before—"*Marie Samuels, Los Angeles.*" And because we knew her already, we saw the fakery of that name spring up from the page. He gave her a cabin; he invited her for chicken sandwiches and milk.[4] Naked for us but not for him, here is Attic Marion, thrilling sight, albeit fragmented for delight into parts, this part, that part (sculptures in the British Museum) as though she is not actually a person in the way that any one of us is, as though we have forgotten that when a person is naked before us the thrill comes not from how good-looking she is but from the conjunction of the very nakedness and our acute eye, the uncovered body and our uncovered eyes; from us watching what, having been taught not to watch, we want desperately to see. Naked, unknowing Marion. A vision to thrill, and proof of humanity. Marion of the Everyday. Marion innocently available to sight, and how quickly that sight would be rotted if just once she saw the seer seeing.

If she saw the looker, she would only be gesturing, and therefore implicating. Much better she be a stage performer who does not at the moment know where she is—sees no stage—is not aware there is an audience, does not think a show is in progress.[5] If we can snatch a *frisson* here, then, for us now, as there was in the everlasting past for anticipatory Norman, there *is* an event, and the sound of the running water soon afterward, for us a sound heard and for him a sound expected, with her standing ready at tubside, is a (non-Wagnerian) prelude. As Coleridge wrote, too,

I moved, and could not feel my limbs:
I was so light—almost
I thought that I had died in sleep,
And was a blessed ghost.

Marion lets the water run, run long enough that, before she pulls aside the curtain and allows us to step in with her, we can register the situation and also confess to ourselves that we are registering. Then, from inside the enclosure, at her side, we are given the ultimate proximal view, the most intimate of intimacies. The water pouring over her is all but upon us. We are all but cleansed, thinking to wash our own pasts away.

Here I pause yet again, but I will not be holding back from sharing some of *Psycho*'s secrets.

We are in the know, either because we have seen *Psycho* before or because we have heard considerable talk about it or because we have read the reviews (heaven assist us!) or because scholarship has blared its interests in our ears, that something not so very nice will happen to Marion in this shower, and very soon. We know whither she goeth. Or else, seeing the film for the first time, we project an imagination of a new tomorrow. That new tomorrow is what one has when the past is washed away. Either remembering to keep an eye out for Death, then, or else daydreaming of upcoming happiness, whichever it is, as we watch the *Psycho* shower scene, this altar of justifiable celebration, we can fail to grasp something palpable but invisible:

That Marion is already not alone. That *we are there*.

"Naïve," virginal, stepping into the tub with her, we feel no shame, no embarrassment, no hesitation. No distracting pinch. We want to be there; or at least we *don't want not to be*. This is where we belong, the tabernacle of release. If for even a breath one can feel comforted under this stream, inside this shower at the Bates Motel with this woman who has arrived out of the driving rain, if we can sense truth inside a shower *in a movie*, then through the embracing sound of the water running it becomes possible even to forget that this is a movie, forget ourselves, forget the world. The camera makes us strikingly present, takes us through the screen (the shower curtain) into the cell of eventfulness. And the water is the signal of that eventfulness, never ceasing to remind our ears.

Yet sharing space with her, one is also a little separate from Marion. Inside, not outside the shower, to be sure, yet absolutely not part of the world of which Marion is conscious. In the space, but not in the diegesis. While it is one thing to recognize that in cinema and other theatricalities the audience is generally unrecognized by the characters, here our separation feels stranger, more acute, because the shower is a very small auditorium in itself, and with the water running, still running, still running, and our viewing consciousness established inside there, we can sense no effective "stageline" or "axis" bounding us away from the action—save cinema itself, of which we would wish to notice nothing.[6] If we are in such a place while Marion is, too, it is a queer sensation to accept the implied tissue keeping her away, to sharply realize that she does not see us, even though of course she cannot and must not. We are invisible but *so close!* Of all cinematic moments, all instantiations of our following this Law of Watching, here is one in which our acknowledgment of a character's being innocent of our presence presents a challenge in itself. Innocence challenged and thus not such innocence.

Could these filmic events, just as I am describing them, survive on their own? That is to say: a healthy young woman strips and turns on a shower. Enters the shower. With us. Is repeatedly stabbed there and dies while we watch. Blood speeds down the drain, the eye in her face superimposed to become the drain hole, so that the blood is flowing into the victim's eye, this victim's eye which only a moment ago, in "life," recognized or signally failed to recognize us. And so on. All that business of the shower: would it, could it work? Would it be, as Paul Goodman prescribes, "long enough to solve the formal problem that it poses" (*Structure* 17)? Could the shower scene survive if it were ornamented and elaborated out to ninety minutes? Surely as a narrative it would seem too disconnected, slashed, arbitrary, explosive, unfinished. Not only unfinished but far too unfinished, just as Marion Crane, now dead in her youth, seems to be. Something has to have come before this, something sufficient to make it easy for us—nicely involved as we would wish to be—to step through the bathroom, past the inevitable toilet, into that shower. Something about a call for wetness, or for a sanctum. Something about the magnetism of Marion.

Because the shower scene is the single souvenir of *Psycho* that viewers have always most assuredly retained, unforgettably so, even while the surrounding story is completely or only half forgotten, even while the prelude and epilogue are lost, even while the film itself becomes a nightmare jumble. The shower scene, *The Shower*, cut away from its context, sliced and stored, stored and vaulted. Cut away from context just as the killing knife cuts Marion away, offering that little demonstration of what can be done with a blade. What can be done, too, far more than is necessary to produce her death: jab, jab, jab, jab, jab, and on and on. Our filmmaker knows that since it is not *any* character who can be successfully stabbed in a drama, since only *some particular* character can, it is necessary for him to elaborate—and consequently for me respectfully to elaborate here—the victim, which means, a carefully etched history of insufficiencies, each requiring the next, that will lead us inexorably to follow Marion with enough abandon stewed with fascination that, when we arrive at the Bates Motel with her in the first place, there is no nuance of any moment of her experience we will not wish to savor. And this motel does seem a place amenable to savoring. Here for America at the end of the 1950s is the absolute epitome of hospitality, succor, warmth against the storm, set into the reserves of the rolling countryside. It is a bucolic haven that entertains, there can be no doubt, values of the most civil and humane sort. This is the adjunct to small-town society:

> The social mores of the small town at every opportunity demand that only those facts and ideas which support *the dreamwork of everyday life* are to be verbalized and selected out for emphasis and repetition. People note other people's successes, comment on them with public congratulations and expect similar recognition for themselves. Mutual complimenting is a standard form of public intercourse, while failures and defeats, though known to all, are not given public expression. (Vidich and Bensman 303; emphasis mine)

The Bates place isn't far outside Fairvale, and we will come to Fairvale by and by. Fairvale, *beautiful and peaceful valley*, . . . but not yet.

Let us move backward from the flesh in the shower, the water still running, the water still running, the water still running, the water still running, because Marion's hand, that turned the water on, cannot turn the water off. Turn off the water, Marion; turn off the water; the water running; turn off the water, for Heaven's sake. The young man running in, "Mother, mother! Blood, blood!" And Lady Macbeth, and so on. Turn off the water. Norman becoming Lady Macbeth on behalf of his mother (who is too enervated and distraught to come down from the house). "Yet who would have thought [the old man] / to have had so much blood in him." Norman washing up the blood. Norman the caretaker. *The water still running.*

And not to neglect a telling instant when Norman, seeing the outcome of Mother's work in the bathroom—yes, when this boy, seeing Mother's blood—swiftly as a fleeing mouse wheels back and swivels against the wall, hand cupped tightly over his mouth. Two very small observations about this, because I have written about it elsewhere at substantial length.[7] First, because Anthony Perkins manages the gesture with such amazing speed, agility, and grace it becomes an eminently noticeable one, it is dance, and because of John Russell's meticulous lighting we cannot help seeing the hand over the mouth to the exclusion of everything else, at least initially. Hand over mouth. *Keep mum.* (Keep mum whilst keeping Mom.) Don't let a word escape. And then, too, the slight quaintness of his move. To act in shock or aggravated surprise by lifting one's hand over one's mouth is a very nineteenth-century gesture, derived from a time when most action and reaction were verbal, when letting words out or holding words in were grave decisions that could affect the tenor of a moment. Norman looks just a little old-fashioned in his move: Hitchcock's signal that we are dealing here with a sensibility, an architecture, a propriety, and an ethic that predate contemporary 1960 by a great deal. Adjacent Norman's lanky body pressed flat against the wall is that brilliantly lit bathroom, and the water *still running.*

Turn off the water. Send out the dove.

Donald Spoto recounts a bizarre little anecdote about Alfred Hitchcock (Spoto is certainly not averse to recounting such anecdotes):

> If he was using a public toilet and another man entered the room, he would quickly raise his legs within the stall "so that no one could tell there was anyone there." For the inveterately Victorian Hitchcock, the quite ordinary business of the human body was fine material for jokes, fine for fantasies—but no one must ever have the impression that such business was part of his real life. (415n)

This, we are to believe, is a story so true to life that it is unsurprising Hitchcock himself repeated a version of it: "Visit a bathroom after I have been there," he told an interviewer, "you would never know I had been there" (qtd. in Rebello 113–14). Stephen Rebello, who has given intensive study to *Psycho*, sees this obsession with tidiness reflected more generally in the film, not only with Norman's desperate labor to keep that bathroom spic 'n' span.[8] For the design of the room Hitchcock "insisted upon dazzling white plastic tiles" and "gleaming fixtures" (114). The space, the wipe-up, the tidy erasure—all purely auteurist.

But enough of this white cloister for the moment. Let us, as I say, back off. Step by step, back, further back. Let us see what it was that led us here, unavoidably, tauntingly. Let us put the waterfall behind us, go into history in order to go forward. The water can keep running, we'll get to it.

Yet wait, wait! That water we can't wait to get to!

Mopping, looking, mopping, mopping, looking, Norman has noticed the water still running. (Finally!) He peremptorily turns the handle. Sepulchral silence. Silence you can taste. Bless you, Norman. Thank you for saving *us*.

THE CHAIN OF CHANCES

There's no such thing as a mysterious event. It all depends on the magnitude of the set. The greater the set, the greater the chance of improbable events occurring within it.

—Stanislaw Lem, *The Chain of Chance*

Saturday morning. She is off to encounter her boyfriend Sam in Fairvale, having had one of those not-so-pleasant nights of sleeping in the car at the side of the road. Today becomes grueling, capped with a storm that drops with the falling light. Exhausted, even hypnotized by the wavering washer blades, she wants nothing more than to shower the day off and get to bed. She agrees to a light dinner courtesy of Norman, who settles her in his private den, surrounded by stuffed birds, and regales her with quiet stories of his mother and how judgmental the old woman can be. Such a pretty boy to be such a very sad boy. Something missing there. A life of stuffing things, indeed! A life full of stuff. But what can one do, the world is full of sadness and beauty. "'Tis an unweeded garden, / That grows to seed; things rank and gross in nature / Possess it merely" (*Hamlet*, I.ii.139–41). When she takes her leave he waits a few seconds, then goes to his peephole to watch her in thrilled silence.

Are the sandwich dinner and the conversation foreplay?

And how could it be that Marion, an unknown, would dine with Norman, a captain of strangers? He was at the desk checking her in—he runs the Bates Motel all by himself—"We have twelve vacancies. Twelve cabins, twelve vacancies"—business having fallen off since "they moved away the highway." (They picked up the highway and trucked it away.) Just beyond the precincts of whatever nearby town are to be found roads like the one Marion drove in the rain, the capillaries that bring life there and guide it away. "Almost all groups ... including the excluded ones, have a central interest in roads" (Vidich and Bensman 156). Yet what a charming, and childish, imagination for Norman to picture in this sad and charming way an unhappy fact of modern highway development. An entire world of roadside entertainments was eclipsed around 1955 as the interstates were studded with McDonald's and Howard Johnson's:

> That, [Kemmons] Wilson later realized, was the real fun of it—picking the sites, choosing the franchises. He would select the best areas and the best applicants and then chart a trip, going, say, west from Memphis, through Arkansas and Texas and New Mexico. He would then fly off in his single-engine Bonanza. He would eat his meals while he was up, flying, checking out these towns and small cities in the early morning and early evening—the best times, he thought, because you could see the traffic patterns.

The Wilson eye became legend in the business. Years later, when the world of chain motels had become much more competitive, Wilson attended a conference in New Jersey along with executives from Howard Johnson, Sheraton, and Ramada. At one point a young man got up and asked Marion Isbell of Ramada, "Mr. Isbell, what criteria do you use for picking a location?" "It's really simple," Isbell answered. "All I do is go into a city and find out where Kemmons Wilson has a good Holiday Inn and I put a Ramada Inn right next door—it's a good system and it really works." (Halberstam 178–79)

How did Marion come to find herself here with Norman? She had been standing at the desk, fresh out of the storm. Outside the heavy downpour and in here this warming, softly lit office. He was getting her key ready: This one? No, *that* one (the cabin nearby, that, as we will discover only after dinner, is a stage). Norman is clearly lonely, happy to meet a girl who has "something that ... that puts a person at ease." Lonely, yet he "[goes] right ahead lighting signs and following the formalities." Lonely: the kind of loneliness one doesn't mind confessing to a stranger. "Will you have supper here?" With or without meaning kindness she reaches out to his loneliness, in this warm place, out of the storm ...

When she says yes to his invitation, he gives us a subtle reminder that before we met him we saw *Vertigo:* NORMAN: "All right, you get your dresses hanging out and ... change those wet shoes." Scottie Ferguson doesn't tell Madeleine, fished out of the Bay, to get her dress hanging out; he removes it and hangs it out. But our Norman: he's not going to touch anybody's dresses! (Not Norman.)

While she eats, he sits patiently watching. "You eat like a bird."

And then a comment about how we are all in our little cages. Janet Leigh said of Hitchcock: "His camera was absolute. Every move was planned before any performer even talked with him. He said, 'Here's your piece of the pie. What you bring to Mary other than what I want is fine. You can do almost anything with Mary and I won't interfere, so long as it's within my concept'" (qtd. in Rebello 61; Marion was Mary before script changes). All inside a frame, a little cage. (A premonition of the opening of *The Birds* [1963]).

Retreat again:

How would Marion Crane have come to the Bates Motel of all possible places? BATES MOTEL. NO VACANCY. The word NO is both not illuminated and plenty visible nevertheless. NO VACANCY. VACANCY ≡ NO THING HERE. No vacancy ≡ there is *not* no thing here. But that is the shadow thought, since the sign reads VACANCY. Come here, you'll be the only one on the premises. Come and populate this empty little world. The rain pelting down so very hard, it's almost impossible to see the road—we were behind the wheel with her, we could see what she could and could not see. (Rainwater coming down like knife blades.) Windshield wipers slashing (also like knife blades, as has been much observed). When Marion is in the shower, will knife thrusts be *rained down* upon her? This in train of a long and agonizing drive, with vehicle headlights oncoming and oncoming, and magnified in the raindrops against the inky wet pavement; with the rain water not swiftly enough washed away by those hypnotic wipers.

She was more than tired, she was bone tired, she was tired beyond thought, and the young male voice soothed, "No point dwelling on our losses." She was, as some say, weary unto death. We have all driven the road, a voyage pressing forward, and in such horrible exhaustion we wish only, above all things in life, not to be there, not to be voyaging.

Backward again: why was Marion driving at all—on that road, in that rain, or for that matter on any road anywhere? Why is Marion in the car? Because she was in Phoenix and had to get to Fairvale to see Sam. And this need she felt was insistent, wouldn't let up. Go with urgency, right now, don't delay. Find Sam, get to Sam, find Sam, get to Sam, find Sam, see Sam, find Sam, see Sam, be with Sam, be with Sam, be with Sam. Desire, one could name this, but there's more to it than that, because Marion did see Sam, and not so very long ago. She was with him only yesterday, with her clothes off, or at least some of them. Friday lunch was Sam. (Innovative at the time for Hitchcock to deliver us into a sexual liaison occurring *in midday* and between decent types. Generally speaking, 1960 was a time—or was made to look like a time—of serious conventionality regarding sex.) Today some matter has been urging her on. She is not only in flight *to* but in flight *from*. She traded in a car in a thorny climate of suspicion, to a distinctly suspicious salesman (John Anderson) (who's not in the mood for trouble first thing in the morning but women will do anything they have a mind to!) and was screened by a suspicious policeman (Mort Mills) who already, behind his Godzilla-size sunglasses, thinks she is odd. Too evidently the salesman was giving her the eye, too; she eyed him doing it. Who knows what trouble this could lead to, with him, with strangers, with the police? She wants to get as far away as possible from this used car lot, and with speed. To put this—put the entire past—behind her, let it drift in the wake. "Go, go, go, said the bird: human kind / Cannot bear very much reality."[9]

And that policeman who seems to think her odd: why should he think her odd? We cannot know about him but she thinks he sees her that way, and Marion's consciousness is the one we have adopted at this point in the film. Marion's reaction is our gateway. Having slept all night at the side of the road, she awoke to his face right up against the driver's window: gigantic, expressively neutral, his monstrous insect eyes hidden behind darkness. A policeman on the road concerned to be helpful might remove his sunglasses. Why did Marion instantly fear this one (and we with her)? Or: why was she predisposed toward fear?

Because: backward yet again: Marion wasn't just driving; she was driving away from a crime. And the damned spot will not come out. Crime tells, crime lingers.

[Thus far, then: (a) crime >> (b) flight by car >> (c) exhaustion and sleep >> (d) encounter with the police >> (e) trading in for a new car, with the same cop watching >> (f) driving all day and into the night, a storm spilling >> (g) losing the road >> (h) the Bates Motel >> (i) dinner with the proprietor >> (j) a soothing shower >> *CURTAIN*. Note how at each transition (">>") chance plays a role but also how the transitions form a tidy chain. Chance: Marion is carrying money she doesn't deeply believe she should have in her possession, the cash *being under her care by happenstance* even though it is *in her purse by design*; the cop *chances* to pull up behind her car at the side of the road but *her purse with the money and her license are on the seat beside her*—she's not breaking a law but *she is breaking the law*; she *chances* to find the side road (the old main road) with the motel but *she absolutely has to get off the road somehow*; the proprietor *chances* to have the impulse to house her in Cabin 1, the one with the peephole, by means of which he will stimulate himself but *he has access to all the rooms in the motel...*]

Further back: What crime?

Lowery, a real estate agent (Vaughn Taylor), her boss, has just completed the sale of a house to the flagrantly *nouveau riche* Tom Cassidy (Frank Albertson), a chap who spends too much money on his daughter and, wink wink wink, I'm cute to the girls. She is to hang onto the $40,000 in cash—any moment it will be after hours Friday night—and deposit it at the bank first thing Monday morning.[10] She's not feeling well, she leaves the office early. Then, swiftly changing her clothes, and with the money stowed in her purse, she heads out of town, not so luckily that she can avoid a traffic stop where Lowery, crossing the street in front of her, squints querulously as though in recognition. Why, in Marion's estimation at the moment, is the boss giving her the eye? Giving. The eye. Because, thinks she guiltily, he knows that I have stolen his money. Although of course he couldn't know such a thing or even suspect it: he thinks the money is going to the bank. And for all we can be certain, whatever his state of mind, he's not actually thinking anything. But her guilt: *He knows what I am thinking, he knows when I'm awake. He knows when I've been bad or good.* The amateur thief is always quickly arrested in his own imagination, but Lowery doesn't know Marion's plans for the weekend or whether usually, when she's not feeling well, she goes for a drive. She'd been complaining of a headache (possibly to avoid the advances of too-randy Cassidy), a discomfort so horrible that her office mate Caroline (Patricia Hitchcock) offered medical advice unbidden. She needed, needed, needed to go home, but here she is, headed, headed, headed out of town—yet, who knows she's headed out of town? Oh well: women'll do anything they have a mind to. Lowery keeps walking. He's had a drink with his (rich) new bud Cassidy, very tranquilizing. He's just made a bundle, very very very tranquilizing. *So far, Marion's only crime was placing the money in her purse, if that*; she couldn't have gone to the bank anyway.

Back still further. Why is it that, as she grasped $40,000 in an envelope, the thought came to Marion that instead of banking it she could drive up to Fairvale, find Sam, and fund a marriage? It's hardly an illogical thought, nor is it exactly probable. *Chance.* And another Hitchcockian construction: immorality wedded to tidiness. Marion was prurient with Sam at "lunch," but now, is she having a second thought about their future? (Women will do anything they have a mind to.) The money is a palpable resource, a weight, hefty in the hand. As a concept it is an easy thing to administer, file, transfer, regulate. As *materiel* it is real, indeed offers the "resistance to the hand" that for Ortega is the prime definition of the real (111). Reality brings potentiality. She *did intend* to deposit the money, but *there are other possibilities*. Sam, Sam, Sam. Stealing in this case would be as easy as driving away. *Driving would in fact be stealing.* Voyage as theft. Yet our Marion is not by nature a thief, and she knows that if she steals the money she will be culpable. Perhaps, given her amateur status, even more than culpable: CULPABLE. (The car is a machine, and the machine can do the crime.)

But still earlier, as she was sitting at her desk in Lowery's office: why, we may reasonably wonder, was Marion, surrounded by large framed photographs of Arizona landscape, thinking about Sam (quite possibly without a headache)? Because here and now, late Friday afternoon, while the sun was still shining, she was freshly arrived from her tryst with him, Sam the Glorious (John Gavin), who drove all the way down from Fairvale for no apparent reason other than having his clothes off with her. Off or partway off. *We leave it to your imagination.*[11] The issue of sex before marriage came up[12] and, dressing again, Marion was firm and upright with Sam's boyish insistence. A love story. Frustration and hesitation on his side because he doesn't make enough at the hardware store to finance their union. More than frustration, hunger; because at this "lunch" neither of them "ate any lunch." Lunch | "lunch." We were there, right there in the hotel room watching the two of them argue, argue and touch, as the bodies got progressively covered up (read: as the naked intimacy moved farther and farther away). In the same way that we don't quite get this little dance out of our minds, Marion doesn't get it out of hers.

And—back yet again: how did we come to be present in that particular hotel room so that we could observe the passion leaving its prints? So that we could examine these particular specimens: because there may well have been other quite "proper" trysts in that hotel, at that moment; or, perhaps more intriguing, there may have been meetings of another, more mysterious kind, attractions for some hungry eye. Were we invited here, by word or gesture? Hardly. We wafted in like a cooling breeze through a partially opened window,[13] in sun-bleached Phoenix, Arizona. Friday, December the Eleventh. Two Forty-Three P.M. And that slow, lazy, pleasurable, fateful wafting-in was at the beginning of the film. Wafting in was the beginning of the world of *Psycho*. Hovering outside the window, seeing it partially open, we made our move. We insinuated ourselves. Seeing the slit, we penetrated. He "told me exactly how the camera was going to go into the window and follow the characters, all for concise effects," Leigh said (qtd. in Rebello 61–62).

One retreat more, the implicating retreat, the hook:

With what conceivable motive would people like us—people such as we would readily take ourselves to be—slide into that primal and private darkness? Proper people, as we surely are. Proper, even trysting with Hitchcock. Away from the fresh air we glided, from the view of the cleansing desert, from daydream. Into the bubble of other people's lives. Why would we lean forward and sneak into that dark space? Look, look!:

three hotel rooms in a row, and the middle one has the window partially open! Look!!!

Lean forward, have a look-see.

How would that happen? It would happen because this is how we watch a film. Look through your eyelids half-closed, into the cavern of that darkness. Follow the leader. There are no invitations. The voyage *is* the invitation.

Step by step, then: (1) open window in a building, (2) hotel room, (3) sex?, (4) marriage talk, (5) real estate, (6) money, (7) escape, (8) mollify policeman, (9) change cars, (10) worry about salesman, (11) rain, (12) motel, (13) loneliness, (14) dinner, (15) weariness, (16) shower. A positively inexorable line of circumstantial happenings chained unbreakably, each following clearly what came before but also no one definitively implying what comes next. How *very happenstantial* that, moving into that particular hotel room, we should find these particular lovers since before moving we could not have known. That these particular lovers—did Marion "eat like a bird" with Sam, too?—should have that particular argument of all possible arguments lovers get into, with money at its root. That money should *chance* into Marion's hand directly afterward. That she should *chance* to think the money might bring her together with Sam. That traveling to meet Sam she should *chance* to be frightened on the road by that *chance* encounter with the law. That frightened on the road she should *chance* upon that motel. We can imagine how the Marion who returned to work in Lowery's real estate office was, as some might say, fated to die in that shower. From real estate dealer to real estate. Die or be reborn: "The shower was a baptism," Leigh reported Hitchcock to have briefed her (qtd. in Rebello 109). Chaos theory, no. Logical contingencies linked, yes. *Fated* to die?—well, the invocation of *Fate* would put us in classical Greece, an age and a setting of balance, proportion, arrangement. Here is one probable impossibility that would seem real enough but would kill our story: On the highway, looking into those gigantic cop blinders she is not only surprised but also reminded that there are police in the world. There are police, they look for criminals, she is a criminal, he has been looking at her. Thank him for his kindness, turn the car around, go back home and on Monday first thing put the money in the bank. Repent, repent, and ye shall be saved!

THE SOUND OF SILENCE

Hello darkness, my old friend.
—Paul Simon

What is it that we could have hoped to see by sneaking into the Phoenix hotel room in the way that we did? Because, not knowing we could only hope. We slid in, what did we want? We slide before seeing who's there and what they're doing. Move first, see later. To what paradise is our curiosity directed? Surely to what people smoothly contrive to prevent us from seeing in the everyday. What they do when the door is closed. Inevitably something physical. Stanley Cavell wrote: "The possibilities of moving pictures speak of a comprehensibility of the body under conditions which destroy the comprehensibility of speech. It is the talkie itself that is now exploring the silence of movies" (*World* 149). We may hear talk, but we will penetrate to the pithy silence under it. If the hotel room, then Lowery's private office. If Lowery's private office, then Marion's bedroom where she changes clothes. If Marion's bedroom, then Marion in the bathroom at the car dealership, fishing out $700 in front of the damning mirror. If Marion in one bathroom, Marion in another bathroom. If a bathroom, a shower. As we have found ourselves penetrating all these pieces of real estate with Marion, we must obviously get into the shower stall, the smallest cage of all. Why, after all, would we think to hold back, suddenly, from sliding forward into the undiscovered?

The queerness of being inside that shower stall, next to a young woman who is cleaning herself with the water blissfully streaming, her wet and slick self very close (yet not at all close) while we are there only in the imagination—yet, what is the imagination? And from the tub the bathroom beyond, seen through that semi-opaque liner fully drawn: a zone of moderate, diffuse light. The water sound, the softened light, reassuring, an envelope. In such a setting the fact of a stranger intruding becomes palpable, the running water even emphatic now as it flows with what might seem a more staccato sound. *There being no other sound*, the curtain of water aside we are confronted with a silence, but as Rowan Williams notes, "We cannot imagine an 'unframed' or pure silence: we can only imagine the silence in which *we* are not hearing anything, not hearing what we might expect to hear—that is, it will have to do with what has shaped our expectations, our history and fantasy and so forth" (157), a history and fantasy, we might add, that speak in their silence because "the spirit of things is not in words" (Artaud qtd. in Corbin 68; see also Goodman, *Speaking*). The advancing figure approaches the shower liner, darkening, tall, angular, slightly jerky in movement. Note two things:

[1] At first we cannot know what is happening here, whether for us, watching in anticipation (as always with Hitchcock), this feels like or does not feel like a welcome visitor, although something about the angularity and speed of the movement leads to the conclusion that the visit is unwelcome. But we cannot, we do not, *know*. Quickly invoke rationality: our rational thought tells us this is not Marion's home, she could not possibly be welcoming anyone entering; but inside the shower, the water has rinsed away our rational thought as we actually see the moving shadow, and curiosity is mixing with trepidation. Rationally we would arrive at a conclusion without seeing the figure, basing our calculation on the very fact of the silent intrusion, the coming into space, *this sacred space*, and moving forward in it. Penetration as threat. The filmic action entirely previsualized. But to look carefully at the image here is not to be rational. We see it organically, we organicize it, before knowledge.

[2] And more: at this moment in the diegesis, Marion is still unaware—entirely unaware—of what is happening in our field of sight because while she shares the shower with us (unkenningly) she does not share our sight. The shower is coming down on her face. Hitchcock is here making a strange and wonderful division. Since we are in the shower as much as she is, so very close to her, we are in the diegesis almost as she is, yet since she is wrapped up with her eyes closed and we are wrapped up with our eyes open we are outside the diegesis. This may not be Marion's shower, it may be ours: she is only a stranger come to a motel but without possessing the space as we possess the space. We have been engaged all along in a different way, and this is surely our shower, in our bathroom, a place into which some friend might walk. She is overcome by touch, we by sight. Hers is the skin; ours is the light.

A few further considerations about this powerful moment in the shower:

- Depth is a principal structural concern here, not merely a spatial indicator (as in: the sink is far away from her hand but not as far away as the door). Hitchcock having fixed the camera position inside the shower, the advance of the unidentified figure at the doorway could have been made crisply visible—even were Marion looking as we are looking—only in deep focus, f16 or f32; but the shower liner is assisting to blur the focus in any event and the aperture is set for f5.6 or f4, not deeper, so that when the bathroom door all the way at the back of the shot (at f16) comes ajar that action is far enough away and indistinct enough that we get only a hint of it. A visual whisper, and not a jarring one. The increasingly proximate stranger on the other side of the curtain is also given as a mere hint without detail because of that liner and the flat bathroom lighting, the vagueness of the figure both spurring and reining in our sense of threat. (I try here to capture the *first* experience of seeing this film; later on, when the viewer sees the future, the experience will be different.) Soon the viewer's encroaching feeling about the encroaching stranger is anticipated and mirrored in the darkening optics of the screen presentation. But Marion, directly beside us, remains just outside both our visual periphery and the action as we are sensing it. The eye is wary of the approacher now, but the ear is enveloped by the protective water sound. And what we see she doesn't see.

- As to our *presence inside* the shower, it is in more than one way that we are a little separate from Marion. She is somewhere by our side, but her consciousness and our consciousness are, at present, unaligned. It would be incorrect to say we are *in the shower with Marion*; and even more incorrect to say that the camera turns us into "Marion in the shower" or indeed someone who is fully "identifying with Marion in the shower." We are and are not there with her, equivocally. We are intruders who would not stay out, to Marion as unknown as the stranger we are watching, yet visitors with permission, if such beings can exist when one is taking one's shower. Let us say, we have a ticket; and the form advancing toward the shower curtain does not. To be blunter: every sense we have of this visitor's apparently unacceptable inappropriateness must be parried with the fact of our own apparently acceptable inappropriateness, furnished by Hitchcock's camera placement.

- However perverse this presence of ours may seem, however odd or inexplicable when examined from a cold-hearted remove, it is a dramaturgical requirement, because when a shadowy glyph materializes in the space beyond the opaque curtain and comes forward, becoming by steps less an abstract form and more a creature, our precise placement in the wet zone *next to Marion*, offering us the knowledge she is absorbed with getting clean, *permits us to see it before she does*. Were the camera to have been positioned more conventionally, outside the shower enclosure—so that we would see Marion's naked self only vaguely through the curtain[14]—the entire structure of the scene would have been disrupted because the intruding element would be crystal clear to us from the outset: so very clear, and thus so very menacing, that we would lose a sense of proximity to Marion altogether and also lose a conviction that she is oblivious. And if, by contrast, inside that shower we were led to such an identification with Marion, such a unity of consciousness, that we "wore" her body there, certainly wore her proximity to the water and its sound, took on her self-cleansing, if, in short, we were attending to the water as Marion must be—acoustically virtually inside the sound—the anticipatory visualized beats of the silent footsteps and swelling form would be elided, just as they are elided for her, and the invasion thus made far too imperceptible to catch until a point far too late. Then we would be shocked. She is certainly shocked, but viewers must not be. Shock is not the explosion of lightning bolts one sees in cartoons; it is an utter collapse of the system. Shocked, we would fall out of the film (much as she will). Our proximity to her founds Hitchcock's dramatic architecture. We must be decisively willing to step into the shower with someone who is essentially a stranger, someone who has an attractive body, someone whose personality we have only touched, with all its many defining ambiguities—to step into the shower with her, and yet stay modestly apart, so that finally our knowledge can precede happening. Between knowledge and happening falls the shadow.

- Here is a trademark maneuver of Hitchcock's: the "familiarization" of the character to the viewer, the building of an empathetic relation. Familiarization as in familialization, as in *the family and the familiar*; to be of the same family as in *to be blood related*. "Strong and vague odors." Her blood, our blood as we watch. Some of the knife slashes are designed to make the viewer feel the object of the stab, stab with a knife so sharp there may be no particular sense of the penetration, yet the blood suddenly flows. One perishes from loss of blood; Hitchcock catalogues this in the sequence: a steady and progressive depletion, quite as, in any poetic progression one starts at a position of high potential and methodically *loses potential until the end*, when there is no potential left (a theme that will return later; see Goodman, *Structure* 14–17). We are made to feel the killer is stabbing us, although we can see quite plainly that the killer is stabbing her. While we are wrapped in the movement, the killer is sparing us, stabbing the person with whom we are happily—but impregnably—sharing the shower. Leaving us safe in our aristocracy. The person to whom we have perhaps allowed ourselves to come too close is paying the price, is the sacrificial lamb. Through this, the second phase of Hitchcock's trick: de-familiarization, de-familialization or separation. There can be a story now, and it can continue, because we are left alive to endure it, Ishmaels all.

- Because we are so close to Marion (caged by the camera), we can feel ourselves sharing her experience, feel that this is *our* shower; that the cleaning here is, and will continue to be, *our cleaning* in some magically unliquid but absorbing way. As Marion daydream-washes, we do, too. Letting the events of the day and the previous day fade into the near past and the more distant past. And as in her daydream presence she hears an inner voice, shower babble, so do we: this is a voice that cannot actually speak because the spirit does not possess a speaking apparatus, is not a body. But now, seeing the figure enter the private room—*our private room as well as hers*—and advance there, we hear not exactly alarm, not exactly warning, but a voice terribly interior, one that articulates without having words, timbre, pitch, or vocal color. Call it a responsive voice. A particular kind of *acousmêtre*, absent yet present, articulate though undefined. A voice from nowhere and anywhere.

If this voice had words—and it does not have words—it would surely say: "Someone ... Someone coming. . . !" Then, "Too near!" But it *cannot be that any voice says this*, because Marion is there to hear such a voice, and for dramatic reasons she must hear and anticipate nothing. And that is what we catch. A nothing that will lead to an express nothingness.

This voice I invoke, entirely an internal projection of the viewer's, allied sensibly with a hypothetical mirror voice inside, but inactive in, the still unkenning Marion—a voice we might like to imagine she *would have if only she could see what we see*, if only she had motive—makes a figurative and non-real sound, a clarion call that only the single viewer can hear in the back of the auditorium of the mind. It has no material acoustic components. Without this internal voice of notice and growing alarm, this voice that speaks without sound, we would watch the advancing figure from within the shower in a dumb silence that matched the figure's dumb silence; would watch in an acoustic emptiness save for the water; would watch literally without the breath of speech; and I think audiences do not watch *Psycho* this way. They watch with the breath of speech, but without the kind of voice that can outer speech. With enunciation but no words.

- But Marion, who we like to think *might* have a voice such as the voice inside us, not only does not have such a voice but also, as Hitchcock has determined, could not seem to have it. It is a voice from and to the inside, *my inside* as I view Marion whose inside I cannot view. If she had such a voice we would never catch it, but perhaps it would awaken her and, of course, if it did it would ruin the scene. Affiliating with her position under the shower stream I remain, and must remain, separated, certainly because of modesty but also technically, by my ability to detect what she does not detect. Hitchcockian choreography: Marion looking away, looking up into the water, looking into herself, but the viewer standing properly at her side, impotent bodyguard, looking out through the shower liner (at the new, oncoming entertainment: everything that even begins to appear in film, we grasp).

- Regarding the camera (us) so close to this scrubber, modesty is an insufficient address: real modesty would have kept us from entering the shower at all. Hitchcock has forbidden us real modesty. Standing eagerly with naked Marion under the water makes us safer than putting on the air of good manners would. Notwithstanding that Hitchcock's camera does show a modicum of modesty: he films the shower as no other filmmaker—surely none today—would, by keeping the camera's eye away from the naked body of which we are interminably aware; and notwithstanding that even a circumspect partial vision, with the camera cutting off the frame at Marion's shoulders, is at this moment artfully avoided, our principal ideal being to look out—look out because Hitchcock has given us nowhere else to look; look out because ... better Marion than us. Looking is escaping. Looking is a voyage to freedom.

- Were we more closely bonded with this woman and were harm to fall upon her, it would also of necessity fall upon us, upon our consciousness. But in that event (an event Hitchcock knows he must prevent at all costs) such harm could be nothing but "harm" for us, who know we are in an audience where no harm can fall. (In the most horrendous of horror moments onscreen we know we are inviolate.) Harm would dissolve the project. Yet if we are to be close enough to Marion to catch her heartbeat, we must never be forced to admit to ourselves that we are not really there. Escape but remain present: the ghost.

- And there is a second, dramaturgical logic for separation. Were Marion to see what we see she would panic and become hypergestural, on one hand confounding our isolated position at her side, barging into our space, and on the other making it virtually impossible for the filmmaker to maintain his practice of providing a very clear view. As Marion's daydreaming is pictorially essential, so, and for the same reasons, is tranquil silence upon the stranger's entry, aside from the sound of the shower water. Nothing can disturb her placement and composure since her placement and composure are the camera's, too. And our anxious inner voice will be inaudible, if not pointless, should Marion start to scream before we do. We scream first, in the mindless hope that she will follow the sound of our inner voice and, superhuman, take a step that will transcend the moment altogether.

But she cannot take such a step, anymore than she can hear us. We get a sense of the impotence many Hitchcockian characters share.

- The shower curtain is parted sharply, the knife comes down, and the Bernard Herrmann score fills in the acoustic space because his violins are screaming. But those violins are part of the film. So, the film screams whilst the character is silent. The violins scream and Marion holds herself in, quite as though she were in a concert hall listening to a beautiful cantata whilst also being naked and wet and slowly dying.

- Discussing screams (particularly in the canvasses of Francis Bacon), Gilles Deleuze suggests a relationship between "the sound of the scream and the forces that sustain it" (42). The following prescient comment seems to me directly applicable to the shower moment in *Psycho*, although Deleuze is not trying to make this connection:

    > But the forces that produce the scream, that convulse the body until they emerge at the mouth as a scrubbed zone, must not be confused with the visible spectacle before which one screams, nor even with the perceptible and sensible objects whose action decomposes and recomposes our pain. If we scream, it is always as victims of invisible and insensible forces that scramble every spectacle, and that even lie beyond pain and feeling. (42–43)

    Produce the scream, convulse the body. Not Marion's eclipsing scream, should it ever come, but the silent scream we hide as we see forces at first "invisible," soon enough "insensible," and surely "scrambling" the spectacle we are eagerly taking up (on Hitchcock's use of the silent scream motif more broadly, see Weis). Not only Marion's but already the viewer's mouth is a "scrubbed zone," when evil enters.

- If it is true, as Murray Schafer suggests, that "man likes to make sounds to remind himself that he is not alone" (256), we must wonder that our own private sounding—which is to say, our liking to make sounds—results in nothing audible at all; that in "screaming" without screaming we eschew the opportunity to remind ourselves that we are not alone. It is a way of affecting aloneness in the dark, even though we are not alone. To feel alone without being alone.

- "I am here—," John Cage writes, "and there is nothing to say" (109). A little reflection on Beckett's "nothing to be done" (with Beckett a redisposition of Lear's "Nothing will come of nothing" and a prescient mirroring, too, of Cavell's "The world *is* silent to us; the silence is merely forever broken" [*World* 150–51]). As we stand in the shower and see the shadow coming forward—as, frozen in the waterfall, we have what Stephen Bottomore has called a "looming response"—as we see the shadow, which is only indexical of a thing, there is no speech that can be effective, since words do not stop the forward rush of mere indices, or even of things. Having nothing to say—no words in a script; no place for speaking—is the trigger for saying to the self. Always when we watch a film, but somehow in a special way when we watch Hitchcock, we have nothing to say. The voyage of silence.

- In *The World Viewed*, Stanley Cavell makes the crucial observation that while the development of sound technology during the early 1930s[15] freed up "the actor's stiff bondage to the microphone, and the camera was free to stray again," nevertheless

    > the technology did not free it from a deeper source of bondage, the idea of synchronization itself. On the contrary, the possibility of following an actor anywhere with both eye and ear seemed to make their binding necessary. No doubt that source has to do with the absolute satisfaction of a craving for realism, for the absolute reproduction of the world—as though we might yet be present at its beginning. (147)

    It would seem that the internalized sound of silence might work for the viewer to provide a kind of "synchronization," too, my voice in its hollow chamber accompanying that movement beyond the curtain, craving to turn the gaping silence of the moment from expressionist to realist representation.

- The withheld voice is an internal acknowledgment of the recognition of horror, as in "horror movies," a nod that allows us to ascertain for ourselves that generic conventions are being followed and that we are in the presence of the "horror movie" we took the film to promise. In conventional horror cinema, the terrifying moment provokes the viewer to swallow the internal scream, hold it in at all costs, and endure the torture of that packing and capping in silence. Were there no utterance suspended inside, the holding-in of blank but expansive emotion would have no power and no meaning. It may be that the particular denial involved in swallowing and retaining is central to the working of horror cinema. That the "pleasure" of horror is the endurance by the viewer of the torture of holding something in, not the torture being produced in the tale. It is always painful to feel obliged not to speak when one feels speech welling up.

- A disturbing feature of the *Psycho* shower scene is the trap. Norman invoked it a little earlier in his parlor. As Marion is in a private bathroom with only one door, now settled inside a shower stall with only one exit, to leave the place she could not avoid confronting the intrusive stranger. Rather than being nudged into confinement by an advancing trapper, she has already trapped herself in the trap, if innocently, in the prospect of self-pleasuring body management as a token of freedom. Yet she did say that we sometimes deliberately step into our traps. While prior to 1960 nobody in Western culture thought of the shower as a trap or cage, after they saw this film many people did. And with the word *Psycho* they uttered the word *shower*. As Cavell has warned, "The voice has spells of its own" (147).

BOY'S BEST FRIEND

In watching Hitchcock's work, one is always finding that the question "What is going to happen?" is balanced precariously against "What ought to happen?" Moral principles on one side, consequential realities on the other. Nor is Hitchcock ever so facile that moral principles automatically triumph, always and inevitably, over happenings. He knows that while moral principles illuminate or enshadow our response, patterns are arranged by a higher Artist in a Work of immeasurable complexity. Some have tried to understand this dualism in terms of Hitchcock's Catholicism, although

Catholicism was something he had in many senses rejected. Some have called it his sanity, his mastery, his film.

Norman—despondent, fragile, sensitive, and dutiful Norman—is worried for his mother, "a boy's best friend." We never have a doubt, for even a breath, that this worry, this concern is genuine. Mother has clearly had another one of her (countless) episodes, has flamed over in possessive jealousy that any of those brazen young women might attract her Norman's pristine attention. Overprotective, yes; but she *is* Mother. She has exacted what, to a civilian of the Victorian age, might seem justice, having undoubtedly read Olive Schreiner and agreeing wholeheartedly with the lesson the author's unidentified Woman offers an unidentified Man: "'A man has a right to look for what he needs. With a woman it is different.... Two people who are to live through life together must be able to look into each other's eyes and speak the truth. That helps one through life. You would find many such women in America,' she said: 'women who would help you to succeed, *who would not drag you down*'" (91; my emphasis). Mother has her eye out.

Protect Mother, at any rate——come what may. She cannot help herself, poor thing. She is loving and kindly, to me at least, and always. She would never perpetrate evil. If she could see herself, she would be shocked to the heart and would make herself different, I know for certain and have always known. Known always. She is a clean woman, in the truth of it. She is a tidy woman. She requires only that the world should be without stain, entirely, and really, there is nothing unreasonable in that. Protect Mother from the "Blood, blood!" Mrs. Bates is therefore to be shielded at all costs from the smear of official investigations, all official investigators being nothing more than bloodhounds who wallow. What has to happen is the erasure of stain, the undoing of the macula, the removal of evidence. The cleansing of the world. When Norman mops the bathroom, we see him acting in a kind of obsessive frenzy, far too easily read, I think, as caution on his part lest prying eyes arrive to watch; we know already that not much traffic comes by this road anymore, that nobody is coming to follow. But stain, stain! Blood! Blood! Mother! Mother!

Make clean. Above all things, make the world new.

No more crushing evidence can persist than the body. So: the wretched woman having torn down most of the opaque shower curtain in falling against it, he brings the thing down altogether, stretches it upon the floor, and lays the body on top. Rolls it up. Carries the package to the door with its blood and bloodstains safely wrapped away and then, looking carefully to see that no one is outside (again: who could be there?), deposits it in the trunk of the car he has pulled forward in readiness. Always already ready. Make up the beds. Back inside, check around, get that folded newspaper she left on the night table. (Inside it are the $40,000 in notes, minus $700 for the car, but he doesn't know that, dutiful Norman, because don't make the mistake of thinking he isn't circumspect. Also, only a viewer could know, and here in the deserted Bates Motel, off the main road, who on earth could be viewing?) Rushing with mop and pail he was both frantic and diligent—notably frantic, notably diligent—in getting rid of all the blood, inside the tub, on the rim of the tub, the wall, the floor. The water finally off, the nagging, incessant water sound finally silenced. The bathroom clean and tidy and white. Surgical. White and tidy and clean. Priestly, at the mass. Any motel room anywhere can require a new shower curtain at any time. Make the body disappear. The body and the newspaper thrown in with it. As Norman did not unfold it (why on earth would anyone unfold anyone else's newspaper?) the money is still safe.

The money is as safe as safe can be.

He will disappear the troubling Marie Samuels, but first let me ask what any sensitive viewer would ask, at least to herself: how is it that Norman can act with such cold objectivity to our friend Marion, to her fresh body? Cold, calculating, meticulous, almost scientific. This body that his mother slayed: has he no personal regard for it at all? Not an ounce of feeling? He treats her so very mechanically. And only a short while ago they dined together and she ate like a bird. How can this boy be so detached? Was he detached when he looked through the peephole?

Are we detached when we look through our peephole at him looking?

One probable answer, disturbing as it may be, sheds great light on the contours of the scene. Norman was never for a moment shown to have an emotional connection to Marie Samuels. Politesse is one thing, feeling another. She was one of the few (but long forgotten) guests who come his way, and that name of hers was undoubtedly made up. She ate the sandwich I gave her——well, she was hungry, it's no matter.... He spied on her disrobing so she became, temporarily, a thrill. Nothing wrong with a thrill, but also nothing lingering. No tingle that does not dissolve into factuality. The very worst is this: her presence in any manner, to any degree and through any wisp of material deposit, will be a compromise to the guiltlessness that must come to be presumed and accepted of Mother-who-cannot-help-herself. She cannot have presence, this Marie Samuels. Presence as stain. And Mother was right, she was one of those who would drag him down. She was, after all, young and attractive, an absolute terror. Norman's car glides away behind the cabins to an expressly dark, splotchy, entangled swamp and he pushes it in. Stands at the edge to watch. Down goes the car into the black ooze. The white car, the black ooze creeping over it like a parasitic growth: perfect graphic construction, so that the image says everything, and indelibly.

Oops, but it stops.

"The idea was to make each audience member an active conspirator in the agony—and, by implication, the madness—of Norman" (Rebello 126).[16]

Norman is watching, biting his lip anxiously. Sink, sink, or they will find you! Then they will find dear Mother. Sink, so that Mother will be mine, only mine, untrammeled. *Sink, in the name of all that's holy.*

The car goes down a little more, hesitates again ...

This is maddening.

But now, finally, it obliges by vanishing. Sweetness as erasure, erasure as sweetness. Norman's lips curl up a little. An efficient clean-up efficiently managed. Might we say *another* efficient clean-up? There are so many of these women trying to drag him down, and a woman will do whatever she has a mind to. Mother, Mother, Mother! This young man is surely a master of efficient clean-ups. Taxidermy as clean-up; stuffing a bird a way of cleaning up the mess of death. *Susannah and the Elders* in a tiny frame covering his peephole, cleaning up the hole and cleaning up the peep with its sanctity or sanctimoniousness. The woman falsely accused. The lecherous voyeurs ...

But viewer, face thyself. Is our Norman, ready to rid himself of this Miss Samuels, actually colder, more dispassionate, more creepily disturbing than anyone sitting around you in the theater and becoming "engaged" with, "interested" in her—but *only* that? If, before the film is much more than half done, she disappears from the screen, do you feel a twinge of pain, genuinely? Or, having at first taken her up, do you ravish yourself with her and then throw her away, just in the way that we do with all screen characters borrowed into our cozy dens (kidnapped) for the brief sojourn of a film's unspooling? Is she not one of those mere strangers one meets on a voyage across the sea? So warm to chat with, over and over; so easy to dispose of. But so alluring ...

And is our own readiness to follow the rest of the story, absent Marion, really and truly disturbed by her rather exemplary death? Are we unable to keep going, as though the shower and its aftermath are a brutal rainstorm come down upon us so that we need respite? In the story as a whole, *does her killing matter?* Does it so disempower our observation, so vitiate our hunger, that none of what follows can truly be seen? As a viewer one is maintaining several phenomenological positions, several "identities," at once: wrapped into the story, wrapped into our padded seat, hitchhiking the free narrative ride, but not forgetting having paid at the box office; sincerely and deeply engaged with the character yet able to see and know that she is in truth an actor. More: fixating upon Marion Crane as though she is the jewel, but then tossing her like a mere stone; or feeling pulled down by her and climbing above? And for each of these angles of view there comes a grouping of aesthetic and ethical principles to which, whoever we are at the moment, we must adhere. We are empathetic in the shower with Marion; fully empathetic, and so much so that the action feels as though applied to us. Yet, through a mercy we fully apprehend without comprehending, it is not. Sacrificial lamb. *Mere* sacrificial lamb. Soon afterward we are cold and businesslike, hopping onto Norman's broad young shoulders and watching assiduously as he cleans up every last drop of her. Don't forget that little bit. Don't forget anything.

But there is one tiny bit he doesn't see. Oh, oh! There! Just in the center of the outside of the tub, at the bottom. Don't forget that, don't omit cleaning up that. Protect Mother. Look, you didn't see it! (Audience complicity.)

But no sympathy. Sympathy gets in the way.

We quite readily accept that a young woman named Marion Crane was never here. She was never here *now*, already. We did have a guest named Samuels, but she went off after one night. Nobody else. Back road. Very little traffic. Make up the beds. A long long time. Once they put the highway through ...

Marion Crane? I have never heard of Marion Crane. Well handled. The hand of an artist.

The bird who wanted to get married. Marryin' Crane.

INTERLUDE: A HAND JOB

One sets hand to a place, one handles persons, one is handy with a hammer and nails, one can be ham-handed, glad-handed, sure-handed, back-handed. One puts a hand to knowing and working things through. And *Psycho*, if we regarded it with care[17] would reveal itself as a film that depends entirely for its progress on applications of the hand. The film is a hand job. Here is what we see if we begin at the beginning and, hand over hand, move through:

[1] The hotel room from the outside, Venetian blinds drawn down except for that slit at the bottom. How could those blinds have been lowered, how could they be raised again when the tryst is done, except by hand? Let us imagine that in order to produce his thrilling interlude, Sam darkened the room. Sam, quiet, retiring Sam: the stable hand who propels us, who brings on the secret cave of darkness at mid-day.

[2] A handy but attenuated sex scene, lips feeling lips while Sam's hand reaches up to Marion's face, then hers reaches up to his. Lying on the bed semi-nude, her hand around his neck (a coupling, as in trains). Sam lying on the bed, grasping the comforter/security blanket as, standing, she (somewhat too) tidily buttons up her shirt, button by button, using both hands.

[3] As he tells her he's all hers if she wants him, she is turned away from the camera to regard Sam seated at that window, his legs spread open a little, his starched shirt draped over his crotch, his torso bare; and his arms are outstretched with the palms up, as though in preparation for a crucifixion. Marriage, even the thought of marriage, as sacrifice.

[4] At the office, Marion handling a sales contract, handling her face powder, finally handling $40,000. Flirting with her, Cassidy handling his wallet to show the picture of his "little girl." Marion's hands with their own life, meticulous in slipping the bills into an envelope, the envelope into her purse.

[5] Marion has a "headache." She stands meekly in front of Lowery's desk, two hands folded together in supplication and deference, until he says

it's okay to leave early—just make sure the money is safe until you can put it in the bank on Monday.

[6] Marion's odd bedroom, with its patterned wallpaper, small and inexpensive pictures, tiny lamps that do not match, curtains over the window that don't go with the wallpaper: did many hands decorate it, and is it thus only a rented room? Pushing a suitcase closed with two hands: definitive, certain, final.

[7] Two hands on the wheel as she drives away, the shots often constructed to show the hands clenched at the bottom of the frame, a kind of "musical" accompaniment for the expressions on the face.

[8] Waking by morning at roadside, with the cop mug peering in the window. "Have I done something wrong?" Fiddling nervously but cautiously with her purse, hands perhaps frozen in anxiety as she hunts the paperwork produced by the hands of the State. She has one hand draped on the wheel, its very long fingers hanging down at rest like the tendrils of a bromeliad.[18]

[9] Reading a newspaper in the car lot as the salesman walks up, a cool cowboy, hands casual and secure in his back pockets.

[10] After the deal, Marion in the bathroom alone with her mirror image, four hands opening two purses simultaneously, and then, presumably, fingering through the hundred dollar bills to get fourteen of them for the twin dealers. The framing ensures *we do not see the hands* directly or in the mirror: the shot is "empty handed"; it is prelude to what T. S. Eliot called "a condition of complete simplicity."

[11] When Marion drives away in her new car, the salesman stands watching with his mechanic and the cop. His arms are dropped military style at his sides. (Lined up one behind the other, at an angle, they look like the Three Musketeers.)

[12] Driving until nightfall, lights glaring from behind and those sure hands, at the bottom of the frame, tight upon the wheel. The hands will bring her through to safety.

[13] In the motel office, Norman demonstrably opens the ledger and hands it over for her signature (she uses her pen hand to make a vital sign that will be a vital non-clue: deeming it advisable to make up a name, she is ensuring that no one will be able to trace her presence in this place). Then he reaches up for her key with a long supple hand. She has clasped the purse in two hands again, her left hand curled around it with the fingers spread as though in playing a cello. Marion's hands in careful protection against fear: of being caught, of losing the money, of not following the best course of action. Is this purse, full of money, an instrument through which she will play a harmonic melody?

[14] Norman showing the room, parting the curtains with both hands (with the calm fluidity of possession, as in the way Mrs Danvers parts the curtains of the dead doyenne's west wing bedroom in *Rebecca* [1940]).

[15] Marion's handiwork of folding the cash into the *Los Angeles Times*, stowing it on the bedside table.

[16] Standing with her arms folded, hands tucked away, as she enters Norman's sanctum for dinner. Hands that did the deed, now in hiding.

[17] Clasping her fork with her forefinger as she looks at spieling Norman. A calculated pose, showing off delicacy (when she is conscious of being anything but delicate).

[18] Norman's elegant hands as he talks about his life with Mother, the long, long, long fingers tightly folded together. Is he gesturing or holding in gesture here?

[19] Marion buttering her bread. The bread is held on the palm of a left hand the fingers of which stretch out again, straining, yearning, trying to climb. Eating with the bread held by the tips of the fingers, a tea party in the English countryside in the Victorian era. Norman reaches out a long arm to point into the "air" where his birds are motionlessly "flying."

[20] Norman examining his ledger again after dinner, a little smirk on his face. His hands hold it like the music he would be singing if he were in a choir. He does have the look of an exceptionally gangling choirboy.

[21] At the peephole now. Marion is bending over, hand on hip, as she undresses.

[22] Norman retreats to Mother's house, sits at the kitchen table leaning over his folded arms. The left hand projects into the air as though it has a mind of its own.

[23] Marion takes a moment at the desk in her room (to help viewers follow the mechanics of the theft). An open bankbook. A little notebook in which she has noted $700 coming off the $40,000, leaving a balance of $39,300. Tearing out that page. Ripping it into pieces. Back in the bathroom dropping the pieces into the toilet and flushing.

[24] The shower, sweet sanctity. Hands raised in cleansing, expiating her sins.

[25] The creature beyond the curtain, arm upraised with a knife. Stabbing rhythmically as Marion, helpless, reaches out to Nowhere.

[26] Marion's hand pressed against the tiles, touching but not grasping, touching but not moving. She reaches out and clutches the curtain, tearing it away as she falls.

[27] Norman running down from the house, bursting into the room, staring into the bathroom. He wheels back, hand over mouth. Hand as shock; hand as cessation; hand as lid.

[28] Norman doing wonders as he handles the mop, swop swop swop. Hand-washing in the sink. *Out! Out!*

[29] Norman hand-loading Marion into the car, sinking the car in the swamp. His hand to his face again, pensive, worried, hoping, calculating as the car pauses and then sinks.

[30] Sam's decisive hands writing to Marion on SAM LOOMIS HARDWARE stationery: "So what if we're poor and cramped and miserable, at least we'll be happy!" *At least.*

[31] In Sam's hardware store, an old lady examining the insecticide, pointing her finger as she reads the manufacturer's claim.

[32] Lila, hand to face as she muses while Sam speaks to her.

[33] Arbogast, handing open his identification for Sam and Lila to examine.

[34] Norman on his porch as Arbogast arrives, calmly nibbling candies from a paper bag. Finger to mouth, better than what birds can do. Marion ate like a bird; Norman doesn't eat like a bird. "Norman's nervous hands constantly fidget and pop candy into his mouth, uncontrolled hands a bodily symptom of uncontrolled desires," suggests Sabrina Barton (67) in a comment that does seem to imagine controlled desires may not, in their essence, be bodily to begin with and somewhat abbreviates observation of Norman's constant hand motion. As we are seeing, he *is* his hands but that does not necessarily mean his persona is a fidgety one. As to fidgeting: *Idle hands do the Devil's work*, and Norman does not have idle hands. Never idle hands.

[35] Norman holding up Arbogast's business card in the office: the fingers closed around it, as though it were a treasure or a poison. When he stares down at the ledger, Arbogast holds the same card, but loosely, casually; for him it is nothing.

[36] Questioned by Arbogast, Norman has to think a moment. Head dropped into shadow. Right arm lifted and the fingers open as he touches his forehead. Musicians will be interested to note (on music see below) that the fingers are opened upon the forehead in a perfect close position, the exercise a serious player of the piano would use for cupping the palm.

[37] Arbogast at a telephone booth nearby, fingering the dial mechanically.

[38] Arbogast checking out Mother's house, handing the bannister as he climbs the stairs. Stabbed in the head he tumbles backward, his arms stretched out helplessly to grasp the air ("promise-cramm'd").

[39] At the sheriff's: This man doesn't dial his own phone calls, he has his loyal wife ask the operator to connect him. Holds the phone as though it were only, but wholly, a tool.

[40] Inside Mother's, Norman lifting her down the staircase, tenderly, as with an invalid. Shhhhh.

[41] Outside Fairvale Church, as Sam and Lila tell the sheriff they've lost track of Arbogast. The sheriff has clasped his dear wife by the arm.

[42] Sam and Lila plot as they drive. Sam's hand tight upon the wheel. This grasp is for purpose and decision, not anxiety. At the motel, he takes Lila by the elbow much as the sheriff did with his wife; a coupling at least by image. Talking outside with Norman, he holds Lila tighter and tighter.

[43] Sam sneaking into Norman's study, fingering the desk. Lila holding the wall as she looks into Marion's room.

[44] In Marion's bathroom, Lila noticing something in the toilet, taking it out. It's a tiny fragment of paper, that she and Sam examine holding it in their hands the way lab scientists use pincers to hold specimens.

[45] Lila having climbed the steps to Mother's house. Her left arm reaches out and she clasps the door handle (with her right hand extended gracefully—a ballerina's—to the world that is behind her).[19]

[46] Upstairs in Mother's bedroom, Lila touching the door jamb with a tentative hand as she looks around. (The hand exteriorizes her thought as she sees.)

[47] The bronzed hands upon the dressing table. "Cut off" at the wrists, but laying upon what looks like a bronzed cushion: iconic hands—hands as icons.

[48] Lila reaching out to finger Mother's bedspread. (Fingers as explorers.)

[49] Lila handling Norman's room: the hand opening the phonograph, the hand picking up a bound volume and opening it so that she can read.[20]

[50] In the office, meanwhile, Sam's and Norman's hands all flattened on the countertop as they verbally spar. (Men giving open demonstration they are prepared, but not eager, to fight. Finally they will grapple with each other, but not now.)

[51] Lila hiding behind stair rails on her way down to the fruit cellar, fingers delicately touching the lathed wood as Norman, suspecting, makes entrance.

[52] Lila in the dank, dusty cellar, seeing Mother in a chair looking away. Then touching Mother and the chair swiveling around.

[53] Lila's horrified retreat causing her arm to reach up and swat the hanging light bulb, which now swings like a pendulum.

[54] The raised hand of the woman striding in, but Sam is behind her and seizes the body from behind. The wig comes off.

[55] The psychiatrist gesturing emphatically and politely with one hand, then both hands, as he lectures. Sam, listening, fist under chin. The sheriff beside him, one hand open receptively on his thigh and the other clasping the arm of his chair for support. At the end of the lecture, Sam's two hands are tightly folded together, and the sheriff is no longer using his chair arm to keep himself in the action.

[56] Norman in his cell, wrapped in a blanket. His right hand sticks out, the long fingers flat upon his thigh as in a half-hearted peace signal. But we get a macro-close-shot of this hand as in one confusingly multi-toned voice Norman and Mother together affirm that he wouldn't hurt a fly. A little fly is crawling upon the thumb.

The manual quality of the film goes considerably beyond implying a chain of gestures or expressions of feeling, because although the hands do make gestures that is not all they do. We see, in a stronger chain, an extenuating array of mechanical movements, hands and fingers geared for accomplishment, deftly arranging things in space to make events come about. The hands are actors here, hands as agents, because, clicking along moment to moment the film is a mechanism, an arrangement of parts each of which will turn in a particular way because of its gearing into the part that turned before. One could say: the story is passed from hand to hand.

The perilous danger in *Psycho* is not to be found in the Bates Motel shower stall or in the stairwell at Mrs. Bates's house, not to be associated with the torn bodies of Marion and Arbogast. Marion's is a horrendous slaughter, but the slaughter of Arbogast not so long afterward should cue us to a key structural fact: she is not and was not the center of this tale, is not and was not the central performer on the stage. And nor is he. Marion's role, in fact, was not to center the story or frame it, but to lead us *toward* the story that, during her "lifetime," does not fully develop. She is an initiator, a schoolmarm pointing the way to advanced theories that will be explicated only later, by professional authority. Pointing the way, with hands on the steering wheel.

How sad it was for fans of Janet Leigh, at the time of the filming "a darling of the fan magazines, a member of the Peaches-and-Cream brigade with Debbie Reynolds, Doris Day, and June Allyson, who were counterpoints to sultry mantrap types Elizabeth Taylor and Marilyn Monroe" (Rebello 60–61). Her brief tenure—"He wanted a name actress because of the shock value" (Leigh qtd. in Rebello 61)—works in the film substantially because of its brevity. That a figure played by an actor of this repute could be so abruptly introduced and stolen away, so blatantly erased from the scene (in typical exhibition practice of the time this could well have happened before many had arrived to see the film,[21] so that they would be in a position to demand and get their money back, a threat prompting Hitchcock to make that unheard-of exhibition contract),[22] is some strong indication of the weight of the development to come after her, some hint that her presence and her death together merely draw back the curtain on something else.

The something else is the principal voyage of the film, to which Marion Crane invites and accommodates us but which (as a new Moses) she is not permitted to undertake herself. What she does is precisely what I have outlined already; she brings us to the Bates Motel, and thus to an encounter with young Norman, hero of the tale (if I may). Her sexual dalliance with Sam in the opening scene is to lure and pinion us, it being a foregone conclusion that audiences will tune into sex if they are permitted (as Norman will demonstrate he is permitted) to peep. We are caught by her naked body in underclothing, we are carried along briskly to her place of work, we follow her bizarre escapade, we endure the tempest, and we arrive at the strange island in the dark.

HARD WARE

Once Marion has been swamped—"Thus do men's fears become women's fate," writes Tania Modleski (109)—we are transported for a scene of astonishing surprises to Sam Loomis's well-stocked hardware store in Fairvale. Raymond Durgnat nicely notices the array of pronged rakes and other dangerous-looking tools Sam has on clean display. A young woman makes entrance and says to the sales boy behind the cash, "Sam? Sam Loomis?" He is somewhere between an old teenager and a young man, perhaps eighteen, perhaps twenty. But she is mistaken, of course: Sam is in the back room. Now he steps out. This is Lila (Vera Miles), Marion's sister, mentioned to Sam before. Lila, prim and proper. Lila, shy and modest. Norman's mother's idea of a dream. Great trepidation: Where is Marion, gone for several days at this point, big hunt on for her and the money she took, where could she be? (The urgency of the conversation could easily make us overlook Lila's fabulous faux pas in thinking her sister could be romantically hooked up with the boy.)

"Yes, let's talk about Marion," interrupts a deep male voice, something of a radio voice.

Coming through the screen door is Milton Arbogast, private detective (Martin Balsam). Could Lila be in league with her sister, and Sam in league with the two of them? A skeptic about everything. (Except himself.) After several moments, Arbogast is assured these two are blameless, and that Marion has in cold fact disappeared. He goes off to canvas local boarding houses, has doors gently shut in his face. He goes to the Bates Motel and questions the proprietor, since it's near the main road and she *was* driving, after all. On stammering Norman he uses that glorious voice, that radio voice, that voice from the past.

Speaking of voices: Arbogast's is one of three soothing voices we hear in this film, all of them interruptions of a storm. And the storm is a bombardment of viciously shrieking violin glissandi, pummeling rain, hypnotic wiper blades, the knife blade coming down and rising up like a piston, repetition, repetition, rain, rain, knife, rain, knife, knife, repetition, repetition. The film is a storm of repetitions, blinking headlights, rain. The film comes at us and comes at us again. In text, pure text, one can blithely say, "Oh, you've made your point, thanks," but this isn't pure text, this is cinema. It must be that we are subjected. It must be that we feel the thrust of chance, and feel it, and again, and the only way words can even begin to convey such a fearsome mechanism is by way of verbal repetition. The only way words can even begin to convey film's fearsome mechanism is by way of verbal repetition. And in the filmic version, the repetition seems like only fact, only the way the rhythm of reality beats upon us, whereas when one writes it the words leap up antagonistically. Three soothing voicers: the sheriff (whom we shall meet); the psychiatrist (whom we shall meet); and

Arbogast, dear Arbogast. Dear rude, pushy, intrusive, pasty-faced Arbogast with the voice from above the clouds.

Shall we say that Arbogast has a nose to match his glorious voice? The detective must have a nose. He must tweeze out the tiny detail that does not belong in a scene, the telltale fact, the discrepancy. And the operation of the detective is based on the supposition that action in the world is impossible without traces, that every movement leaves a print of itself. Moving backward from the telltale print one can arrive at the (supposedly original) event. And, smells Arbogast, this proprietor stinks. Something one cannot put a finger on (putting a finger upon a smell—a call-up of the priest in *I Confess* [1953] claiming he has heard there are *pain[t]s without smells*). "If it doesn't gel it isn't aspic."[23]

What was it, then, that "blocked the gelling," Norman's stammer? The decrepit look of the place altogether? That this Norman Bates fellow is too eager by half offering the detective help? The situation is an interesting one dramaturgically: if Arbogast does *not* pick up a clue when his identity as detective has led us to suspect that a clue is there to be picked, he is not such a great detective; at which point the story collapses. If he finds a clue too quickly, much of what follows in *Psycho* flattens, becomes almost silly. The actor manages to convey that the character *very well might* be catching something here, and Perkins helps by hesitating just a little more as the scene goes on, in nuanced ways, so that Norman seems to gather that Arbogast has been gathering.

"If it doesn't gel": as Arbogast is staring at Norman while he says this, we can take Norman to be the anchor of the metaphor. And as anybody can plainly see, looking at Norman standing nervously behind his counter, he isn't aspic, and he doesn't use aspic, though he may seem to quiver like a gel. Is the word "aspic" intended by Arbogast to sound to Norman a little scientific, a little sharp-edged? Does "aspic" mean to Arbogast, the secret wit, "in the manner of an asp"? If there is meat around here it has not been laid in aspic, it means that for sure. Though admittedly, aspic is a very fine (and very, very old) way of preserving meat. If there is meat in this vicinity it is rotting.

A detective with a brain in his head, Norman must be thinking. A humorist. A man who could find the one microscopic trace of Marie Samuels that I failed to mop away. A man who will put the finger on poor cherished Mother, whose blamelessness must be preserved! She's so easy to put the finger on! Norman is at loose ends, thinking, Save dear Mother from the lethal Arbogast. Arbogast who is sniffing for a mother, as seems. Is he motherless Arbogast? And then, too, Arbogast: a good old-fashioned name, that's been around since at least the fourth century. A wisdom even older than aspic, which comes from the late fourteenth.

Lila is not the only visitor to Sam's Hardware. A lady has been there all along, searching for an insecticide. What she wants, and about this she could not be more explicit, is a method of killing insects that does not cause pain.[24] "I always believe that death should not be painful." We are given no perch from which to see her find success. The conversation fades out and she more or less disappears, which is to say, suffers the same fate, functionally speaking, as Marion did but—and here is the fact to be marked—with no pain. She is there, she is not there. Whereas Marion's story is far more complicated, and was surely a torture. The opened dead eye that dissolves into the tub drain is the dark eye of horror as well as the evacuating eye, the one that by seeing erases or even erases by way of sight.[25] Georges Bataille: "I shall never forget the wonder and violence of the determination to open my eyes, to look straight at what is happening" (266).

Durgnat only hints at this but Sam's store is repletely stocked, in short fully operational, if also, as appears, somewhat unvisited. We can wonder whether it is on a "back road," in some ways like the Bates Motel. Off the beaten track could mean a depreciation in clientele, and the insecticide lady does present herself as the only customer in the area. At the same time, we are given no visible clues that Sam is suffering in his business here. When in the hotel room he demurred to Marion that trying to sustain a marriage on the income from a hardware store was a chancy proposition, he was conversationally pointing to something we are given sufficient opportunity to see in this scene, but actually do not see: that he is hard up for money. Sam does not know all the things we know about Marion, knows nothing from that hotel tryst onward, in fact, and it is safe to guess, should we wish to, that had she arrived with the cash he would have been, at the very least, happily surprised. Yet could it be that Sam has been dodging for some time to keep Marion away from this hardware store, away from the reality of his business life or his life altogether?

Lila is searching for Marion with dedication and an outstretched hand, as it were, but we do not find a look of terror or panic on her beautiful face. For a woman whose sister has gone off the map, and one who has come a long way to hunt, she is remarkably serene. Joining her in the chase, Sam, in fact, shows the spirit, the urgency, and the nerves we might have expected from her. Is she in truth Marion Crane's sister? She has come out of the blue. Sam has never met Lila. Marion isn't there for verification. I don't pose these questions in order that we might be encouraged to think seriously about Lila as a fake, but in order to show how very little Hitchcock needs to do to establish a convincing situational moment. Marion and her whole story beginning with an argument about Sam and his hardware store and an invocation of her sister >> Marion taking money and fleeing town >> Marion in the shower >> Marion gone >> Sam and his hardware store (the link to Marion) >> Entry of a young woman who says she is Marion's sister. Given this chain, who else would she be? Well, given this chain she could be anybody. A probability is established by the chaining itself, and little else. Who else would audiences believe her to be? Yet since her behavior does contradict expectation the establishment of Lila's bona fides sits in Hitchcock's architecture, the careful arrangement of scenic moments one atop another, each moment filled to the lip with information—but only some information. In the same way that Lila becomes real as Lila, this place becomes real as the hardware store that Sam claimed ownership of, that is, Sam's Hardware. And now we have Marion's boyfriend and Marion's sister teaming up, with ostensible desire to locate her, as far as they know. Deeply aware that she is in the depths and that they will not locate her, we are freed to see another choreography, however. Handsome Sam, beautiful Lila, and the pregnant secret: that nothing is keeping them apart, except their fear that something is; and they will overcome that fear in time, if joylessly.

Arbogast wants to meet Mother so he climbs the wood-paneled staircase in Mother's old house. Mother swiftly sees in him yet one more pestiferous intruder from the city! Adieu, Arbogast (and with his eyes so very open!). No detective alive will ferret out Mother. Or: Mother is beyond detection. Detection is for the fraternal order. Norman is again dutiful, evaporating into thin air all the signs that some other nosey detective, on the hunt for the missing Arbogast, might find. Mother is again mistress of the old (modest) Queen Anne Victorian house on the hill. Carey McWilliams describes California houses that "look as old as time, as old as the iron hills" (357).

It is hard to deny that Mother has become interesting (because in part she is history). We have the desire to see her, perhaps even watch her converse, hear some of those imperious dicta emerge from between the parched lips. What sort of attitudinal substructure can be in her arcane personality? How out of tune is she with the modern world, and in what specific ways is she out of tune? Bernard Herrmann's cues for this film, scored for strings only, and exquisitely precise in the way that all his film cues are, sometimes put an "out-of-tune" chill up the spine. Hitchcock knows that with respect to a film story we cannot have anything we should chance to want unless one of the characters chances to want it, too, and goes searching. Thus Sam and Lila must look for Mother *so that we may find her*. Hearing her voice wafting down the little hillock in the direction of the motel isn't nearly enough—all it does is confirm her age and her sternness of manner and pique our curiosity. But because the man officially hunting for the missing sister has himself gone missing—a missing Mister—they need local help and visit the sheriff late at night at his home. The sheriff is law. The sheriff is local knowledge. The sheriff is jurisprudence, wisdom, logic, saneness, and stability. Go to the sheriff, tell him the whole story, see what he says. Plant the facts and see what comes out of his garden.

THREE JOURNEYS OF *PSYCHO*

To understand the journey on which Marion started us, her voyage upon the high seas of the Future, and the earthbound destination to which her journey is headed, it is necessary to consider three vital moments, each of which, in an idiosyncratic way, mirrors that lady in the hardware store wanting to kill without producing pain. Let us say that each moment is lethal to its depths, but also painless; so much so that we might mistakenly think it marginal or decorative, forgetting as we so easily might that Alfred Hitchcock never decorates and never dallies on the margin.

[A] To and From the Past

When Lila and Sam come to the sheriff's house, they find they are bringing him and his wife (John McIntire, Lurene Tuttle) out of bed. An elderly pair, in pajamas and robes, pleasant and sociable to the degree that anyone might be if awakened by strangers in the middle of the night. The word "puzzlement" would nicely summarize the attitude of these two, standing and patiently hearing Lila's tale.

> SAM: If [Norman's] back he probably isn't even in bed yet.
>
> SHERIFF: He wasn't out when you were there, he just wasn't answerin' the door in the dead o'night like some people do. This fella lives like a hermit! You must remember that bad business out there, about ten years ago?
>
> LILA: Please—call!
>
> SHERIFF: (*nods to wife who picks up phone*)
>
> WIFE: Gloria? The sheriff wants you to connect him with the Bates Motel. (*pause*) Here (*handing over phone*).
>
> SHERIFF: Hello Norman? Sheriff Chambers. Th'—I've been just fine, thanks. Listen, we got worries here. (*listening*) Yeah, have you had a fella stop by there tonight? (*listening*) Wellll, this one wouldn't be a customer anyway. He's a private detective. Name of—
>
> LILA: Arbogast.
>
> SHERIFF: Arbo-Gast. (*listening*) What? ... And, after he left ...? (*listening*) That's ok, Norman (*hangs up*). (To LILA and SAM): This detective was there. Norman told him about the girl. The detective thanked him. And he went away.
>
> LILA: And he didn't come back? Didn't see the mother?
>
> SHERIFF: Your detective told you he couldn't come right back because he was going to question—Norman Bates's mother? Right?
>
> LILA: Yes.
>
> SHERIFF (*smiling*): Norman Bates's mother has been dead and buried in Greenlawn Cemetery for the past ten years.
>
> WIFE: I helped Norman pick out the dress she was buried in. Periwinkle blue.
>
> SHERIFF: 'Tain't only local history, Sam, it's the only case of murder and suicide on Fairvale ledgers. Mrs. Bates—poisoned this guy she was ... involved with when she found out he was married. Then took a helpin' o'the same stuff herself. Strychnine ... ugly way to die.

WIFE: Norman found them dead together. (*Stage whisper*): In bed. (LILA *turns head.* WIFE *smirks a little.*)

SAM: You mean that old woman I saw sittin' in the window out there wasn't Bates's mother?

SHERIFF: Now, wait a minute, Sam. Are you *sure* you saw an *old* woman?

SAM: Yes!! In the house behind the motel!!! I called and pounded but she just ignored me.

SHERIFF: You wanna tell me you saw Norman Bates's mother . . . ?

LILA: But it had to be! Because Arbogast said so, too. And the young man wouldn't let him see her because she was too ill.

SHERIFF: Well if the woman up there is Mrs. Bates, who's that woman buried out in Greenlawn Cemetery?

Puzzlement increasing in the direction of consternation in Sam, whose brow, finally, is knitted tight; confusion for Lila, whose eyes are helplessly open; and metaphysical doubt for the sheriff (and his wife), who attended that funeral. Whatever could be the voyage this young woman from the city is proposing we take, toward the kind of understanding she would wish us to have of something we were pretty convinced we already knew?

The sheriff, meticulously performed,[26] is a revealing character. He is one of those old locals who live at the foundation of small rural communities like this one. Through the first part of the conversation, with his wife silent and obedient at his side, he carries a wry smile of very slight condescension, since the prerequisite for the moment is to humor this young lady who doesn't know anything about our ways up here, doesn't know the history, has stepped into a strange new world like Alice in Wonderland and thinks, the way all them city folks think, she immediately knows more than anybody up here about what's going on up here, because she's more educated. That's what she thinks, and the point is to humor her because she is a visitor, after all, and a friend of our fella Sam's, and there is never any cause to be rude. But golly, she's just spinning a tale. And on his face, as he nods and finally agrees to make the phone call, the sheriff has just exactly that notably patient smile one reserves for children and strangers who think they are in a position to speak their minds. By the end of the scene his attitude is completely different. Something *does* sound out of sorts now, something he can't put his finger on, and one can see on his face that he's even beginning to question his own perceptions—or at least his present memory of them—because he saw that casket go into the ground up in Greenlawn Cemetery. Who is in that casket, indeed? And how else could it be that the woman who's been buried ten years is sitting up in the window of that house?

The sheriff's wife sees herself as implicated because after the death she helped Norman pick out the burial dress. What that does is convert the funeral, and the death that inspired it, into *her* ceremony, a ceremony for which she played a vital and necessary role. And as to Norman himself: the sheriff's gentle inquisitor voice on the phone, his attentive pauses, and his entire failure to doubt what he is hearing from the other end of the line are all convincing signs that he and Norman have had a trusting relationship for some time, that is, that Norman has been the sort of person this sheriff feels he can take at face value. And the very last thing this sheriff seems to be is a fool. The sheriff's wife even has a slightly maternal way of gazing forward expectantly to surmise what it is that Norman, her dear Norman, is saying to her husband.

This is an informational phone call, the sheriff makes perfectly plain, not a pleasantry; indeed, he wouldn't use the phone for pleasantries, and wouldn't address pleasantries to a young man like Norman in any case. "We got worries here" means "there are some questions to which I need answers, and I am asking you to give them." Arbogast is similarly perfunctory on the telephone, all business, all questions and answers. The police procedure, as spelled out in *Psycho*, is: if you want to know something, ask a question, and be sure you ask the right person. Questions bring answers. Answers mount up to the truth. All of which is, of course, entirely spurious as a hypothesis about the way the Mechanism of Reality works. The sheriff is a trusting man, however. A gentle man. It pays to be trusting. Especially in a tiny community where you are going to have to relate to the same people all the time, and where good manners and good feeling are essential to social balance. The rationale of adultery to explain Mrs. Bates killing her lover. Indeed, the circumspection that dictates *not calling him* her lover. The implicit social bond of sympathy that leads the sheriff to opine about Mrs. Bates's suicide method, "Ugly way to die!"

He is the local arbiter, but more: he knows that it is his job to protect the community by maintaining good feeling among the citizens. No time ever arises when mutual good feeling is more crucial than one in which there has been a suspicious death, or a death now provoking suspicion. Tread slowly and softly, the sheriff knows. And this is what he does. Do not antagonize. And if this young filly from the city is really convinced, and our fella Sam is convinced, too, we've known him since he was knee-high to a grasshopper, well then, tread slowly and softly and keep your powder dry. Keep your powder dry, don't let the cow out of the barn, a bird in hand is worth two in the bush. And every dark cloud has a silver lining.

Guided by Sheriff and Mrs. Chambers, the journey has now brought us to an unidentified body in an unconventional coffin, an *old* woman in the window who cannot be there unless . . .

The tidy, carefree, Christian ceremonial of small-town death is now made problematic. What was said at the graveside may have been wrong. Something wrong pervades this whole story, like a chemical one can't put one's nose to.

Whereas until now the film as voyage has been routinized and rational, every killing attributed, every death laboriously "handled," now we have entered a post-rational territory where innuendo, myth, supposition, doubt, and destabilization control the game. Raymond Durgnat wisely comments that in this scene, "Sam and Lila's redoubled bewilderment qualifies as a new climax. . . . Even more important is the bewilderment, by new information, *of the spectator*" (181; emphasis original). And yet in prefacing this wisdom with the comment, "Narrative event-wise, this detour is completely unnecessary to the plot" (180), he falls into the same trap as catches so many commentators (not always as brilliant as he) about Hitchcock, that is, misreading the actual plot by falling for the superficial canonical account, in this case, that this story is about murder and camouflage of a certain kind. Camouflage, yes, but as we shall see, not of the kind so many think they detect. Part of the salient, but so very often unperceived, eventfulness of the sheriff scene is the moral character of Chambers and his wife. What sort of folk they are in the world, the small-town Western California-Nevada world hankering back to the mid-nineteenth by adaptation in the mid-twentieth century. In America as in England (Hitchcock's twin territories), small-town conscience and consciousness is a rarefied, sharpened, and clarifying microcosm of the nation as a whole and of its values. Chambers knows *everything* about Fairvale and environs. Not only is he officially paid to know, he has made it his business, and the wife has been his helpmate; he recognizes that he is not only the repository of legality here, he is the historian. What happened in Fairvale's past *is what the sheriff, Official Rememberer, remembers having happened*. In *The Birds* (1963) we will see him transmogrified as the owner of the general store (with the quirky memory). In *Marnie* (1964) he will be both Rutland Sr. and Garrod, owner of the horse farm. In *Torn Curtain*'s (1966) Communist East Germany the old Countess. In *North by Northwest* (1959) he was an elderly gentleman who noticed a crop duster dustin' crops where there ain't no crops. In *Vertigo* (1958) he was, of course, Pop Leibel.

Because the sheriff is so important (and firmly imposing) a figure, owing to his social position notwithstanding his kind personality, the suggestion-become-revelation to him that his historical memory is flawed, flawed because he has been deceived, is no small or trivial event. The seams of history are unraveling. Chambers's conviction that Mrs. Bates has been dead for ten years and his wide-eyed wonder as to who could be in that coffin if she is not are both germane to the plot. The door is open now to questioning, undoing, and reestablishing a past, a voyage if ever was. But that voyage, as it urges us into the future, by means of its darknesses spreads light upon an unknown territory we (and Sam and Lila) are in no position to declare clear or evident.

As to questions, we met the supreme questioner, who had a lot of things he wanted to know but vanished before he could learn them. "Arbo-Gast." Arbo, Arbiter, Arbitrary, the man who knows that he knows and therefore, as far as we are concerned up here in Fairvale, where nature just takes its course and things have been this way for donkeys' years, a man who *knows* too much. And Gast. Gast, Gastric, Flabbergast. The know-it-all who flabbergasts. The flabbergasted Arbiter.

[B] Place

When Lila and Sam go inspecting the motel, their plan is to have Sam waylay and distract Norman on some pretext while she sneaks off to look around. She ends up climbing the hillock to the house, spying the veranda and the front door, gingerly stepping up, reaching out to the door, letting herself in. She will descend into the root cellar for the surprise of her life (and ours), but more perplexing and provocative than her discovery there is the arrangement of objects in two rooms at the top of the stairs (the stairs "Arbo-Gast" couldn't quite manage to climb all the way). It is worth bringing to mind how dangerously thrilling it is to walk into someone else's rooms: to discover the other, to see the extent of the space and the configuration of its use, the strength of the illumination from without and within, the inviting or uninviting furniture old or new, the state of tidiness, the aroma that loiters in the air, the mixing and melding of colors, and the peculiar objects other people choose to treasure for themselves and to pose against each other without the least thought that some stranger's eyes will be coming in to inspect. I recall a recognition of Guy Davenport's: that in *Still Life with Onions* (1889) Van Gogh's having his onions

> resting on F. V. Raspail's early home-health manual was a message, in recovery still from severing his ear, to Gauguin, whose decadent carousing had disgusted him during their falling out. Inside Raspail, we are told, were recommendations of a camphor smear to forfend wet dreams, putatively to reserve potency, and of onions, a nutrient nearly Calvinist, revolutionary in its affordability. (Blanchfield n.p.)

Language is a certain flexibility within a constraint, Talcott Parsons told me.[27] In the stranger's private space we find a language, alteration of a form. When Lila goes into Mrs. Bates's room, and then Norman's, it is as though, one by one, she pervades their bodies and souls. She becomes a member of the high priestly class, alone permitted to enter the sanctum sanctorum.

Of rooms such as these Edgar Allan Poe writes,

> There could be nothing more directly offensive to the eye of an artist than the interior of what is termed in the United States ... a well-furnished apartment. Its most usual defect is a want of keeping. We speak of the keeping of a room as we would of the keeping of a picture—for both the picture and the room are amenable to those undeviating principles which regulate all varieties of art; and very nearly the same laws by which we decide on the higher merits of a painting, suffice for decision on the adjustment of a chamber.

As to the way chambers are furnished,

> Very often the eye is offended by their inartistic arrangement. Straight lines are too prevalent—too uninterruptedly continued—or clumsily interrupted at right angles. If curved lines occur, they are repeated into unpleasant uniformity. Undue precision spoils the appearance of many a room. (243)

Davenport, reading Poe, was able to imagine an "ideal room" offering a sumptuous collection of pleasures, including "figured rugs, marble-top tables, tall narrow windows with dark red curtains, sofas, antimacassars, vases, unfading wax flowers under bell jars" (*Geography* 5). Poe's critical point, and the pre-Veblenian issue Davenport finds to consider, is America's having "no aristocracy of blood and having therefore as a natural, and indeed as an inevitable thing, fashioned . . . an aristocracy of dollars" (qtd. in Davenport 5). The display of wealth "has here to take the place and perform the office of the heraldic display in monarchial countries" (5).

Let us say that the style of Norman's bedroom and the style of his mother's bedroom are two distinct, unmarriageable styles, reflecting two unmodifiable languages of design, so that following Lila into one space and then the other we have the experience of two discreet journeys.

The mother's room is late Victorian, and the framed landscape oils and the portrait of a dignified woman, all set upon patterned wallpaper, fit the bill prescribed, exactly, by Poe. There is a marble-topped washstand with a crystal goblet; a high wardrobe with double doors, these pried open hesitantly by Lila as prelude to a quick inspection of the long, sheer dresses arranged on hangers and the singular fur coat. A cheaper construction of the same social pattern (a different linguistic expression) is to be found in her room at the Empire Hotel as Judy Barton steps forward to remove her garments for an escape, in *Vertigo*. A different arrangement still, call it refined language, is shown in the west wing bedroom in *Rebecca*. As to Marnie Edgar, a beast in continual flight, from the police, from creditors, from anyone and everyone, her wardrobe is in her suitcase, the most casual language of them all. Mrs. Bates has a dozen or so dresses, all floral as far as we can see, all dainty, and some of them a little rumpled as though recently worn and quickly stowed away. The high windows are draped with luminous shears and extensive curtains (Poe again), and beside them is a needlepoint on a standing frame and a high-backed chair upholstered in satin. A hanging light fixture is set with tulip glass. By the bed is an ornate wooden stand bearing a tall vase filled with high flowers, Birds of Paradise, perhaps, but surely flowers that bring loyal Hitchcockians back to the somber garden of the Mission Dolores. Standing still to gaze at all this, but then pivoting a little, Lila sees, upon another wooden stand, a bronzed Orpheus, head thrown back, arms akimbo, making to move forward but frozen in time, his lyre at his feet. Davenport's still life:

> A tabletop in its own intimate space, a musical instrument that has been put aside for a moment, a book or sheet of music, a newspaper, a pipe, a bowl of fruit, a bust, usually classical: such is the traditional still life for the past five hundred years. The musical instrument displays versatile affinities from age to age. Most archaically it is Orpheus's lyre . . . summoning the dead to speak for a while on stage. (*Objects* 38)

In the far corner is a quietly posing, richly covered dressing table laid out with perfumes, creams, brushes, and so on. In discussion of Arthur Conan Doyle's Sherlock, Davenport notes, "He could feel exhaustion in the symbolic content of an art when all its materials had become bric-a-brac" and then quotes Walter Benjamin: the interior "is not only the universe, but the case of the private individual. To inhabit means to leave traces" (*Objects* 31–32). As Lila looks toward the little table, all swagged in front, the camera tracks in to simulate her view and we see that centering the still life is a bronze sculpture of two folded hands. Long slender fingers. The vision lingers just a little. Up close. Close and lingering, but we haven't time to be sure whether these are male hands or female ones, or to feel any certainty about whether the gentle folding together indicates tranquil patience or the silence of death.

Perhaps there is hardly a difference between the silence of death and tranquil patience.

Lila is tranquil and patient, in any event, and remarkably so, quite as if she has put aside any thought of her chum Sam doing his magic act in the motel office. Tranquil and patient, remarkably stylish in her long coat, remarkably proper and self-possessed, albeit curious, until . . .

Until out of the corner of her eye she sees that she is being watched.

She wheels.

And it is no one but she herself, in a full-length mirror, stunned in gazing at the cause of her stun. Of course. I am alone. (Awakened from reverie.) But also, in a way that ought to seem troubling Lila is not alone. Lila is in the room with her doppelgänger, so identical, albeit isomorphic, that she must be stunned at the resemblance before recognizing how to rationalize it. Before we explain the double away, its presence, the vision of it, the presentation itself are captivating and traumatizing. In her trauma she turns now to examine the bed, nook of repose.

A queen-sized affair, ornately carved. The spread has been pulled tight, snow white, by a careful hand, and on the near side it is impossible to mistake the depression caused by Mrs. Bates as, of an afternoon, she lay for a nap (the depression is on top of the spread). The bed sags altogether, this emphasizing the body print. An old mattress, an old bed, the bed of an old person who has been sleeping in it for countless years. The bed has taken the shape of the sleeper's body, yet one more of those things who become their user—

> A man sets himself the task of portraying the world. Through the years he peoples a space with images of provinces, kingdoms, mountains, bays, ships, islands, fishes, rooms, instruments, stars, horses, and people. Shortly before his death, he discovers that that patient labyrinth of lines traces the image of his face. (Borges 93)

—and Lila cannot help but notice this sleeper's body is long and hardly frail, else the depression would be only slight.

The room has two predominating and contrasting appearances. It is in use, now and here, although to be sure Mrs. Bates is hardly a vigorous soul: she is dressing here, she is sleeping here. At the same time the room looks like a museum setting of a bedroom from the 1880s or '90s, the furniture burnished, the space dusted with an eye to presentation, oddly since it seems forbidden to human entry. Lila cannot be sure whether she has stepped into a display, which is to say into the past, or into a privacy, an urgent present.

Norman's room next. This is certainly a child's room, as we see instantly by the eight-inch frieze beneath the ceiling, decorated with elephants and carnival carousels. Norman's jacket hangs on a hook near the door. There are framed pictures on the walls here, too, one of them showing a schooner at sea. (Voyage within the voyage. Who is on that schooner, and where are they going?) A record player and a stack of records. Lila turns away from this, in the direction of the camera at something we cannot see yet, a look of disturbed fascination in her features. It is the bed. A narrow twin, the sheets and pillow rumpled, a quilt cover thrown back. In the near corner is a huge stuffed bunny, a frown sewn onto its face. This bunny is ancient, easily from Norman's own childhood and perhaps even inherited by him from a time long before. Lifting its lid, she looks down now at the record player, where a disc is still on the turntable. A "Premier" recording made in England: Beethoven's *Eroica*, with the Symphonette Philharmonic Orchestra conducted by Claudio Caselli. She lowers her head toward and withdraws from a space we cannot know, a bound volume the cover of which has no marking. We see a portrait shot of her face as she gazes down, presumably reading. Norman's diary? A yearbook? A philosophy that will explain?

Whiling the time in these upstairs rooms, Lila—and we with her—can have a provoking sense of having voyaged to an indeterminacy. Again the language metaphor: the language form in both rooms is plain enough—bedroom—but within that constraint the actual expression is ambiguous: old yet not old, artistic yet bourgeois, vibrant yet lost. Climbing the stairs, Lila indubitably thought she was a hunter after facts, at the very least after imagination, and believed she would find success: Marion's traces. Or Arbogast's. Or at least Mother's. We mounted with her, similarly enthused. But there is no information here. "For here there is no place / that does not see you."[28]

[C] Profane

Norman O. Brown wrote in 1960:

> I sometimes think I see that civilizations originate in the disclosure of some mystery, some secret; and expand with the progressive publication of their secret; and end in exhaustion when there is no longer any secret, when the mystery has been divulged, that is to say, profaned. (4)

Among watchers, appraisers, and scholars who have considered *Psycho* for its historical and thematic importance, far too many have been convinced that the mystery is profaned in the fruit cellar. The action of *Psycho*, for them, is brutal, repetitive killing spiced with a liberal dose of perverse sexuality. A single and unified recipe for sex and violence coupled. The action resolves as Lila strikes the light bulb.

Thus, when looming over delicate Lila in a garish dress and with kitchen knife upraised, the antique wig dropping over his cheeks, Norman is revealed as the secret killer, the film reaches its ostensibly proper explosive climax. *It was him all along!* That nice, sweet, gently smiling, politely mannered young man, who showed such courtesy and promise, such consideration and gentility, was not a person but a mask, only a performance, a cloak covering something ineffably darker and hellish. The mystery invoked in the shower, and then developed in the multiple investigations, is now (apparently) opened fully to the shocking light. Be careful in thinking people are what they appear to be. And then we can look back on prim and proper Marion, with her high values yet in her depths a craven thief. Or even Sam, unable, as he claims, to support a legitimate marriage with his meager income yet nevertheless quite ready to strip for a hotel-room noontime if it will bring a modicum of pleasure. Watch out for what things look like.

There are, of course, good and suitable reasons for doubting this view of the film's structure, and even for doubting that viewers of *Psycho* ought to have learned from it to be wary of what things look like. Cinema is an art form for which, finally, the camera sees only what things look like, although a great deal can be hinted or suggested as to what may lie beyond. Film is unrelentingly visions, and for us to doubt what things look like is to doubt the very most essential quality of the viewing experience. We have a thrilling climactic shock, as Lila meets Mrs. Bates in her swivel chair, exactly because we were happy to trust what things looked like. To preach in culmination that such a commitment was either silly or misadvised or wrong is to deny ourselves the sincerity of that shock, one of the great pleasures of the screen. But, too, the scene in the fruit cellar is *not* the profanation of the mystery Hitchcock has brought forward here. There is a long scene to follow, one that has with little serious regard been thrown off as turgid and pointless, a faulty cadence; one that can be considered mere decoration if the film's theme is fully developed before it begins.

Present in an office at the police station, beside Sam and Lila and Sheriff Chambers, are a county chief of police and an assistant district attorney, both of them in serious-looking business suits, and, commanding the scene, a psychiatrist. This last is played by Simon Oakland, who later was Schrank in *West Side Story* (1961), Steve McQueen's captain in *Bullitt* (1968), and, including his film and television work together, a man with more than two hundred screen credits. Here, he uses a very deliberate, calm, intellectualized, and patient explanatory voice in the manner of a kindergarten teacher revealing to eager young pupils how it is that A stands for Apple and B stands for Banana. We find him easy listening, with all his emphatic pauses, his soothing tone, his expressive raconteur's eyes. Psychiatry is the talking cure, after all, and the therapist is inevitably the talker's talker. So it is that we are opened to a deep engagement with what he tells us (by way of telling the people in the room with him), a deep engagement that is marred or obliviated only as we proceed down the path of taking the film as already complete beforehand and the scene with this man as an incompetent's tack-on.

The psychiatric message is at once as definitive as a glass of water and as challenging to our understanding as new, unheralded scientific theory—what, say, in 1910 relativity would have seemed to those who feared to grasp it.

"I got the whole story, but not from Norman. I got it from his mother."

"Norman Bates no longer exists," the man begins, improbably. Very improbably. Too improbably to shunt off. With profoundly chilling improbability. "He only half-existed to begin with." This is, instantaneously, a cluster of powerful contradictions of so much the viewer has already digested as "given" or "to be taken for granted": (a) that if anybody were going to explain Norman to anyone else, that person would of course be (the articulate, if stammering) Norman; because (b) we are each of us so fully in touch with, and in control of ourselves, that self-knowledge is paramount; (c) that it would be inconceivable for a keen listener such as the psychiatrist, or anyone else in the know, to *hear* the story from the mother at all, that it could ever come from her mouth (because in the fruit cellar scene we have just finished, and of which the psychiatrist has been apprised, we have learned two things irrevocably about that woman, first that she is a skeleton and second that her son has been impersonating her); (d) that sweet Norman, surely the main protagonist of everything we have seen, *does exist*. By this point in the film, one is convinced, very little does exist at the swirling center *aside from* Norman, who most assuredly must exist if one is to have watched this film. To all our construction, then, centering on our construction of Norman, the psychiatrist is saying "No."

Further: Norman hasn't existed for some time, since way before this story began. The psychiatrist's opening statement thus neatly operates to sever us from the entire structure of analysis we have used to grasp the action thus far if we are sailing the canonical route as we voyage to understanding. Hasn't existed for some considerable time. We never did meet Norman. His mother has been speaking. His mother was always speaking. It was her behind the desk at the motel. It was the mother who sank the car. And the idea that Norman could give us the story of his life is preposterous. Perhaps no one of us is equipped to tell the story of our life.

"Did he kill my sister?" Lila sensibly wants to know. Two questions conflated as one: has my sister been killed? and is he responsible?

Hence, a double-edged answer: "Yes . . . And no." Again, consider this as architectural structuring to see its elegance. We saw with our own eyes (as much as cutting would make possible) the murder of Marion. And we saw with our own eyes how the personage who emerged from behind that shower curtain with the knife and the one in the fruit cellar were one and the same, that is, Mrs. Bates, that is, "Mrs. Bates," that is, Norman. So "Yes" seems at this point the entirely correct answer. Except that our psychiatrist—raising his finger!—has added "And no." Thus, again, the film's structure is turned on its head. Something we do not know is slowly manifesting, something on the other side of the boundary of our knowledge.

". . . and no."

Hands comfy in his pockets, the lecturer now brings us back in time, ten years (a moment the sheriff and his wife dimly invoked, and with periwinkle blue!), "the time when Norman murdered his mother and her lover." Ah! Not only is Mrs. Bates dead, she is dead by matricide, not self-administered strychnine! (When asked to compare two official sources of information, a country sheriff and a city-trained psychiatrist, we choose, Hitchcock knows, the latter.) "Now, he was already dangerously disturbed. Had been ever since his father died. His mother was a clinging, demanding woman. And for years the two of them lived as if there was no one else in the world." What kind of living can this have been?[29] Clinging to Norman means constantly observing, judging, expecting, evaluating, so that the boy can never exist outside of Mother's scope of definition. And is the partnership incestuous? Well, physicality entirely aside, it can hardly have been otherwise. *Lived as if there was no one else in the world:* a coupling in hushed withdrawal, a secret marriage, a marriage to the exclusion of society. Hermits, both. "Then, she met a man. And it seemed to Norman that she threw him over for this man. And that pushed him over the line and he killed them both." This is not hard to grasp: if he thought himself her entire world; if his entire world was Mother and the thought that she thought of him as her entire world, then this other man destroyed him. And so did Mother. "Matricide is probably the most unbearable crime of all. Most unbearable to the son who commits it." Here is one of those wise comments that seem so very obvious they easily pass unnoticed. Most viewers of the film do *not* want to go down the route of imagining themselves killing mother, so they stay outside the idea, listen to it as patent diagnosis, typify it and put it away. But for Norman to kill the mother is beyond killing partnership and years of co-habitation; more than killing off the demanding, judgmental voice; it is undoing his own past, and thus a prospect that cannot be borne, just as, after the erasure of his past, he cannot be *born*. Matricide means undertaking one of those voyages that writers of science fiction love so much to elaborate, in which through some mechanism of Time Travel the hero gets to go back before he began in order to make some vital change. Norman was going back and killing the bearer of the foetus, making the Norman Bates we have been seeing all along—read, imagining all along—*actually not exist, actually never have been born.* That is to say: *now*, after killing her, he was never born, since his origin is gone. "So," says the psychiatrist, and with what might now seem profound insight, "he had to erase the crime ... at least in his own mind." Erase because he cannot both *be* and *undo his birth*. He cannot have time traveled, as the fantasy requires. And thus the fantasy must be done away with. He must wipe away all thought and memory of killing the mother. The mother, killed with certainty, cannot have been killed by him.

Again, so that we may understand this psychiatrist: I am not telling you what you might see and understand. I am telling you what Norman, that is, the Mother, sees and understands. I am telling you about Norman.

Some perfunctory information now, because Sheriff Chambers and the assistant D.A. need to know what on earth happened in perfunctory terms.

"He stole her corpse. A weighted coffin was buried." Ahhhh. "He hid the body in the fruit cellar. Even treated it to keep it as well as it would keep." Yes, yes! Norman was doing taxidermy. A needle and thread. We saw that it didn't keep so very well, that thing, that *stele*.

The cellar was not the best keep.

The keep: the most internal structure in the castle, from which one could have a view. The looking point.

And now the psychiatrist opens his greatest light, the light he shines from beyond the border of our imagination and that bleaches out the terrain we have been treading so far:

"And that still wasn't enough."

What—beyond killing, stealing, and mummifying a body, still something else? Yes, in effect the birth of a puppet:

> PSYCHIATRIST: She was *there*. But she was a corpse. So he began to think and speak for her. Give her half his life, so to speak. At times, he *could be* both personalities, carry on conversations. At other times, the mother-half took over completely. He was never all Norman. But he was often only Mother. And because he was so pathologically jealous of *her*, he assumed that she was as jealous of *him*. Therefore, if he felt a strong attraction to any other woman, the mother side of him would go *wild*. [*Pointing to LILA, stepping toward her (toward the camera)*] When he met your sister—he was touched by her. Aroused by her. He wanted her. That set off the jealous mother, and *Mother* killed the girl.

Now, *after* the murder Norman returned, as if from a deep sleep. And like a dutiful son, covered up all traces of the crime *he was convinced his mother had committed*. (Hitchcock convinced us, too.)

The crime he *was convinced* his mother had committed: not the crime he wished to commit himself, and for committing which he used his mother as cover, rationale, self-justification. No no. No no no no. Norman was the dutiful son, just as the psychiatrist tells us. Or: this is what the psychiatrist believes.

Then, in summary, a statement of abject horror: "You see, when the mind houses two personalities, there's always a conflict, a battle. In Norman's case, the battle is over, and the dominant personality has won."

Michel de Montaigne: "I fear that our eyes are bigger than our bellies, our curiosity more than we can stomach. We grasp at everything but clasp nothing but wind" (80).

What is being revealed here is a form of cannibalism.

And also a form of self-cannibalism.

Norman devoured his mother (as Pinocchio devoured Gepetto), incorporated and adopted her persona so fully it was inside him utterly, inside him and at some times devouringly so: *he was never all Norman but he was sometimes only Mother.* The ventriloquist's dummy takes over, owns the space, owns the ventriloquist. In this case, Mother's values. Mother's language. Mother's principles. Mother's dictates. Mother's shibboleths. Mother's gestures. Mother's defenses. Mother's anger. Mother's indomitable will. The boy became, one could say, what his mother taught him to become, without limit, without hesitation. Her puppet. But because he was so enthusiastic in his incorporation, his devouring, the internalized mother finally took the place of the son who had eaten her and her world. He became what he ate. And so Norman as Norman was no longer there, only Mother. And she came alive once again, through his unkenning agency, eating him from within where, eaten, she waited. He awoke, *as if from a deep sleep.* He ate up the woman who was eating him up.

But now . . . a twist of the knife:

There are two ways an actor could perform a scene such as this, with such impeccably devastating words to utter. He could be bombastic and spectacular, finally opening a Pandora's box and revealing something diabolically radiant, akin to what Robert Aldrich reveals in such spectacle at the end of *Kiss Me Deadly* (1955). He could build his phrases, finally soaring out like a prophetic eagle, screaming his verdict from the skies (Peter Lorre in *Hotel Berlin* [1945]). *This!*, our psychiatrist friend could scream: *THIS is it! Here it is! This is the CREATURE inside the egg!!!*

Or he could do what Simon Oakland quite stunningly does: speak calmly, rationally, directly, and largely without emphasis, merely as though explaining a technical phenomenon, almost a part of nature.[30] Just point it out. See, this piston fits in here and moves this rod . . . . Don't harangue. Don't make Norman a monster.

Do NOT make Norman a monster.

And in this chilling way we are brought to the ice-capped destination of the voyage that is *Psycho*. The boy who learned from mother. The boy who took mother seriously (father was gone) and who took learning seriously, too. (Hitchcock adoring his mother back in Leytonstone, coming to her at night with stories of what he did today.) The boy who found the world daunting and amazing but who trusted that Mother knew the world, Mother *was* the world. The boy who learned the world from the mother who knew too much. The boy who believed in Mother so faithfully that he gave himself to her, took in her every syllable as his own. Gave himself to her; was her meal.

And who is this only-apparently ravenous child-victim, finally, we must ask, when we hear Herrmann's deep, ominous, discordant, sustained note of the conclusion,[31] but ourselves? Each person learns at the mother's side. Each devours the mother's universe and is devoured by it in turn. The problem is to find a doorway that will let us breathe on our own. A gateway out of the Oedipal dungeon. In taking her lover, how could the mother have known that she was abandoning a child who had taken her as his craft upon the seas? Oedipus's problem is his problem, after all, not Jocasta's. He must find the way out, or, as we see with Norman, not. The way out, on the deck of the schooner on the wall, upon the high seas.

> Having failed as a musician and as a journalist, [he] had become a mnemonist, met with many prominent people, yet remained a somewhat anchorless person, living with the expectation that at any moment something particularly fine was to come his way.
>
> —A. R. Luria, *The Mind of a Mnemonist*

A LIVING ENCYCLOPEDIA

Mr Memory has left his brain to the British Museum.

    A little man, tidy dark suit. Very small self-effacing moustache, slicked hair. The hands keep folding into one another, clasping and unclasping, as in molding clay or searching nervously for salvation. He begs people to ask him questions that are serious, not the frivolous ones they are too casually hurling out. His audience is full of hecklers, who think he is a pie. At audience-right is Hannay, a young man whose tone is quite serious and respectful, the tone of someone who believes in Mr Memory (Wylie Watson) and really does want to ask an arcane question to see if he can solicit an arcane

answer, or any answer at all. It's a game. He knows how to play a game. And courteously. "How far is Winnipeg from Montreal?" Youthfulness rising from the crowd, eyebrows lifted querulously and sincerely, a bright and shining face (Robert Donat). The sort of face one wants to entertain.

Plenty more heckling, overshouting. "Where's my old man been?!" Camera darting from one to another pocket of the audience, plenty of mirth and self-satisfaction among the standing-only crowd who've had a pint or two. Very Globe, 1605. An old man, seemingly daft, with a wife beside him who is clearly put out that he has the brazenness to speak up, keeps pestering, "What causes pip in poultry?" "Shhh," she says sideways, "Don't make yourself so common!" But this man, too, is overshouted. Mr Memory is begging now, please, please, a serious question. The audience is having a raucous good time with this dollop, not necessarily in response to his act. One can taste the sauce of anti-intellectualism here, a theatrical crowd not interested in the gathering of facts into the warehouse of the mind. Another pint, if you would be so kind. Gawd, look a' 'is fonny fyce!

"How far ... is Winnipeg from Montreal?"

"Oh, a Canadian!" he stalls, holding the stage. "Winnipeg is one thousand four hundred and fifty-four miles from Montreal."

Aha! But Mr Memory is wrong by somewhere between forty-five and one hundred twenty-one miles, depending on how one travels, by road or by rail. And when he says proudly that Winnipeg is "Canada's third city," meaning, no doubt, third-ranking by population, he is wrong again, since in the mid-1930s the third-ranking city in Canada was Vancouver. Winnipeg was next. But he's a game one, this little man. He's playing for real. So somehow, odd as he is, we rather like him. What is it?—it's that he's trying. He's keeping up the side. We like people who do that.

And his errors are picayune, after all. Given that Mr Memory shows off pretty well with sports and horse-racing statistics from the past, declares himself a kind of living encyclopedia, and that he really does seem in his manner and appearance a paragon of serious intentfulness and honest devotion to his audience, one forgives him for being a little off with a country that was not seventy years old at the time, and a few thousand miles away. Numbers, distances, betting statistics: he's particularly fond of the numerical, and of a kind of flat-toned direct drawl (prologue to what, thirty or so years afterward, popular culture productions would attribute to vocalizing computers, HAL9000, for example, being a notably gracile version of Mr Memory).

If he doesn't have a memory, Mr Memory—truly there is no possible way one could ascertain whether or not he has—this man seems to possess a library of facts at his disposal. His "remembering" is a feature positioned at an incalculable position between reading a lot of books and committing all the facts in them to deep storage; or else having the bulk of the audience's questions prepped in advance with well-placed shills happily inquiring. Hannay we take to be distinctly *not* a shill, but to be asking out of both genuine curiosity and genuine desire to help this performer deliver his act. A friendly, helpful, polite, and no-nonsense young man is this one, and keep that in mind. Not British, not an Englishman at any rate, not a limey.[1]

John Buchan (Lord Tweedsmuir), who published *The Thirty-Nine Steps* in 1915 (it was serialized in August and September and published as a book in October), was no Englishman, either. He was a Scot, born in Perth in August 1875, then raised in nearby (and utterly charming) Fifeshire, in a town on the Firth of Forth (more than familiar, therefore, with the Forth Bridge [1890] that Hitchcock uses quite signally but that does not appear in the novel). Partly because of a strong recommendation from his close friend William Lyon Mackenzie King, who would soon be the tenth prime minister of Canada (and lead his country through World War II), Buchan was chosen by King George V as Governor-General of Canada as of 27 March 1935, only nine days after shooting finished on *The 39 Steps*. He lived in Canada for the final five years of his life (he died in 1940), celebrated as a warm-hearted, generous, intelligent, affable, and honest man, certainly one who was welcomed in Canada, repeatedly (if with a little stiffness in

Québec) in the same gregarious way Mr Memory, reaching out spontaneously, welcomes Hannay to England. While the Hitchcock film reaches its darkest depths in a number of scenes set in rural Scotland, it also finds its humor there, its precariousness, its morally articulate if romantic sense that the future of great nations perches upon the small shoulders of stalwart, dignified loners. The film's noisy beginning and early violence, then the highly charged conclusion, take place in the center of London.

The form of the voyage subtends virtually all the action in *The 39 Steps* (1935), sometimes broadly—as when Hannay travels northward into Scotland—and sometimes much more narrowly, for instance in the visit to the crofters' cottage. T. S. Eliot's mysterious 1942 pronouncement in *Little Gidding*, "We shall not cease from exploration / And the end of all our exploring / Will be to arrive where we started / And know the place for the first time," written to reflect the bleak sentiment of wartime England, nicely echoes the prewar tension, the need for moral illumination, and the fragility of hope demonstrated, all, in *The 39 Steps*. But if voyaging fills the contours of the story, a grander and more mysterious voyage envelops it, namely, Richard Hannay's trip from Canada (did he live in either Winnipeg or Montreal?) to England, culturing his presence as a Canadian in London.

One might reasonably wonder—although many who think and talk about this film do not seem to—why this Canadian is on a voyage at all? He seems on the surface pleasant and mild-mannered, comforting, exquisitely civilized: could such a person possibly have run afoul of the law over there? He makes no contacts that would substantiate such a thought. Does he simply want to see what England, perhaps his ancestors' England, surely the England people talk about so much, is all about? Is he, in this music hall amid the jumble of working-class rowdies taking their delirium together, having a go at the authentic side of the London scene, if not a mere tourist then an anthropologist at heart who is bent on seeing who this "Englishman" is, and who the Londoner, how he lives, how he speaks, what he speaks about. "What causes pip in poultry?" indeed.[2]

That one, by the way—and I am not supposing our foreign-born Hannay gets this—is hardly a Londoner at any rate. He and his wife have come in from a farm, Hertfordshire, perhaps, or the Home Counties, maybe even Sussex, to see what all this London London London fuss is about—"You watch who crosses and gossips, who saunters, who hurries by," Robert Browning astutely wrote in his "Up at a Villa—Down in the City"—and here they are, in their heart of hearts unable to get a plain man to tell them the one practical thing they want to know. (Presumably our rural questioner keeps chickens.) When a chicken is in respiratory distress, it breathes through the mouth and the tip of the tongue can blacken and die off, and this is one meaning of "pip." The chicken becomes speechless, we might think. This farmer can be imagined a man who spends his early mornings, before the sun is up, chatting with his birds in the coop as he feeds them, as he gathers up their eggs, and if they do not chat back he becomes worried, thrown out of his daily routine. Who, unused to such conversations, could care about "pip in poultry"? Alternately, the chick "pips" the shell from within, twice, in order to make it breakable so that he can emerge into the world; this "pip in poultry" has a Cause very Great, and surely no farmer would be concerned about, or less than knowledgeable about, chicks pipping this way. The farmer, something of a naïf, sees a man on a stage, especially lit, higher perched and dappily clothed, and thinks, "Authority . . . Wisdom . . . Agent of the Lord. Give 'im a teaser." Hannay is catching some of this. Are we?

Yet this querulous man, this bumpkin, is only one more "Londoner" in the "London crowd"—this music hall might be especially popular with strangers to the city altogether. Hannay is tucked in here, eager and also, it seems, happy to be part of this Notably English multitude. His comfort could not better be established than by his steady composure when from immediately behind him a young man pops up like a Jack-in-the-box to ask Memory a question, resting his hands for support on Hannay's shoulders. Yet, too, the very distinctive and quite variegated local accents are not fetched up by Hannay's intelligence; he merely waits through the din of the questioning for an empty spot in which he can talk. When Memory identifies him as a Canadian, is this because of the way Hannay speaks, or because of the referencing in his question? We might have good reason for supposing any Canadian such as this man is purported to be would know, already, how far Winnipeg is from Montreal. Oh, yes, he *does* know, and the point of his question is not to glean information but to give Memory a stage for his show. An act of kindness.

This may be what Memory's whole act is about. "Am I right, sir!!!" the man beaming like a lighthouse, reaching out an index finger to point at his questioner (look back to the artist's painting in *Blackmail* [1929]). "Am I right????" It's not a search through the living encyclopedia at all. It's a verification structure, for ascertaining whether the man putting himself up as a living encyclopedia is giving the impression of one in fact. It's a ceremony for impression management and the assessment of claims. *Are you who you say you are?* Whilst in everyday life we assess claims all the time, swiftly and often without conscious deliberation, the dramatic arrangements in this film bring the issue to the forefront, open the door for us to consider this vulnerable hinge of experience.

STEPS

The "main events" of the film (that is, what we are to understand takes place, not what things look like):

[1] In the music hall at the end of Mr Memory's routine, shots are fired. Pandemonium. (The theatrical panic is reprised in *Torn Curtain* [1966].)

[2] In the frantic crowd, Hannay finds himself face to face with a desperate-looking woman, who identifies herself as Annabella Smith (Lucie Mannheim) once he has led her to the safety of his flat on Portland Place where she produces some disturbing behavior: keeping the lights off until she has looked outside, begging him not to answer the ringing telephone, gulping down a Scotch as though it is medicine. She confides that she is a spy—"agent" is the word she prefers—trying to catch a gang who have stolen military secrets. "Persecution mania," he chuffs, but she is grave. The leader has a joint missing from one of his fingers. A macro-close shot of her hand holding his, and caressing his pinkie. She mentions the curious and mysterious phrase, "The 39 Steps" and speaks of the secrets being hustled out of the country. She asks him for a map of Scotland.

[3] But in the middle of the night she bursts in upon him, gagging, "Hannay, you're next!" and collapses upon him mortally stabbed.

She is clutching the map in her hand, a British Ordnance map of Perthshire, with a farmstead called Alt-na-Shellach marked near Killin, at the head of Loch Tay.

[4] He escapes the building dressed in the clothing of the morning milkman (see the reprisal of this costume change in *North by Northwest* [1959] once Roger's train has reached Chicago).

[5] Aboard the Royal Scotsman he sees a newspaper headline that lets him know the police are on his tail for Annabella Smith's murder. Seeing policemen searching, he rushes into a compartment and kisses the female occupant (Madeleine Carroll) possibly as a way of hiding his face (a moment also reprised in *North by Northwest*). She pruriently signals the police, and the train is halted on the Forth Bridge (just north of Edinburgh). Hannay escapes onto the structure,[3] evading capture.

[6] He continues his journey on foot, begging a night's stay at a crofter's hut. The crofter (John Laurie) and his young wife (Peggy Ashcroft) give him a berth, the jealous and malevolent crofter watching his wife converse with the stranger through the kitchen window. In the middle of the night, the wife sees police coming across the moor and warns Hannay, gifting him her husband's coat. Racing over the hills and streams,[4] he finds safety at Alt-na-Shellach.

[7] When the maid asks his name at the door, he advises her to say to the owner, "Miss Annabella Smith." Upstairs, Professor Jordan (Godfrey Tearle) welcomes him in an equivocal way: "You're from Annabella Smith?" with a terse smile poised somewhere between politeness and sly menace. Jordan is hosting a party with the help of his "genteel" wife (a relationship reprised in *North by Northwest*), but once he is alone with Hannay the fugitive confides to him that he is tracking some foreign spies led by a man whose finger joint is missing. "Like this?" says Jordan, lifting a hand with a missing finger joint and soon afterward shooting Hannay dead on the spot.

[8] But Hannay awakes alone to discover that in the pocket of the crofter's coat was the man's (bullet-catching) Bible. He tells his story to the

local police, not catching that the chief is a chum of the Professor's and one of the guests at that party. Jordan is his best friend, indeed. He moves to arrest Hannay, getting a cuff onto his wrist. Hannay bursts through the window and into the street, joining a Salvation Army band for cover.

[9] He finds his way into a crowded building where a political speech is about to be given, and discovers with alarm and some real perplexity that *he is the man about to give it*: of the politician he must now tout to the crowd, the man's politics, the crowd's pleasure, he knows absolutely nothing. Ad-libbing deftly, he sees police enter the hall. Pamela, the woman from the train, spots him and sends the police after him again. As they lead him off, she is asked to come, too.

[10] But as the police car zooms past the police station he realizes these "policemen" are actually members of the spy gang. The car stops on a tiny stone bridge, held up by a flock of sheep (a moment reprised in *To Catch a Thief* [1955]). In order that the men sitting in back to guard the passengers can get out to disperse the sheep, one of them "fixes" the situation by anchoring Hannay to Pamela with the cuffs. As soon as they are alone, he and Pamela make an escape and hide beneath the bridge. The two stumble across the countryside and find an inn, offering themselves as a newly married couple and artfully disguising their linked wrists.

[11] During the night Pamela wriggles free, but looking down from the balcony she sees the two false policemen, one of them on the telephone. Overhearing him, she comes to realize that Hannay has been telling the truth all along. She goes back to him, in the know now. But when she says the men left after the phone call he is furious: "Four or five hours wasted!" There's no problem, she assures him. They're going to the London Palladium, and he can catch them there. He sends her to London to warn the police, who search but cannot, as it turns out, find any missing military documents!

[12] At the Palladium Hannay hides himself in an audience while onstage a performance begins by ... Mr Memory! Pamela joins him. Just as

the police are about to take the two of them away, Hannay spots Professor Jordan in one of the boxes, watching the stage. In a flash he recognizes that Memory has seen the borrowed plans and committed them to memory, so that they could be returned to their safe cache and the fact of the theft hidden. Jordan must be planning to shepherd Memory out of the country. Our hero turns stageward and bellows out, "What are the 39 Steps?!!" Memory is jolted, and blurts out that the 39 Steps is a spy organization working on behalf of the Foreign Office of . . ." whereupon Jordan shoots him.

[13] In the ensuing hubbub Jordan is caught. Memory, in the wings, spells out the military formula and sighs, dying, what a relief it is to finally have this off his mind. And Hannay and Pamela are left holding hands—uncuffed—at the end.

With the "military plans" that we never quite fully know, and the importance of which is never established, Hitchcock provides yet another instance of his celebrated "MacGuffin," the null object or principle around which the elements of a story appear to revolve with urgency but that at the end of the film turns out to be nothing at all. Such a reading of the "military secret" is, of course, as facile and empty in itself as Hitchcock's own claims about his MacGuffin. No serious thinker, such as Alfred Hitchcock knew himself to be, could be satisfied knowing that with the long chase for the secret plans resolved, there was nothing much else to the film. Fluff packaged around an artfully created vacuum.

There is more to see beneath the surface.

In the early winter of 1935, while he was filming *The 39 Steps*, Hitchcock was no foreigner to London; he lived there. This was his territory, and he knew every point of focus intimately not only for its appearance and what it could be made to seem onscreen but also for its history and cultural background. To give just one tiny example: all the scenes in the London Palladium were filmed on location, with a real audience (a setup reflecting Hitchcock's use of the Royal Albert Hall for *The Man Who Knew Too Much* [1934] and foreshadowing his reuse of it in 1956). The Palladium was generally on Hitchcock's radar, being a rather elegant and, for London, large theatrical venue (seating just under 2,300) on Argyll Street behind Liberty of London. As of 1945, the theatrical impresario Val Parnell was managing director there, importing numerous big-name stars from America to perform on that stage (where also, for years, the Royal Variety Performance took place), and hosting, from 1955 onward, an ATV variety show based in the premises; in 1956 Hitchcock made him a character (played by Alan Mowbray) in his *Man Who Knew* remake. The Palladium attracted a genteel crowd, and while it reflected all the attributes of fashionable London theater, a true West End atmosphere, it was secluded enough to be both above and a little outside the orbit of conventional West End stages (on or around Shaftesbury Avenue or near Piccadilly Circus). While the finale of *The 39 Steps* could have been set in any theater at all, it was necessary to invoke a setting appropriate for the presence (in a box) of Jordan, whose home in Scotland had already been shown as opulent and spacious; this was not a man who would wonder what causes pip in poultry. The Palladium as a structure dates from the early eighteenth century.

But the placement of Scotland in this film is similarly purposeful and evocative on more than one level, entirely notwithstanding Buchan's roots there—"He thought of himself as [a Scot], through and through" (Lloyd 23)—since Hitchcock never felt awkward about making changes to the texts he used when it suited him. It suited him here to invoke a certain "Scotland" for Hannay to visit, crawl around in, taste deeply from the flowing burns to the rambling hills.

IN A CROFT

What, indeed, was Scotland for the English in the 1930s?

> The heathery moors slope down to a distant valley. The sun is setting. The sky above the Lammermuirs is red and troubled. The wind drops. The autumn mists far below are creeping from wood to wood. The smoke from chimneys hangs motionless in the air. Thin veils of grey wrap themselves round the foot-hills. Faint white serpents of mist twist above the greenwood, outlining the course of stream and river. It is a study in blue. In the foreground, like a promise of the Highlands, and as notable as a ship at sea, rise the tall peaks of

the Eildon Hills, blue as hothouse grapes, standing with their feet among the woodlands of the Tweed. To the far sky lie hills, always hills, fading in graduated subtleties of blue; ahead the long slopes of the Lammermuirs merge westward in the outline of the Moorfoot and the Pentlands. And it is quiet and still. (Morton 6)

What was British Railways' Royal Scotsman that Hannay rides? What the heather-covered hills over which he climbs? Or the Forth Bridge that saves him, the farm tucked away that succors, the curling roads among the bleak stone fences, the sweet and warm little inn with the innkeeper's wife who was unutterably charmed at the thought of a pair of newlyweds? What of that crofter, a bitter man old enough to be his wife's father, and his heavy tweed coat, and the deeply buried Bible? All this betokens a certain blithe, bucolic romanticism, an eye toward distant streams plentiful with salmon and woods running with stags, lavender sunsets; a Scotland radically altered from the wildland haven of mercenaries, revolutionaries, and brutalists who characterized the Jacobite Rebellion, now transformed, wholly, in train of the Victorian enchantment. In September 1848 Victoria wrote to her uncle from Balmoral:

> The scenery all around is the finest almost I have seen anywhere. It is very wild and solitary, and yet cheerful and beautifully wooded, with the river Dee running between the two sides of the hills. (qtd. in Dolby n.p.)

She enthused, too, over the deer forest and the hill laid with grouse, black cock, and ptarmigan. Good healthy wilds, good refreshment from solitary meditation, after the press of the city. Worth a journey. If not to eat one's catch, to breathe the atmosphere one's catch had breathed, something diviner than London air, as Victoria wrote:

> It was calm, and so solitary, it did one good as one gazed around; and the pure mountain air was most refreshing. All seemed to breathe freedom and peace, and to make one forget the world and its sad turmoils. (*Leaves* 65–66)

The queen's was an enrapturement, whereas in 1786 Boswell had noted that his companion Dr Johnson expiated to me on the nakedness of that part of Scotland which he had seen ... when Dr. Johnson talks of trees, he means trees of good size, such as he was accustomed to see in England; and of these there are certainly very few upon the *eastern coast* of Scotland.... About eleven at night we arrived at Montrose. We found but a sorry inn, where I myself saw another waiter put a lump of sugar with his fingers into Dr. Johnson's lemonade, for which he called him "Rascal!" (69; 72)

London was keeping a post-Victorian sentiment, and Scotland was not only a freshened paradise but also an ideal site upon which Hannay could target his travel. It made sense that in a far-off and secluded zone, where one would be alone with nature (Alt-na-Shellach was in the Grampian Hills; the term means "river by the glen"), a secret organization might base itself and conduct its operations; and that, desperately in flight from the London police (for a crime he did not commit—a repeated motif in Hitchcock), Hannay might seek blissful rest, at least to catch his breath.

Hitchcock's Scottish lowlands are windy and unforgiving, but majestic for all that, and shot by Bernard Knowles (whom Hitchcock would have known at Gainsborough when he made *Number 13* [1922] and who had earlier lent atmosphere to *The Hound of the Baskervilles* [1931]) with an extraordinarily sumptuous range of lambent mid-tones and deep-contrasting blacks, most especially as Hannay flees to Jordan's hideaway with the local police in pursuit, tiny figurations whistling on the far distant hills. The same painterly geste is used to figure the stone bridge where Hannay and Pamela flee during the obstruction by sheep, and the nocturnal landscape, a virtual dream space into which the fake policemen drive their captives after Hannay has made his little oration (a Hitchcockian joke being the complete stranger's ability to mimic a *perfectly typical* political speech). The long, elaborate Forth (Railway) Bridge is shown as a true monument to modern engineering, both a supreme hideaway (because of the thickness of its iron beams) and a splendid and triumphant form, socially important for two reasons: it facilitated the extension of railway travel, born in the 1840s, northward into the Highlands, with all the concomitant expansion of trade and commerce;[5] and it celebrated, much like the Eiffel Tower in Paris, the new idea of constructing with iron. Hitchcock's use of this bridge goes far beyond the facility he tended to show, noted by

Truffaut in his interviews, for using whatever local landmarks were available when he shot films: the Dutch windmills in *Foreign Correspondent* (1940) or Copenhagen's Newhaven (Nyhavn) in *Torn Curtain*. The Forth Bridge and the Grampian Hills are utterly characteristic, and also telling, but used in the film not just for pinpointing of dramatic locale but to establish cultural meaning and to develop action realistically.

The location: *not* London. With some eagerness we will follow Hannay as he walks from the bridge into Perthshire.[6] This is not a land of sophisticates and cultural manipulators, not the home of the Bank of England and the Stock Exchange, not a land running over with barristers and solicitors, not a venue for glib circumlocution and smarting one-upmanship. Country people in a nation with a small population, many of them farming on the rolling hills under bleak skies. Hannay will encounter old-fashioned behavior, strange modesty, biblical principal avowed and clung to, ancient proprieties, a culture of genuineness that does not tolerate insincerity, a place without amenity under God. And as to Hannay himself: whyever he came to the United Kingdom—"I'm only over here from Canada for a few months"—he would need to have had money to do so and we can therefore presume him to be in the Canadian educated classes. He knows literature, he has wit, he recognizes irony—and he will therefore see distinctly that literature, wit, and irony are largely absent in this harsh bucolic zone. He will be entering a zone of moral high contrast, the Good being very clearly different from Evil there, hence the high-contrast black-and-white photography of mountainous territory filled with sunny splotches and dark shadows. When he comes to the crofter's hut, only the simplest of human virtues and the most honest of etiquettes will see him through.

As we come upon him the crofter is leading a steer to barn. Hannay is direct but sweet and imploring, while the crofter is taciturn and abrupt, speaks the way one does when the wind is continually threatening. Yes, there's a professor type who lives over at Alt-na-Shellach, but you won't be going there tonight, it's fourteen miles. No, that lorry is going in the other direction. Could the crofter give him a place to sleep the night? "For free?" No no, he can pay. "Can you eat the herring? ... Can you sleep in a box bed? ... Two and six." At the door a much younger person is instructed to bring him in. Quiet, quite beautiful, feminine without proclamation. "Your daughter?" The crofter scowls, but with an unexplained amazement. "Mah wife!"

She is young, Margaret; younger even than she knows. Crofter John has never been young. Hannay sits to table at Margaret's behest and sees that beneath the packages the lorry delivered rests a copy of today's paper, with a lead article involving the Portland Place killing. Not noticing it, she gathers up the paper with the food packages and lays them aside. "Won't y'sit down, please, while I go on with our supper." She lets him know she is from Glasgow, "Did y'ever see it? . . . Oh, you should see Sauchiehall Street with all its fine shops. And Argyle Street on a Saturday night, with all the trams and the lights!" And is it true—holding breath—that in the big city (London) the ladies all paint their toenails? He has been, he says, to Edinburgh, Montreal, and London but never saw one so fair as she. There is not the slightest intimation of insincerity in his voice. In strides the husband, glowering. Hannay asks, "Could I read your paper?" A close-up of Margaret's hand lighting the lamp, the glass holder shaped like nothing so much as a crown.

The newspaper story is chilling. PORTLAND PLACE MURDER TRACED TO SCOTLAND. EXCITING INCIDENT ON THE FORTH BRIDGE. GUARDS STORY. One of the most horrible crimes of the century. . . . She is beside him, looking down at the table as she sets the places. The crofter is behind giving a stare but unable to read over Hannay's shoulder. They sit while the crofter, at the head of the table, lowers his head and gives the blessing. Not a happy prayer but a cold, even resentful one, as though the Good Lord could, had He wanted, have afforded a sweeter life. Margaret, eyes open, has spied the headline and is reacting with wide-eyed shock in pure silence—literally as in a silent film. Hannay tries to gesture with his eyes and lips (in a situation that will crop up again in *Saboteur* [1942]). (No intertitle is required here!) The crofter sees the two of them, his dark, fire-poker eyes darting this way and that. Suddenly he remembers that he forgot to lock the barn so he stands up and goes out. But cutting to the outside we see him pause, as though in doubt or recrimination, and proceed to the window where he can spy upon them. They are standing over the table, leaning toward one another conspiratorially. A stunning medium close-up of his greedy face (greedy for vengeance) through the window glass from the warm inside, showing the cross bars of the window (reprised from *The Lodger* [1927]) and the crofter peeping askance, his lips stitched, his eyes thirsty.

The middle of that night. Margaret fully awake in bed, with her husband asleep—possibly? really? does surveillance ever rest?—at her side. She hears the very distant bray of a horn, leaps up, goes to the window, and sees the approaching light of a car in the far hills. Letting herself into the main room she awakens Hannay, but the crofter is right behind her. "Behind my back! Get out!" Hannay gives a perfectly simple, perfectly clear explanation: that she has been trying to help him because he is fleeing from the police, and now they are here. "The police!!!" a look of surprise and possibly concern. He will agree to open the door and keep his mouth shut for five guineas, but when he leaves the shot (when he leaves the room; when he leaves his promise; when he leaves rationality) the young wife expresses grave concern, going so far as to lean into the camera listening in with doubt and trepidation. "Yes, he's asking if there's a reward...." She gets Hannay out a back door, draping him in her husband's long tweed coat, dark for the darkness, heavy to keep out the damp. He gives her a swift peck of gratitude and we are left with the crofter's wife, her head slowly falling as the scene fades, a look of lost hope, lost opportunity, a lost pathway adorning her beautiful face.

(In *Torn Curtain* Hitchcock will bring this noble woman back, in the persona of the Countess Kuchinska [Lila Kedrova] who wants nothing more than to come to the United States of A-mer-i-ka! with Michael Armstrong and Sarah Sherman as her sponsors. But they flee, leaving her to whimper pathetically, "My sponsors ... my sponsors ...")

As story surface, the little crofter scene fulfills the function of giving our fleeing hero a place to sleep for the night, or at least part of the night, and a decent meal. In the cold damp hills, a haven of warmth and rest and conviviality on offer at least on the wife's part. A fair exchange with the husband is two and six. A fair exchange with the wife is information about city style for a decent meal and a box bed. The advice not to trust her husband and the warm coat are gifts free of charge. But from this scanty information—I would call it the "plot read"—we do not catch hints of the quality of the scene, its tone, its carefully effected look, its echoes. To emphasize: working through the actions, one does not *see the screen:*

- The tidiness of the crofter's cottage arrangement on a tiny rise among the majestic hills. Whitewashed wattle-and-daub with a thatched roof: wattle-and-daub and thatching are artisan creations. At screen bottom a typical curling stone wall: stone wall building the same: with the crofter leading his steer leftward to a darkened shed.[7] Above, a lorry backed against the house. Overcast sky (trouble coming), vague outlines of the hills (this is a lonely area with no special landmarks). Already visible on the crofter, a sleeveless jumper and a shirt and necktie: he is at home, he is alone in the country, he is with his steer—but a shirt and necktie! Man should always be modest before his Lord. And Man is never *not* before his Lord. One has the strong sense that this man is settled *into* the perfectly shaped and crafted space; that he neither leaves it nor plans to leave it; that beyond being his home it is his world.

- Leading up to this, enchanting long shots: the braes and glens with a teasing patch of moving sunlight. Lonely, forlorn, magnificent, perfectly remote, a study in form, graphic and geographic. The cry of any single human would not be heard in these emptinesses. A detail shot shows a stone bridge Hannay crosses, with a purposeful stride and an optimistic bounce (a bridge not very unlike the one Constance Peterson and John Ballantine will cross for their picnic in *Spellbound* [1945]). All the structuring in these wildlands is done by hand, trades passed from generation to generation to tradesmen whose expertise in handling their materials is very pronounced.

- Hannay and the crofter are the only humans we see at first, in this sequence. Not the wife yet. Nor the itinerant lorry driver. Nor the inhabitants of the manse visible in the far distance. Surely not the "odd" professor living at Alt-na-Shellach. A lone man, his lonely but cozy domain, the raw natural world. Hitchcock uses several shots here not to set the scene—any one shot could do that, and without artistry—but to place us cognitively and emotionally where the winds howl, the sheep fight the recalcitrant scrub, the curvatures of hills and valleys never cease enchanting. We are meant to be enchanted, murder mysteries entirely to the side.

- Hannay must make himself familiar to the crofter, and here in the lonely countryside, where every person is either a familiar or a stranger, one becomes "familiar" by honesty and truth, not by a quick superficial recognition. For the crofter, Hannay is either someone whose background and purposes can be seen somehow and trusted or someone who comes from beyond the boundary and whose purposes may be evil. It is not ingratiation that Hannay must accomplish; it is joining, clanning, being civilized. To the degree that the crofter is made to look dark and unpredictable to us, somewhat dark surely, somewhat unpredictable, the audience is led to hold back from trusting him and attention strays from the regard a man like him must have for a man like Hannay. Already we are on Hannay's team, seeing other people from his point of view rather than seeing him from theirs. We are ready to neglect the view of the crofter, an outsider to Hannay's world (and, in truth, "outside" like our view of him and all characters in cinema). Hannay surely knows he is a stranger, but also that no veritable stranger can expect to be given much comfort here. Georg Simmel:

> Throughout the history of economics the stranger everywhere appears as the trader, or the trader as stranger. As long as economy is essentially self-sufficient, or products are exchanged within a spatially narrow group, it needs no middle man: a trader is only required for products that originate *outside* the group. (403; emphasis mine)

Outside, in the universe that is *not known*. This crofter, we can directly see, has long been suspicious of, even repelled by strangers.

Hence the simple sense of the crofter's query to Hannay—which will seem abrupt and money-grubbing only to those of us far outside the little community in which the crofter has been making his life, those of us for whom he is, already, dark: "What'll your business be?" And the swift, yet notably constructed, answer, "I'm a motor mechanic looking for a job." (Or *is* Hannay trained in car repair? We are never informed.) Constructed along the lines of tradesmen, those who come near because they can do something for you that you cannot do for yourself. Strangers are all about economy, as Simmel teaches. Or: it is only by reference to employments that the stranger is strange at all. The technical problem for Hannay is that he is in no position to cite a local farm at which he is a worker, and a man like this crofter wouldn't take a recommendation from anyone who wasn't local. As a stranger, Hannay "intrudes as a supernumerary, so to speak, into a group in which the economic positions are actually occupied" (403). To leap away for a flash: this crofter has been living here for a considerable time already, and has been quite self-sufficient. Hannay needs him but he doesn't need Hannay.

"What'll your business be?" comes instantaneously after the exchange of mutual greetings. No nonsense. I don't listen to the music of your mouth because I don't know you. What do you want here, why are you standing at my croft? But there is also no cursory dismissal. This stranger may be an angel in disguise, after all. Think of the need for civility above all, elementary courtesy, decent fellow feeling at the simplest. And think of the crofter, no longer a young man, with his childless wife, and recollect the angels visiting Abraham (Genesis 18):

> 1. Again the Lord appeared unto him in the plain of Mamre, as he sat in his tent door about the heat of the day. 2. And he lifted up his eyes, and looked: and lo, three men stood by him, and when he saw them, he ran to meet them from the tent door, and bowed himself to the ground. 3. And he said, Lord, if I have now found favor in thy sight, go not, I pray thee, from thy servant. 4. Let a little water, I pray you, be brought, and wash your feet, and rest yourselves under the tree. 5. And I will bring a morsel of bread, that you may comfort your hearts, afterward ye shall go your ways: for therefore are ye come to your servant. And they said, Do even as thou hast said.

Hannay is no angel, we know: but the crofter isn't going to hedge his bets. Fervor has given the crofter sufficient doubt, sufficient reason, day after day, to fear. Fear if not man then the Lord. And if not the Lord then the Lord's messengers. Fear and fervor, harbingers of revelation.

As for Hannay, "Assume a virtue if you have it not" (*Hamlet*, III.iv.161). He claims a trade helpfully imported from the outside, since it can easily appear that this croft is standing so far out in wilderness that the crofter (who may or may not think this a wilderness) could have need for a mechanic. But there's a blunt riposte: "Ye'll find no work here." Simply put; honest; direct; not the kind of ornate, sociable tease one would encounter in the city, in, as the crofter would think, Satan's Province. The man does not mean either friendliness or unfriendliness, merely to give an honest comment about what the stranger has just said. Not only clarity but forthright clarity, even light. Two indeterminate faces, each sizing the other up, neither certain of sanctity.

"No houses around?" Hannay wonders affably enough—if not you, is there somebody else near here who might need my labor? But the answer is perturbing. "Sir Andrew has a chauffeur who's been with him forty years." Hannay is curious about this: "I didn't know there's been cars that long." The film is shot in contemporary time, 1935, and Vauxhall was building automobiles in England since 1903. For all this cold taciturnity the crofter is standing at screen left, his right arm up behind him on the top of the gate to the sheds, a coat draped over his left forearm and his trusty walking stick clasped in hand. He looks down, distinctly not into the stranger's face. At his side Hannay takes a sideways view, giving no appearance of being put off by this withdrawal. Something must happen to resolve the tension of this face-à-face.

Yet we must first wonder at Hitchcock's arranging a face-à-face in the first place, wonder critically, that is, from outside the film and looking back, because the crofter as a personality has only marginal effect on the action here; it will be his wife who is preeminent. Without him, and his brusqueness, and his general state of withdrawal (into the mountains) the experience of Hannay in Scotland would be far too sociable, far too much like London; and so what would be the point of setting him there? Scotland has to be the kind of place one wouldn't find near Piccadilly, and to be that kind of place to the full it must harbor citizens like the crofter, who meet strangers in this seemingly equivocal way:

- As Hannay is introduced to Margaret at the doorway, the crofter turns his eyes back to look up into the stranger's face with his lips turned down (an expression urbanites should not interpret too quickly), while she stands in the door, hands clasped peacefully (idle hands do the Devil's work) and her face a mask of neutrality. Dappled (that is, friendly) sunlight. Will this be an amicable situation or not, for our fleeing hero? We hope the sun will shine. So far he has followed the tack of giving very curtailed (if not so very honest) answers to the crofter's honest, but very curtailed questions. "Mah wife!" The easy reading here—the popular reading—is that the crofter is not only a suspicious man but a jealous one and an aggressive one, a man who probably beats his wife regularly but certainly will have no truck with any other man's presumptive sallies. He is showing off the suspiciousness and jealousy immediately, as a warning to Hannay possibly but surely as a signal to the audience. Much more complex, and much more interesting, is reading this moment as the crofter's awkward, uncomfortable way of socializing, since he knows he's in a social situation but he's very not used to being there. "Ye keep yer filthy hands offa'n mah wife!" one can hear him grumble, but be wary of hearing what isn't being said in these hills. At any rate he walks off.

Does Hannay at all fancy the wife? Does Hitchcock wish us to imagine that he does, and that in this gallant and handsome stranger the imprisoned woman sees a chance of freedom? Her eyes do not show this, because they have dropped, but the placid light that floods her person does suggest a delicacy perhaps not unfamiliar to Hannay and that the husband cannot match. The scene will play dramatically if it is unavowedly structured around a potential bonding, if the viewer is led surreptitiously to hope for salvation. (If salvation is the MacGuffin.) But would Hannay, shown carefully in his flat with Annabella Smith to be a man of etiquette and decorum, really think about the wife so cravenly, immediately upon greeting her?

And is it quite certainly dominating possessiveness that possesses the crofter? Wife as property?

He is a lone man without family, speaking with a country dialect. While no doubt he has it within his power to be tender, on an appropriately blessed occasion, he is nothing like the model of handsome masculinity one finds, even without looking, in Hannay. When he spies Hannay he cannot possibly be unaware of this. Further, we will learn very soon how the wife started out in Glasgow with its trams and lights but has somehow found her way to this wasteland:

> Winter kept us warm, covering
> Earth in forgetful snow, feeding
> A little life with dried tubers.[8]

We can see the homesick nostalgia in her face as she recalls Sauchiehall Street and its fine shops. "And Argyle Street on a Saturday night.... It's Saturday night tonight."[9] Hannay tries to show sympathy: "You certainly can't get those things here," but before she agrees, "No," there is a long, richly nostalgic pause. We can imagine how strange it must have been for her to make a home in this alien place, not so long ago—how the strange aura of Glasgow may still glow in her heart. What, she may well wonder, is she doing here with this cold man? This man whom she met how, exactly? When he courted her was he a softer man?

Or was courting elided? This could be a marriage arranged at long distance, through intermediaries, possibly by way of the church. A meeting one day when he came to the city on business, say to purchase some lamps for his croft. Love as a business arrangement between two incompatibles. And has she been locked here, with this Bluebeard, a long time, say, since she was fifteen or sixteen years old? Locked and guarded. All the Scots landscape portions of the film serve to offer visions of an unyielding openness—the untrammeled air!, lofty peaks, shadowy vales, endless stretches of sky, mysterious trickling streams with origins in The Nowhere. Thence attention can be drawn, by contrast, and subtly, to rigid confinements: the wife's, the crofter's himself, Hannay's in the face of the police on one side and Professor Jordan on the other, those two "sides" being in truth, and for Hannay so deplorably, only one. For the wife, her sentence seems an eternity yet she is radiant. Radiant with lost feeling, or with yearning, or with the tang of memory? She has come from a Glasgow she may have patrolled by herself on a Saturday night. Perhaps she is twenty-three or twenty-four now. As to an arranged marriage, for John to have found a lone woman of maturity was unthinkable at the time, because such a person would likely have gone into a convent or become a governess, if she did not head for the streets in a more pathetic way. Margaret knew she must find a husband. And as to him: alone in the country, man will not survive materially or socially without a wife. Did an intermediary in the church go out of the way to be helpful, knowing someone who knew someone? Was the coupling an accident? It is a delicious complication that through the characters' gestures and the variant lighting that falls upon them Hitchcock conveys the relationship to the viewer as unresolved, as perplexing, as both evident and impossible, without venturing to make a resolution, without bringing the crofter and his wife forward as principal elements in a story that must take another highway. Even in the crux of this marital coil, just as in the windy world outside the croft, we see tonal emptiness signaling a grave plight of confinement, borderlessness that enunciates borders.

Setting eye upon Margaret, the sour crofter must surely have asked himself, "How could this good fortune have happened to me?" He must think, "This is a beautiful young woman, how is't sh'has become mah bride?" How a bride, indeed, and how a partner in life for someone so plain looking, e'en so dismal, as he knows himself to be, for someone who is (and who knows he will be seen as) no gallant catch? Further, given his obsession with commandments biblical, how vitally important it is in any event—he must have murmured in his conscience—for a man to take a wife before the Lord! A wife to have and to keep.

That is: to have; and also to keep. To keep by one's side, and to keep near in the storm of life. To clutch, perhaps. But surely to preserve.

Could it not be that when Hannay appears out of thin air, this crofter is already terrified of losing his treasure, has been terrified since they met? When he sees her cozying with the man (in his eyes, an ideal suitor and a stranger, with no ties to the community—no ties, no moral obligation) might he not be sore afeard she w'run off? (In the early morning, when he barks at the two of them to "Get out!!!," what can he imagine happening next but that she might accompany the stranger?) She is precious, to be sure; she loves him (because she has learned to love him); she cares for him (through his days); she cares for his home (cleanliness is next to godliness); she was hard to find in the first place, and ... *how many other young women would be free for his proposal in a lonely, deserted, forlorn, blustery, challenging environment like this?* Did he meet her on Argyle Street on a Saturday night?

Might it, perhaps, not be jealousy we see in the crofter's narrowed eyes laid askance, but fear? And are the sideways glances not so much gestures of arrogant superiority (the local man above the stranger) as gestures of deference and shyness, gestures that speak an instantaneous regard of the city man as (holy or unholy) King? So much silence ...

- As for Margaret, she goes about her business with a silent devotion, she shirks no duty. She does not quite fully belong in this place. Her mind is in the city, her childhood was in the city, her dreams were city dreams. She is wearing a tidy and entirely unobtrusive shirtwaist dress with a Peter Pan collar, prim, demure as demure can be. Even in a place where visitations are a rarity, never to give the least hint that she might wish to show herself off to any man other than the one she married. All his fearful suspicion is matched by her stolid loyalty, hushed as it is. The silence takes physical form. It inhabits her postures, her smiling face, her hands. The silence is the emptiness of the hills, the bars of her cell. Why does the crofter not notice her loyalty? Because his business isn't reading faces, it's tending to his animals in this wasteland.

- The crofter wishes to sell Hannay out. We could very easily (mis-)read him as a venal man, hungry to profit upon any exploitation whatever, a man who, immediately upon learning that Hannay is in flight from the police, sees advantage for himself, yet advantage of a moral not only an economic kind. He is better than Hannay, and he will be the proud (oh, so proud) means of Hannay's capture, imprisonment, and, if the wheels of justice thresh the chaff from the grain of human affairs rightly (and righteously), hanging. We could read him this way. Or we could use the Scots stereotype of money hunger, cheapness, hard bartering, forgetting that a stereotype like this grows into its hyperbolic form from a commonplace germ, that there is a great deal of poverty in rural Scotland, a poverty hardly changed since the Jacobite wars (read Stevenson's *Kidnapped*). Forgetting, too, that this crofter is "eking out a frugal subsistence" with "small-scale farming" (Pryor 484). His life of decency and moral propriety is his bulwark against the battering force of the wind. He cannot with reason deny himself a chance to make extra money, even a small amount. He is not betraying Hannay from personal disregard, because it is clear he doesn't especially like or trust the police and doesn't have a negative view of Hannay for being in flight from them. He is bartering hard, not being one of those city sophisticates who can afford to let money breeze by. We will meet the Professor and his wife and his blithe daughter and his good chum the police inspector, and see how these folk do let life breeze by.

- A startling shot has Margaret peering out her bedroom window at the hills by night, dark and almost living forms, with the light of the police car beaming as a small point among them. It is not only by daytime rationality, the practical light of a workman's day that one sees the lonely croft in the lonely countryside. It is a place that is also a condition, always, forever, unchanging.

- The expression on the wife's face once Hannay has slipped away, such a very special moment: her chagrin, as though it would have been ideal to keep him as a friend always; the pain of withdrawal: she has not fantasized him as a lover but she may very well have fantasized him as good company; the pain of a particular abject knowledge: that there is a world in which others race and climb, act and prevent action, a world *out there* (among the hills, beyond the hills, beyond even Scotland altogether, because this man is not from Scotland), and she is fixed permanently *here*, under the aegis of this sanctimonious man who has little hope of rising above his station, above the beast in the shed. She is caught here, trapped here, yet willingly, yet by marriage, a sacrament. Sacramental but caught. Caught in her social identity as young woman; caught in the memory trace of her urban roots torn away; caught in his judgment, when she has a moral life of her own that she must not take the liberty to express. There is also a hint of melodic sadness, her sense that she has been gifted a solitary moment of wonder to be cherished, a moment that sparks an inner life in her, a vivid life, yet now as quickly as it came it is gone. Perhaps it happened only in a dream, a dream so provocative that, far too like Caliban, she would cry "to dream again."

- The crofter wants to know, with some irritation, what Hannay (Hammond, as he knows him) is confabulating about with his wife. "I was just saying to your wife that I prefer living in town to the country," Hannay dissembles. The crofter passes left-to-right directly near the camera, between us and Hannay, saying, under his breath but not so muffled that we cannot hear, "God made the country." Invocation of a relation between the Deity and nature. Stipulation of the superiority of rural living: it is safely distant from the degrading and sacrilegious filth of the city. *I am closer to God*, a statement not a boast; perhaps a self-reassurance. He is wearing a warm, combed cotton grandfather shirt. His waistcoat is a little too large: he has been eating poorly, or else he has to wear whatever he could find in the lonely thrift shop at Killin.

- But finally, and in ceremony, the Deity is openly invoked, as Hannay and Margaret sit across from one another at table, signaling with their eyes, and the crofter, hands folded, head dropped a little, speaks to his God. Yet without taking eyes from the other two. The eyes shift left and right nervously, and the two listeners sit as still as gilded angels on the altar. "If ye'll pet doon thet papr, I'll say a blessin'":

  > *Sanctify* these bounteous mercies to us miserable sinners. O Lord, make us truly thankful for them and for all Thy manifold blessings. And continually turn our hearts from wickedness and from worldly things unto Thee. Amen.

Impossible not to hear and retain certain resonances of apocalyptic Puritanism. Not to imagine that the crofter has invented these sentiments or tonalities for himself; no, he was taught as a little boy, long long ago, at the tableside of another martinet, and he has picked up his character as a natural matter of course, there having been—in what I imagine to have been a very cloistered youth—no other influences. The crofter cannot behave otherwise than he does; cannot use other phrases. Bounteous *mercies*, as though we are dependent on Grace, not only helpless but destitute, most likely because of our low position. *We . . . are . . . low.* And then, *miserable* sinners: we suffer misery, or many miseries, because life has been unbearably difficult, and thus we are "miserable"; or else in the objective estimation of others we are nothing but miserable—rude, dirty, starving, poor. *Turn our hearts from wickedness:* that is, from the manifold wickednesses which we persist in ogling, from the font of wickedness which is our sorry altar, from the disease of wickedness that will never be redeemed. *And from worldly things.* Precisely: The spare table, but a table. The spare hospitality, but hospitality. Turn our hearts from the sorts of things one picks up on Sauchiehall Street in the lovely shops. Or on Argyle Street of a Saturday night.

It is Saturday night now. A simultaneous conflation and expansion of space by way of a simultaneous affirmation and denial of time.

It is Saturday night now.

MEMORIES

The act that features Mr Memory is interesting in itself. It is immaterial whether he has used prepared shills in his audience some of the time. He clearly has an acute visual memory—a quick glance at the military secrets on paper and he has locked them in his vault. But the act, as performed before an audience, is notably *acoustic*.

Not only is Memory's appearance announced by a jaunty, if nonsensical musical riff, a scherzo, which for some reason bears striking resemblance to a person crying "Oops!"; but we are shown in the film how that musical theme has embedded itself in Hannay's deep consciousness. On his visit to the Palladium, the instant the theme is struck up he jolts awake with the memory that he has heard that before, and yes, it's the same little man. The sound of the past. In the police car in Scotland he whistles the tune, but it isn't possible to be sure whether he knows what it is (in *The Lady Vanishes* [1938] a haunting but elusive tune plays a key role).

There is more than this ditty, however. Mr Memory is distinctively bland to look at, he has a face very similar to a blank page. The cheeks are chalky and broad, flattened by make-up and the lens. His piercing dark eyes seem to be screaming a question, "Do you see me? Do you see my astonishing power?" He has a tiny mouth, odd for someone who uses it for pay. Above this is an even tinier moustache, just enough of a line to decorate the face with a modicum of character. Nobody would pay money for Mr Memory in order to see him. Is the design of him vaguely from Chaplin's tramp? Is it from a tranquilized Hitler? No, we cannot remember where we saw that face before, or whether, but there is pain to feel when we see the little man flustered onstage because his music hall audience taunts him. Meek, possibly inheriting the earth, except that his memory will damn him.

When Memory speaks, *listen*.

Listen with the greatest care . . .

. . . a challenge so easily unmastered. The film's finale is a little choreography involving Memory at its center. From a hidden cave in the audience, the voice of Hannay barks out, "*What are the 39 Steps?*" Pointless now to look for meaning or value of any kind in the huge audience spread laterally across the auditorium, or in the nervous posture of the man on the very brightly lit stage. Pointless, too, for a moment, at least, to recollect that the Professor is perched in a box over the stage. Or to take serious note of the police who have entered the hall. "The 39 Steps ... —" Mr Memory repeats to buy a second or two (an obedient grade-school student, standing and repeating the teacher's test question; posturing reassurance that he's done his homework, that he's studious and well behaved, that he hasn't a negative bone in his body). Hannay is at wits' end, realizing in a flash—realization always comes in a flash—that Memory has committed the military plans to memory, Mr Memory and his treasured (very non-public) memory, and here is Jordan planning to shepherd him out of the country. But just as Hannay has noticed Memory, the police have noticed Hannay. The police—a noxious element—want to take him away, since although Pamela told them of the conspiracy plot coming to a head tonight, deeply buried in their mental files he lingers as the murderer of Annabella Smith. It's his realization about Memory coupled with his desperation at the sight of the uniforms that leads him to scream that interrogative mantra, "What are the 39 Steps??? Come on, answer us, what are the 39 Steps?????" It is desperation voyaging in a breath to realization.

> MEMORY: The 39 Steps is an organization of spies, collecting information on behalf of the Foreign Office of—

Gunning him down, the Professor races off, leaving Hannay and Pamela to scoot onstage to Memory's aid, cache him in their arms in the wings, hear him spill the military plans before dying.

How easy, how direct and unimpeded it is to voyage to the conclusion that a foreign power has put the spy organization to work to extract that vital information, that the information is to be ferried by Jordan out of the country by way of Memory's embodiment; and that Jordan, masquerading as a stolid middle-class academic with a substantial reputation in the countryside, is now and has long been an instrumental power in this foreign spy group, a moving force. Annabella Smith would have uttered all these truths had she not been cut off too young (and in the first reel!). How easy, how painless to conclude this, to travel to this destination.

But there is something mesmerizing about that reply delivered onstage in a robotic trance, Mr Memory's inexpressive monotone intended to mark it out from all the acoustic hubbub of both the scene and the film so far, all the shouting out we have come to expect from him, all the frantic back and forth. The reply is a kind of printed memorandum come to life and speaking for itself. It's not the words that convey this; it's something about the stunned look on Memory's face, shown quite abruptly in a markedly tilted shot and from up close, as though we are looking at a different part of the man's brain, as though we have tapped into an Aladdin's cave never known about before. A new source of knowledge, a New Memory, and in gaining access to it the little man has come alive, a robot suddenly activated, Frankenstein's monster after being jolted. Again—the script wouldn't reveal this. One has to see the way seeing is slanted, exaggerated, sucked in. He's come alive to answer exactly as if by movement of some rote mechanism, after a similarly rote act of memorization, as though he was hypnotized a long time ago, conditioned operantly to spring awake on hearing the words, "What are the 39 Steps" spoken as a question. Question as code. Question as mechanism.

The 39 Steps is an organization of spies. Collecting information. On behalf of the Foreign Office of——

Two blunt queries demand to be raised:

[1] *Regarding espionage.* How significant might it be that a simple link is implied here between spying and collecting information? Not that we might reasonably doubt what spy films have taught, that spies do busy themselves with collecting information. But that the reverse may be as true or truer, those who collect information are spies? Collection of information is espionage. One spies upon the world, one examines the minutiae, the date on which Florence Nightingale died, the distance from Winnipeg to Montreal, tidbits of information wherever they lie, scattered, deployed, organized, thrown loose, yet all picked up in the net, sifted, catalogued, placed in their separate battalions. Collecting information is the life of the mind. Mr Memory, if anyone, is surely a spy, then, and naturally so, a man who has diligently culled full libraries to glean the information contained therein: he is a model for the researcher type, in fact. A nice psychological game-test for memory strength: recall a list of numbers in order; recall it backward; state every third number. Or blunt spying: look at this picture, now turn it backside up, count to five, and tell me everything you saw. The amassing, preservation, contexting, and retrieval of relevant details. What causes pip in poultry?

When we see a film like this one, complicated, jumping around as at an enormous soirée and meeting so many different people, this one and that one and this one and this one, and taking it all in, and trying so very hard to make the puzzle pieces come together into a rendition ... when we do this we are spies, and the watching is espionage. Gather enough intelligence to make the logic plain. As if in cinema the substructure is a logic, not a look.

Professor Jordan is a spy, too, and not as much in the sense—conventionally appreciated—that he is head of the 39 Steps as in the simpler, purer sense that as an academic he gathers and holds information, supremely: his collecting and filing of facts, texts to quote, theories to toy with, and his subsequent public demonstration of that accomplishment by way of lectures and publishing, are given such assiduous practice, with such rigor and such determination that he can be little other than a paragon to match Mr Memory, except that to preserve his class proprieties Jordan would never be caught lecturing in a place like this or secretly memorizing classified documents. Better for Jordan to memorize what's in the British Library. Consider this professor and his loyal coterie, but very generally speaking, beyond the hills and valleys of this film: the academic world broadly speaking, filled to spillage with ravenous collectors amassing so much worth knowing it spreads all around them, surrounds them like an atmosphere, and soon they no longer have the power to organize it but fall into arguments about what is and what is not important, what theoretical tool to employ for prying out hidden relationships, and who did or did not pick up which specific tidbit. A society of aardvarks, and every aardvark a spy. *What is Hitchcock's* The 39 Steps? *What is* The 39 Steps *really about?* Hannay and Pamela never find, touch, read, or return the stolen plans. We never find out whether Jordan's cronies are still at work after he is caught and Memory is dead. We never find out that Hannay and Pamela link, as they were linked in metal or otherwise, after the film. And how safe can we believe anyone is, really, with all these inquisitors burrowing into the archives, teasing out what seem like facts, doing their esteemed espionage? As the Ambassador says to pathetic Drayton in *The Man Who Knew Too Much* (1956), "You English intellectuals will be the death of us all."

The superficial reading of Mr Memory's claim, that the 39 Steps is nefarious and threatening, a group to be feared because its agents will steal information they should not have—outsiders trying to get inside dope—while incontestably daunting and chilling the viewer, is hardly as daunting or chilling as the far more quotidian reading, that the 39 Steps is a model for those who go around amassing facts before handing them over to unidentified others for organization and deciphering. Unknown others: the priests reading the eagles' entrails. The priests eager to talk their readings to one another. The priests of the High Religion, not the religion the crofter practices, the one that houses his God, his God who made the country, but a Religion of practicality and measurement, fragmentation and recoding, illuminating and burying.

And also *having* knowledge, as one presumes, by having facts. To collect facts in order to possess them, working in an arcane economy where information is value. He who has the greatest amount of information shall be sovereign. Footnote counting.

With respect to the Hitchcock film, that sovereignty is the viewer's alone, by some curious, indecipherable "divine right," given that Hitchcock is the force mobilizing the world we apprehend to our benefit. We are the ones mining his scenes for information, surely on behalf of an office foreign to the world of the film, since in a Hitchcock scene there is a very great deal indeed that surpasses information. We pick up and assemble his pieces, we try to make sense of every aspect of his every view, treasuring some winning perspective for assembling which we have gathered our facts, reveling in the breathtaking view. To show us our obsession with shows, our espionage, I would suppose, is the motive behind the oblique angle in which Memory's face is shot at the instant that, with eyes bulging open in twin ricti of disempowered astonishment, he taps into his vault and delivers the answer to Hannay: Hannay and the nearby world. (In Buchan's novel, there is in fact a stone stairway with thirty-nine steps leading down from a precipice, and these are the steps of the book's title. Hitchcock loved changing the materials he worked with.)

[2] *Regarding angle.* Notwithstanding all this cupidity for secrets . . . in the end, which Foreign Office was Mr Memory—and are we—talking about? Which one, that is, was Mr Memory about to name before his tongue was stilled? It is so facile to rest on the assumption that we are on the cusp of hearing about a nefarious foreign power, a power one would have to voyage far from London to find in some horrible

anti-Utopian miasm, given the appeal of the jarring word "foreign." Jordan as a foreign agent, then; operating in Britain to steal secrets and clandestinely export them. An Englishman on the payroll or "payroll" of another country: the British aristocracy's sympathy for German fascism in the early 1930s (principal photography for *The 39 Steps* ended 18 March 1935), or for Oswald Mosley (head of the British Union of Fascists since 1932), or latterly for Edward VIII (accused during World War II of being a Nazi sympathizer) isn't beyond recollection. However, some riddles are raised by this proposition of foreign affairs. If Jordan knows—as he must know, having organized the theft in the first place—that Memory has the secrets in his head, he must also know that if his purported enemies, if he is essentially foreign we would think the British, were to steal this little man away from him scant advantage would come to them, since, in military fact, the British already know the secrets in Mr Memory's head. Getting Memory out of the theatre and then out of England (away from punishment) is the project to be engaged in, not killing him. Fire into the air, create pandemonium (see as well *Torn Curtain*); then, when people are confounded with one another, quickly make way to the stage, seize the performer by the lapels, and disappear with him. Perhaps the professor is frustrated while his protégé babbles down there onstage, stuck over in the boxes and feeling himself quite unable to seize the man and carry him off. Instead, however, what he is evidently trying to do with his gunshot is to stop the uncontrollable expostulation in midphrase: to close that mouth, close it for good. Keep Memory's information from getting not to the foreign powers so many viewers of this film think are waiting to procure it but the British public. Consider the stringent economic quid pro quo operating here. If Memory has the secrets in his head, and if these secrets are valuable to Jordan and whomever he is working for, no good can come of killing Mr Memory. Dead men tell no tales, not even secret memories got up as rhymes or what have you. Given that we do not actually hear the message from Memory, it is worthwhile to trouble the presumption that we already know what it is. Hitchcock could have made certain we would know, had he wanted to.

A more direct approach to the problem can be found if we ask why Memory must be silenced, not for the Professor *but for Hitchcock*. He is ensuring that the audience watching—not the one in the Palladium but the real one, in front of the screen—is given *only the very slightest hint* of the great mystery lying beneath the quotidian realities of this story, only a few words upon which to speculate (as I am doing) rather than a complete utterance at this instant. Action is the byword, after all, and what the filmmaker wishes is that we must have the gunshot followed by Jordan's withdrawal, Memory's collapse, pandemonium in the Palladium, and the rush into the wings, all swift and sweeping as a finale.

And consider a different calculation:

That there is another possible country with a Foreign Office, one in which the word "Foreign" does not point to distant climes. A "foreign" territory, then, that will call for a very different kind of voyage. I refer to the British Foreign Office, the governmental department responsible for relations between Britain and the world, the British equivalent to the American State Department. Any spies working on behalf of the British Foreign Office would be in MI6. Such collectors and assemblers of information as these would guard their identities to the death, and would also make arrangements for safeguarding their treasures should light fall upon their activities. After he says "the Foreign Office," Memory may very well have been on the verge of adding "... of His Majesty's Government," in which case the professor would have been outed, at least to Hannay and Pamela, as an agent of MI6 operating a project to steal military secrets from the home government's military wing for purposes far beyond anything we, or anyone outside MI6, could imagine. Such a thought would seem preposterous only to those who know nothing at all about the kind of work agencies like MI6 do in this world. If "the Foreign Office" were the British Foreign Office the gate would be opened to many avenues of speculation, all of them beyond the deep arrangement of the film: that the script is written, and the scene artfully choreographed and performed, in order to leave a wake of ambiguity, not one of certainty. To remove secrets from the War Office and use them for some purpose involving international intrigue, perhaps, but not necessarily a purpose opposed to the purposes of Britain even if it is a purpose that must not be permitted to come into public view. Let us imagine what Hitchcock makes it at least as easy to imagine as that Jordan is a foreign operative, namely, that the spy intrigue is a top-secret British intrigue, and that as regards the purposes of MI6 it is preferable to have Memory, treasurer of the secrets, dead than alive and revealed. If Memory is openly revealed as an MI6 operative, or a tool of one, it becomes known that MI6 has found a crafty way to steal governmental military secrets for its own (wholly unsurmisable) purposes and *this* may be the professor's real problem. Imagine the chilling possibility of an entirely *internal* power struggle in Britain, with the stranger Hannay getting caught up in it by pure happenstance. Hannay, a man who is eager to like but is a long way from knowing the British people.

The bottom line here: when the film is done, although we learn something of what the secret is that Memory has been hauling around from stage to stage, we know nothing about who he really was, for whom he was really working, what the secret was to be used for and by whom, what government or governments local or distant are involved in whatever plan. We know nothing...

THE UNION

We know nothing... except, of course, that we are bound up with our condition; bound up as Hannay is bound up, and his new friend Pamela with him. He comes to London and visits a music hall, bound up in frivolity, caught in his search for a laugh. He scurries out with a streaming crowd and is attached to Annabella Smith, bound up in protection. When he brings her home he is bound up with her troubles, then with her corpse, then with his anxieties lest he fail to escape the building. He becomes romantically "bound" to Pamela in her train compartment, then "imprisoned" in the Police Gaze, which he escapes upon the Forth bridge. At the crofter's, he is bound to patient deference, although in truth he is eager to move on, and then, soon afterward, having escaped the police manhunt upon the hills (an extraordinary long shot of dozens of policemen in a chain, moving forward over the turf), he is bound to social convention at Professor Jordan's. Then, of course, stopped by a bullet. He will almost be trapped, bound, incarcerated in the police station, he is bound on the lecture platform by the imperative to seem like a proper lecturer, bound with handcuffs in the car driving off. Bound in a mystery, bound in a concatenation, bound in a turmoil, bound in a combat against nature and the world. But if the idea of being bound is absolutely central to *The 39 Steps*, there are some provocative and fascinating instances in which it is evident that social ties literally disempower, even as they guide us.

- In the crofter's cottage, the marriage is its own cell. Margaret entered into it through force, if not physical force then the force of a community's esteem, because in mid-twentieth-century Glasgow marriage was the state not only to be sought but to achieve at all costs, lest the wrong thoughts circulate.[10] A young woman had to have a husband and John presented himself. John with his upbringing and his ideas, John with eyes askance, always checking to see who is checking. It could not be more evident that she is trapped in that marriage although, truth be told, only because a stranger from London like Hannay (Hannay the visiting Canadian) has come to stay does she seem so very bound to her duties and her place. "Supper ready, woman?" The crofter is a man who follows dictates, in his case chosen biblical ones, and his conscience is entirely cultivated from without. All of what he does and does not do flows from principles of "correct" husbandly behavior. Pleasure would be absent from crofter life, and when the man sees that Hannay's conversation is bringing his wife some small pleasures he is incensed at the ungodliness of the situation, eager to invoke the Heavens just as soon as he can. "God made the country."

    Let me suggest that the crofter scene is inserted into the film expressly to introduce the young woman as captive in her wedded "bliss," a prisoner of the kirk if not of the state, for either or both of which the man has been acting as eager agent. The crofter scene lays the tracks for a voyage into "the marriage as trap," so that very soon we will be prone to seeing another trap of the same kind, one that initially presents itself as only comedy.

- Hannay becomes handcuffed to Pamela in the fake police car being driven away into the countryside by night. The car will arrive at a stone bridge, forced to halt by a flock of sheep. The two will manage to escape and hide beneath the structure until the thugs have moved off, but they are still cuffed. They will scramble across the terrain to a cozy inn, still cuffed, hide their hands and check in as a newly married couple, ascend the stairs still cuffed, be shown their room. Now what to do? Maneuver like contortionists, the landlady standing at their side enchanted by the new couple (so freshly married, so enthused that they will not part from one another for a second). Sharing a sandwich at the end of the bed, Pamela crouching to get her nylon stockings off so that when they stand together he can place them to dry over the hearth, Hannay offering her to drink from a glass. They move bedward and she climbs on, yanking him after (!!). Impossibly close now, she sits up to finish eating while he lies back. A conversation founded on distrust. A suspicious glare from her. And she drifts off. We cut away to Alt-na-Shellach, where the professor is bidding his wife/co-conspirator goodbye as he heads to London. Back to the inn, where Pamela is awake now but Hannay is sleeping the sleep of the jailed. Being the clever one, she manages to slip out of the cuffs while he snores. She will escape the room, escape him, escape this chapter of her life, but on the landing, looking down, she hears the two thugs on the telephone down at the desk, confessing the truth of the situation. With sudden knowledge that her bed partner is in fact not a bad man hiding under the cape of a good one, she returns to him and they make a plan of escape (redemption), a desperate plan once he knows the clock is ticking. But back to those cuffs, and the odd—even carnivalesque—situation these two must be finding themselves in as they realize their present experience and their immediate hopes for the future are inextricably bound together.

- The notable length of the scene, as though the taffy of discomfort is being stretched to the limit. How long will they have to stay bound this way, and we with them? Indeterminate.

- The humorous touches, both to ease the spectator's nerves (because we are led by the photographic setups to commiserate, even "share" the experience of being locked together) and to establish that these are ultimately pleasant, heroic types who can crack a smile under duress: how to eat with one hand, decorously, for example; how to get liquid into a glass; how to get one's nylons off . . .

- The problem of sharing the bed, with all its implications and confounding physical challenges. They hardly know one another, and so each person's sense of the other person's far-too-near body will be the most generalized sort of knowledge, Anatomy 101 rather than some more nuanced intimacy. The bed will offer a condition of repose and relaxation, something Pamela does not wish to offer, because she is still frenetically calculating Hannay's possible motives, even in his trapped state. Further, what might the two bodies do, unconsciously, when their owners are asleep? Might the bodies move, roll, embrace?

- The severe problem of impression management. Never to be forgotten: we are watching a story unfold in the prim, hyper-conservative Scottish countryside during the Georgian reign. There are Proprieties. Single life is one thing; married life another. A couple gains a certain respect and admiration *simply by virtue of being what it is, regardless of the individuals making it up*. Respect, admiration, and, if a *new* couple, intense curiosity, especially, perhaps, with much older innkeepers whose romantic hearts easily fly back to their own romantic youth. In sum, locked together these two are going to seem bonded in a way that they do not feel they are. They will be enduring forced impression management, not the performance put on by two people who would like others to think they are married so they can find a way to share a bed but the one put on by two people who would prefer others to think them single, prefer to be placed in separate beds, in separate rooms, but who now for purely mechanical reasons impossible to disclose must *seem* married. "Married," because in this culture, with people who are obviously sexually mature, closeness of the kind Hannay and Pamela will be required to demonstrate can *properly* indicate nothing other than marriage. Thus:

- The requirement laid upon them to peacefully, even smilingly, tolerate the lingering presence of the landlady, whose personal quirk it is to examine the minutiae of young newlyweds' interpersonal gestures. To tolerate her kindness, her offers, her impossible but also benevolently made demands.

- On top of all this, Pamela's is a special case. From the start we have seen her as a person very well put together, that is, self-conscious and self-protective, but also wary, distrusting, a full-fledged worshipper at the altar of "Beastly Men." The handsomer he is, the more one ought to watch out for him. He is after your money, your good name. Even your virginity. After whatever he can get. He is here, now, always, everywhere focused on getting and having. Watch out, watch out. Therefore she kisses him in the train compartment because, and only because, fighting him off would be unseemly (if not also discourteous, messy, and perhaps injurious), but her brain is not involved in the kiss. Easy to turn him over to the police as quickly as possible. And all through the cuff episode she has the same point of view, until the moment of revelation. The fact that he seems dignified, genteel, sweet-looking, even innocent of the affairs all around only aggravates the situation, makes him seem to be wearing an elaborate mask, because Pamela has been warned in advance *against men*, not only against this one. He merely typifies a class. Therefore:

- In this bonding, which masquerades as weddedness (and in fact the two *are* wedded together), she is constantly looking "out of the corner of the eye" for an escape route. Constantly wondering how to get away from him. Constantly thinking—nay, assuming—that over the hill there is a brighter tomorrow, a clearer sunshine, more heather on the hills. (We may take Pamela to be English, not Scottish, and to have been on the Royal Scotsman on the way to her own holiday in the north.) Pamela's decorous ease in the inn bedroom and earlier, on the hills as she is escaping with him from beneath the little bridge, are all masques. She is not accepting and warming to his presence, she is sullenly acquiescing, but she knows how to mask sullenness under a polite smile. The moment an opportunity presents itself she will get away. And—

- The only reason she does not flee once she has unlocked herself is that she sees downstairs, on the telephone, the two men who took her prisoner before. But this is a crucial moment in Hitchcock. Do focus on just this tiny moment as a fragment, a tiny almost instantaneously passing node. Pamela is free, she can run. She starts to run. But running she sees an obstacle. Were nothing else at all going on here, her natural move, on impulse, would be to turn on her heels and head back into (what she would now, ironically, recognize as) the safety of that bedroom with Hannay. *She does not do this.* Instead of retracing her steps—

- Pamela does something only a woman curious about her surroundings would do. A woman needing to watch the world with care, because she knows it is not truly *her* world. A woman with keen eyesight and keener insight. A woman who would always like to know a little more about situations than what meets the eye. A woman who, unlike men, is not at every instant hell-bent on taking action but knows when a moment has come for standing still with eyes and ears open. And because of all this—something only Hitchcock would build an architecture for at such a point—she can listen in (and from a high perch) on the phone conversation, albeit one-sided, and learn the secret that (a) has been utterly hidden from her until now and (b) will completely change both her attitude and the events that will follow.

UNRESOLVED

Three concluding comments, addressing deeply evocative and unresolved conditions that are sharply pointed to in the film—and in a way only Hitchcock would manage to point.

[1] As we follow through Pamela's impossible situation vis-à-vis Hannay, surely during the whole handcuff episode but prior to that as well, we can see as a kind of afterimage, lingering and echoing behind every shot, the crofter's wife. And having seen, we can perhaps note how in putting the crofter's wife and her perplexing situation, and Pamela and hers, side by side in a single film, Hitchcock is saying something about "the woman's role" (as male lingo would have it) in British patriarchy of the time (a patriarchy he knew well). The earlier episode might well have led to the conclusion that the domination of "the woman" was a laborer's, purely working-class affair, indeed rural and working-class. A farmer in the Scottish hills, living in a tiny croft with a few steers to his credit, would dominate as John dominates, but we could expect all that as part of the "natural" resentment of his position in life. He has taken a wife, after all, because "one must take a wife," not because he wants one, and there is no instant in the crofter sequence when we have an inkling that John desires to be with Margaret. There is no *desire* demonstrated.

But reprising the "contractual" binding with the case of Hannay and Pamela changes the analytical view. The domination is not a matter of class. It flows through all classes. Pamela understands her locked-in status much as Margaret does. Hitchcock arranges that Pamela will come to discover Hannay's involvement in an affair much greater than a mere attempt at hoodwinking her; something grand and heroic and noble, probably having to do with protecting the national interest of a country that is not truly his own—it is Pamela, not Hannay, who is English. She can relax into partnership with him because she discovers that nobility. Margaret is given no such opportunity.

Yet, also, a more startling comparison: while Pamela wishes, at every instant before her revelation, to escape from Hannay, to find the chink in the wall she can slip through, Margaret subsumes any such desire under the protective and gracious armor of duteousness. She has made the pledge to stay with the crofter, and she stays, quietly, usefully, honorably, even if in degradation. Here, of course, is a class matter, since Margaret has no holdings and is thus in no position to go anywhere, especially not in this forbidding terrain. Pamela, by contrast, comes from the same class as Professor Jordan, his wife and daughters, and their social company: she has means of some kind, a grounding on which she could hypothetically stand. The idea of escape is a naturally sensible one to her.

Two dominated women. Two conditions of domination. Two outcomes. A more elaborate analysis would bring the Professor's wife and Annabella Smith into the equation as well. Smith seems as unattached and as free-floating as Pamela, her social position similarly masked and her affiliations unknown. Mrs Jordan is the crofter's wife, submissive if elevated socially. Another chained relationship, another "crofter" but this time one who owes no allegiance to God.

[2] The "police car" is shepherding Hannay and Pamela away from the lecture hall into the future. Hitchcock gives us one two-shot edit comprising what always strikes me as, somehow, one of the most beautiful images to be found in his entire oeuvre (which is, of course, jammed with beautiful shots), indeed in all of cinema: it is night, we were inside

the car but the camera seems to slide sideways toward the window and a darkness seeping in. Swiftly in darkness we hold on that darkness and then feel ourselves swiftly dropping back as the car speeds forward and away down the curling road, its bright beam disappearing into the night. This transition—the edit through the darkness—works as a single, swift movement, declaring that our heroes are off to we-know-not-where, and with some permanence, as, catching our spectatorial breath, we float in the air behind. Part of the beauty is the shadowy shape of the car against the shadowy hills and shadowy road. The beam of light. The movement of the object away from us quite as though we have been dropped into the wake of some elaborate ship on which, as we now suddenly discover, we have been sailing the high seas.

[3] As his final words (and he has been introduced and touted as a creature whose words are everything), Mr Memory confesses to Hannay and Pamela how relieved he is now to have that secret off his mind. About this moment Tom Conley offers a striking observation, that the cuff still attached to Hannay's wrist is shown adjacent Pamela's hand in a concluding vision, this perhaps a reflection of a "premonitory sign" in which, as he tries to take the map from murdered Annabella's hand Hannay's hand is shown in close-up adjacent her dead one, with its wedding ring and gleamy wrist bracelet (140). Memory's coda is also about being cuffed into a kind of chamber. It is an Ecclesiastical comment, surely, about the vanity of knowledge in the face of faith, a notification that all the manifest contents of this (living) encyclopedia finally come to naught. But something further, something mysterious. One can but imagine that Mr Memory, here with his last breath, is in fact quite literally evacuating his mind, at once spilling all the beans and freeing himself. We hear only babble about the military plans, but at least metaphorically we are hearing, too, a vast expulsion of thought. And this makes it a perfectly perplexing conclusion for us to wonder about as, whatever the film's finale, we make a finale of our own. What will happen when, his brain having been left to them, but left evacuated, the curators at the British Museum discover that those who seek shall not always find?

CHAPTER THREE

"WHERE DO YOU COME FROM?"

Hitchcock's Winged Victory

> Personality is the original personal property.
> —Norman O. Brown

> "I'm afraid civilization wouldn't look
> very pretty in a high wind."
> —John Ford's *The Hurricane* (1937)

Let's be logical about this.

It is not exactly a film to revel in, *The Birds* (1963), nor especially lush, nor complicated in the ordinary and intoxicating way one repeatedly finds with this filmmaker, if any way, ever, can be ordinary, and it is not, like, for instance, *Dial M for Murder* (1954) or *North by Northwest* (1959), a film one can claim one was *delighted* to have seen. Spare, angular, spacious. Far too spacious. Far too much empty space in which far too much can happen—the cornfield, taken all the way to a logical limit. And it is both expressive and clamoring in the purest kind of way, pre-musical, pre-linguistic. We remember the cawing and screeching more than what anyone says. The

birds complaining. The birds in pain. And, as is well enough known, there is no music, conventionally speaking. (One has heard over and over how Remi Gassmann and Oskar Sala were contracted by Hitchcock to provide an electronic score simulating bird "speech.") The birds sing like birds pretending they are characters, not like "birdsong." And one moves through *The Birds* the way birds move, in fits and starts, in graceless natural swoopings, jerking the head around to get the eye on things, jumping from perch to perch to perch.

Jump with me, then, if you would, into the warming envelope of a charming little dockside nook, The Tides, a place you go for coffee and a donut after smelling the hunger-inducing sea. The place is so crammed and jabbery this troubling afternoon, a waitress losing patience with a chef who's too sluggish, a bartender who doesn't focus well, an out-of-sorts sailor whose fish are just plain disappearing, an antiquated ornithologist smoking furiously as a volcano, a lady with her petrified children becoming steadily more petrified herself as she listens to chatter about gulls marauding. Sea gulls. Coming down to attack. (Descending from heaven?) A traveling salesman full of blustering opinion: birds are disgusting, birds should be wiped off the face of the earth. When he goes his way, we follow (our somewhat strange heroine) Melanie looking through the window at an attendant filling a car at a gas station across the way. A gull swoops down and strikes him so that he falls away from the vehicle and the gas hose, dropping out of his hand, spews flammable liquid on the pavement. In a wide-angle shot the liquid gushes toward the camera. The stolid hero Mitch and others rush out to help but slowly Melanie is turning (a camera panning) until she spots, in a parking lot adjacent The Tides, a pinkish car next to which that same obnoxious salesman is preparing to light a (self-congratulatory) cigar. Don't strike that match, scream the crowd at the Tides behind their window but of course he doesn't hear. "How can anyone who is warm understand what it is to be cold?" writes Alexander Solzhenitsyn (in *One Day in the Life of Ivan Denisovich*). The match flame licks the pitiable man's fingers so that he must drop it (match flame = swooping gull; match = gas nozzle). He perishes a solipsist in Hell. Ritual immolation, fire spreading like blood. All the racing silence of the flames.

All the racing silence.

And now suddenly—and suddenly now—Hitchcock brings us to . . .

APOCALYPSE

Up in the air, thin air. Very high. Looking down upon the tiny town of Bodega Bay, its wharf, its parking lot now sorely enflamed, The Tides threatened by a ball of fire, cars spread around waiting to explode. All this seen from a tranquil distance. And in the foreground, to establish our position and our reason for being here, some gulls seized in flight. Easy flight. Meditative flight. Observant flight. The flight of spies and peepers. Peepers because the combination of an aerial view of the town burning and this proximal view of the gulls above it immediately commends to us the idea that *the gulls are watching the town burn*. (Of course, they needn't be.) *Watching the town,* and with a certain *Schadenfreude.* One can hear them whispering, if birds can whisper, "Better them than us." Gliding, too, with a certain confident pleasure of accomplishment, as though the events below were planned by them, orchestrated, engineered, "produced for the stage."

And that camera, so very Hitchcockian:

"Serene" doesn't come near the quality of the shot. Unearthly we are, up in the *au-delà,* in a too brief, hovering, drifting, floating trance borne on the wind, self-empowered, breathing with time. "Nothing but order and beauty there, / luxury, calm, and voluptuousness," Baudelaire could have sung of this.[1] And the birds are keeping us safe from the chaos below, in their being not only oriented for keen observation but removed from the heat—the fiery heat, the human heat. Distanced from passion, say? Distanced by a shadow, as another poet sang? "Between the emotion / And the response / Falls the Shadow / Life is very long."[2] Certainly from up here the burning chaos is but a graphic array, the multiple fates of humankind down below reduced to a miniscule pattern in the carpet of civilization, a flaw in the carpet. The gulls do not call out in alarm or pride, they have no need to boast or demur, nor—perhaps very strangely—do we ourselves recoil at the sight. The sight is all-encompassing, all-absorbing, all-directing.[3] The camera is like a bird, lifted on wing. The camera *presence* is the presence of a bird:

> MRS. BUNDY (an elderly ornithologist): Birds have been on this planet since archaeopteryx, Miss Daniels; a hundred and twenty million years ago! Doesn't it seem odd that they'd wait all that time to start a ... a war against humanity?

And ... what if it should seem odd? That for so many eons the birds have waited and plotted and peaceably kept their silence. The retreat into received thinking will make all sorts of phenomena seem odd. Hitchcock's work, from the beginning, is all about what might seem odd, about the oddness of that seeming. And "all that time"? When he began shooting *The Birds* (1963), Hitchcock had been working for more than thirty-eight years, had made forty-nine features. Doesn't it seem odd that he'd wait all that time to look down from the sky. . . ?[4]

Because very clearly Hitchcock is a bird.

Hitchcock is a bird whose camera eye rests inside the flock. It is *his* desire to go aloft for that supreme view. For that treasure: not just the fire as people see it, flaring in their faces, but the fire more universally, as birds see it, as Any Being might see it *from above*. In God's eye.[5] We are birds, too, in that we predictably desire to have such a sight, else, knowing our state of desire so fully, Hitchcock would never have troubled to deliver us one. The aerial shot comes without warning, without overt preparation—there is no grounded shot of a character staring *up into* the sky in preparation for it. We simply jump up, expand our horizons, in fact cross a border and enter the domain of another kind of creature: a foreign domain, from which anything and everything of the story thus far might seem strange, dislocated, unintelligible. One can well imagine the gull brains hard at work when they happen to look down as we do: "What is this? What are those creatures?"

THE SALESMAN (who will self-immolate in a moment; now standing at the bar [Joe Mantell]): Gulls are scavengers, anyway. Most birds are. If you ask me, we should wipe them all out. World would be better off without them.

"What is this? What are those creatures? Where did they come from?" Rational query, that we project into the spirit mind. How can *this* array be displaying *the* fact of the case? And the projection of rationality onto the gulls is with hope and faith, as though the answer to every question can indeed be known, as though knowledge is always the supereminent tool.

As though we may climb into history only by knowing. "We propose, then, to place together under the name of the *Prometheus complex* all those tendencies which impel us *to know* as much as our fathers, more than our fathers, as much as our teachers, more than our teachers" (Bachelard 12). Filmmaker as scavenger, grabbing up and holding in storage what fragments he can of the human everyday, mounting them, filtering them through narrative conceit, arranging them, setting them to accompaniment as on a concert stage. The audience as a gathering of scavengers, grabbing up what images are on offer, filtering them through narrative conceit, arranging them as a meaningful story. The salesman's negativity is almost instantly negated in the story, through his carelessness, his mindlessness, his death. But far above, anyway, float the querying gulls for us to eye unknowing....

Gulls *en masse*. Gulls will indeed hover in this fashion, tightly accompanied, following a ship's wake, in hopes the propellers have stirred the fish or the human passengers have thrown off the tail feathers of their sandwiches. Once I looked up at a flock of gulls like this one, hovering just above my head, at the stern of a small boat coming into Trouville harbor at twilight. And still once again, above the green wake, from the stern of a boat heading away from Istanbul. Gulls of the world. Gulls all over the world, not just California, though it is just California these gulls appear to be scavenging (like good moviemakers, like docile moviegoers). Flying with ease and with composure, relaxed in the face of intense action, sweetly observing the details of an agony that needn't aggravate them. Perhaps, like Hitchcock (now, here, and all the time), conjuring the aggravation viewers would feel while witnessing moments like this. Steering, shaping, unbinding that aggravation.

How could a shot like this have been made? Off the cliffs at Santa Cruz Island a second-unit team filmed hovering gulls in the air just below a clifftop, these to be inserted into a composite later. The bird shots were processed to internegative and reprinted in extreme high-contrast interpositive, so that only the creatures showed against a completely transparent ground (the Disney studio's sodium yellow matte process was used).[6] A second, reverse high-contrast print was made of the identical shot, the birds becoming black and the ground transparent. Now, a second piece of film was shot, showing an aerial perspective on the town. The interpositive with "black" birds was sandwiched (optically printed) with this to make a strip of film showing the town below and empty gull-shaped spots where the birds would be in flight. Then this film was rewound and the earlier interpositive with the actual bird images was sandwiched against it, and presto! the birds "appeared in the air above the town." Of course it wasn't the real Bodega Bay down there (where much of the film was shot)—it would have been virtually impossible to get a stable helicopter shot, and one could hardly set Bodega Bay on fire. The background was a matte painting, by Albert Whitlock. It measured four feet across by three and some feet high. Painted with a very tiny brush in minutest detail. A black splotch spread across its center, so that this painting, too, could be treated as basis for a matte by being sandwiched against separate photography of fire. The fire—photographed at Universal—would fill in the black splotch. All very mechanical in process whilst also supremely artistic in rendition (Whitlock [1915–1999] was a veritable master of matte painting, one among very few working in Hollywood at the time). Elaborate arrangements were made for the setup shots and follow shots before and afterward "on the ground," so that, onscreen only briefly, the bird shot would stab.

But why, one could wonder—as many in The Tides do—why would the birds plan and execute an attack on humankind? What could be their motive? Can the notion of motive even find reference with birds? What human crime invoked this revenge? And of course nobody can think of a solid reason (certainly not that we've been eating birds for a very long time). Least helpful seems the hyper-rationalizing ornithologist (Ethel Griffies), who begins to seem doddering and stupid as she protests avian innocence against the background of real attacks:

MRS. BUNDY: Because there are 8,650 species of birds in the world today, Mr. Carter. It's estimated that five billion, seven hundred and fifty million birds live in the United States alone. The five continents of the world ...

SALESMAN (muttering): Kill them all. Get rid of them. Messy animals.

MRS. BUNDY: ... probably contain more than a hundred billion birds! ... I have never known birds of different species to flock together. The very concept is unimaginable. (Laughing) Why if that happened, we wouldn't have a chance.

The woman with the two small children (Doreen Lang) is at her wits' end with all this talk, all this stalling, given that the sky is falling. How do I get my fledglings out of here? "I'm glad you all think this is so amusing. You've frightened my children half out of their wits.... I'll never feed another bird as long as I live!" Note the resentment: I've been good to birds, why are birds not being good to *me*? Now she is convinced it's this young lady come up from the city, this Miss Daniels ('Tippi' Hedren) who made it all happen, provocateuse! She!—she is the infernal cause and there is no other. *"It's her!!!!!"* (Well, Melanie arrives in town and the bird attacks do begin more or less at the same time.) It's definitely her! all her! only her! there she is! in her chrysalis green suit and with that look of scorn in her eyes.

If birds of different species flocked together we wouldn't have a chance, no, but why would they flock except to attack and why would they want to attack? Conversely: if in fact we wouldn't have a chance, what is the point in wondering or asking about the enemy who would certainly vanquish us? Is there a reasoning on earth that could afford us that *chance* we wouldn't have without it? Yet, still, in a drone, the ornithologist preaches: "Birds are not aggressive creatures ... They bring beauty to the world ..." A world that, imaginably, did not have beauty until the coming of the birds. Until— perhaps—now, since it seems to be now that the birds have come. Come to "bring beauty" to mankind's as yet unbeautified world. A world in need of the birds. A world hungry for bird life.

HELEN (the waitress [Elizabeth Wilson], going to the door leading to the kitchen): Three Southern fried chicken, Sam. Baked potato on all of them.

INTERLUDE: 'OLOGIES

Ornithology, indeed. For a breath let us stand back from the academic life of which we claim such admiration—all those esteemed professors and -ologists getting interviewed on the Evening News for their learned, their advanced, their special, their arcane opinions—and make observation, if this is at all possible, from the outside. I say "if this is possible" because getting outside of "teachers" and "teachings" is not as easy for us as for the birds: that educational system to which we have all been subject—long ago, when we were forming and were far too young to understand—taught us one lesson, principal to all others, one stupendous lesson, that *knowledge is the single supreme value and the teacher knows*. The knower is therefore quite sensibly the person to evaluate the knowledge—and experience—of all others. Not any particular teacher, standing in front of any particular blackboard, but the *teacherly role*, the edifice we call *Repository of Knowledge*. The idea of "having knowledge," knowledge as possession and accumulation, is altogether fraught, an arbitrary and somewhat rigid construction, a way of imposing order and, as with other ways of imposing order, a way of apportioning and stabilizing power. As John Le Carré writes with perceptive distance, "It's facts. One fact more, one fact less. Then you do the logical thing at the end of it" (323). The issue Hitchcock is posing for us, in this film but not only in this film, is knowledge taken in a certain facile way: that one might glibly presume to have it; that for all events and all conditions there is and can be *a supremacy of knowledge*; that *knowledge* unquestioned and in itself is something worth achieving and something we can, always and everywhere, achieve. Knowledge as the only royal upshot of a voyage from innocence, or as the most satisfying rationale for that voyage. Not street directions or the time of day or what causes pip in poultry, but what the world is all about in its germ: what motive truly is, and what the grand terminus on the twisting pathway, and what the vision on the other side of the fog—that kind of *knowing*. What exactly is happening. How ideally to be. We were urged from the beginning to believe that one could know with sureness, perhaps even disparage those who aren't on the inside. That one might think *knowing* is not only an expression of life, a flowering, but even what life is all about. Winners know the secret, losers don't. And knowledge is the courier of reward: long life, wisdom, capacity, truth, verve.

Yet sympathizing isn't really about knowing. Does not the 'ologist's mind, such as our complacent Mrs. Bundy shows off here, have too much in store, perhaps? Does it energize a quest that persists in calling upon knowledge in place of other similarly powerful and less pompous treasures that might bring, if not understanding, at least peace? It is one arrogance, after all, to claim to know when one actually does not know; but a still greater one to claim to know when nobody knows and nobody can know. Rationality does not travel beyond Keats: "Beauty is truth, truth beauty, —that is all / Ye know on earth, and all ye need to know."

As a demonstration case Hitchcock often uses the intellectual who puts forward a claim of (only partially evidenced) knowledge in order to gain status and advantage in a difficult social situation. "Listen to me—," that is to say, "*I* am the one to be listened to." With a little more hesitation, "If you ask me. . . ." Here, then, the ornithologist whose tongue drips with astonishing figures, bird counts, bird populations, worldwide coverage, historical time, species differentiation, not to say words hard to pronounce; drips without the least effort, since she is concentrating on the pleasure of her cigarette and merely allowing the army of facts she has marshaled to spread out onto the landscape. (Mrs. Bundy's spilling knowledge; the pump's spilling gasoline.) It was important to Hitchcock to have someone "sophisticated" like this mixing with the town locals who "all seem to be the same village types and speaking the same language and, as you know when we were up there, there were other elements" (Hitchcock to Hunter).

But I think Hitchcock is warning his audience to question those who proudly make claim to intelligence, who announce their knowledge from a high podium beneath a rippling flag, who brag about their closeness to a source of information, their keys to the vault, and who are always, it seems, prepared (uniformed) with data. The Hitchcockian world, as I see it, is more complicated than data will allow, and revealed to us, through his mastery, by astounding arrays that at once inform and riddle.

A more complicated universe, more frayed, teetering near darkness:

> Our speculations may run the whole qualitative gamut, from play, through reverence, even to an occasional shiver of cold metaphysical dread—for always the Eternal Enigma is there, right on the edges

of our metropolitan bickerings, stretching outward to interstellar infinity and inward to the depths of the mind. And in this staggering disproportion between man and no-man, there is no place for purely human boasts of grandeur, or for forgetting that men build their cultures by huddling together, nervously loquacious, at the edge of an abyss. (Burke 272)

In The Tides, Melanie Daniels finds herself distraught, disoriented, and mentally disabled because she has just come from the Bodega Bay School where the birds—crows, this time—have perpetrated a genuine catastrophe. Children are lying wounded, bleeding on the road. She has not discovered yet, but soon will, with Mitch, that her new friend Annie Hayworth (Suzanne Pleshette) is dead in front of her clapboard house. A frenzied vibration is in the air. In the face of the crisscross argumentation to be heard in this restaurant, this jabbery vortex, she has to move slowly, hesitantly, almost insensate, her eyes and ears glued open but without the ability to focus: the incessant order-taking and food delivery in the midst of chaos, the opinions, the questions, the maternal concern for children's fear, the dry, dry, dry academic pronouncements, the repetitive mewling about fish stock depletion. For Melanie, and for the viewer who has bonded with her presence, the world around, this fishing village on the California coast, is coming apart: and abruptly, without storm clouds. She has no inkling of exactly what is happening, who she and all these people have suddenly become in the face of the blitz.

The blitz. More accurately the Blitz, some awesome California-utopian recreation of the 1940–1941 German bombing campaign directed against Britain. Hitchcock and family were in the United States but Daphne du Maurier was in England. Although the details of her biography are not exactly clear as to her exact location at the time, there can be little doubt that Daphne du Maurier was in some way affected by the Blitz, as was England altogether. As with these bird attacks now, the aim then was to destroy resolve, cripple the economy, demolish architecture. "The Birds" appeared in 1952, relatively early postwar Britain and still a time of desperate austerity. (Du Maurier's play, *Rebecca*, opened six months earlier in the West End.) Writing "The Birds," she could not have failed to understand the planner-architect Max Lock's "experiencing the shock of familiar buildings disemboweled before our eyes" (qtd. in Kynaston 35). On the image of disemboweling we jump to Hitchcock's rendition of the Dan Fawcett farm massacre (perhaps the very first cultural instantiation of this theme). Yet the Blitz metaphor is far too distinctly only a metaphor to be more than momentarily useful as we struggle with the developments in Bodega Bay. This is nature, not the Third Reich. This is a kind of "intelligence" with which we have not, as humans, come to terms. Closer, perhaps, to *War of the Worlds*:

> There is many a true word written in jest, and here in the Martians we have beyond dispute the actual accomplishment of such a suppression of the animal side of the organism by the intelligence. To me it is quite credible that the Martians may be descended from beings not unlike ourselves, by a gradual development.⁷ (Wells 181)

Motive, reason, logic, impetus are entirely obscure when the birds come down. Yet our calmly puffing academic has all the answers, nicotine wisdom, now risen far above the merely mundane, exemplar *totale* of Hitchcock's helplessly ineffectual, even evil, professor type. In *The 39 Steps*, the spymaster with a severed finger. In *The Man Who Knew Too Much*, the intellectual thug got up as a minister. In *North by Northwest*, the quirky little man organizing the intelligence operation of which George Kaplan is so signal a part. In *Torn Curtain* the brilliant and scheming, if also hilariously charming, Lindt: "They thought I was crazy! They didn't know I am Lindt!" Hitchcock also has kindly, gentle, encouraging, wholly human teacher types, formal and informal, who never boast of knowledge or show knowledge off: Brulov in *Spellbound* (1945), Isobel Sedbusk in *Suspicion* (1941), Annie Hayworth here, even the ultimately befuddled Rupert Cadell in *Rope* (1948).

The nature of Hitchcock's query into false knowledge has a Wittgensteinian flavor. It is a query into verbalism, the established link between guttural formation, meaning, and nature, not dissimilar to that famous query about colors, for example the relationship between the color of that apple and the word "red" (*Tractatus* 17ff). As Wittgenstein was interested in our methods and manner of using words to mean things, interested to note that what we see when we look at the apple is not actually redness though we make use of the tag, Hitchcock is interested in the problem of knowledge taken very broadly, knowledge too confidently expressed and believed in with too much facility: and this is language in its relation to happening, action, and event. We must never forget that his storyline—what so many people (mistakenly, I think) take to heart as the true center, film by film—is something he could have expressed in writing had he wanted to; he knew how to write, and with sharpness and effect. The reasons his films *are films* is because something of what is to be found onscreen—indeed most of what is to be found onscreen—must be seen and understood as transcending language, as existing beyond language and ideas as we receive them. Existing beyond.

NEW WORLD

When we see Miss Melanie Daniels emotionally staggering into The Tides after the crow attack we are witnessing the beginning of her moral education, even more importantly her sentimental education, since before this moment she was a person perduringly self-assured in a cool (superior) knowledge of the world. Her father being a newspaper publisher, she knew where she was going, she had capacity at hand. When she begged information (from the postmaster: Where is the Brenner house?; from Annie: How can I get a boat out there?) people gave her answers obediently, as though her city manners (read, testiness) or her strangeness to the community (read, awkwardness) or her (too) noble manner of presenting herself (read, self-consciousness) commanded attention and response. She had been stiffish in the pet shop with Mitch (Rod Taylor) as the film began, she was diffident and proud, if sweet, when she met his mother (Jessica Tandy) and sister Cathy (Veronica Cartwright). She was cool with Annie, even cooler with Mitch (for whom we may well imagine she has been feeling attraction since first sight and who, indubitably, she imagines to be attracted to her). Something about Annie's students seizes her: their youth, their innocence: and somehow she bonds with them enough to show genuine concern about them somehow escaping the onset of the crows. When the birds peck the fleeing children, pushing them to the ground, causing havoc,

> Things fall apart; the centre cannot hold;
> Mere anarchy is loosed upon the world,
> The blood-dimmed tide is loosed, and everywhere
> The ceremony of innocence is drowned...[8]

and Melanie is galvanized. Now in The Tides, as she tries to report all this first-hand, she is trembling with purpose. Trembling because instead of floating above social affairs she is thrust into them, she is inside the maelstrom the newspapers will calmly be reporting (thus, suddenly cast away from the protection of her father). Soon the film will show her tormented even more, even to the point of near death, and finally, at a crucial moment, entirely bereft of pride, so that she is able to permit the Brenner family to embrace and cover her, this surrender being the subject of the portrait three-shot we see at film's end. Melanie was nothing if not knowledgeable at first, knowledgeable and opinionated, opinionated and (as one of her lips-sealed / eyes-open facial gestures suggests) smug, but now in Bodega Bay—"Surely some revelation is at hand"—her platform has collapsed.

Bodega Bay, whither she blithely motors upon a splendid empty curling road in her splendid sports car, top down, with two splendid lovebirds green and happy in a cage next to the gear shift.[9] Go north, go to the coast. The sea air is invigorating, a certainty, and also salty, air that preserves, as in a salt cellar. Bodega Bay as a living salt cellar. But, indeed, a *bodega* is a cellar (Spanish). This is not Hitchcock's creation (*creare*: to fashion, create) but his invention (*invenire*: to find). And nor his first foray into cellars. Think of the finale confrontation in *Psycho*: if you keep your fruit cool in a cellar it will last long past the summer's harvest and you won't need to use expensive sugar to make jam for keeping it; preservation. Or, think of the nefarious Otto Keller (German: cellar) (O. E. Hasse) in *I Confess* (1953), a bug crawled up from the cellar of the world. And the dangerous shadowy cellar beneath the stage in *Stage Fright* (1950). And the church cellar as stipulated locus of child murder in *The Man Who Knew Too Much* (1956). And Lindt's (Ludwig Donath) office/classroom stowed in the basement at Leipzig University in *Torn Curtain*. And Adamson's padded basement cell (the cellar cell) in *Family Plot* (1976). And the secret stowed on a dusty shelf in the Sebastian wine cellar of *Notorious* (1946). But Melanie wasn't headed for a cellared Bodega; she was headed for a blissful Bodega, driving the lovebirds to (she thinks arrogant) Mitch Brenner for his (presumably not arrogant) sister, but now, after some serious bird attacks—attacks notably vicious and personal, attacks to her very skin, and dropping from the capacious, universal sky—she has descended into the Special Cellar where are kept the props and struts of civilized culture, the hold where the elements of human intercourse are shelved and fondled *before* being brought on deck and assembled according to the instruction manuals; fondled, admired, put to the test. Yeats's "foul rag and bone shop of the heart."[10]

A bodega cluttered and catastrophic. "An unweeded garden." The gulls have descended on The Tides, at any rate, and having stumbled outside Melanie is locked in a telephone booth, pummeled from all sides. We see the gull faces swooping in from her perspective and then, in alternation, aiming at her from the birds' angle as she shrinks inside her glass cage.[11] Beaks fracture the glass. Melanie collapses. Mitch rescues her, wrapping her in his arms, bringing her back inside. And there she holds herself, half-dazed, half-shuddering, still attempting poise but no longer boasting rationale or standing up to the moment. But someone else *is* standing up. Slowly from a crowd of defeated souls in a small corridor, the nerve-wracked mother moves forward toward the camera, swelling with "passionate intensity"[12] as her mouth uncontrollably moves:

> WOMAN: Why are they doing this? Why are they doing this? They said when you got here the whole thing started. Who are you? *What are you? Where did you come from?* I think you're the cause of all this. I think you're—*evil! EVIL!!!*

The waitress, some of the customers, and the ornithologist sit slumped into themselves or stand abjectly, the ornithologist withdrawn into a cave of silence with her Humpty-Dumpty knowledge smashed at her feet. A group of women stare daggers at Melanie, boring into her with their drill vision because, we may think they think, she has dared to use the secret power we all share, our summoning humanity. Melanie is too deflated for ceremony, too diminished to feel significant. "They also serve who only stand and wait." Each of these silent, cold faces seems to scream, "You!" The moment of the birth of the ego.

Who can this princess be, frequenter of Davidson's Pet Shop (like Alfred Hitchcock, who is marching out with his twin Sealyhams as she walks in), inhabiting, as Mitch Brenner would have it, a gilded cage, trapped in her good fortune, blithe, superior, capricious to a fault? Is she, like 'Tippi' Hedren who embodies her, lifted from the pages of a fashion magazine? The pale green suit she sports with such élan, from the first moments in the film and all the way through it, come what may, is styled (by Edith Head) with supreme elegance and simplicity, the kind of garment available only to the limitlessly rich.[13] Is she a lonely one, this princess, seeking a bird for companionship, or is she a collector, seeking a living trinket? And once she has been piqued by Mitch (piquing but also piquant Mitch) and has gathered up her lovebirds, is she tailing him to Bodega Bay because she wants to see him again (curiosity)[14] or because deep in her heart she feels stirring the spirit of generosity and wants to give him a present by gifting the sister who is dear to him? Is she trying to get his attention? And if it is attention she seeks, does she now try, and has she tried in the past, to get the attention of other men? There are no other characters in this film who make any play to gain attention, not that we do not wish to attend to them. They do not style themselves as she very evidently has done—walking into the general store, say, in a full-length mink. They do not take every step in life the way a model on a runway takes steps, because Melanie does. Or is it that she wants to pay Mitch back sarcastically for his comment about the gilded cage, this because she is fiercely competitive and will not be one-upped and let things lie? A much-touted society girl, she gets into the papers, especially, perhaps, the papers owned by her father: apparently at one point, too notoriously, she drew the wrong kind of regard by throwing herself naked into a fountain in Rome. Can this possibly be the kind of girl for Mitch? In Mitch's estimation? In his mother's? Or was she only an impressionable girl who watched *La Dolce Vita* (1960) one time too many, hunting for her own Marcello?

In the pet shop is established the root of the love story that is undertone to the avian action of this film. Mitch and Melanie, supportive as they are to one another in moments of terror (as all good people ought to be), seem chemically inert when blended, an impossible pair. He is a practical man, spirit of his late father: jurisprudential, handy with a hammer, Mom's best boy. He is dutiful and loving to his very young sister (his sister who seems almost thirty years younger, enough to be his daughter—is she his unacknowledged daughter in masquerade, the family secret?). Sharp-eyed, quickly attentive to business, suave as an Italian lothario (if not quite a Mastroianni, as much a one as could be found in a quintessentially American place like Bodega Bay). She, on the other hand, is frivolous, profligate with money, too casual by half in her assumptions about people but at the same time shy and withdrawn in new friendships. We never find out much about the Melanie inside Melanie, her desires, her calculations.

Can these two make a go of it? She would need to have a heart... This setup befits a standard screwball comedy, *It Happened One Night* (1934) or *Woman of the Year* (1942), where the woman seems too sleek, too successful, too dominant in the social world to be able to love a man who has his feet pinioned to bedrock: but is she? And to unite with him, if ever, must she be lowered from her stalwart pose more than he is lowered from his?

Melanie's proximity to Mitch results from young Cathy insisting at dinner that she stay in town in order to attend her birthday party the next day. It is so easy to forget that Melanie's actual plan was to zip up to Bodega Bay, deliver the birds to the Brenner house with a little note, scoot to her boat, row across the bay, get into her car, and drive back to San Francisco. And at that point:

[a] Go tomorrow morning to Davidson's Pet Shop, look at birds again, meet someone new, steal a glance at his license plate, and drive off with another pair of lovebirds to another utopia ready for wrecking. "To-morrow, and to-morrow, and to-morrow, / Creeps in this petty pace from day to day."[5] Or:

[b] Back in town, park her car on Nob Hill (just where Scottie Ferguson parked that first morning, waiting for Madeleine to emerge); sit slumped behind the wheel thinking, "Oh, what a fool!" Or:

[c] Back in town, take off that green suit, have a long relaxing shower (!), wipe Bodega Bay away, go to sleep, wake up the next morning with no memory of Mitch or the lovebirds or the town. Or:

[d] Feel immense regret, pull off the road in Millerton or Olema, turn the car around, and head back to Bodega Bay, but now, it being too late and there being no place to sleep, curl up somehow and in the morning awaken with muscle aches and no idea what the best move is. Will a highway patrolman be staring through her window?

[e] Or else... by some happenstance linger in Bodega Bay, get involved, get caught up in the town's spirit of place. Something entirely off the game board, something unlikely, unexpected. A sea gull swoops down from the sky as she rows back to town and takes a swipe at her head. Gull consciousness, bird consciousness, unfathomable, inestimable.

Because she is wearing that fur over her suit, the gull thinks she is an animal predator? Or the gull finds her attractive, remembering fondly a day many years ago when it (its friends and ancestors) hung out at the Trevi Fountain. Or . . . ?

Melanie's plan was to drop and leave, but in the process of leaving she is wounded, and now the wound must be looked at, and Mitch must be encountered, and dinner must of course be proposed, and Cathy must be given opportunity to take to her, grateful for the lovebirds she has already excitedly made her own and desperate, in her young dream, to escape Bodega Bay.[16] And the night must include a bird smacking into Annie's door, accidentally, unfortunately: outside of Fortune. A voyage away from plan, a series of likely inevitabilities one after another, unheeded steps away from the Melanie whom Melanie once was. A voyage into the New World. (But it was only a drive up the coast!) For such a voyage one cannot prepare, cannot foretell, can barely—caught up in the flow—use memory. There is only patience, riding with the wind. "I can hardly understand, for instance, how a young man can decide to ride over to the next village without being afraid that, quite apart from accidents, even the span of a normal life that passes happily may be totally insufficient for such a ride" (Benjamin, "Kafka" 812–13).

IDÉE FIXE

Is Cathy thinking of Melanie as an appropriate lovebird for her brother? Do all little girls arrange lovebirds for their older brothers? Cathy is certainly lonely, this perhaps accounting for the speed with which she brings Melanie into the flock. Was she at school in San Francisco before her mother moved up here? Had she grown accustomed to a different class of friends?

Lydia is beleaguered,[17] first by the demand that she be hospitable to this somewhat brittle stranger in mink that matches her hair, and because the chickens won't eat the feed that Fred Brinkmeyer sold, then by the sparrows fluttering down her chimney—birds don't come down chimneys! birds don't *want* to come into the house!—and much more generally by the loss of a husband who clearly directed her life. She was enthralled to him but must now rule the realm herself, as Mitch can come up from the city only on weekends. How fortunate that he is in Bodega Bay now; or are the birds attacking precisely *because* Mitch and Melanie are together in Bodega Bay? A chemical reaction not so inert after all, and with cosmic effect. Note how the mind keeps leaping back, again and again, to the unanswered question, "Why are the birds doing this?" as though an answer can and will be found if only one struggles hard enough with the materials at hand, these materials being wholly—and only—the characters with their private passions (taken not as sensations but as facts). Why the avian masses, why the formations, why the wild attacks, why the antipathy? Did that gull swoop down over the bay and peck Melanie's temple because her very presence in the area, specifically near that residence, triggered some environmental switch? Are the repeated bird attacks on Melanie and those close to her focused in the way that they are because *she is the one the birds want to get*, or is it the happenstance that she decided to find this Mitch Brenner who scooted up to Bodega Bay that put her in the circus, that and nothing more? She placed herself on the flight path (somewhat in the way that Marion Crane placed herself in a shower).

We find ourselves gripped and aggravated, because on some (entirely irrational) impulse we pursue the *idée fixe* that the attacks from the air should be connected to something, and in this scenario every something is a *someone*.

Who are you? Where do you come from?

Maternal Lydia Mitch's amiable friend (and former girlfriend) Annie portrays, if only through implications, as a neurotic, controlling, possessive harridan, making it plain in her cozy little sitting room, with her LP album covers decorating the shelves and the night as black as crows' wings outside, that her affair with Mitch was doomed from the start because Lydia just wouldn't have it.[18] It is important in reading Annie Hayworth to attend to much more than the spoken script. By meticulous casting, Hitchcock literally orchestrates his "score" by having performers of specific vocal tone and physical appearance say certain words: in the case of Annie, the very dark-haired, dark-eyed, alto-voiced Pleshette whose rendition about Lydia shapes, colors, and electrifies the vision she gives. Lydia, Annie leads us to conjure, just wouldn't let go of Mitch. "Her son, an extension of herself, was free and mobile, and she could live her life through him" (Slater 31). Mitch is a figurine bound to apron strings, a totem Melanie clearly doesn't accept though she won't say so. Annie is plenty good looking, so much so that Mitch could easily have fallen for her, but as he could not go against mother's advice nothing could come of nothing: thus Annie's diagnosis. He could not—as Annie would have it—disconnect himself. (He could not be born.) In the film his only physical link to Annie is the courteous gentility of covering her face with a coat once she lies pecked to death in front of her house. Or might Mitch be more the hunter than his mother or Annie have credited? He could well be working to catch, to cage, to keep Melanie Daniels, treasure of a lifetime from the moment he saw her (which moment followed several unwitnessed previous ones when he read up about her, learned the secret history of her life after watching her tarnishing in court). He could be imagining (even building or planning to build) a special gilded cage in which she can live out her future. He could be chasing her, just as, hat at the ready as improvised net, he chased the liberated bird in the pet shop (with such astonishing aplomb). Have the birds descended to protect Melanie from this hunter, then: to fly between them, scar her face, puncture the man's hand-made defenses?

> "All right," he said aloud, "I've got boards over the windows, Jill. The birds can't get in."
> He went and examined all the windows. His work had been thorough. Every gap was closed. He would make extra certain, however. He found wedges, pieces of old tin, strips of wood and metal, and fastened them at the sides to reinforce the boards. His hammering helped to deafen the sound of the birds. (Du Maurier 21)

Must Sir Mitch battle and defeat the bird protectors (the bird monsters, the flying dragon), a supreme challenge, in order to have Melanie safe in his arms? More: is there any evidence onscreen, at any moment, that Mitch desires to be with Melanie? To protect and salve her is gallantry, but gallantry is not desire.

Gallantry is chivalrous. But chivalry is not desire.

The events depicted in *The Birds* raise all these questions—whisper them, shout them, print them in the newspaper Melanie's father owns. But no answers fly by. We are offered no clues, no logical connections, no substrate of evidence or intuition that could lead to what Western ontologies have deemed Reason. Indeed, there is nothing presented in the film to even hint at the suggestion that the birds could, or do, have reason although surely we are invited by that aerial shot to imagine that they do, and although there is no mistaking the viewer's committed belief, from very near the start, that they reason very well: better than we do (the old monster-movie formula, projecting outward onto the Other a supreme capability that far exceeds our own?—or: ejecting our own liveliest capabilities as monstrosity). That aerial shot, majestic, where the gulls soar peacefully just below the eye. Of course we can see what they can see, but not in the way that they see it, not in that special, unfathomable, horrifying in part *because* unfathomable way. We can never know how they see anything or anyone in Bodega Bay, why, for instance, they should choose innocent (or is she innocent?) Annie Hayworth to slaughter. Hundreds of thousands of birds amassing and making military formations and attacking strategically: certainly the audience sees strategy, else the film has no pith. Hundreds of thousands of bird eyes watching the "lovers" struggle together, watching the maternal anxiety, watching the innocence, watching the civilization. As for the enemy spying the social construction it intends to violate, we might give attention to something that, in the West at least, has been largely neglected, the so-called Baedeker blitz of late April and early May 1942, in which the Luftwaffe systematically targeted Britain's landmarks of historic charm. On 9 May 1942, Mollie Panter-Downes, the *New Yorker*'s observer, wryly noted the Germans' "new cultural policy of visiting Britain with an open Baedeker propped above their bomb sights":

> The general feeling seemed to be that much as one might lament the disintegration of a gem of eighteenth-century English architecture, it was more sensible to reflect that Nash's elegant inspirations had served a good purpose as bait to draw more German bombers away from the Russian front. (275)

A tiny coastal fishing village like Bodega Bay is a landmark of historic charm, too. An American landmark. Appreciated by American birds.

A good cast is worth repeating: Alfred Hitchcock is a bird.

The mystery of the birds—the presence of the birds *as mystery*—is the motor of the film. They are ongoingly here, emerging from who knows where. "*Where do you come from!?*" Every time they appear there are more of them, and still more, and on each visit they are more ferocious, less simply curious about human affairs. Ferocious visitors, at any rate: indeed malevolent ones, consciously so, as would seem. Birds with a design (shaped by the master designer). They have been plotting. The gulls we see hovering on high, are these the general and his adjutants? Bodega Bay has been chosen as a site-specific target, maybe to test the armament for a future grandiose attack, perhaps on the West Coast altogether. Have they been lured here, because of the town's bucolic plainness that promises a country paradise? Are they marauding? Melanie, for all her grace, all her sophistication, all her evident wealth, never seems less than a marauder herself. Is she their leader? The birds are advancing, the birds are up there. Position of tactical advantage. Kill the unworthy. Plummet down toward the human heads, beaks first.

Where do you come from? indeed. Where do any of us come from? This is one of those painfully facile questions, open to a far too easy and far too unconsidered reply. If we really think about it, we find we cannot say where we come from, cannot map and identify a source or give a trajectory by which we migrated from there to here, by which we undertook this voyage. There is an overtone to the vocal hysteria of the woman in The Tides: she seems to think Melanie is not only alien but *an Alien*. By her dress, her way of speaking, her initial shyness this woman seems alien to Bodega Bay, too, so that her implicit denigration of Melanie seems especially cold. *Where do you come from?* There is but a single allusion in the film to Melanie Daniels's mother (written by Hitchcock himself), offering the information that she abandoned her family.[19] This we learn on a dune peak where Mitch and Melanie stand flirting (not without affection; yet without touching) against a charming (but artificial) shoreline backdrop.

As the question "Where do you come from?" settles in our considerations, so does a direct application of it to the presence, the movement, and the tactics of the birds. Not where geographically do they come from but out of what cauldron of motivation have they lifted themselves to fly? What force has led them to mass in the sky? What troubling echo of human ignorance and abuse has called up this vengeance, if vengeance it is, if it has been called up? By giving us not even the slightest indication, Hitchcock causes all possible motivations, vengeance, curiosity, anger, play, *Lebensraum*, and also *nothing* to float as mere hypotheses, ungrounded (!), unstable, both possible and impossible in a breath. There is only a visual elaboration of the birds arriving, manifesting themselves, then being on scene, *out of thin air.* Say that in the Brenner living room there might suddenly be detected nervous flutterings at the bottom of the flue. Say, at the birthday picnic for Cathy there might come sudden plummetings out of a high nowhere, higher even than the special aerie to which Mitch and Melanie have climbed in mounting that dune for their private tête-à-tête. At the school we have the much-celebrated sequence in which blithe Melanie, sitting outside to wait for Annie to finish teaching and calmly smoking her cigarette, doesn't at first take note of, but finally becomes more and more startled and then shocked by, the crows zoning into the kids' jungle gym. From far and wide the jet-black invaders seem to come, as though homing in, as though drawn by a beacon: the children's song? They are concertgoers? Something in the human vein is attracting them by its smell, by its unyielding presence down below—perhaps. Children have not yet built up the thick defensive armor so challenging to pierce; children have the flavor but do not know it.

As the children run down the road the crows descend on them from a very indeterminate "above," simply a zone over the top of the screen frame, presenting the effect that each charge is coming out of nowhere, since the space above the screen is a *nowhere. Where do you come from?* The gulls hovering above the town while the fire burns: we did not see them take off, they are like those Air Force fueling tankers always aloft, twenty-four hours a day, to keep the defense system on point.[20] Simply flying, simply up there. (In the blue. In the heavens.) And down below the attack springs with paralyzing suddenness, the birds again perceptible only as they are in close approach, here, now, heading for one's eyes. One cannot even deduce the eyes as targets when the birds come, so defensively yet so paralytically does one eye them coming. "He could see his hands and his arms because the eye and the hand are separate; but the eye cannot see itself" (Sartre, *Baudelaire* 25). The finale, an attack in the Brenner attic, is perhaps especially confounding since when Melanie sneaks into the room she can see dozens and dozens of gulls and other birds perched in silence but also—*but also*—a gaping hole in the roof through which a greater multitude can come ... and of course will come, now that she is here. A gaping hole made by the birds, like the two gaping holes in Dan Fawcett's face. Substance emptied. They come in, they are in action, we are caught; but: *where do they come from?*

At the very end, a strange suggestion is made visually. As Mitch, his mother and sister, and helpless Melanie struggle out of the house, across the veranda, and down to his little sports car, carrying the caged lovebirds (who "didn't do anything"), they pass dozens of birds sitting peaceably like sentries on the ground, on the railing, on the veranda, on the roof: every conceivable angle of view. Sitting, watching, noting, watching, thinking, sitting, watching. Watching. Watching. (The way we are watching, and watching, and watching.) Žižek remarkably suggests that at this point "the birds are no longer needed, their role is finished" (*Awry* 106). Then as the car glides off, slowly slowly slowly, and we have the final extreme-long shot of it disappearing down the long road under the cloudy, sun-streaked sky,[21] the screen is spread with what seem like billions of birds all standing on the alert, watching, guarding, watching, watching, watching. The birds have landed. They are here.

The birds are on the ground, as we are.

The militant birds, or the birds who have just finished being militant, who used the air to attack, are now shown as residents. A beautiful reprise of our experience at the very beginning of the film, our slightly awkward though not yet fearful experience, of watching Mrs. MacGruder, the proprietor of the pet store (Ruth McDevitt), speaking to Melanie and having the strangest sense that she behaves like a parrot. Something about her eyes, her nose, the way her mouth opens and closes. And in the cages all around her, sweet and sociable and living in complete harmony, the various birds in their little society. Birds like human beings. Human beings like birds.

I REMEMBER MAMA

We come to learn that Lydia Brenner is far too swiftly stereotyped as a controlling shrew. She is, on the contrary, an unmistakably educated woman but also a wounded one: we have the sense that she has not been a widow long. When her husband was alive, he showed her the world. Here in Bodega Bay she knows very well how to keep to her territory yet also how to be neighborly, a perfect example of old-time agrarian yeoman civility. There is a quality of class in her bearing: she may have descended from monied Northern California interests and married down. The portrait of the husband over the piano, admittedly a painter's conceit,[22] shows a dignified but unexpressive pose, a shirt collar just slightly rumpled in front, a folded handkerchief in the breast pocket. Mitch does not wear slightly rumpled anything, and does not carry the reassuring handkerchief: that wouldn't be modern enough, relaxed and jaunty enough. Though Mitch does the hard labor to render Lydia's house secure from attack, hammering boards, wedging furniture against the doors—all straight out of the Du Maurier—it is not to Mitch that Lydia turns in her hour of need.

She sits partially crouched into a straight chair beside the piano, just under the protecting presence of her husband. Atop that piano are plaster figures in the eighteenth-century style, Watteauesques. Her complexion is almost as pale as they are, certainly gray. Earlier, after she had a traumatic shock at Fawcett's—a shock that would be traumatic to anyone; and that is surely traumatic, for an instant, to viewers—it was under Melanie's tender care that she began to warm again. And it was Melanie, of course, playing Debussy (Arabesque No. 1 in E [c. 1888]) at that piano under the portrait of the (approving) husband.[23] Melanie and the husband are linked in the imagery, the family plot of the film making clear that through Melanie (and, implicitly, the memory of the husband), Lydia will be returned to sanity and to a wholehearted but uncontrolling relationship with her son.

For some reason not made clear, Annie Hayworth, her charm, wit, and savvy notwithstanding, didn't—couldn't—see Lydia's pain and vulnerability, wasn't able to care for her with the assured quiet and respect Melanie has, perhaps because of the accident of fate, that Melanie and Lydia are coming to know one another in the context of the weekend of horror; whereas Lydia and Annie met some time ago, certainly outside the bounds of this nightmare. Annie certainly knew, and knows now, that a son's dependence on a mother's presence and judgment can shape him even if the mother does not extend herself to micromanagement. She was perhaps too much like Lydia to be capable of contact—they both scan their territory like hawks. One might sense that in this story Mitch is finally able to be comfortable with Melanie because he can see that his mother is; and yet there are many teasing moments—teasing, not affectionate—between Mitch and Melanie before Lydia is in the picture. If Mitch is turned on by Melanie—it is interest, even curiosity, he shows, not a flame—he needs his mother's blessing, but this may be far less because she is a dominating and manipulative woman who will not let her son have an independent life than because Mitch has sympathy for Lydia's widowhood and physical dependency and knows that whatever woman he chooses will have to be in the family in every way. At least for the present, the Lydia we see in the film is not a woman the son can blithely leave on her own.

Lydia is a serious, no-nonsense type, a person who says what is on her mind. As such she is vital to a certain twist in the story that has powerful resonance but in a strange, improbable way. Melanie has been pecked on the head by a gull, a gull circling around the zone where Lydia lives (since the event happens while Melanie is rowing back to the town from the Brenner house). She gets some cleaning up, some sympathy, some curiosity directed her way. But when she is in the Brenner living room she is party to Lydia's making a telephone call to the local feed store. To have one of the characters, even Lydia, make a passing comment about chicken feed might on its own be provocative, more than "chicken feed," but Hitchcock establishes an entire telephone call (of which we hear only Lydia's end) not only so that the two bird events—the gull; the chickens—will reverberate against one another but also so that a certain pricking challenge can be made to our conventional way of distinguishing between probable and improbable action. A pecking gull might be a pecking gull. But a pecking gull followed by a flock of chickens who won't eat seems like a lot more. Lydia seems not to be making the link, because what is concerning her is the chicken feed and nothing more. But her distinct *presence* on the phone makes *us* detect the link. She is foregrounded close to the camera. And Lydia is formal on the phone: neither a phony nor a phoner, she talks to people face to face unless the sky is falling in.

The birds in the chimney make a third charm on the bracelet, one too many to be an accident. Had they come down Annie's chimney or any other person's, these birds would have seemed inexplicably weird and problematic, yet not fitted into what now begins to look like a program. Lydia is the connective chain holding them in association: Lydia hosting the wounded Melanie (gull-struck: recall that the gull attacked and quickly *flew off*), Lydia worried about her chicken feed (not just that the birds won't eat, but they are *off* their food), Lydia attacked at home (not far from the spot where her husband lingers patiently on the wall: she tries to defend herself *by waving the little birds off*). When Melanie is pecked we think, "injury." When we learn about the chickens we think, "Odd ... eerie." Once the birds come down the chimney we think, "Something is happening," that *something* being greater by an immeasurable magnitude than what we are seeing. Something involving these birds *and also other birds*, but not non-birds. Thus, The Birds. The birds are up to something. Something has gotten into the birds, something that is not their feed. The chain now continues, with the birthday party a seeming continuity from the chimney ("Get them where they live!" "Get them where they celebrate!" "Come at them from a *long way off!*") and the school attack a focusing and sobering of the birthday party ("Get them where they educate!"). A *chain* of events built up, extended through an accretion of happenings, one following, yet also seeming to build upon, another. Events seeming to build, mostly because they involve characters who are apparently comparable and are thus subject to mathematics. One bird plus one bird equaling two birds, notwithstanding that the ornithologist gives a lecture, as persuasive as any lecture anywhere on any subject, about the variegation within the avian species, and how birds of one type do not associate with birds of another. Yes yes, but here is *addition*, theory be damned.

Consider the mini-lesson being offered the viewer by Hitchcock at—where else?—the school. He would like us to see that there are two different kinds of addition. One is simple agglomeration, a counting that does not amass; a linear ordering that does not have gravity. For his example: a group of students is in a classroom with Annie,[24] available to us mostly by way of the soundtrack. They are chanting a repetitive building rhyme, *Risselty Rosselty*,[25] in which, although there is discernable modulation verse to verse, the static repetition of the five-line stanza's second, fourth, and fifth lines, combined with the monotone quality of the children's aggregate voice as they sing, suggests simple "againness," a formula of aggregation, the many verses *adding*, yet *not building*. In simple cumulation is a counting that is not a collecting:

(1)
I married a wife in the month of June,
Risselty rosselty, now now now,
I carried her off by the light of the moon,
Risselty rosselty, hey bombosity, nickety nackety,
Retrical quality, willaby wallaby now now now.

(2)
She combed her hair but once a year,
Risselty rosselty, now now now,
With every rake she gave a tear,
Risselty rosselty, hey bombosity, nickety nackety
Retrical quality, willaby wallaby now now now.

*

Etc.

A second kind of addition or accretion results in aggrandizement. Swelling, ascending, multiplying variations that produce a condition markedly new and alarming to the senses. Melanie is in the quiet sunshine while this rhyme rings in our ears, as a crow flies down and perches behind her. *One* crow. Soon there are *two* crows. Then *three*. Then *many more*. Then *more still*. Then *a platoon*. This addition is definitely a swelling, a mounting, an elevating, a building, an achieving. Yet why should it be thought a strategic parade and not a simple repetition, except by way of the conviction that mounting their action together, in company, the birds can exercise a motive? *Risselty Rosselty* seems to have no motive.

Hitchcock makes one further step that seals the display for us.

He arranges for the black black black crows to be photographed on a black black black jungle gym posed against a white white white morning sky. This is a very pure graphic construction showing form, multiplication, the construction of a crowd. Now—and only because of the composition of the shots and the graphic design through exposure control—the identity of the grouping of crows as *an ever-increasing avian threat* is emphasized over what could also, all other clues absent, be seen more calmly: (a) birds present nearby, (b) birds conveniently perching, and (c) birds casual, apparently peaceful. It is literally the swelling of the pattern that transmits the threat. *Threat as growth*. It is not the crows who build the platoon, then, it is the audience, with Melanie giving signals to guide—she is a leading member of the audience; she is bonded with us—as the birds' number climbs (and finally takes off). This crow ... another crow ... now another crow ... and still another crow, and then without warning we suddenly realize a border has been crossed. How many crows does it take to reach, and then to cross, a border? And what a journey it is, the passage from casual crows to crows who kill.

TRAUM(A)

I will not elaborate discussion of Hitchcock's inventive method of showing Lydia's approach to Dan Fawcett, her walking in his door with a slightly stiff propriety, her pausing in his kitchen to note (what is in the same shot as she is, noting it): a row of hanging teacups from each of which a significant morsel has been chipped away. Or her walking down his shadowy corridor toward the room at the back. Or her stepping across the threshold. Broken window, wind blowing in. A turn to the right. The body on the floor, pajamas, the eyes.

The invention of the triple jump cut to give us, in the middle of the dead man's face, black, **BLACK, BLACK** ... no eyes, **NO EYES, NO EYES** ... fall, **FALL, FALL!** Looking and pulling away *at once*, gaping and fleeing, we feel our own eyes being gouged, pecked, sucked out of our heads. Enucleation, writes Martin Jay of Georges Bataille's *Story of the Eye*—*l'oeil qui ne voit pas*—"is, in fact, a central theme of the story,"

> which reproduces an actual episode Bataille witnessed in 1922: the ripping out of the matador Granero's eye by a bull's horn in Seville. Until he saw the famous scene of the slit eyeball in the Surrealist masterpiece *Un chien andalou* by Dalí and Buñuel in 1928, about which he wrote enthusiastically in the pages of *Documents*, he had no more vivid image to express his obsessive fascination with the violent termination of vision. (220)

I will not go on about the Surrealist fantasy of the severed eye's insertion into bodily orifices, now that it cannot see. Nor will I go on at length about Lydia Brenner's gasping, that Žižek calls, inaccurately I think, yet respectfully nodding to Elisabeth Weis's marvelous book of that title, her "silent scream" (*Symptom* 134), her being unable to breathe, her hands stretched out as though in blindness to seek a hold—blindness because, for her, the birds *have* gouged out her eyes. And her stumbling down the corridor. And out the door. And past the stablehand, his face querulous. And into her pickup. And the macro-long shot with the prepared dirt road so that as the truck races away screen right a cloud of dust trails after it like the miasm of hell.

Instead, let us think about this stunning enucleation as a property of—not the story but—the film. Not that our victim in this bedroom is a man, a farmer, a neighbor, a friend of our friend Lydia although unknown to us, a worker now permanently disabled in death—not any of that. Not that Lydia is thrown into consternation, losing physical control, losing calm, losing sanity for a moment. Not even what must be a major revelation for her to share with Mitch, Melanie, and Cathy, that something has gone far, far, far out of balance in nature, that the birds have trespassed. Nor even that it would be impossible now to look into Dan Fawcett's eyes, to see the gleam, the tint, the fragility, the purity. This ravage having been done to Dan Fawcett we have so vague and so little purchase on him as a personality. Not any of these albeit authentic dramatic possibilities, but instead . . .

The merger of emptiness and sight.

Sight, mirror sibling of our own powerful will. The taking in of the world through the portals of the eyes. Eyes as receptive centers, the hunger of the eye. It happens that when we see the eyes of film characters in general they can easily *not* signify for us the activity of our own eyes looking at them, our eyes looking at those eyes, but instead be projected outward as story elements: the eyes of Mitch looking at Melanie, the eyes of Melanie looking up into the sky. But when the eyes are notorious absences, they touch us, and the *absent eyes become our eyes*, seeing what only absent eyes can see. And that To-Be-Seen, that invader, is the conjunction with nothingness, our sense of presence with empty space, a complex world with a hole in its center.

This idea of *integral absence* is invoked by the conclusion of *Vertigo* (1958) with Scottie standing in the bell tower, his arms open because he has lost his grasp. But in *Vertigo* the idea is tactile, not optical. The eyes become hands, sight becomes contact, the hold, the possession. In *The Birds* the hand becomes an eye, the touch becomes a gaze. Birds, not other creatures, because of the penetrating gaze of birds' eyes. All-seeing birds. And because lacking hands birds can fly.

The gaping blankness that Dan Fawcett's face signals, instigates, inspires. And then the matching blankness on Lydia's not-yet-comprehending face. A blankness unto eternity. A bottomless blankness, and a blankness without form. Do the birds intend to make an inscription upon this blankness? Would they use their beaks? Would they peck out their message like so much Braille, so that Dan Fawcett can read it?

But a stepping away is called for. Retreat from the body, from Lydia's observation, from Dan Fawcett's disordered bedroom, from the silence of the farmhouse, even from Bodega Bay. Had Hitchcock wanted to show an unmistakable murder, a resident torn apart by the birds, in order to attest unequivocally to the power of the aggressors to enact human destiny, to show conflict gone out of proportion; and to inspire in the viewer a heart-pounding fear of what would be to come, what could fall upon our beloved Brenners and their increasingly familiar guest from the city; had he wanted this, expressly this, he could have opted for blood, a body with discernable cuts all over the arms and torso, blood everywhere in the bedroom, the neck gashed open. The bedroom and exterior colors in the scene are washed out, pastel. Blood would have jumped out as a shocking stigma. There would not have been need to show pecked-out eyes, nor even eye sockets without blood. These are *black* sockets, not just biological locations where organs have been removed crudely (because however vicious the birds may be thought to be, they are not surgeons). To go even further, when we see the face, the **FACE**, the **FACE**, there is something pointed about the black sockets, the **BLACK SOCKETS**, the **BLACK SOCKETS**, the voids, the **VOIDS**, the **VOIDS**, something quite beyond two eyes that have gone missing, beyond *absence instead of presence*, because the black sockets are a protruding, leaping presence in themselves. Not only does Hitchcock contrive a black vacancy where no black vacancy is required, he makes that vacancy emphatic: first through doubling, this eye that eye this eye that eye; then through a graphic composition—the black spots against the pale color of the face, the face against the pale pajama, the body against the floor and pale wall; and then, brilliantly and memorably, through the leaping inward, the unheralded cutting. Cutting to suggest the journey of the weapon that did Fawcett's eyes in, cutting to suggest the beaks darting forward, Hitchcock's "beak" darting in, cutting for cinematic effect—all these together, at once. We swallow the effect before apprehending it. We have it before we think it. Experience prior to naming.

And the general, even meditative vacancy at the Fawcett farm is also indication of something so very simple it could easily go without notice: the fact that we have been given an emptiness where we expected to find a thing. We have been confronted by that emptiness. Dan Fawcett, his farm, paralyzed Lydia—all this is to frame the black holes on the face. And the black holes are a bald spot on the surface. Since these black sockets are emphatic in the design they stand out as paradigms of disappointment, telltale signatures of what is not there, and attestations to the fact that part of the "natural" world has been removed. But because the dense blackness—the extraordinarily dense blackness—of the sockets is so very dramatic, it signals itself as a signal, rather than a mere journalism. What of other absences, other lacunae, things missing where they should be present and yet not as dramatically missing as these eyes whose absence is given emphasis through design? Confronting this particular absence, does Lydia begin to come to terms with the hollow in her own being, so that from this moment on it becomes possible that she be reached? Is this the beginning of Lydia's grief? Melanie, so far in the film, has not been given to witness such an absence: for her all the bird effects have been presences, accretions. The scar upon the scrubbed face.

It is because there would have been numerous ways to present a shocking reality here—*some* shocking reality—yet only one way that could work for Hitchcock, that I consider Dan Fawcett's eyes to be a directorial gesture. A signal is made about the film as a whole, about what could be called the true subject of *The Birds*. And that subject is emptiness. Not diminution or poverty of form but entire emptiness where we would expect material substance. The film's rhetoric articulates the same emptiness, posing again and again the supreme question, *Where do you come from?* and offering not even the semblance of an answer. When we look at the film's protagonist with the figuration of emptiness in mind, it is hard not to see the astonishing emptiness of expression on her face, throughout. After she is attacked, the emptiness becomes flaccid and surrendering. At the film's beginning it is a proud, an assertive emptiness. *You will not know me.*

Emptiness is the elemental building block of *The Birds*. We never really escape its call, for all the twittering, questioning forms, all the tearing of paradise. Yawning blankness of expression, flatness of contour, waiting instead of acting, the whole thing somewhat Pinteresque. To wit:

LACUNAE

[1] An as yet unidentified Melanie Daniels outside Davidson's Pet Shop (on Union Square), gazing up into the sky at the passing bird army in the air. A model's pose, a model's face; the blank-canvas face one would see on the cover of *Vogue* or *Life* (the face in the negative "Jeff" Jeffries had nearby him, in the opening shot of *Rear Window* [1954]), blank so that every looker can fill it in to one's heart's desire. The eyes bright but entirely unexpressive, unfeeling.

[2] On Hitchcock's face as he walks his pups out of Davidson's, studied blank neutrality. A fulsome profile lending form, iconicity to be sure, but hardly a reaction to life. No interest in Melanie or in anyone else. He strolls screen left where two strangers are staring into the near window while in the window at right a tiny kitten looks up at Hitchcock incredulously.

[3] Mrs. MacGruder, addressing her customers with a blank stare, interrogating, deciphering, a descendant of Alexander von Humboldt. A face on which one could inscribe a bible. Eyes open in perpetual surprise, the world so astonishing as to be incomprehensible, unspeakable. The face a mask of perplexity and readiness. Long chalky cheeks. Melanie's head tiltings and vocal wavering constitute social pose (and poise), not an attitude. Mitch Brenner is far more expressive, always appearing to take a position (like a good lawyer), but he positions himself toward the empty space of The Law.

[4] Lovebirds in hand, Melanie searching for him at Mitch's apartment building. The neighbor (Richard Deacon) stands with artificial dignity, his face an open book.

[5] A clue to Bodega Bay: Melanie first arrives at a store boasting GENERAL MERCHANDISE. This is the repository of everything people in town might need, as well as the post office (the point for

sending communication to anywhere on earth, and receiving it from same). In short, nothing particular, nothing appertaining to any particular endeavor is to be found here because materially speaking this is the local encyclopedia, where one finds *everything* in order to do *anything*. The store is a blank check, to be filled in by the consumer. This particular consumer wants to know where the Brenners live, and what the little girl's name is. (In short, she has purchased and trafficked a present for a cipher.)

[6] The clerk (John McGovern) perfectly matching slight suspicion with slight friendliness, slight coolness with slight warmth. He both knows a little and doesn't know a little. There is a general feeling, in this repository of general merchandise, that Melanie is getting help from this man, but the more one reflects on what he says the more one sees he likes to gab but not to reveal. He may know more about her than she does about him.

[7] The Bodega Bay School. A solitary little building under a vast sky. When students sit in here they are isolated from the world. The world becomes a set of signs, only. Actual life is suspended.

[8] At Annie's house, asking for a room. This house is next door to the school, so Annie is the "girl next door." She has a perfect girl-next-door demeanor, an alabaster complexion, a relaxed way of holding a cigarette in her hand. Too relaxed, perhaps. She shows both local and amicable and—awkwardly—professional relaxation. The empty pose of a marble in the British Museum, all shape, all curvature, no voice that is not hollow. Melanie does not at all dislike her, nor has she found a way to like her yet.

[9] At Annie's advice, renting a boat on the pier from an unexpressive, even secretive fisherman (Doodles Weaver). Rowing across the placid (and empty) bay, docking in empty silence, pacing along the boards of the empty dock, stepping inside the empty Brenner house and leaving the lovebirds and a little note. Into the boat again, but not without a look back. The vague smile—is this a come-on or a calculation or a critical appraisal, jumping as it does out of the blonde fur coat? Mitch

has binoculars and is watching her watching, but an uncrossable gap separates them, a no-person's-land.

[10] Melanie pecked by the gull. She reaches up. There is blood on her finger. Mitch has taken all this in, has raced around the edge of the bay so as to be at the pier ready to welcome her and gently lead the way into The Tides. The owner (Lonnie Chapman) and his wife pump Mitch for information while he tenderly applies a cloth to her head. Melanie loves the attention in a smug and disconnected way. Mitch's mother comes in and hears the gull story. Thoughtful eyes, purposeful mouth, but another one holding it all in; a woman who does not intend to show her cards. Meanwhile, the story of the pecking is bizarre if not entirely incredible. Something of a black hole.

[11] Back at Annie's. Annie uses her posture to express domination of the space in the face of this urban sophisticate. But as to Annie herself, her background, her desires, her doubts—nothing. Something of a black hole.

[12] Melanie at the Brenner house for dinner. The indefatigable Cathy adopting her instantaneously, letting it all run out. She is utterly charming, completely candid, even effusive: but because she is very young there is no experience yet to give off to the world. She must wait to absorb the experiences of others, and so at Melanie's side she is thirsty but unsated, ready for input but at the moment still empty.

[13] Melanie sitting at the piano, turned away and chatting to Cathy. We are confronted with the golden corona of her hair, a vortex but also a treasure, and a hairdo that gives away very little information about the woman sporting it. It is sophisticated, but this isn't different from anything else about Melanie. It is urban, even European (a foretaste of Marnie's hair), yet it would have been crafted by a closed-mouth professional while Melanie sat speechless in a chair. The silence in which personality is shaped. The unadorned figure upon which identity is laid. All the way at the inside, past the furthest door, emptiness.

[14] Doing the dishes with her, Mitch sensing that his mother, patient, respectful, and thoroughly polite, is still, in some way a little perturbed

about Melanie, but he knows she cannot be plumbed. Lydia is a blank, too, and Mitch has been living his life with her.

[15] At Annie's for the night. A nice glass of wine. But space yawning between the two women, despite their friendly smiles. When one learns a single fact about someone, one is provoked to fill in others and is stymied when there is no avenue for doing so. We learn here that Annie's relationship with Mitch broke off because of the mother. Annie seems to have been disaffected at the time, yet now she is smooth, even sarcastic, but only a little. The tone is a cover for lingering feeling or just evidence of a naturally catty personality. By telephone the invitation for the birthday party tomorrow. Melanie showing off the (for her unfashionable) nightie she has bought. Then, in cosmic percussion, the thud of the bird at the door. *I hear ya knockin' but ya can't come in.*

[16] In the birthday party chaos, Melanie open-mouthed with curiosity. She is a question, not an answer. On the dune, perhaps too much modesty from her—more, at least, than makes for heat. An otherwise empty dune, a mere rostrum for a curtailed autobiography about an empty relationship with mother. The stretching sky all around seems empty even though it isn't.

[17] Melanie pensive, retentive in the Brenner living room that night. What are her thoughts, her concerns, her sensibilities in this strange place in the face of these strange events? And how does she feel herself connecting or not connecting to these people? No clues. Uncomfortable silence. But then:

[18] The sight of a bird pacing the hearth and with no delay a flutter of sparrows coming through the fireplace, disorienting Lydia, causing Mitch to flail, scattering through the air speedily like dangerous projectiles aimed in all directions at once, the fluttering of wings making the image blurry, the place turned into space. Lydia down near the floor, dutifully picking up the shards of broken teacups. Broken teacups as a signal that will return. That fireplace, that flue: a black tunnel.

[19] Lydia visiting the Fawcett farm, the extreme long shot showing her little pickup far in the distance moving past an enormous empty field.

The empty house. More broken teacups. The endless corridor (*Vertigo* again): we watch from a stationary position as she walks all the way down it. The bedroom, the eyes. Eyes as spaces. Lydia escaping, her mouth agape. Voice empty, spirit empty, mind empty in panic. The chorus of Lydia's sounds absolutely *not* emerging. Lydia without language, Lydia reduced to the prelinguistic state of childhood when the world is apprehended but not pointed to. Meanwhile, a lingering afterthought (an ineradicable afterthought): those black sockets where eyes had been.[26] The eyes that had been there. The eyes that were.

[20] Looking down upon Lydia in her bed, while Melanie serves her tea and brings along (a daughter's) comfort. Melanie's ability to touch a shelf, to lean over the bed, to express herself to Lydia all indicate her emptiness on the voyage to fulfillment, a gap closing. (The teacup is not only a restorative repetition of the chinaware events earlier, it is a signal from the deeply British Hitchcock about therapy: on his set, there was always a tea break.)

[21] Melanie alone outside the school, the emptiness of the jungle gym. As the children race away from the charging crows, a sense of their idealism, their innocence, their sweetness and presence all being emptied into the air. The birds not only charging at them but sucking their innocence away.

[22] Melanie in The Tides, slick on the phone but in a conversation the other end of which is not to be heard, so that she is locked into a conversational emptiness. The ornithologist always looking away from people talking to her, as though facing an eternal abyss.

[23] The Brenner house as Mitch prepares for the Great Attack. The faces of Lydia, Cathy, and Melanie show abject fear, frozen anticipation, while Mitch must focus on purpose and action. They are all empty of civility, warmth, trust, joy. During the birds' violence, the sounds upstairs building, climaxing, almost vibrating the house, Melanie is curled on the sofa—at one end of the sofa, "out on a limb"—her arms extended to grip the sofa back and her legs drawn up in self-protection. The moment is shot so that the empty spot on the sofa beside her rings with hollow reproach, but reproach to whom? To the birds?

Soon it is dark and Melanie has moved to the other end of the couch so that Cathy can stretch out and sleep (empty her consciousness).

[24] As Mitch drives them all off to what we would love to hope is safety, the empty, brightening horizon. Neither a commentary nor a promise.

IN THE COUNTRY

Melanie's elaborate voyage, a voyage that may easily appear sparser than it is, less fraught for the soul, less succinctly relevant, her voyage that is the thread of this film begins with a slight disorientation, the tone being set instantaneously that she is a figure far too steadily perched on a special branch and thus in need of a little shaking up. Mitch is in the pet shop at the same time as she is, by happenstance (happenstance: something we will gladly entertain here and now, but surely not once the escapades begin) and he is looking for lovebirds. He "mistakes" her for one of the employees, and she presumes to try to help him (is he, coding himself in curiosity, a young man looking for love?). He turns out to be a very particular customer:

> MITCH: These are for my sister ... her birthday, you see. As she'll be eleven and ... well, frankly, I wouldn't want a pair of birds that were too demonstrative.

A particular customer and a circumlocuter, too, keeping the naughty details of life away from this emboldened Maisie[27] who surely isn't his eleven-year-old sister poised on the cusp of knowledge and who bridles, one might think, at the implication that she could be satisfied with allusions rather than facts. A great deal of socially relevant information in a gulp here: (1) Birds to be acquired not for himself but for someone else, in short, it is not actually *him* needing the lovebirds. (2) He has a sister, for whom he cares enough to get such a charming present. (3) This (beloved) sister is becoming eleven, so she is far younger than he is. Melanie appears not to catch this as especially meaningful at the time and, since we follow her instincts, we don't either. (4) The sister becoming *only* eleven, he doesn't want "demonstrative" lovebirds: that is, he doesn't want a pair of lovebirds who will relentlessly make love. Here are a couple of distinct ideas. First, that Mitch supposes—or makes the assumption that this particular young woman would suppose—that lovebirds are called *lovebirds* because they frequently or continually make love (which they do not). Next, that this particular young woman would understand why, if the birds *were* that kind of bird, it might be good to tame it down for the young sister; in short, this young woman knows the arcane secret of what lovemaking is and knows how a young girl would not know. And then, Mitch is identifying as a lovebird and indicating that *he* would not be overly demonstrative were some shopper (Melanie) to pick him up. The scene is played for quiet comedy, the two of them sparring with a kind of natural impulse as he taunts her by asking questions about birds that (he knows) she cannot answer and she makes up answers (she thinks he will not detect as made up). She says some of them are moulting and he asks how she can tell:

MELANIE: Well . . . they get a sort of hangdog expression.

At which point the screenplay actually stipulates what we see onscreen, a close shot of a caged bird from Mitch's point of view. "The bird is wearing a distinctly hangdog expression." The punch line comes as one of the birds flies free and is being chased around the shop.[28] Mitch snags it in his hat and gently puts it back where it came from with a pedagogical tone: "Back into your gilded cage, Melanie Daniels," which of course startles her.

A pickup of sorts, handled so deftly and so casually by this man that he never loses his serious demeanor as he looks at the various birds, never loses his quietly questioning tone (a lawyer's style of questioning, but a curious layperson's questions and tone). He has had her, and now she must get him back. Of course there is no formal imperative, nor does she really have to act as though she's been had because the dialogue was all in fun and nothing more. But she's a competitor if ever was, and he's not above raising the ante:

MELANIE: I don't know you.

MITCH: Ahhh, but I know you.

MELANIE: How?

MITCH: We met in court.

MELANIE (irritated): We never met in court or anyplace else.

MITCH: That's true. I'll rephrase it. I saw you in court.

MELANIE: When?

MITCH: Do you remember one of your practical jokes that resulted in the smashing of a plate glass window?

MELANIE (defiant): I didn't break that window!

MITCH: No, but your little prank did. The judge should have put you behind bars!

MELANIE: What are you? A policeman?

MITCH: I simply believe in the law, Miss Daniels, and I'm not too keen on practical jokers.

Her feistiness gets the better of her, pinches her composure, and soon, without fail, she is trailing after this arch fellow to ...

Bodega Bay. "Up on the coast. About sixty miles north ..." Where reside folks who believe in the law and don't make practical jokes.

This small town, epitomizing many small towns across America, is filled with serious neighbors who have made a life there in simplicity and civil courtesy. Those uppities from the city think they're above all this, think they rule the world, and they could come down a notch or two. Nor is it hard to discern, the moment Melanie enters the general store/post office, that she is a City Type, as locals do not drive sports cars and prance around in full-length fur coats. The clerk, an older man who has evidently been standing behind this counter for decades, is busy with something and does not look up. Let her wait—these city folk think everything happens *now*. And then a conversation in which, like someone well trained by Mitch in how to behave on a witness stand, he utters the truth, the whole truth, and nothing but the truth, so help him:

MELANIE: I wonder if you could help me.

CLERK: Try my best.

MELANIE: I'm looking for a man named Mitchell Brenner.

CLERK (still busy, not looking up): Yep.

MELANIE: Do you know him?

CLERK: Yep.

MELANIE: Where does he live?

CLERK: Right here. Bodega Bay.

MELANIE: Yes, but where?

CLERK: Right across the bay there.[29]

MELANIE: Where?

He has soon taken her outside and pointed the way. "That's where the Brenners live." Melanie slams into a brick wall. "The Brenners? Mr. and Mrs. Brenner?"

But surely this man has at least part of his tongue in his cheek. "Where the Brenners live" is a daily, commonplace phrase for him, but he cannot doubt that for this uppity from the city it will be more—and for him observing her discomfort, more delightfully—ambiguous. Is he really "trying his best" to help by being clipped? To say in response to "I'm looking for a man named Mitchell Brenner" only "Yep" gives indication only that he can recognize her having stated a fact, no more. Does he know him? "Yep" again, but nothing about context, duration, quality of knowing. And to "Where does he live?" to offer "Right here, in Bodega Bay" is surely a way of momentarily toying with knowledge. She is right here in Bodega Bay, so presumably she knows that already, and he is just showing her a mirror. Again, these uppities from the city expect everything to be given on a silver platter when they snap their fingers. Let 'em stew a little. And "right across the bay there" is the kind of direction that would be sufficient and complete for a resident of the town—there's only one bay there, only one residence on the other side of it—but a resident is the last thing she seems to be.

She is not one of us. "One of us, one of us. Gooble gobble."

What Melanie is really learning from this teacher is that she will find out the answers to all her questions, but only by waiting. A taciturn man, a country local, he doesn't need to tell most people things because most people know things to start with. He can converse, he's learned his manners, but he's no conversationalist. And as to this uppity in her fur, what does she want with Mitch Brenner, anyway? Country locals only become curious, even hyper-curious, in the face of those uppities from the city, who always, always, always have something up their sleeve. Anita Page in *Sidewalks of New York* (1931): "I've met your kind before. You're too polite to be up to any good." Melanie, from the start, oozes with politeness, a kind of veneer. Civility is another thing, responsiveness still another. Politeness means you have something to hide, and those uppities are overflowing with it. Country locals know everything is always on the surface, easy to see in the sunlight, easy to understand.

THINGS FALL APART

Things do fall apart here. Regarding the central emptiness of the film, the center of Bodega Bay and of the Brenner world that is unable to hold, the odd sensation one has, watching and thinking in later reflection, is of the bird armies in attack mode, the swift darting, the zooming approach from all angles and taking off to all angles, the general sense of the air itself fragmenting, and the body fragmenting in response. In short, an emptiness derived from things falling apart. And that center, whatever it once was, holding no longer—perhaps never ready to hold again. But what is the center that "cannot hold"? How is the center that cannot hold like a bird, whose wings beat to "eat the air, promise cramm'd" but cannot hold? ("You cannot feed capons so" [*Hamlet*, III.ii.96–97].)

What is the center?

Because if this film riddles any sensibility in the devoted viewer it is the penchant for, the recognition of, the need to situate oneself in—a center, and here the center is reached by voyaging. There are a number of ways one can imagine centrality in *The Birds*, and thus a number of ways of understanding the fragmentation, ways to show how the voyage of which the destination is a center is no longer viable.

- *Town life*. Bodega Bay is the American small town in microcosm. Residents who know one another. An attitude of wary helpfulness toward outsiders, especially outsiders wearing full-length mink coats when the sun is shining. Local, geographically based values: here, the importance of fishing, the importance of loneliness, the truths of the sea. Salt in the air, salt in the soul. Salt, "a permanently renewed resource" (Kurlansky 335). The kids in the schoolroom are learning how to be adult members of this community, growing into their parents as in some unexplained Grand Circle one generation follows another to till the land, farm the sea. They will learn fishing tales. Melanie has a definite appearance of sophistication, education, finish, her stories come from Mary McCarthy, Joan Didion, Doris Lessing. She's been around, our voyager, has crossed the sea, has woven her way into forms of language the locals here have never imagined. But her elegant plumage, her haughty poise, her guarded silence all work to mask a deeper and more historically grounded identity; that she is symbol and harbinger of modernity, bringing urban savvy to a small town with its own mode of consciousness. Is modern life, perhaps, fragmented, sharply discontinuous, arbitrary, capricious just as the bird attacks are? When the desperate mother looks at Melanie in The Tides and says, accusingly, "They said when you got here the whole thing started," is she touching upon a deep truth: that as modernity in fashionable disguise Melanie is the source of the decentering of Bodega Bay? The Tides is no longer a haven, the pier no longer safe. The bay is a site of danger. The school no longer harbors innocence. An 1824 country sampler from San Francisco, by Mahalath Richardson, suggests that innocence confers freedom on the mind, "and leaves it open to every pleasing sensation."[30] With innocence lost, are pleasing sensations of the countryside gone, too?

- *A young woman's faith.* Plainly, Melanie Daniels has been not only self-possessed but also self-reliant. She makes decisions with express alacrity, takes what she feels is necessary action without delay, forms her own opinions, celebrates life in a way others find eccentric. Her beliefs flow from her opinions, in the sense that she focuses belief on the world *as she sees it* rather than on officially sanctified precepts and arrangements. One could call her a "purposive" woman, always involved in a project however slight—such as the drive up to Bodega Bay—and always committed to that project in the face of the universe. When the universe comes crashing down, and crashing *specifically upon her*, Melanie must be shaken to the very depths. Her posture, which has kept her in such high regard and given her such a towering point of view, now collapses, first with a gull attack and then with worse, in a long chain of miseries. The pretty little town (ideal for an afternoon's wandering) is reduced to a war zone. People one could ordinarily take at face value for civil and decorous folk now reveal themselves in spasms of frustration and fear. The world she knows, a world protected by her father's money and her father's knowledge, now contradicts itself, now produces reportage nobody anticipated or dreamed. A sign of this transformation of the world is the chain of accruing metamorphoses of the jungle gym, ordinarily a place for children to play and now a perch, then a multiple perch, then a multiply multiple perch, and finally an army barracks. All is not right with the world; or, if all *is* right with the world, then Melanie's world was all along a shambles she did not recognize.

- *"Male" knowledge.* Of the ongoing thematic importance of knowing, knowledge as the target of a quest, the pithiest clue is given by the general store proprietor, who is quite convinced the Brenner girl's name is Alice, no matter the corrections he receives from his helper. "Yep. Alice." John McGovern affects with such precision the stolid bucolic canniness of long-time small-town residents that the character's effortless intelligence seems entirely natural. But of course Mitch's sister isn't Alice, she's Cathy. An absence of knowledge where knowledge is so casually presumed. A man who was the perfect first destination for Melanie, the local arbiter/historian/postmaster purveyor in complete certainty of the repository of facts he carries, sure of what is in his knapsack. But the ontology here is purely rural. He knows because he has always known and, further, has always known that he knows. Another example is in the subtle facial expressions of Mitch, the well-trained lawyer, certain that he knows how to make two and two come to four. One sees his repeatedly furrowed brows as he considers Miss Melanie Daniels as a case for evaluation. Another is Annie the schoolteacher, perceptive in a subtle, almost ethereal way, canny, intuitive: she knows what makes Mitch tick, what makes everybody tick, so long as she can find the child in them. She is in every way feminine except one: that her name and her image resonate instantly with memories of a Mitch-before; that she is Mitch's girl *as was*. And consider that long-gone Brenner whose portrait hangs on the Brenner wall: perhaps he knew more than anybody, possessed a sum of general knowledge tantamount to the sum of agricultural knowledge in his neighbor Dan Fawcett. But now the father, the farmer, the schoolteacher are all three dead. The general store proprietor will be horribly confused to see the birds come down, he's never seen anything like this before except that, indubitably, he knows that such things don't happen. As to our presumable font of sagacity, the ornithologist: the glowing sun of her knowledge will set into a gray and silent sea as she is confronted with something beyond her ken. And Mitch, who knows his strengths, will learn what it is to have weakness, to be vulnerable to forces beyond control (the court, his arena, is a control room, after all). In the finale he steps out of the house, across the veranda, down the steps one by one, toward Melanie's car, toward her car, toward her, toward her car, toward her, then into the car; then slowly ... slowly ... slowly glides the car through a barricade of sea gulls; and slowly ... slowly ... drives off into the future—the actions of a man no longer flaunting his power, his smartness, his obedience to duty, his military-jurisprudential savvy. In Bodega Bay, knowledge cannot hold.

- *A woman's grief.* Even grief itself cannot hold. Lydia has been clinging to a semblance of it, holding the memory of her husband alive in her thoughts, looking at Mitch again and again as his replacement and inheritor, her protector. Her sense of loss and her dependence on her son are one and the same. It is only when she can begin to bond with Melanie, to sense that Melanie sees the personhood in her, and feel that she can see the personhood in Melanie, that grief can dissolve. Nor, until that revolutionary moment—nothing more than a compassionate regard and a gently offered cup of tea—is there a character in the film not caricatured by some social role he or she has long been forced to play. Lydia: distraught widow doing her best in protracted grief. Cathy: impressionable, energetic, idealistic child. Mitch: Mr. Practical Reality. The postmaster: helpful John. The schoolteacher: wisdom personified (the good witch). The ornithologist: repository of fact. The waitress: bringer of food to the table while still hot. The traveling salesman: a creature with no time to spare, not for conversation, less for aesthetics. Melanie: polished and superior, the mirror in which all other characters see themselves, until finally she drops her pose and becomes compassionate. Although Mitch tends to her when she is wounded (more than once), and although Cathy admires and looks up to her, Melanie is the only one in the film to show compassion. And her compassion seems grown of a grief for the self, an acknowledgment that Melanie's time has passed and that Melanie's time is born.

The voyage of *The Birds* thus takes us, by way of the girl in green, from the metropolitan seat of power and movement toward a kind of island on the land,[31] a place where the air is clean and the personalities sharply drawn, where a shining future awaits, but also a place that, Caliban warns, is "full of noises." He is quite convinced, this monster, that he has heard "a thousand twangling instruments that will hum about [his] ears" (*The Tempest*, III.ii.142–43), and who are we to say that Melanie Daniels, monster of another kind, has not heard them, too?

EPILOGUE

When our heroes make their *adagio* march from the house to the little sports car at film's end, there is a slight hitch (!) in the proceedings. The problem has been devastation, bleeding, death. The task is escape. The route to freedom is short and clear. But little Cathy seems to be on another planet. Wait, wait, can I bring the lovebirds? They haven't done anything. Good heavens! She wants to go back for a package? And more, she wants to go back for *birds*? She wants to bring *birds* into the car, when it is sickeningly clear all these birds have been communicating with each other, and for all anyone can know her two adorable little creatures have been instructed to peck out everybody's eyes before Mitch can get a hundred yards away! But yes, she does want, and because she wants to do she does. In the tiny tiny tiny tiny car, everybody squeezed in tightly as sardines in a can, the birds come, too. The birds are part of the civilization that is left to us. Albeit in their cage. Peaceful. Innocent. Meek. Sweet. Tender. The birds, *our* birds.

In . . . their . . . cage.

One speedily recalls the film's opening scene, where trouble started when a bird escaped from its cage. A moment invoked when, as a bounding principle and mechanism, the device of the cage no longer worked. Metaphorically, the doors were opened.

And now, standing upon a peak of sorts, let me make a wild surmise:

The Birds is not, itself, an ornithology, a report from a pet shop habitué as to the nature and biological essence of birds. The film could not exist without its birds, principally because it is about the cage, ultimate repository of emptiness. The cage as a pure principle of containment. The cage as boundary and framing. The cage as limitation. The cage as form. The cage as civilization. The cage, present even when—especially when—no creature lingers inside, the cage *a priori* to habitation, before life. Hitchcock's great and perduring fascination is for etiquette, control, withholding, suspension, restriction, and discipline all seen through the elaborate mechanisms of social propriety, technical arrangement, cultural form, and public order, a broadly defined cage that shapes—by bounding—our experience. Funereal proprieties in *The Trouble with Harry* (1955); the formality of the concert hall in both versions of *The Man Who Knew Too Much*; marital loyalty and disloyalty in *Vertigo* and *Notorious* and *Suspicion* and *Dial M for Murder*; the rules of tennis in *Strangers on a Train* (1951); hostelry and hospitality in *The Lodger* (1927) and *Psycho* (1960); psychiatric confidentiality in *Spellbound* (1945); naval order in *Lifeboat* (1944); civil obedience and civil disobedience in *Saboteur* (1942); love and honor in *Blackmail* (1929); family love in *Shadow of a Doubt* (1943); moral principle in *Rope* (1948) and *Sabotage* (1936); patriotic courage in *The Lady Vanishes* (1938) and *Secret Agent* (1936); fidelity in *Torn Curtain* (1966) and *Marnie* (1964); class privilege in *The Skin Game* (1931); doubt and faith in *To Catch a Thief* (1955), *The Wrong Man* (1956), and *I Confess* (1953); performance in *Stage Fright* (1950); mortality in *Rebecca* (1940). Energy and impulse and hope are vital, but containment is all. The charge of illumination is sustained and augmented by the composition of the frame.

Thus, *impetus caged*.

What *The Birds*'s birds are is not, as might appear, a fact. They are an unbounded inexplicable presence that we feel a quite civilized need to bound and explain. That *we* feel the need to bound. We, it seems to me, far more than the characters. Hence the perturbing riddle that hounds us when we walk away from the screen: what were the birds? And as we watch, the birds reflect back to us that need for enclosure, taunting, pressing, reiterating their inscrutability and engendering our bent for order. Frame them. Understand them. Come up with some theory to explain what cannot be explained, here in God's chaos.

CHAPTER FOUR

SAY NICE THINGS OR *DIAL M FOR MURDER*

> Nijinsky's tragedy lay in the fact that he could not invent dances for himself, that his choreography and inventiveness were at cross purposes with his legs.
>
> —Serge Lifar

To begin this voyage at the beginning, a lovely distraction: the dial of a public telephone (our connection to the world, the Umbilicus) bigger than life (as seen by an infant or an admirer of Claes Oldenburg's sculptures), with the "M" blazing away in blood red. Distraction, yes, but not of attention, because in fact this image is a lure; a distraction of intelligence, an artful misdirection. On the British telephone of 1954 there was no dial position marked simply "M," although here in the opening credits of *Dial M for Murder* (1954) there is (and, we instantly feel, should be). (Hitchcock the Showman.) The number 6 was tagged "MN" in those days—evident in the phone scene at Wendice's club. 5 had "JKL" and 7 "PQR". o for Operator was in the bottom center. Well into the 1950s, in England and in America, telephone exchanges had often exotic or charming names preceding the number such as, in Maida Vale, where the Wendice apartment is, CUnningham. To get, for instance, CUnningham 4-7899, one would dial up 2-9-4 (for C-U-4) 7-8-9-9. In print formats, the first three letters would be bolded: **CUN**ningham. If the Wendices had been closer to Marylebone Road they might have had a **WEL**beck number, but it is not possible to go further with this speculation because Tony (Ray Milland) informs his new chum Lesgate (Anthony Dawson) that he lives at 61A Charrington Gardens, a street that did not, and does not, exist. There is, however, a 61 Harrington Gardens[1] in London and, oddly, "Harrington" is the word Lesgate mistakenly thinks he hears, virtually as though, very early in the film and sliding in and out of the script, touching but not touching the streets of London, Dawson's Lesgate is saying, bluntly, "You're in the real world!" and Milland's Tony is replying, "Not at all."

At the crucial moment in which the murder is to be triggered—the title promised a murder; we have to have at least a good try—Tony should ring his home by dialing 2 for **CUN**ningham or 9 for **WEL**beck, but his finger goes to the 6. "M" is on his mind: "M" for Maida Vale? "M" for "Murder"? "M" for "Money"? "M" for his wife Margot (Grace Kelly)? "M" for Mark (Robert Cummings), Margot's friend or "friend" (a conundrum never absolutely clearly resolved; or let us say resolved as far as such things could be onscreen in the mid-1950s)? "M" for Master of Suspense? Very signally, at a crux of the film, we see the world upside-down. "M" upside-down is "W." "W" for Wendice? or for Whelan (Hitchcock's mother's name)? or William (his father)?

Or is Tony in his moment of urgency dialing the wrong number?

The Wendice residence itself was an interesting choice (for both Hitchcock and the playwright Frederick Knott, from whose work the film is taken). North of the Regent's Canal, below Kilburn, this little district was largely constructed around 1835. "In the southern end," writes Harold Clunn in 1932, "between St. John's Wood Road and Hall Road, several magnificent new blocks of residential flats have been erected of late years, giving it the appearance of some high-class residential thoroughfare in the West End of Paris . . . only people who are in very comfortable circumstances can afford to rent an apartment in one of these buildings" (244, 245). *Magnificent new blocks.* Worth crossing to England to visit.

It is important in Hitchcock's design, as I see it, that viewers use the phone-dialing trope as a way of catching instantly that there is an element of good-humored wit in this otherwise dark, also unabashedly conventional, film. "Conventional": the film replicates, with a detail that could only have brought pain to multitudes at least in England, the fine details of British upper middle-class life at the time, an assiduous and unrelenting image, so that without the (sommelier's) soupçon of good humor the film might easily have seemed far too much, even too critically, a mirror: Tony's dominating ease, his thug chum's too burnished cleanliness and twisted smile, eagerness for a thousand quid, moral lassitude. Or think of the modesty with which Margot dampens her astonishing beauty in order to become nothing more than the softly responsive wife, *pro forma* for gender organization in the 1950s, in America and abroad, giving not even the smallest hint as to who she more atavistically is.

The Wendices are one of those apparently satisfied (if childless) and comfortable London couples of the middle postwar period, a time when things are still only promising to look up in England. Meat rationing still on after ten years, unbelievably, although as Tony and Margot are not seen eating or using their kitchen we are not forced to discover this. The NHS is but five years old. The unions are fulminating because the Labour government's nationalization schemes are not bravely working. The Attlee government is on a precipice, having failed to deliver the plenitude of victory that had been promised more than once. The pairing of Margot with Tony, we may easily imagine, is from an infatuated romance of a certain kind, she having netted a major sports star (a row of shiny trophies lines the mantle) yet not for an economic uplift since, as always in Hitchcock films, Grace Kelly's character already has class, position, history, and *an admirable family,* and even a cursory look at Tony will show that he has none of these, really. There is something burnished but false about his manners, ever so slightly brutish about the way he talks with cheap, too-well-learned ornamentations of the voice. The upper-class boy who voyaged from Winchester or Eton to Oxford and a cozy berth in the Foreign Office smacks a tennis ball around at the weekend country-house visit, and for frivolity only—good hard exercise involves waking at six and taking a cold shower with one's housemates, then running around the fields under supervision—he doesn't collimate his talents, whatever they are, and put them to work earning him a living as a tennis pro; and he mumbles. Tony's a prole, but our heroine has the soft good grace that comes only with breeding, only from a childhood sitting to tea with a marquise or a duchess or if need be the wives of magnates, lips closed. Margot is above Tony, as Lisa Carol Fremont will be above "Jeff" Jefferies in *Rear Window* (1954) and Francie above even the supremely classy (but not classed) John Robie (Cary Grant) in *To Catch a Thief* (1955). Margot is the (age-old) support (of the Empire). Tony's intention is that the climax of this film will have this woman fall "from a great height" (as Vandamm plots in *North by Northwest* [1959] for Eve).

The Wendices reside in a cozy flat decorated and furnished much more in the comfy 1930s style than anything else—that is, by early 1950s standards, a style that would have been regarded as old and established, and if not exactly proportioned as a manor house would have been still offering chintzy ease for languid meditation. Tony, we are going to discover, has been languidly meditating. Too languidly, perhaps, and not in a morally upright way. At any rate, the sitting room, where we spend almost every moment of our time in this film, has plush things to squat on, not the neo-Scandinavian modern design that was becoming a rage (Heal's was offering modernity dishtowels and drapes memorializing the 1951 Festival of Britain[2]).Art is framed on the walls. Pleasant side tables hold pleasant table lamps. Lush upholstery is plainly evident and in cozy use, an interesting feature of modernity. Wolfgang Schivelbusch notes how upholstery began as a reduction of the industrial experience, "a central cultural-historical phenomenon of the nineteenth century ... its initial purpose was simply to protect the human body from the mechanical shocks caused by machinery" (122)—here, the "machinery" is civilized pretense and the call for proper comportment. Facing the camera are plain, not modishly papered, walls. Margot and Tony are living for ease, not to make a design statement. The place has been lived in, a sense conveyed instantaneously as the scene opens. She came, she saw, she conquered. Rich American girls did, rather generally, want to visit Europe: in a way the film shows the result of their voyages. Some of them fell in love and desired to stay. Some picked up the mannerisms, became the New Britons. And they had love affairs, with reliable, boyish American types from back home, of course. In the Wendice marriage, things are arranged for mutual convenience and with a view to a soothing politesse. We are shown no view of a husband and wife swept away in love, or else going adulterously amok. Passion will appear (but three months afterward) in *Rear Window*, coming soon to a theater near you. Margot and Tony go about their unconnected businesses, casual, friendly, cool, faultlessly courteous to one another. In the silences, which are legion, one reads ... silence.

Tony Wendice knows his way around Wimbledon and has voyaged, for tennis, thrice around the world: a master at the escapade. But Margot has gone further still, reaching out of her *royaume* to find someone like him, then locking herself inside his pretensions, in self-sacrifice. In the early 1950s—present-day aficionados of deregulated air flights, red-eyes, air terminal chaos, body scans, and pay-as-you-go peanuts might have trouble believing—crossing the ocean in comfort (Margot's crossing is in her voice) was for the very rich or very famous only. She carries a certain innocent disregard for the material contingencies of life, the ones Tony values so very much: not blithe carelessness but a reliance on her own natural state, her own automatic bufferings, all attached in childhood whilst she wasn't noticing. A girl like this can be taken advantage of without a great deal of effort as her confidence disarms her, but as long as she stays in the company of others who share her class, the Right Boys, she will be guarded by their sense of decency, their own code of class loyalty, their sweet diligence toward the girls (so that mama and papa would never disapprove). Margot can daydream in her bubble, can primp, can go to the National Gallery and take tea near Bronzino's *Allegory with Venus and Cupid* and Titian's *Noli Me Tangere* and Tiepolo's *Procession of the Trojan Horse into Troy* without worrying about the flutterings of the strangers who shuffle by in chatters.

And her domestic privacy will not be invaded, not by the milkman, not by some complete unknown in a trench coat with an uncomfortable grimace on his face.

INTERLUDE: A ROOM WITH A VIEW

In her cozy cloister, the room in which she is comforted, then trapped, then condemned, Margot has on the wall a lovely view, the sort of thing that would appeal to a city girl who hasn't had this sort of thing outside her window. We see it again and again, a quiet landscape oil in what looks an early twentieth-century mockup of the Constable style: vivacious sky, expressive clouds, wavy trees, a rolling dip in the green, green, intoxicatingly green ground that whispers of Arcadia.[3]

Margot and Tony may bring us to think of E. M. Forster's Lucy Honeychurch (in *A Room with a View*), wishing for but not having a view from her room in a *pensione*, and finding herself arguing with her chaperone at table near "one of the ill-bred people whom one does meet abroad." This "ill-bred" young man (in James Ivory's film [1985] the stunning Julian Sands) "leant forward over the table and actually intruded into their argument," saying, "I have a view, I have a view." The young man's father, the noble Mr Emerson (Denholm Elliott), speaks up to suggest that Lucy and Miss Bartlett (Helena Bonham Carter, Maggie Smith) exchange rooms with them, but the women are diffident, clinging to fragile proprieties. "But why?" he persists. "Women like looking at a view; men don't." Emerson is perhaps right, and Forster will show him so. Here, Margot does not look at her view in that Arcadian canvas, nor, for that matter, does Tony when he stands next to it to pour drinks. Nor does anyone in the story. *We* do not stop our gaze, our thirst to inhabit this green paradise without the kinds of boundaries that tie people like Margot and Tony into their (perhaps, for them, only slightly) painful everydays.

But we have two little voyages to undertake, still, before coming fully into the film.

THE WRONG FUGUE

Speaking only in terms of composition and graphic form, *Dial M* has a perfunctory tameness, a trenchant civility. The cozy flat with its pale sea greens and its pale yellows. The plush furniture, much utilized. The fire in the hearth. The civilized, even elegant conversation. The figurae: Tony, tall, clean-looking, in pleasing gray; Mark shining like a star; Margot with a radiance *nonpareille*, even the two visitors holding themselves agape with unbroken poise (until, of course, one startling moment). The eye is always at rest, if in motion simultaneously, yet as we listen we discover, perhaps in a little (well-designed) confusion, another film. *Dial M for Murder* must be listened to with the eyes.

Jump back, if you will, a few hundred years. Johann Sebastian Bach began composing the first volume of his *Well-Tempered Clavier* in 1722. The progression of the pieces is chromatic, beginning with C major and C minor, moving upward to C-sharp major and C-sharp minor, and continuing up the scale until it can terminate at B minor. This step-by-step continuity was not invented by Bach, although there is no question he made more of it than anyone had before him. His great invention, beyond the composition itself, was in pairing, for each of the twenty-four key signatures, a prelude with a succeeding fugue. There are, thus, twenty-four Preludes and twenty-four Fugues. What can one say of a prelude except that it proposes, moves toward, builds expectation for a fugue? And what can be said of a fugue but that it eventuates from, follows up, resolves problems raised in, or in other ways reflects back upon a prelude? A Yin and a Yang. A Question and an Answer. A diptych. A Before and an Afterward.

Before what? Before what comes afterward.

After what? After what came before.

Frederick Knott's play *Dial M for Murder* (1952; performed first on BBC radio, thus an intentionally talky piece) picks up on Bach's proposition of a twofold revelation, a B surmounting an A, and the Hitchcock film is careful in the way it *follows* Knott's play, rather as though Knott has given a Grand Prelude for which Hitchcock delivers a Grand Fugue. But inside this cinematic "fugue" there is another, inner doubling, a division into two acts, the second one a resolution of the first. Act I—I call it The Prelude—shows a calculated murder attempt turned out into an actual murder, and ends with a soothing bustle of police officers collecting evidence around the corpse. Act II—The Fugue—works through what happens as (Queen) Margot, found guilty, awaits execution whilst her lover works against time to find evidence of her innocence. The story ends happily for her, as must be for a Hitchcock comedy, but not as happily for someone else. This is the gross structure: violent prelude—violent if mannerly—and detective fugue. A crime story from Bach, as it were.

What makes the chain of events—as Hitchcock reveals it—both riddling and fascinating is a deeper structure still for Act I, our "Prelude," because it is itself subdivided into a structure of Prelude* (a contracting and rehearsal) and Fugue* (a performance), the Prelude* being further divided—confoundingly!—into a Prelude** (the contracting) and Fugue** (the rehearsal). To move backward: in the Prelude**, a man is shown making plans with a stranger to murder his wife, then in the Fugue** taking the stranger through a complex residential choreography to show off each part of the abode and what the stranger must do in order to succeed there: effectively the rehearsal (Fugue**) is a variation upon the plan (Prelude**), as all fugues must be to the preludes that precede them, with two actors walking through a scene, checking out the blocking (whilst also talking about it, of course, in quips, reflections, and rationalizations). The Prelude* containing the Prelude** and Fugue** was a seduction, a drawing by a kind of spider into a kind of web; and the Fugue*, culminating a playing out of the entire scenario, this time "on show," all the way down to having a scarf yanked tight around the wife's neck, ends finally with the entrance of the police, the photography, the gentle speculation. It is a deep pleasure to recognize ourselves watching a performance of the routine for which we sat in on rehearsal (a rehearsal from which the victim was of course excluded). Margot Wendice does not know, as she squirms for her life, that she is in a "production" inside the greater production by which she is created. She does not know that she has voyaged, unconsciously, from the effortlessness of an everyday routine—put on some lovely clothing; go out for a lovely lunch—into a tightly staged dance of death. Not all voyages require consciousness.

Four times over, Margot is innocent. She:

[1] does not know, and could not imagine, that her husband, of all people, has malicious intent;

[2] does not know there is an actual murder plot, in which she will be on a precipice;

[3] is actually, legally, technically innocent of the crime (of killing her intending killer) for which she is about to die on the gallows; and

[4] doesn't know the intended murder is a routine, worked out step by step, and that she is presently, in her agony with the scarf around her neck, playing out one of the steps, if unwillingly (that is, without will but with arrangement). This is what happens to props when a rehearsal is put into performance, and, here purely a body, Margot is a prop. It is the performance, not the rehearsal, that begs our attention once the curtain is up and the stage is alive. The Hitchcockian gesture here comes in showing how, whilst things *do* go wrong, spectacularly wrong, for the intending killer Lesgate (Lesgate today; yesterday named Swann), his rehearsal having been clearly, too clearly, inadequate to the contingencies of his performance, nevertheless the knot unwinds for reasons that are almost unconnected to the dead man, except in one tiny regard. By the way, we are immensely relieved that Margot is left alive, but the relief is short-lived since far too soon she will face the judge wearing the black cap.

Margot slays nefarious Lesgate desperately, single-handedly, even expertly, with a pair of sewing shears to clasp which she reaches awkwardly behind her head in a rear shot that puts her upside-down.[4] With the blade in his spine the man gives an orgasmic spasm—a beautiful noirish shadow hurtled onto the wall as he arches—then throws himself backward to a death pose on the carpet. Some details about this death (the deity is in the details), since, plain enough on the screen, they are easily overlooked:

- Margot has no idea who it is that she is stabbing, since he has come upon her from behind and in surprise. This theme of *the unfamiliar (die Unheimlich)* is carried forward as she speaks to the Inspector, gazing down at the body and admitting, with excruciating honesty, that she has never seen him before. To be looking for the first time at a man when he lies dead on the carpet before you, and when you have put him there! There is an irony to this, since during his briefing to Lesgate/Swann Tony drew down a framed photograph from the wall showing the two of them at a Cambridge dinner (along with Hitchcock), a photograph that was all along hanging on the wall, that is, on Margot's wall. She does not recognize a man whose picture has long been hovering near her, yet, of course, why would she know or recognize anybody in Tony's university reunion photograph?[5]

- The clipping shears that Margot strenuously seizes from the desktop behind her head were obtained for her, just before he left for the evening, by Tony. He wants her to stay home, not go out. But if, willingly or not, she is to function as his icon of *Heimlichkeit*, one of those women who, on the trail Betty Friedan identified, avoided "political activism and lashing out at experts who promoted domesticity" (May 201), he must have something for her to do. Why not those clippings that have been waiting so long—clippings presumably, although not demonstrably, regarding his tennis career, that is, tearsheets of paper with, among other content, photographs of him. (Again, the photograph.) To do the clippings she will need scissors. So he fetches the scissors, as turns out the single reason she remains alive. To say this differently is to spice it more: Tony provides Margot with the tool she will use for killing, much as he provides Lesgate/Swann with the situation that he would have used. Tony as provider. Hopeless provider since Lesgate/Swann cannot make effective use of the situation made for him and Tony would not have Margot using the shears as she does. (An *auteur* at war with our *Auteur*.)

- The death itself: Margot stabs Lesgate in such a way that he goes into nervous spasm, but it is not until he crashes to the carpet face-up, pressing the scissors deeply into his back (against the carpet), that he dies. Accidental death, as far as murder goes. Hitchcock places his camera in a pit in order to shoot supine Dawson at carpet level (Truffaut 210) so that we actually see the dorsal side easing down and pressing the blade all the way in.

- By absenting himself in order to script an alibi, Tony has reduced his access to the events at 61A Charrington Gardens to what can be heard through the telephone line. We are given an extraordinarily revealing depiction of the action involving Margot and Lesgate, and it is easy enough to imagine that this depiction is transferred to Tony, since he planned it. But he did not plan things going awry, and he does not know that they are, until Margot's voice comes on the line. From this instant he is in panic-action mode, inventing every response to every twitch of muscle or word. I will return to this moment.

The legal problem, not morally but technically speaking, is that because the rehearsal was so meticulous in preparing Lesgate, as Tony prefers to call him, to enter the apartment in a hermetically clean way, carrying no hard evidence of the surgery he is about to do, his body is merely an unidentified corpse as far as the police are concerned, and Margot, tucked away in the bedroom and represented by Tony's "helpful" claims, will merely seem the killer. When finally she speaks, she is confused, barely present: "He was trying to kill me." This sounds plenty convincing to us, but only because we attended both the rehearsal and the performance: that is, regardless of Tony's secret knowledge, bad planner that he is, and given that Mark accompanied him for the evening, we and only we are witnesses to what actually happened. Police Inspector Hubbard (John Williams) has no earthly reason for believing her (and here, as in *To Catch a Thief* for Hitchcock, Williams onscreen is a man who wishes to be sympathetic but has his eyes and ears open). Can a sweet and beautiful woman such as Margot Wendice, as played by the sweet-and-beautiful-looking Grace Kelly, be imagined a murderess? We did see her commit the killing, and without hesitation or mercy. Can we bring ourselves to wonder, along with the Inspector, that beneath her appearance and beneath her claim to decency she could have had a motive to produce this death?

It is the architecture of a situation that intrigues Hitchcock without cease, here the division of information—our knowledge split from Tony's and from Hubbard's, split also from Margot's; the separation between motive and appearance; the fierce mechanism of contrivance. Separation, as in Prelude and Fugue, a music based on doubling, echo, repetition (in music recapitulation), variation, haunting. The astuteness of Tony's planning is no accident. He is playing a championship game against the police, in order that his wife should hang for a killing he arranged and paid for Lesgate to commit; in order that with her hanging her fortune will fall to him. This film is not about a crime of passion, and indeed crimes of passion do not frequently interest Alfred Hitchcock who, François Truffaut handily observed, films his killings like love scenes (345). Bill Krohn says that with *Dial M* he "finally finds the colors with which to film sex and death conjoined" (*Hitchcock* 53).[6] The murder here is as cold as coin, worked out for rational gain, in short an intrinsic part of an essentially capitalist, modern world in which the supreme value is rationality, planning, the organized mind. It is against this brick wall that heroic dignity must strive, as we see again and again (for instance, in *Vertigo* [1958] and *Family Plot* [1976]). A very broadly structured voyage away from sense and sensibility and toward calculation and gain.

It will be with utter and grossly displayed rationality that Wendice goes to his club where we will catch him playing a quite rational game of cards. At precisely 11:00 p.m., the plan dictates, he will telephone home, and when Margot has picked up the receiver Lesgate will strangle her. The entire affair has been crafted like clockwork, thus upon a medieval model. But Wendice's wristwatch stops. An important man, at least to himself, Tony may well be wearing a Jaeger-LeCoultre self-winding wrist watch (made in Le Sentier, Switzerland, between 1953 and 1956). If he is, he has neglected to twitch his wrist and forearm, carried away, perhaps, by the twinkle of his own brilliant mechanism, or even suffering belatedly from tennis wrist. For Tony, the Fugue** played out after the Act I Prelude** is the *wrong fugue*.

TENNIS WRIST

Wendice's wristwatch stops, and not only stops but stops at 10:40 p.m. (as though by its own rehearsal), so that, a few minutes past 11:00 he must hie to the club telephone where, of course, he is stymied by an old codger who won't get off the line (and cannot, we instantaneously think, have anything important to be saying). Here once again is that old, never tired, and never less than enchanting Hitchcockian merger of villain and viewer. We murmur incessantly, "Get off the phone! Get off the bleeding phone!": all so that "poor" beleaguered Tony may have the chance to call his wife—and precipitate her death. No matter. Just as Lesgate is about to leave the flat in disappointment (no murder, no money) he hears the phone purr, quickly runs to tuck himself behind the arras—a thick curtain covering the French door that leads outside into the garden—and catches Margot half-asleep saying "Hello?" over and over and over again as the person at the other end keeps silent. As Lesgate makes his move, no clearly decipherable sound is transmitted. When, the horrid action complete, she struggles to the phone and finally Tony announces himself, she starts to speak, horribly confused, and he is instantly not the happy husband delighted to hear his wife. His shock and dismay need covering quite as much as the ugly deed he attempted.

A tiny observation in reflection of Hitchcock's casting, which always "rings." Milland had been a somewhat sleek, somewhat dark, and very handsome leading man, even decrepit for Billy Wilder in *The Lost Weekend* (1945), yet here he has fleshed up a little, not at all to the extent that his clothing fails to sparkle excitedly as though he is a highly paid model but only sufficiently to suggest that this man, who raced around the courts, races around the courts no longer. Cummings here: what he always appeared to be onscreen—film or television—gentle, extremely courteous, handsome in a notably clean way, American, open-minded, bright, but not exactly active, so that near the ending, as he excitedly attempts to persuade Tony to a redemption plan, the energy really bristles (and touches us): he is the perfect American on a voyage far from home. Williams sports the dignity, bearing, quietude, precision, tenderness of a doting grandfather, whilst showing again and again that he has what people call a mind like a steel trap; if his masculinity has a cerebral origin it extends to the best British tailoring. Dawson is an unctuous sort of male, gliding over Tony's carpet as though on gimbals. What is attractive about him, what could entrance a landlady, for example, is the lusting twinkle in his eyes. Milland, a Welshman by birth, was forty-seven when shooting started. Cummings, from Missouri, was forty-four. Williams, from Buckinghamshire, was fifty-one. Dawson, from Edinburgh, was thirty-eight.

Grace Kelly, a Philadelphian, was twenty-five here in her first appearance for Hitchcock. She was one of the women who epitomized female beauty onscreen at the time, but in addition carried herself with a deeply inbred American aristocratic bearing, having been born into an East coast elite. Not much more than a year after making this film (and two others for Hitchcock) she left the business in order to become a princess. But in *Dial M*, where she is required to collapse and degrade onscreen, she begins as a princess already and is transformed by circumstance into a full-fledged human being.

BEST LAID PLANS

Steven Jacobs has provided a floorplan that will help make clear the silent, risky dance of death that is the central mechanism of the film. In the longish flat there is a capacious sitting room lit with what seems a very fine golden mist. At one end, a desk (the fatal desk) is set into an alcove that peers out upon the garden; then, some furniture: armchairs, a sofa, tables and lamps; and at the other end a hearth with a mantel holding trophies. Behind the hearth, with its door on the left side as we look, is the bedroom leading to the bath. Nearer the alcove is the kitchen, which is visited only for the briefest time. The Wendice telephone sits on the desk, pearly white.

As Margot is intended to be slain at the desk while holding that phone (wearing, Tony must guess, the pearly white satin peignoir we observe),[7] and at a time when Tony can with convenience not be present, the following facts become salient:

[1] The event had best be planned for evening or night, when he can slip out with an acceptable (and therefore accepted) excuse. He even prepares Lesgate for a room that will be swathed in darkness but slashed through with a shaft of light when she opens the bedroom door to emerge (not only a director of action but a lighting cameraman as well!).

[2] Since by night: Margot could well be occupying the salon instead of in bed, reading or daydreaming but in any event blocking the killer from making entrance secretly. This would never do. Thus,

[3] In order that Margot be positioned not only at home but in the bedroom, the key action will be scheduled for later, after she normally retires, say 11:00. Note that the hour must not only make sense in terms of the habits of a woman like Margot, it must ring to the audience as sensible. She cannot, without drawing too much attention away from her pathetic role here, be one of those who retire at 9:00, or a nightbird who doesn't retire until 2:00 in the morning. For example, 11:00 is roughly the time when a 9:00 or 9:30 screening of *Dial M for Murder* would be letting out.

[4] When she hears the phone ring—if Tony's plan is accurate—Margot will rise, put on her robe (a habit), and walk through the bedroom door, along the full length of the salon, to the desk, where she will pick up the receiver. Lesgate, tucked behind the alcove curtain, will now have unfettered access to her. As happens, Margot doesn't put on a robe. But she does do everything else Tony would wish, the perfect "assistant." As to picking up the receiver, Margot could naturally do

this from the side of the desk (so that the killer is in her right periphery), not behind it (with the killer behind her). Hubbard has noticed this and questions her about it, resigned to acceptance when she says she always does this, so that she can write a note if she needs to. *But Tony knows this already: his whole choreography is based on her standing behind the desk.*

Rehearsal will be a very good idea, since this is by no means a simple or simple-minded plan and requires patient working out. Involved are complexly related pathways in the Wendice space, precise movements of two unfamiliar bodies, habit, responsiveness, interior décor as blind, and clear wings by which at least one of the principals can make entrance to and, most importantly, exit from the stage. Moreover, as with so much performance, notably including all of what is given in this film, Lesgate and Margot must both execute a choreography—her unkenningly—composed by someone else: though Margot's actions will seem natural to her, they will all have been foreseen. Thus we have the long (bravura) (Prelude**) section in which the murder, once settled, is rehearsed like a kind of dance. But into this Prelude** there are two obtrusions:

[A] The intended killer is certainly a churl, but not already an accomplished killer, and he must be egged on to make the quantum leap. More, this sort of man must be found in the first place (the contracting), a needle in the great haystack of London, and sucked into the Wendice apartment for tutelage leading to: "Blackmail?"—"Influence." Tony followed him ever so long, we hear recounted afterward, one little story within the story: "There were times when I'd felt you almost belonged to me." Lesgate is a kind of virgin, and the Prelude* is to show that.

[B] As to seducing Lesgate: no apparent stranger is going to visit a man's apartment upon a blunt request to commit murder for him, so some entirely sociable pretext must be found, as well as a scene in which this pretext can be played calmly, comfortably, decorously, without raising alarm. The sitting room by the hearth. Warm light. Soft furniture. A nice little glass to celebrate and lubricate a car sale.

A genteel conversation between two men of the world. Convenience, money, masculinity, privacy, honorable exchanges of honor. Because they are "men of the world," Tony will find it comfortable and unquestionable to share his life with his new friend, the pain of his marriage, the pain of his lost career, pain in general. A man will understand a man's pain, after all. This Prelude* is a real *andante*.

Tony's cleverest invention, displayed in the rehearsal, is that the latchkey to the apartment, pilfered in advance by him from Margot's bag, will be tucked just beneath the carpet lip on one of the stairs directly outside the flat's door. He escorts the man outside and gives him a chance to play at retrieving the key, all this simultaneously giving *us* opportunity to see the hallway and the staircase area outside the flat, a space that will come to figure importantly in the drama later on. We have meanwhile taken in, as on a museum tour, all aspects of the salon. We have noted the bedroom door, have examined the desk even to the extent of checking into Tony's bankbook to be assured, with Lesgate, that he has withdrawn and secreted away enough money for the payoff and this in a way that won't ever be detected. And by the time Lesgate's walk-through, the Prelude**, has been accomplished we have prepared ourselves for the Fugue**, the outplaying of the act, the thrilling leap from ordinary rehearsal to glorious show. In the bedroom, beside the beds, but not to be discovered until later, some windows peer out onto "Charrington Gardens," which we will have no trouble discovering as a rather quiet, definitively sedate street, the kind of place in which nothing nefarious ever happens.

A CHAIN OF RINGS

I am calling the movement around the Wendice apartment, in rehearsal and then in performance, the central mechanism of the film. It is surely a voyage. Hitchcock also presents a finer mechanism, more definitively modern, and that is the telephone and its elaborate system extending, we are to believe without expressly being told at the outset, all over the great city. Every telephone is either in a call box or, for those relatively few who can afford one, set handsomely and sweetly upon a piece of accessible furniture. And generally the telephone works.[8] You can call from any point X to any point Y simply by dialing, so telephone traffic can be imagined flowing heavily all through the city, this in distinction to the emptiness of the quiet road outside the Wendices' flat. Already in the early 1950s, if they can, people ring up rather than run around (the story contains key calls from the Wendice apartment to the local police constabulary, and one call going the other way). Yet the Wendices are above the average. "Before the age of telesales," writes Paul Feeney, "when most people didn't even have a telephone, the door-to-door salesmen were very active" (39–40), and "If you went sick during term time then you might get a visit from the school board man to check up on you (most people didn't have telephones back then)" (177).

The murder by telephone envisioned here is a criminal act devised to be not only accompanied by, but also charged to, a publicly organized system, a kind of machine killing, reflective, perhaps, of the use of the guillotine in France since the Revolution. Not the human hand expressly but the mechanical system triggers the kill (although of course the human hand is a requirement). Here, a man with a garotte is waiting for a victim to be distracted by a ring. When Tony hears his wife speak, "Hello? ... Hello? ... ," he will know that she is on point of dying, as specifies the "score" he has composed. When too soon afterward she begs help, Tony is caught on the horns of a dilemma, since as her husband he can do nothing but flee homeward whilst as the mastermind behind the crime he is stunned and deflated by the failure.

Like all systems, this system doesn't work as planned—setups of elaborate systems generally prepare audiences for a dramatic collapse—and now we face a further trio of paths to follow:

[I] The viewers are placed halfway across a fence separating judgmentalism from sympathy, since at the instant of the missed schedule (Tony in the club finding his watch has stopped) it is possible both to sigh with relief in finding that sweet Margot will not, in the end, die by strangling as this horrible man planned; but also to wince with irritation, since the dance of death was so beautifully choreographed, so slickly rehearsed, and so pristine in its subtle, tiny, mechanical movements—step over this way, reach out there, check that, step over there—that it took on the quality of a beautiful ballet, and now the ballet has closed.

[II] But at the same time a great vulnerability is revealed, because now, as can be seen all too clearly, mechanical systems, harbingers to and monuments of modernity, don't work flawlessly. The stopped watch. And the occupied call box: such receptacles are in public or semi-public places, accessible to whoever might wish to make use. There is never a guarantee with a call box that one can get to the phone instantly. Nor is there ever a guarantee that a wrist watch won't stop. But Tony's plan has been timed, worked out literally to the instant. Thus, the holdup is signal and horrid.

As happens when technologies slip their way into social affairs, improvisations of etiquette soon follow. In this case the ultimate taboo is dragging any other person away from a phone call. A call in progress is sacrosanct, regardless of who is saying what silly thing to what silly listener. A pair of ironies: that the man on the telephone can be presumed by the viewer to be saying nothing of importance yet seen to hold up Tony, whose ability to have the phone is the linchpin of the kill plan. But also, that we cannot know whether the man using up the call box is ringing his own home, where yet another wife murder is being carried out.

The nature and shape of time, surely as understood by the audience on their voyage of discovery, are critical in this murder mechanism. There is a plan for precision, in that all timepieces will operate in synchrony to the very second. This recalls the attack-theft sequence near the beginning of Fritz Lang's *Dr. Mabuse, der Spieler* (1922), in which temporal synchrony is the operational arrangement bringing together different aspects of a crime composed through fulfillment of different tasks by different team members situated in different places. Here, and much as we see performed by very idiosyncratic others in *Dial M*, is an organization that, like Lang's, "tackles the way one form of technology interacts with another to create the abstract and fully co-ordinated grid of space and time that forms the terrain of modernity" (Gunning, *Lang* 96). Lang wrote that he had in mind "the man who prepares his crimes quasi-scientifically before executing them himself or having them carried out by others with a mathematical precision" (Sadoul 532 qtd. in Gunning 96). Lesgate's watch and Tony's were meant to be—and we were to think them—in match step, and it is because of this presumption and all that is linked to it that Tony is so alarmed and put off guard to find, inadvertently, that his wrist watch has stopped. (To find, in sudden dismay, that one does not know "what time it is," whereas it is, of course, *now*, always and forever.) The mechanical gears of time and communication are explicitly rendered by Hitchcock when Tony finally dials, with the image shifting away from the callbox into the hidden machine of ratchets, gears, and springs by which an electrical connection is established. The detail here inspires a pair of New Wave homages, the vision of the Paris sewer system, with the hanging street signs, in Jacques Becker's *Le Trou* (1960), and the underground tube system that extends across that city, and through which official messages can be transmitted, again moving past street signs beneath the pavement, in François Truffaut's *Baisers volés* (1968).

[III]   There is another ironic strangeness produced as Margot quizzically hesitates in picking up the phone. Clearly, in the Wendice household there is no custom of receiving telephone calls at 11:00 p.m., so she is thrown off already, by the ring itself. But when, receiver to her ear, she doesn't receive a response to her seven hellos, each one more tremulous than the hello that came before—in a vacuum expressly arranged by Tony—she is confronting yet another way in which the phone system can operate less than perfectly, and to some annoyance. The line, she has learned in England, can be imperfect, so that it transmits only one way, and someone may be speaking whom she cannot hear. Or else, the system permits, among other possibilities, prank calls, in which case someone is deliberately teasing her. Or else, the system guarantees a certain invisibility, so something may be happening at the other end that she cannot see and that is preventing someone from speaking. Or else, the caller has not yet pushed in his coin. She faces a "garden of forking paths," in Borges's phrase,[9] and cannot tell one from another, therefore cannot know what is going on—with her at present, or with the world outside. At this intended penultimate moment of her life she is thrown into utter confusion. The telephone, intended systematically as a means of communicating, here at a crucial instant fails her spectacularly.

A further turn on the telephone voice—Margot's, for instance, as Tony is hearing it. Here, and in other cases both cinematic and noncinematic, the voice on the other end of the line exemplifies the figure of the *acousmêtre*, discussed in depth by Michel Chion:

Sound films can show an empty space and give us the voice of someone supposedly 'there,' in the scene's 'here and now,' but outside the frame.... We can never praise Pierre Schaeffer enough for having unearthed this arcane word [*acousmêtre*] in the 1950s. He adopted it to designate a mode of listening that is commonplace today, systematized in the use of radio, telephones, and phonograph records. Of course, it existed long before any of these media, but for lack of a specific label, wasn't obviously identifiable, and surely was rarely conceived as such in experience. (18)

One can never fail to notice that the murder in *Dial M* is acousmatic in nature, from both ends. That desperately reaching forward, both before the attempt is made upon her and then, staggering, afterward, Margot knows herself to be in the presence of a *thing unknown*, this even when Tony's "distraught" and "concerned" voice comes on, but tinnily, as in a place invisible, infinitely far away. Tony hears the sounds on Charrington Gardens acousmatically, too, putting together a picture in his mind of what must be happening, with the help of his memory of the rehearsal that he guided and the plans he made up. What is most shocking is something else: that *we* are seeing in plain view what Tony cannot, does not see; and that when we cut to him waiting eagerly on the phone at the club we are seeing what Margot cannot see either. And these two, separated from us at a very great distance and over a substantial time, are *acousmêtres* to us. On separation, the essential element of voyages, more to follow.

MOTIVE AND MOTIF

Yet why would a man comfortable in life, such as Tony Wendice, a man with a glorious enough background and a marriage one could not fail to call glorious as well, with quite a nice flat in quite a nice part of town, plenty of quite nice glasses of Scotch to look forward to, a career to be proud of, wish to kill his wife? Why get involved in that abysm? And why mar lovely Margot? Even through green jealousy. Even through resentment. Why, too, elaborate such a very dirty plan, seduce the perpetrator off the streets, walk through the rehearsal with the care of a ballet master, let the thing actually slide into happening? Money, we are informed, yet looking at Margot, notably early on as she models her carmine red gown, we find a radiance that money cannot touch, a radiance that is surely not to be completely devalued in the film's gross structure. This person is obviously beyond money. (In watching Hitchcock, it is a mistake to fail at noticing the casting, the choice of a face, of a profile, of a voice.) Is Tony a boor, simply incapable of an aesthetic response to her? If he is a boor, he is a slick boor. But since his deeper motive, the wellspring of his movement, is not the subject Hitchcock would most wish his viewers to focus on and wonder about—this film is not, and should not be mistaken to be, about Tony's motivations—it must be a fairly simple one and hard to question, something out of the textbook: gross infidelity. Which is to say, Tony seeks justice. That our beauteous Margot with all her elegance should have been taking a lover on the side;[10] and that Tony, stalwart athlete and couth dilettante, should, to preserve his honor, set matters aright. A warping of the manners of the courtly romance.

We are informed that the lover is Mark Halliday, the American (The American Boy—Edward Albee will soon give another birth to him in *The Sandbox*). He has been her lover for some time. Even across the sea. Remembering how conversations can be fraught—how this film works to show us how conversation can be fraught—let us peep in again on the conversation between these two, as the film begins. We can grasp that Mark has just come off the ship at Southampton and trained into Waterloo Station, whence by taxi straight to her. Hitchcock's comedic touch: medium shot of Tony kissing Margot bye-bye; cut to Mark coming off the ship; cut to Mark kissing Margot in the flat:

> MARGOT: Let me get you another drink, Mark, before Tony comes. I ought to explain something . . .
>
> MARK: Yes, I've been waiting for that.
>
> MARGOT: I haven't told him anything about us.
>
> MARK: That's not surprising. It's a tough thing to do.
>
> MARGOT: When you telephoned this morning, I simply said you wrote crime stories. And I'd met you once when you were here before.
>
> MARK (with an amicable smile): That has a pretty guilty ring to it. I'd never use it in one of my stories.

MARGOT: Mark, I know you think it's silly. When you get to know Tony, you'll understand why I said that.

MARK (smiling even more warmly): Darling, I understand now.

A barrel of herrings, to be sure, and we are plunged into it directly. Yet also a sea of tentative meanings, across which we might voyage to imagined probabilities:

[1] "*Another* drink," because they have already been drinking. Perhaps for some time now. Perhaps neither of them is particularly sober. Or, in the social grouping to which such people belong—and now, presumably, Tony as well, because he has married into it—one drinks and drinks and the idea of sobriety is beyond belief. Drink is life. Or certainly the paving upon which one walks through life.

[2] "Before Tony comes." She is simply being hospitable, making indication that Tony will shortly arrive and that Mark might wish another drink as his glass is empty. Or else: she is pointing to the imminent arrival of her husband and suspecting Mark might need some "courage." Or: she is cuing us that her husband, soon to be there, is a man who does not like to see his wife sharing his liquor with another man, under any circumstances—possessive, surely, but most definitely about his booze.

[3] "I ought to explain something," which is to say, "There is something regarding Tony and me, Mark, that you do not yet know." And to us: You may think you already know what's going on in this marriage, viewer, but no you don't, not fully.

[4] "Yes, I've been *waiting*." In short, Mark has had the feeling there is something that ought to be said that hasn't been, and he wishes her to know he has made a point of not asking, of not raising issues, not probing. Tender *and* gallant. But not happy to be left out of the know: "Perhaps I shouldn't be kept waiting any longer."

[5] "I haven't told him anything about *us*." Oops, there is an *us* [our first clear indication, or better, clear intimation], and Tony is on the outside, by intent. Tony doesn't know about you and me, about me and

you, *whatever the viewer is likely to take that to mean*. A secret is being kept from Tony. Everyone out there will now know a secret is being kept from Tony, a secret that is perhaps something of a clue. Poor Tony? And also: Might Poor Tony be keeping a secret from them? Secrets are common property, after all.

[6] "It's a tough thing to do." Well, if Margot and Mark have been carrying on a love affair, for her to tell Tony would be to make a confession, to open, if nothing else, that secret, perhaps set off an explosion. Yet, too, note "tough," not "difficult" or "tricky" or "perilous" or any other word. Something rather like cowhide, or like wood, or like iron bars, something very resistant, not liquid, something very recalcitrant to accommodate itself, faces Margot. She is strapped to Tony?

[7a] "When you telephoned this morning": a blunt and brilliant pointer to the telephone, its utility, its swiftness (and right at the film's beginning). "Simply said you wrote crime stories . . . met you here before." Mark Halliday, the author, travels with some frequency to London, perhaps sets his tales there. Perhaps he has an agent there. And if he's a writer of crime stories he sits calmly before a typewriter and invents crimes (not really unlike Hitchcock). We are moved to gaze at him now, this paragon of criminal intelligence: sleek, soft-featured, bright-facedly youthful, well dressed, dignified, sweet. Don't get me wrong, I write crime stories but I myself am entirely disconnected from crime. My crime stories are entirely my fabrications (a motif that will come back with a vengeance). (Fabrications: you don't need to be a killer in order to play one.)

[7b] "Met you once"! Mark had come to London; she lives in London. There were at the time roughly nine million souls in London. How did she meet him? *She* met him, not the other way round. We somehow instantly leap to that. Did she step a little out of her way to catch onto him? The lady who comes out of the audience after one of his readings and asks for his autograph saying what a wonderful way he has with words. How would a person like Margot Wendice meet a person like Mark Halliday?

And Mark picks up these undertones without hesitation:

[8] "That has a pretty guilty ring to it." Not only no slouch, this man has exceedingly well-tuned reflexes and exceedingly well-tuned sensibilities. He invents detectives, after all, and they sniff out clues that are sniffably placed only because Mark has already sniffed them. "I'd never use it in one of my stories": an indicator, surely, of Mark's taste as a writer, but also a little clue for Margot's delectation that what she has just murmured would, indeed, smell if she said it. It would conjure a crime scenario, albeit in Mark's view a cheap one. Margot, don't say it that way.

[9] "When you get to know Tony you'll understand why I said that": well, *what* exactly did she say that Tony would respond to in a revealing way? That she is a fan of crime stories? Or that she is eager to meet a writer, Mark for instance, since writers are famous? Tony is also famous, a major tennis star as was, so he has an ego, and perhaps she would be respectfully addressing his ego by invoking an alibi that involves fame, creativity, looking up to people. Or challenging his ego, the fame she liked not being his. But either way the fragment she has offered Mark is enough to make him see with professional eyes that she has invented something far more complex than it needs to be, promising to be offering up three pieces of information—what Mark does; that he has been in London before; that she met him that way—when one would do: "I met him last April." Will the surfeit of informative clues itself draw Tony's attention, make her seem guilty, or is Margot now confiding that Tony is a demanding man who doubts too often and too deeply, a man who will ask many questions, so that only a complex alibi will work? Under all this is the presumption of Tony's incipient jealousy. He will not easily slide into a ménage, and he will be strictly intolerant of infidelity.

[10] "Darling, I understand now," emphasis on the last word. In other words, you don't have to tell me all this, I picked it up from the start, and this little bit of conversation is over. Another way Mark could have put this, more directly aimed at the audience: "Thanks. I can

see," but that would have made him seem churlish whereas what he does say makes him seem protective, caring, and gentle. Not too many actors can give the word "darling" the ring of truth that comes from Cummings.[11]

To stress a small point: There may have been some sexual dalliance between Mark and Margot, yet nothing we have learned so far points singly and unimpeachably to that. They could have some other secret business (she is giving him money out of charity and admiration, so that he can pay someone to publish his books). And here is one of the key points where the Hitchcock vision of *Dial M* makes its peculiar weight felt. We must see. We must see these two in medium close-up, see the one looking at the other and vice versa, see their expressions while they chat about this "illicit" matter (the absent Tony being The Law) bearing the look of a romantic couple. The speech fails to contain the full truth. Yet at the same time, in regard to looking, we must keep in mind that Mark makes his living by writing believable but wholly untrue stories about people who look the part. It is intriguing to think that if they are *not* in bed together, any suspicion on Tony's part that they are—Tony who is not watching them now as we are—would be tantamount to evidence of jealousy on his part, irrational jealousy even, of a mind gone off the rails. Early in the film, Hitchcock doesn't want us having that thought about Tony, thus the slight tipping of scales toward adultery in Mark and Margot's performance (Cummings and Kelly's performance of performance). Tony will not be irrational if he comes to suspect what we already believe.

THE FIRE THAT PURIFIES

We must always be prepared, watching Hitchcock, to think of his moments being prepared, and being preparations: as both fugues and preludes together. "On a day like today / We passed the time away / Writing love letters in the sand" (J. Fred Coots and Nick Kenny and Charles Kenny, "Love Letters in the Sand").[12]

"Do you remember the letters you wrote to me?" Margot asks Mark. "After I read them, I burned them."

Ouch, what a debacle! What a slap! Letters, note, that we are never permitted to read. Letters that no longer exist. I destroyed you telling me how you love me.

"All except one..."

GULP:

"You probably know the one I mean." Would she have saved one and only one because it was especially ornate in its romance, because in its poetry he had outdone himself? Was it especially confiding or revealing of the writer? Especially tender? Salacious? What a beautiful tease for the audience's smudgy fantasy: the letter, no doubt, with the explicit reference to... to what one does not reference explicitly. Thank you, Henry James, but *what is that, pray?* What did Mark carefully make reference to, addressing his innocent little girl in a communication so provocative she would not toss it away? This decorous, lovely Margot. This unimpeachably untrammeled lady.

And then she drops the bomb: "It was stolen."

Tony and she going off... handbag... platform... Victoria Station. Two weeks later the bag is returned, without the letter. Then a note, "Printed, all capitals," detailing how she should prepare fifty pounds in used one-pound notes and mail the package to John S. King, Brixton SW9. (The residence of Vincent Van Gogh from 1873 to 1874, Brixton is a part of London distinct from, because lower in class than, Maida Vale.) But that delicate letter was never returned. She goes to Brixton and hunts Mr King. Nobody by that name has ever lived at that address. The tantalizing tentacles of a mystery.

Margot in something like this stunning red dress would stand out in Brixton, which is a humble setting. Mark has caught fire from her flaming dress. Tonight he's going to tell Tony about them. But she begs him off, making Mark either anxious or dismayed: "I can see this is going to be a rough evening. All of us saying nice things to each other." (Later in the film, to our horror, the Margot Red will be reincarnated diabolically.)

Listen to the film once again and notice that there is no moment at any point in which anyone says anything to anyone else but "nice things." Nice, nice. Courtesy, courtesy. Know your station.

But then Mark wonders aloud why she didn't burn that letter, too, that singular epistle, that unerased footprint,[13] but before she can frame an answer in strides Tony, the perfect *interruptus*. Smiling, tall, even regal, casual, a commander of every molecule of this place. One can see Margot's muscles stiffening through her alabaster skin. And Mark's a player, he's on the court. Charming to see how charming he can be, how well he can spend an evening saying nice things (that he doesn't mean): in short, give a performance. Never think that performance, the voyage from the self, will be far from Alfred Hitchcock. Tony, sadly, cannot join them at the theater tonight but may come later. Take the tickets. Sell the extra one. Buy yourself a drink on the proceeds. What a kind and thoughtful husband, what a paragon of civility and hospitality! Never imagine that performance will be far away. Await the *pas de deux*.

Note the bouncy pattern of Tony's seductive moves as he leads Lesgate in a voyage of subterfuge and containment. Lesgate, a sleazy but hardly abnormal bloke, Cambridge graduate (if he didn't drop out) who used to call himself Swann and has been feeling carefree and uninhibited in his dark activities ever since, is soon enough moved to realize he has come into the hands of a madman. This little voyage from blithe carelessness into conspiracy happens methodically:

[a] Using his voice of innocence, Tony rings Capt. Lesgate at **HAM**pstead 7899, a number in Camden Town, a plain middle-class neighborhood near the Regent's Canal nowadays gone to used T-shirt and patchouli stores. We learn later that Lesgate has been shuffling around. Camden may be nothing but his most recent conquest. Tony with City voice and dubbing himself "Mr Fisher" says he understands Lesgate has a car to sell. An American car. Having business that will carry him out of town, he was "rather hoping ... you could come to my flat tonight." Come to me. I'll give you a drink. We'll be chums and I'll haggle over your price. Prod prod, tickle tickle. One can see Tony's eyes as he uses the telephone, not pointed straight forward at the nothingness before him but in fact looking askance, speaking one line and thinking another. Twinkling with ... merriment? Self-approbation at his smartness? Childish curiosity?

[b] "Fisher" saw this car at the garage where Lesgate had berthed it, that's how he knows. Good explanation. To justify Lesgate coming to Maida Vale, he claims an injured leg. Physical injury is an easy claim to make on a telephone, where legs cannot speak. Could Lesgate possibly bring

the car? No? But the papers, then? Yes. (Lesgate "sounds" a good fellow. Fellow, *fellah*.[14]) We will observe that Tony has a stick already to hand; in short, he was prepared for the "injury" claim and the need to prove it, before making the call. (But a stick may be a whip.)

[c] Lesgate at "Mr Fisher's" flat. Fisher is using the eyes of a hunter and has polished up his walking stick, on which he makes a show of leaning a little. "I can't help thinking I've seen you before somewhere ..." staring hard like an optician—another tiny performance—and ostensibly reaching back into what someone might call his memory. (Is Tony actually journeying to the Land of Memory or is he delving into the records from recently conducted research? Or just watching Lesgate's cheeks for a reaction?) Oh, but Lesgate thinks Fisher is familiar, too! Tony beats him to the ball: "Wait a minute! Lesgate?" ("Wait a minute" as a way of catching the sleeve whilst stalling, drawing one's interlocutor into affiliation, because it works to hold a listener who can now neither change the topic nor duck away but must hang on to hear what's coming). "You're not Lesgate! Swann! C. J. Swann! Or was it C. A.?" A tiny, effortless, and painless question. An utterly, totally, irreconcilably, ineffably trivial question, which for Lesgate and for us can have no meaning whatever. C. B.? C. K.?? C. L.???? But this nonentity is a central gear in the mechanism: get the tiny details correct, and make a show of being concerned to do that.

And who at any rate could object to being quizzed about his name? Who would neglect to furnish a direct answer, thus both joining in on topic and assisting in the diversion of what might otherwise have been a line of inquiry? Turns out both of them were at Cambridge, but not *quite* at the same time (there are plenty of students at Cambridge). Both men at Cambridge, both not at Oxford, therefore friends for life. Lesgate/Swann being a Cambridge man—we are never told at which college—his new friend "Fisher" wouldn't dream of going forward with his "plan" of pawning the visitor off with a cheap drink. Best bottle now, nothing less! A wonderful tactic for currying favor, if only old Swann will bite, since a good drink is a good drink and a man like "Fisher" would own the right kind of bottle. Between men, it's material relations, not ideas or sentiments.[15] "Come," as it were, "we'll toast to my double blue!"[16]

But brilliant beyond brilliance is "Fisher"'s open admission that he did have a plan in mind, the idea of fobbing Lesgate off with mediocre port to shave the car price, and that he is now dramatically binning that plan. (The speaker at the dais who ceremonially throws away his prepared speech: when you make a plan, let it contain a "bad plan" that can be discarded openly, with a warming flourish.)

[d] They will have brandy, seated face to face, Tony with his stick leaning against the side of his chair and Lesgate oozing into the sofa. But gazing at "Fisher" Lesgate says, "I think I must have seen you somewhere since we left Cambridge...."

Now here, we might think, are choppy seas, *have seen you somewhere*, an unanticipated squall, yet also hardly incomprehensible because Tony could have been seen anywhere in town and is surely now seen posing near his trophies. (We are all visible, after all, and don't ken who might be looking at us.) Indeed, more than visible this Tony, a star, is hypervisible. When cornered, act cornered. "Ever been to Wimbledon?" Swann and Lesgate leap to it in unison. "Wendice! Tony Wendice! What's all this about Fisher?" (Tony has no qualms about Lesgate making the discovery, all too soon, that he is a man who plays by subterfuge, the sort who might try a little trick now and then. It's a smooth preparation for the riposte that's coming.)

[e] "What's all this about Lesgate?" Tony always remembers Lesgate/Swann at Cambridge because of the college ball when he was the treasurer. "Some of the ticket money was stolen, wasn't it." Beautiful insinuation: stolen, Swann, by you no doubt. What are you doing nowadays? Tony runs a sporting goods enterprise, but his wife has some money. *Some* money. "Some" is the adjective would-be Uppers use to point to wealth without pointing, whereas Uppers don't point at all. For our part, we can hardly be astonished to learn that Margot is rich. She seemed rich from the outset. Rich, pampered, finished in Switzerland, no doubt, dressed by someone expensive on the Rue du Faubourg Saint-Honoré if not Hardy Amies or Hartnell. But Tony wants to get Margot on the record. Margot, the tropical isle that is the destination—that has all along been the destination—of this voyage. Queen Margot, with whom things aren't good:

TONY: She tried to make me give up tennis and play husband instead. In the end, we compromised. I went alone to America for the grass-court season ... and returned after the national championships. I soon realized a lot had happened while I was away. For one thing, she wasn't in love with me anymore. There were phone calls which would end abruptly if I happened to walk in. There was an old school friend who used to visit from time to time. One day, we had a row. I wanted to play in a covered-court tournament ... and, as usual, she didn't want me to go. I was in the bedroom. The phone rang. It all sounded pretty urgent. After that, she seemed rather keen that I play in the tournament. So I packed my kit into the car and drove off. I parked the car two streets away, walked back in my tracks. Ten minutes later, she came out of this house and took a taxi. I took another. Her old school friend lived in a studio in Chelsea. I could see them through the studio window as he cooked spaghetti over a gas range.

All those climactic short sentences, bing, bang, bing, bong, bang, like a barrister's summarization to a recalcitrant jury. And here is Tony, the wounded knight, thrown into the humiliating shadows and cast out of the sanctified light that beamed down from the throne:

- She tried to make me give up tennis.
- She wanted me to play husband instead.
- I had to go alone to America.
- She wasn't in love with me anymore.
- We had a row. (It's not nice to squabble. Nice folk don't.)
- As usual, she didn't want me to go. (On and on and on, never letting him out of her sights.)
- I could see ... them. (Them: the enemy. The aliens. The plotters.)

He moors her secure with one single line: "She wasn't in love with me anymore." We might under other circumstances pause to wonder whether this "old chum" from school was Mark, or whether before Mark she had had another lover? Whether she took lovers in, made a bracelet of them? But under these circumstances we are far too eager to know what Tony will reveal next. Man to man comes the unclean secret of what women are all about, and how, thanks to Margot's machinations, his (natural) prominence in their marriage, his presence like a trophy on the mantel requiring constant admiration and deserving of constant polish, was collapsed. For any of us who are watching this dispassionately, with the kind of discerning eye we might like to think Mark Halliday would use if he were there to use it, Tony is giving a textbook display of Narcissistic personality. Not "I don't love her" but "She wasn't in love with me" as she ought to have been. As the multitudes ought to be. *I exist to be loved.* I am the center of all this.

And yes he is, because on one side the fire blazes heartily at his back and on the other his audience stares at this mongoose like a cobra.

But here, too, is a string of claims guaranteed to procure Lesgate's complicit sympathy, bring him onside so that Tony's "case" becomes Lesgate's, Tony's honor the tatters that are to be made whole again. It is valuable to note that all these implicit hints are equivocal, while each is very easily interpreted in the most accusatory way, like this:

[1]   phone calls she terminates quickly when he comes into the room (because they're about him, *of course*);

[2]   an old school friend, that is, another person of interest to her, *of course*;

[3]   her "irrational" self-contradiction, telling him not to play in a tournament, then taking a telephone call and suddenly saying yes, he should play, manipulating him, *of course*;

[4]   his driving off but, wary, the serious husband who takes his husbandry as a law, parking only blocks away and walking back to find her getting into a taxi (to deceive him, *of course*);

[5]   his taking a taxi as well, not so much out of curiosity, we are to gather, as out of the sense of propriety offended: she has lied, he should find out why (since his having the full picture is essential, *of course*);

[6]   his finding her with the friend in a Chelsea studio, watching the fellow cooking spaghetti over a gas range. This last is a *coup de grâce*, because by comparison with Maida Vale, Chelsea's a seriously upclass neighborhood, as chi-chi as one can get outside Belgravia, so the friend who has a studio here is, among many other things, higher

than Tony. Class resentment, Margot sluffing it with a true companion of the blood and giving revelation that with Tony she's been merely slumming for fun.

North American readers may have trouble swallowing this, but in the light of a social class embarrassment like that, a threat not simply to his manhood but to his classed manhood (by comparison with the lower Lesgate's), the word *Chelsea* is considerably worse than the word *sex*. It is so easy listening to Tony prating on this way to lose sight of Hitchcock's architecture, which, I must stress, should not go out of view. Here what we are observing is Wendice putting out his rationale story *to an audience*, Lesgate, not as an objective and neutral report of background décor. He is setting up a rationale for violence, drawing not a picture but a caricature. This tale doesn't get verification, and as Lesgate is the only hearer and not at all interested in going into the details it is also never questioned. Hitchcock knows that if the audience doesn't question this tale, they will have a very compromised view of Margot, which is necessary if soon we are to watch an elaborate rehearsal for killing her, for meting out punishment.

Deeper and deeper into Poor Tony's dingy rabbit hole. Tony was (understandably) devastated. He goes (morosely) to a pub. He thinks of ways of killing the friend, then ways of killing Margot. The friend goes back to New York and the two of them start writing. (Oh yes, it does sound as though the friend was Mark. Her honor is set aright, in that there was, and is, only one lover.) She burns the letters from him but keeps moving one around from bag to bag. He just *has* to see what it says (among the wounded curiosity is blessed) so he pilfers it, then writes ransom letters. "That letter made very interesting reading." Here, a beautiful springboard for projection. Interesting how? "Interesting" as euphemism for what? Does the viewer think, "raunchy"? Was Tony having some pleasure, or some "pleasure," reading an unknown man's eager love letter? Tony has the thing in his hand, "accidentally" drops it out of his fingers—hard evidence—and Lesgate picks it up, graciously hands it back. Man to man, man for man, brain with brain, and all without revelation. The letter is itself dirt—the filthy spaghetti-eating nob who dares to come between man and wife, iconized. And then a punch line:

> LESGATE: Why are you telling me all this?
>
> TONY: Because you're the only one I can trust.

Lesgate, the font of comfort and confidentiality, I love you I love you, although we've only just met. There Tony was, in that bar, thinking of murdering her, and then he saw something.

> LESGATE: Well, what did you see?
>
> TONY: I saw you.

You, Lesgate, moving around town and changing names all the time, not paying rent, taking money from women, disappearing. I saw *you*. (You, whom I started tailing.) Sharply indicated, Lesgate feels the trembles and makes to leave:

> LESGATE: Thanks very much for the drink. Interesting, hearing about your matrimonial affairs. I take it you won't be wanting that car after all.
>
> TONY: Don't you want me to tell you why I brought you here?

Coup de foudre: Let the fish almost get away and then give a tug on the line with a Great Secret: "Why I Go Fishing."

Lesgate is invited to pass over his glass as Tony shyly but without haste admits having followed him around town for some time and having noted Lesgate fleecing various landladies out of significant funds. What, asks Tony, if I went to the police and told them you were trying to blackmail me? You took the letter from my wife, you wrote the blackmail notes to her ("Can you prove you didn't?"), you came here tonight, I gave you money, you gave me the letter ("It has your fingerprints on it"). Were Lesgate to claim Wendice confided a murder plan it would be one man's word against another's—one famous man against a known criminal. All Lesgate has to do is "a few minutes' work" (calculated time again, all this talk but for only a few minutes' labor), and he'll be paid a thousand pounds.

To see the Wendice dexterity is to watch championship at work. He has Lesgate's prints on the letter tucked into his wallet tucked into his inside pocket, and wiping the man's glass will effectively erase Lesgate's drinking in the flat tonight. The story he will concoct for the police is technically incontrovertible (as well as entirely false) and this shows us not just that Lesgate is in hot soup but also that Tony has the wits and talent to poach him there—he can make up a wholly believable but untrue fiction (like Mark). Further still, something much, much more chilling—no chill more devastating than on a voyage—that were it not to speed by so quickly we could hardly breathe: the union of technical incontrovertibility and utter falseness. We can now look back on everything Tony has said tonight and see that not a single statement is proven or provable, there is no unambiguous evidence for anything (not evidence that we can see, since the sacred letter is *not opened to us*). Like so many characters in Hitchcock early and late, Lesgate has walked into a trap. In this case, a trap made of hypothetical possibility and casual claim, the phrase "wife murder" being potentially significant enough to snag any policeman's attention and concentrate it wherever Tony points.

Lesgate will animate the murder. Tony has to be seen as its author. And it will be committed on the principle of male dignity and wanton humiliation. Animator, author, and principle, as Erving Goffman notes in *Forms of Talk*; the three parts of speech, and, as we may conclude, the three pillars of fictional wisdom, the three winds by which the voice sails.

FLAWLESS

Tony is going to leave a key under the stair carpet. Lesgate should let himself in, replace the key, "pretend to rob the place (the trophies), and when discovered in the act by Margot attack her." "Horrified that he has killed her," he should flee by the garden path. Tony and Mark will return from the club about midnight and together they will find the body (Tony's gift to Margot's "friend"). It will be Margot's key Tony hides, she won't be missing it. To get in with Mark, he'll use his own. It's flawless. Neat as a pin. Tidy as tomorrow. Latchkey paradise.

But of course what happens is (and can only be) a Gross Undoing. For viewers of the polarized 3-D version that was originally made of this film at Warner Bros.' urging, one of the profoundly jolting delights is a depth-of-field shot in which from behind the desk we see Margot reach back (Lesgate is strangling her from in front), seize the shears, and plant them in Lesgate's spine that 3-D gives us to feel as our own. His curtailing spasms are pure modern dance, something straight out of Martha Graham. Dead on the floor he is out of the picture. But Tony knows that Lesgate's presence in the flat must be shifted out of the Police Mind, so he concocts the story that Margot caught the man during a simple robbery and killed him. She is definitely the killer (as we know only too well). Notable to Justice, however, is that nothing has been stolen. She must have incautiously let him into the place herself. She must have had her reasons for putting him away.

Tried, swiftly convicted, she is sentenced to hang. At the sentencing the screen is suffused with scarlet.

But before we have a brief look at this second part of the film, this grisly Fugue, let us consider the strange spectatorial position Hitchcock has reserved for us just at the end of Act I, the bobbies silently pacing about the place—it's almost a church ceremony—the photographer recording, the fingers searching, and Margot in the bedroom where Tony has placed her, calmly out of the way. Up to this point, it seems the whole film has revolved around a failure, a voyage to Nowhere and a colossal collapse of narrative, given that in order to detail only what failed to eventuate a tremendous time and space were taken: Mark and Margot whispering together, Tony slyly sending them off to the theater, Tony seducing (most extensively and with agonizingly slow method) then plotting with Lesgate, the elaborate rehearsal, step by step, the night of the event, the creeping in, the darkness, the ghostly movement of Margot toward the desk, and so on—all this baroquerie, this castle with its turrets, this boundlessly decorative garden, everything brought to vacancy. Nothing that comes of nothing. A voyage across the world, over the high seas, through tempests, to a dense island cropped over with growth, and plunging through the jungle, and finally coming upon more or less what in *Heart of Darkness* hopeful Marlow comes upon when he discovers Kurtz: the loss of desire. The end of the road. The melting of expectation:

> "Nothing remains—nothing but a memory. You and I—"
> "We shall always remember him," I said hastily (Conrad 94).

Viewers will always remember the Wendice flat, a marvelous feat of set design in which we come to feel at home,[17] uniquely interesting in its décor, oddly spacious and unbounded as we perceive it, richly if softly colored and textured—all this comfort essentially nothing, because the central turn of the film, something we hardly get to see, takes place at the Old Bailey and in the prison, dank uncomfortable places; and the central actor, eccentric and poised, is nothing but a conventional police inspector doing his job, enchanting to Americans, perhaps, but for Britons so normal as to be almost invisible. Routine, day to day, humdrum questions and answers and a firm, quirky puzzle, a challenge that requires order. Inspector Hubbard has been catching hints of a disorder he cannot disattend. It's finally a story about a police inspector and a condemned criminal, the one redeeming the other. All the trappings of décor and etiquette fall away. A trapper and trappings.

I will come to Hubbard's culminating marvel but first—and not at all, I think, to detour—let us see those "ornamental" trappings. In Hitchcock, everything we find onscreen is there to inform, not to decorate (ornament never has been decoration), and so no detail merits neglect. The trappings are fragments of a puzzle the Inspector is putting together, having first seized all of them, having retained them, having kept them spinning in the inner world of his own intelligent imagination. (Fugues are always puzzles.) We, too, were handed these trappings to collect but, enthralled by the fluttering banners of personality and gruesome intent, we watched the human beings instead. We watched the human beings in the traps, distracted from the trappings that trapped them. It is so easy to forget, voyaging through his films, that the trapper is Hitchcock, not the eager viewer laboring in the dark.

[A] *Aquascutum.* Tony, Lesgate, and Inspector Hubbard all have Aquascutum trench coats. Founded in 1851, Aquascutum manufactured these items to be worn in both World War I and World War II. From the time of Edward VII they had a Royal Warrant. Might we surmise that Tony Wendice fought, or that he seeks some of the aura of gallantry that attaches to those who pretend they fought? If he fought on the courts, might he not also have fought in the fields? Might he not have come back from the war a scarred man? Shell shock of some kind, battle fatigue, wholesale depression, wholesale fatigue? Why would we benefit from such a supposition?

Because more than a vehicle to be understood, *Dial M for Murder* is a vehicle to be watched, and when we watch Ray Milland's Tony Wendice we see gracility, polish, and softness yet a softness and a calmness covering something disturbed. There has been oil (unctuousness) of a kind poured upon his waters, because the waters are not still. He is not at peace (as Mark is). And whilst he regales us with a story of a recent schism in his "loving" relationship with Margot we have no way to be sure, no way to know there wasn't always something irretrievably offside. A figure too shapely, too smooth, too impeccable is Tony.

He walks into his flat and drops the trench coat flatly on a chair near the door. One of the delights of the Aquascutum was that after wear and tear and beating about it would catch a pleasant rumpled look, the look we see in film noir on Humphrey Bogart. Don't be fancy with it, don't be pristine, just toss it. The coat never loses its impermeability. Is Tony Wendice also a creation with an impermeable surface, does he maintain his good form, his implacability, in the face of anything and everything? (Inspector Hubbard certainly does. Image of the stolid British man.) More bluntly: is the Aquascutum the very perfect garment for Tony? Is it in some way inseparable from him, his very skin? He tosses it on the chair and bares himself, as it were. I'm home, I'm safe, I'm really me. Everything you get of me here is authentic, true to the bone. Because we all know that any covering at all, surely including an Aquascutum, works also as a mask and look at me, I've stripped my mask off.

Lesgate will also toss his Aquascutum onto that chair.

The Inspector will pick up and finger an Aquascutum that is lying nearby, a real bona fide detective's coat: "They talk about flatfooted policemen. May the saints protect us from the gifted amateur," he chides Mark. There's a hole in the pocket, though, says he. *He says* he has a hole in his pocket.

In the pocket of Lesgate's Aquascutum post-mortem: a latchkey, a telltale latchkey.

[B] *Hearth*. In the early 1950s there had not yet circulated the blessing of central heating in England. One would find a hearth, or several hearths, sometimes electrically operated, and one would eagerly keep them "on." The Wendice flat has a wood-burning fireplace, and for combating the damp a gentle fire will be lit here, useful rather than plush. Many things other than firewood can be burned in such a fire.

Things like letters one wishes to both discard and destroy. A letter, unread, signals itself by the return address, and one could wish to lose it. Or a letter carefully read has delivered its message, and the message now embedded in the heart need not be held on a page for reminding. Or inside its own heart a letter has words that could be damning, should the wrong eyes fall upon them.

It is interesting in its own right, however, that the Wendices possess a fireplace of this kind. Wolfgang Schivelbusch takes note of how when a new technology has come into vogue the old one that it replaces might linger in a new form, for him in the case of the horse-drawn carriage, entertainment. "The final fate of carriage-riding, the traditional mode of travel, was to become the amateur sport of the privileged classes. In everyday existence, the new technology took over" (14). Here in Maida Vale we have the privileged classes retaining, during a period when electricity was fully in use all around, and when the hearth had become usefully electrified, a technology of the past, a "sporty" decoration of everyday life. Implied here, however, is a certain socially relevant constraint. The electric fire will not burn things. But the Wendice fireplace functions perfectly to permit both parties to the marriage to discard something they would prefer the mate not know of. Tony will burn Lesgate's scarf, substituting as possible murder weapon one of Margot's nylons, now tucked under the desk blotter. One has to wonder how many marriages in this class were inflected by sleight of hand, by such trickery as the "sporty" fireplace made possible; even whether the presence of the fire at this time in social development—intensified social and geographic mobility, leading to marriages between strangers—might have engendered tricked-up secrecies. In the 1950s, the electric fire was "hot" in every way, but to show (and use) sporty class the real fire was hotter.

[C] *Sewing basket.* The presumption we are to make is that people sewed, either in fashioning garments for themselves and family members or in making informal repairs—darning socks, fixing buttons, repairing hems. As long as sewing was a habit in great distribution there was no serious market for pre-fashioned garments, such things as command almost all of costuming today. Early mass-market manufacturers, such as Levi Strauss and Co. of San Francisco, were not yet influencing imitators who would spread across all economic markets. One could surmise, however, that Margot's gowns (like Grace Kelly's) are designed especially for her, that the Wendices enjoy a culture in which home-sewing is practiced only for small repairs. In retaining the sewing basket, Margot participates in yet another retention of a technology well past the time of its heyday. There is something slightly old-fashioned about her, youthful as she is, and the sewing basket is an indicator.

[D] *Shears on desk.* This story takes place in an age before the rabid spread of photography from the 1960s onward and of the spread of digital imaging so taken for granted today. One kept one's own memories not in digital files or via Instagram postings but in diaries or letters, made up through handwriting (which was still a subject taught in elementary school; taught and graded on report cards). The medium of television was communicating news, but for their information about the world in which they lived most Britons still read the newspaper, clippings from which would be treasured by those featured in them. To save (that is, to cut out and save) one's clippings was ordinary professional behavior for anyone in the public eye; not only to procure souvenirs but to have material for aiding later publicity. If there is something forced about Tony's pressing Margot to use this particular night for doing "the" (meaning his) clippings (a wifely chore here, presumably), still the central fact of attending to clippings is perfectly ordinary for him. Ordinary, too, are the shears she will need for slicing up the newspaper tidily. The murder weapon is thus an absolutely perfunctory domestic tool in this household. This domesticity contributes to the Hitchcockian irony: something tediously normal being utilized for an act astoundingly abnormal.

[E] *Chequebook.* Tony's chequebook stubs are marked to show the target of every expense (every tiny voyage he takes), but of course nothing would prevent a man from leaving his stubs blank when he writes (himself) a cheque, then filling them out later on, when a plan and particular usage were firmly in mind. It is a curiosity how open Tony's chequebook is for the inspection of others, since not only Hubbard but also Lesgate feels it entirely within his right to ask for access to it: a backstage that is not fully backstage. The stubs are not organs of privacy, mere recordings to keep tabs on one's budget.

[F] *Drinks.* Always available on a side table. Sipped for relaxation, for therapy, for diversion, for evidence. Of course one would like a drink—always. Easy to pour out for demonstrating sociability. Nothing like sociability to seal a deal. Of all distractions, alcohol is the preferred one. If in London of the early 1950s drugs played a key role, as in Jules Dassin's *Night and the City* (1950) we are told they do, there is no evidence in this film. The drug trope onscreen is very typically of the anti-social; the liquor trope is all sociability, all grace and good manners.

[G] *Accounts.* The account can be seen as "a linguistic device employed whenever an action is subjected to valuative enquiry ... a crucial element in the social order since they prevent conflicts from arising by verbally bridging the gap between action and expectation" (Scott and Lyman 46). Accounts work to join eventualities by making them narrative, that is, seemingly probable, thus establishing voyages toward the Isle of Meaning. Because there are so many accounts offered in *Dial M*, accounts realistic and ridiculous, accounts that can and cannot be verified, accounts heading in all directions, the film is chock full of voyages. Briefly, one is almost always traveling along a narrative line that is built to make sense as rationale or informational fill. When they do not form a narrative line, eventualities themselves do not "make sense," they merely happen in a vague flow. The flow of events is one voyage-like movement, but the explanation, the "accounting" of the flow, is more important still.

Accounts multiply with zest in the film:

- Tony had been to a reunion dinner and the fellows were talking about Lesgate and how he'd gone to prison, stolen that money, blamed it on the porter, and so on. Lovely story, entirely unverifiable.

- Tony, eager to kill Margot for her ninety thousand pounds, needs an alibi so he follows Lesgate around and Lesgate becomes his familiar, but then one day Lesgate disappears from his lodgings.

Lesgate could confirm all this, presumably, *but he does not do so, not to us*. The accounts are not exclusively for the characters, but they are always for us.

- Lesgate, examining Tony's chequebook, notes that he's taken out over a thousand pounds this year, and what would the police think about that?, and the answer, very prompt—perhaps too prompt—is, "I go dog-racing twice a week" (note the delectable detail since all details are alluring *de facto*; not "a lot" or "quite a bit" but "twice a week"). False accounting demonstrated.

- Regarding the instruction to leave the latchkey under the stair carpet again, what would the police be thinking? Again, the immediate return, a proactive account: "You came in by the window. You thought the apartment was empty, so you took the suitcase and went to work. She heard something." A projected detail: "I'll use my own key to let us in. Then while [Mark's] out searching the garden or something I'll take the key from under the stair carpet and return it to her bag, before the police arrive": we picture this as in a little film loop.

- Tony to Margot while she gasps on the phone, a cue for a secret future account: *"Don't touch anything!"* (Things are moving far too quickly here for us to grasp the handrail beside the precipice: a woman has just been almost strangled to death. Why would *she* not touch anything?)

- "He put something around my throat; it felt like a stocking" (Margot's mini-tale that we take as true because [i] we know about the stocking, [ii] we saw the gesture but can't be sure this was a stocking, yet [iii] it could have felt like one, so her truthfulness isn't quite as compromised as it might be).

- Margot confesses to Tony that the police wanted to know why she didn't phone them straightaway—a very reasonable query, actually—and she answered that he had told her to do nothing until he got home—weird, but protective-sounding. But now he confesses to her—*confesses*—that *he told them something different*: that you didn't phone the police "because you naturally assumed that I would do it from the hotel" (entirely logical, entirely plausible, and offered to a woman swimming in confusion who is in no shape to stand back and wonder what's going on). A blanketing account.

All these accounts, and a legion more, add up, just as the chequebook does. Everything has its place, the regular order of the world holds.

- To Hubbard, Tony says, with properly demeaned attitude, that he had to ring his boss and couldn't remember the number so he called Margot for it, "hauled her out of bed." An account with elegance.

- Mark's (unburnt) letter to Margot from New York was found in the dead man's pocket and the Inspector wants to check with her: "You did lose it, didn't you?" An account on offer, pure plausibility.

- The "lethal stocking" was found in the garden, and its mate under the desk blotting pad, or vice versa, and a heel has been mended by silk thread, found in Margot's basket—talk about details!—but Tony has an explanation ready for her to use: "I've heard of the police deliberately planting clues to ensure a conviction" (this an ironic riposte if ever there was one, since Tony planted all the clues here).

[H] *A fitting misfit.* With Margot in the death cell and Mark panicking to convince Tony they must do something to save her, the Inspector has been all along working his own private magic. In the flat he's made up his own fiction about a theft in Ledbury Street that brings occasion for him to inspect Tony's chequebook. "If you got this money from someone you didn't know . . . I mean, that might be the very person we're looking for." But suddenly, "Is this yours?" It's a latchkey he found on the floor, just near his draped Aquascutum. But no-no, it's not Tony's. "It may be mine!" says the Inspector, absent-mindedly, and (smiling happily), "Yes, it is mine," because it dropped out of a small hole in his coat pocket. (A "hole" on the *inside* of the pocket.) "That's the trouble with these latchkeys, they're all alike." Here is a man who has been all over London, inside and out, and he . . . has . . . seen . . . latchkeys! Beautiful little invocations, however: *a hole in the pocket—a hole altogether—my key, your key, me, you—keys alike, people alike.* "I understand you, because you cannot possibly be so different from me or anyone else" ... but of course these words are not said because they would open too many doors Hitchcock does not, at this juncture, want us peeking through: for instance, Hubbard does not understand Tony with fellow feeling, at all.

Mark, meanwhile, is slaving. He bends over backward to convince Tony of his own pet theory devised to persuade the police to reopen the case against Margot, that Tony himself stole the key, that Tony himself wrote the blackmail letters to Margot, that Tony himself planned the whole thing and arranged for Lesgate to be there. But Tony's reply silences him: "Before nearly every execution, someone comes forward like this." In short, "You're desperate, Mark. You're making concoctions." The Inspector informs Tony that there are some of Margot's things at the police station if he'd like to go down and—"I'm sorry to bother you at this time"—collect them. Tony trundles off with deliberation, seizing his cherished Aquascutum. "Goodbye, Mr Wendice. I don't suppose we shall meet again," from the Inspector who—strangely, perhaps, but the distracted Tony doesn't notice—doesn't make any effort to leave, too. Hubbard jumps to the telephone to set "things" in motion. Mark has had a sound idea, that this case boils down to only these three things: "My letter. Her stocking. And the fact that because no key was found on Swann, she must've let him in." But now the Inspector, watching the street from the bedroom window and asking Mark to keep utterly silent, produces a shock. A car pulls up and Margot steps out to walk into the building. Full-length sienna brown coat, stylish if somewhat *triste*; she looks haggard. In a hush we hear her troubling a key in the latch but to no avail. The hush is especially notable because of the small scratching noise of the failing key. Hubbard steps over and suavely lets her in. "Why didn't you use your key?" She did, "but it didn't fit the lock." One can see the light come on behind the official eyes. The light of sunrise.

Hubbard takes Margot's bag from her. "Your husband's explained this, you know. You can tell us all about it now."

She has just come away from the gallows, whither Tony sent her (his clinching tale to the Inspector: "I found her kneeling beside Swann's body, going through his pockets. She kept saying he had something of hers, but she couldn't find it"). "You can tell us," but, ashen with weariness and confusion, Margot *doesn't understand.*

"No," says Hubbard with a kindness that is exquisite, "I don't believe you do."

The Inspector's explanation must now be given to Margot, an abbreviated one but an account transcending all previous accounts, wholly credible (because wholly credible to us, who have been watching) and likely to cause a very deep disturbance. He must be blunt and accurate, but also take care to be gentle. "We strongly suspect that your husband had planned to murder you." Hubbard became suspicious as the police wondered about Tony's accounts—his bankbook, not his tales. He went to the prison, jolly upright Hubbard did, obtained Margot's bag, and filched her latchkey from it (trickster that he is). "Highly irregular, of course, but my blood was up!" (Redeeming blood.) Back at the flat, he found that, marvel of marvels! he couldn't get in.But Tony is returning now. Silent inside, the trio hear that he cannot get in with the key from the raincoat. The Inspector sends his man back to the station, by way of the doors to the garden and clutching Margot's purse: "Not like that, you clot!" the tiny explosive comedic firecracker, because the policeman has slipped the purse over his wrist, wrong wrong wrong! Disappointed Tony now returns to the station and is instructed there (we are told) that the Inspector, *whose raincoat he took in error*, is away for the weekend. Ahhh, so it's the Inspector's latchkey he has—no wonder he can't get in! But he is to be given the purse, Margot's purse, Margot's purse with "Margot's latchkey." Returned now, and back in the hallway, he tries the latch again—Margot's latchkey, the latchkey from Margot's bag—and still cannot get in, exactly as she couldn't with that latchkey, but—count to ten!—in a breath he has obtained the key hidden under the carpet and let himself in, the act of self-condemnation. Swann, the Inspector realized, had done precisely what he was asked to do, opened the door and immediately returned the key. The latchkey in the dead man's pocket, that Tony was using, and that he had slipped into Margot's purse, was Lesgate/Swann's own and on investigation yes, it did open a latch—to the man's girlfriend's flat.

So many consequentialities: both played out and spoken out, both hypothesized and recounted, both made up on the spot and faithfully remembered, that by the conclusion it becomes a matter of great difficulty to sort them, to know who did what in what order, except that the unctuous, malevolent Tony is taken away and the beautiful Margot is left with the supportive Mark while the Inspector combs his moustache calling the Home Office to have the death sentence cancelled. A long befuddling litany of repeated words, Mr Wendice, Mrs Wendice, latchkey, Lesgate, addresses, latchkey, Swann, names of women we never meet, amounts of money spent on this, that, and the other, latchkey, Cambridge, a motor car, latchkey, nylon stockings, latchkey, silk thread. . . .

As to Margot's obvious (and also purported) delicacy: at the instant she stabs Lesgate we see nothing but animal ferocity, muscular abandon. She is as much a beast as anyone at the end of their tether. It's spirit that counts, however, not action.

TALKING POINTS, OR POINTS TALKING

Dial M for Murder is notably (for some viewers, no doubt exasperatingly; and for many readers, I suspect, similarly to this chapter) verbal. "Words, words, words." In other Hitchcock films, characters are inveterate speakers, and usually every word out of the mouth is a pearl from on high, even with the villains (especially with the villains), but they don't make elocutions. Elocutions that, far beyond merely filling the air, amount to voyages: away from the moment, away from a situation, away from a condition, away from a presentiment, away from a problem. A *spiel* carries a listener away. In this film one must go beyond simply noting that characters speak dialogue. With only the smallest variation, Lesgate in action, they do very little but speak, and—most tellingly—speak very often without apparent consciousness that they are doing so. This is partly because we are in comfortable middle-class London, and we can presume that everyone British in the ensemble, possibly excepting Lesgate/Swann, has had a grammar or public school education of some distinct quality, Mark, the outsider, being a writer and thus an expert at language himself. If language counts, however, it is usually not as abstract as it is here. Language here is not the medium of conversation or communication; it is the substance of the film. As Paul Goodman claims, speech is a thing:

> When speech intervenes in the world and shapes experience, it often is, or is taken as, a direct action in the environment, an energy or even a physical thing, rather than the use of the common code for communication. We can show a wide range of important cases where this is so; one cannot understand what language is without taking it into account. (19)

Speech in *Dial M* works in several interesting ways:

- First, all the principal actors—Milland, Kelly, Cummings, Williams, Dawson—being extremely adept at physical movement, there is an eloquent mime in process as subtext to the talk. Standing soberly; leaning over; turning and gazing; pacing nervously; posing casually; pointing out urgently. If one removed the sound, very often the actions, so clearly "enunciated" by the bodies, would be plenty clear in terms of *what must be seen to be happening*. This raises the associated and, for the film, quite central implication that the talk is only tangentially, and by degrees, about what we see going on.

- By degrees? Sometimes it is what we might call back-talk. Frequently we hear someone recount to us in plain, articulate language what we saw transpire earlier, even just a half-second ago. This is a speech pointer, only the thinnest slip away from the movement it indicates. Such talking "walks us through events again," as it were for a second—or a closer and more informative—look, every word being a reference to a sight we have already taken in and already digested; but also a prediction. As Jean Starobinski wrote, "We decipher the past in such a way as to make it culminate necessarily in a future preordained by our will" (112). Sometimes the pointing backward is instantaneous: we see a talker demonstrating what he is saying while saying it. For instance, Tony needs pathetic Lesgate to be painfully aware that he has (unconsciously) left his fingerprints on the telltale letter, so he pulls the wallet from his inside pocket and flips it open in front of the man, showing the lethal object tidily cached inside, but at the same time he says, "Your fingerprints are on the letter." Of course we do not, and cannot, see those fingerprints (not being police experts with the right powder), but we can see the letter being adduced, and we can add two and two. The accusatory glance Tony gives, the bold presentation of the document, and the word "fingerprints" as uttered all sum to a memory of Tony "carelessly" dropping the letter to the floor and allowing Lesgate to politely bend and pick it up for him. Lesgate's bending down was several moments back; but the link between "Your fingerprints are on the letter" and flipping open the wallet is virtually instantaneous. Or: Tony instructing, "She will walk over to the desk"—he paces to the desk, "being" Margot—"and you will be behind the curtain"—we see the curtain and Tony seeing the curtain as Lesgate eyes it.

It is like a lecture. Note this, over here. And now note that, over there. And now, if you'll follow me . . .[18]

- Talk is unfailingly polite in the film, sometimes even gracile: a social class indicator, from the Wendices and their guest; pretention to class from Lesgate, who takes the act of looking up to his "betters" quite seriously, even though he likes to fleece them. We can note that the dirty word "kill" is used with the keenest rarity, and with delicacy. The sentences are constructed to be floral—ornate in construction but also redolent of honey and jasmine. Of all the characters the most prompt, cursory, direct, even blunt is Margot, who just wants things to move along and notices that Tony has a way of hogging a stage. We will return to the etiquette, especially as it is demonstrated by Inspector Hubbard, a fountain of style.

- Often talk fulfills a practical function here. Characters are moving or standing in a relatively contained narrative space (that Wendice living area) and flexibility is provided them when (a) they move back and forth along the length of the space (desk to fireplace, doorway to sofa to fireplace, doorway to bedroom doorway to desk) while chatting, or (b) when they confine themselves (further) within the confinement by settling in a chair or on a sofa, legs crossed perhaps, eyes keenly forward, so that they can direct speech more precisely. All this physical moving around or posing is a kind of extended, but silent, aria that can benefit from accompaniment, and the talk that happens in conjunction with the locomotion works to pull our attention away from the simple body moves into the world of interpretation. It is as though every movement made onscreen is a gesture overflowing with ambiguity, and the verbal accompaniment assists us in making resolution. Leading us, or misleading us, into an interpretation. In other Hitchcock films the talk furthers the action that is set in a chain of spaces. In this film the talk is the space, the talk renders the space, and the geometrical space not only holds but also illuminates the talk. We aren't really going anywhere (except toward release), but we need to hear what everybody is saying, *not for information but for satisfaction*. A voyage of consciousness, as if with enough words floating in the air, even repeating in refrains, some mystical clarity will be achieved. Latchkey, latchkey. Inspector, Inspector. Taxi, taxi.

- Talk is also used as prelude. The long rehearsal scene is a talk-through of action that Tony is hoping will ensue on the schedule he has set for "tomorrow night." On that night, we see, almost silently, actions in the Wendice flat that accord with the talked-out "script" stored in memory, that "script" almost re-speaking itself as Lesgate shuffles around in the darkness actually anticipating Margot. At the moment she stabs Lesgate, or as she will be taught to know him Swann, this memorial voice sharply breaks off. We are suddenly confronting a glitch in performance, something that occurs "onstage" without having been rehearsed, structurally not unlike a line muffing. Talk fails.

- There is a great deal of elision, not only of the keyword "kill." Tony makes a point of never directly alluding to the affair Mark and Margot are carrying on, of which he is in full knowledge. Even when reference must be made for clarity's sake in explaining some small action, the reference is oblique. For instance, Tony makes it plain that he knows about Mark's letter, but he never *says* that Mark was the writer or what that letter was about. Sufficient that we know, and know he knows, because he can point to the same letter we heard Margot talk about. In the final movement when, desperate to save Margot at the last possible moment, Mark walks Tony through a scenario he believes Tony "ought to" offer the police, the scenario spells out precisely what Tony presumably did do, or planned to do; and Mark's talk seems to be flowing from a person who magically figured it out or else an ingenious writer who thinks the claims would hold water. But Mark never says a syllable to indicate that he actually means to suggest he knows Tony is guilty and should seriously implicate himself: it's all a ceremonial to get Margot off, just that, and of course Tony would get only a very short prison sentence. The Inspector is nobly circumspect in sending Tony out into the garden to check a back entrance so that in total privacy he can ask Mark, "How much does he know about you and Mrs Wendice?" (a liaison that, apparently, has become clear to the police); Hubbard delicately doesn't use the word "affair." A careful study of the film in terms of direct or circumlocuted speech could show how very little is bluntly said from start to finish, by anybody, about what is apparently really going on. Creatures dancing around the altar. Or plotters who fear the viewing audience might turn them in.

ONCE UPON A TIME

Most tellingly, however, the talk of *Dial M* slides into and marginally out of a certain age-old, familiar, comforting, and imaginative mode, that of the entertaining story told by a *raconteur*, and in this case there are some rather profound effects. As storyteller the Inspector is a paragon. But all the accounts of the crime, confessed by the distraught Margot, flipped out by the cocky Tony, urgently replayed verbally by the desperate Mark, and calmly rethought by Hubbard, are finally *stories*, tales before bedtime. Like *Rashomon* (1950) the film is about something that happened and many different persons recounting it in their own ways. Worth pointing out is that Tony's spieling is notably persuasive in being filled with more information than a situation calls for, as though he is constantly on guard against some silently and invisibly invoked questioner, fully real to him, a doubting consciousness who will query any and every phrase for truth value against a presumption that this speaker is a lying toad.

Getting Margot not to leave the house for a movie on the night he wants to have her slain is a study in pirouettes, for example, with plenty of ornamental filigree that is mostly an inducement to the listener to mentally "realize" the tale. The martini scene: Mark gently stirring while he stands in front of the bucolic landscape. Margot cooing to Mark about the

Maharajah, "Isn't he dreamy!" "Yeah," says Tony, "Four Rolls-Royces and enough jewelry to sink a battleship and all he really wanted was to play at Wimbledon."

> TONY (to Mark, after chatting about playing tennis with a Maharajah): How do you go about writing a detective story?
>
> MARK (in reflex): Well, you forget detection and concentrate on crime. Crime's the thing.
>
> . . . .
>
> MARGOT (genuinely curious): Do you really believe in the perfect murder?
>
> MARK (swallowing his drink): Mm. Yes, absolutely. On paper, that is. And I think I could uh ... plan one better than most people *(Tony has turned his back)* but I doubt if I could carry it out.
>
> TONY (turning): Oh?? (Both sociable and curious) Why not?—
>
> MARK: Well, because in stories things usually turn out the way the author wants them to and in real life they don't ... always. No, I'm afraid my murders would be something like my bridge. I'd make some stupid mistake and never realize till I found out everybody was looking at me.
>
> . . .
>
> TONY (to Margot, but staring at the doorknob): Darling, did I lend you my latchkey, I can't seem to find it anywhere. (*She goes to the bedroom to look in her handbag because she may have them both in there. Tony goes to the windows and, whilst Mark dons his coat, swiftly draws the curtains.*)
>
> MARGOT (demurring): No, I've only got one here. Are you sure yours isn't in your overcoat?
>
> TONY: No, I looked. May I borrow yours?
>
> MARGOT: Well, that's a bit awkward.
>
> TONY (more than dismayed): Why?
>
> MARGOT: I may want to go out!
>
> TONY (edgy): *Tonight?*

MARGOT: (*standing in front of the trophies on the mantle; she might go to a movie or something. He wants to know: won't she listen to radio? No, "Saturday Night Theatre" is a thriller. She doesn't like thrillers when she's alone.*) In any case I'll be back before you, so I can let you in. (*He is holding the white gloves, palms his key and suddenly "finds" it, holding it up. She holds her key up, too. He eyes her carefully.*)

. . .

TONY (holding up his key): Oh, it's all right. Here it is, it was in my glove all the time!

MARGOT (dropping her key into her purse as he observes): Well, that settles that. (*After Tony persuades her that staying home doing the clippings is better than going out, Margot gives a half-mock complaint about being made to stay in while they go out gallivanting.*)

TONY (in performance): Very well, we won't go. (*Mark on the margins is watching this tête-à-tête cannily.*)

Regard the phrases, words, syllables tucked in for rhythmic pulse and listener entrapment, the verbal construction of real-world talk in this profoundly set up moment:

[1] Margot to Mark, innocently asking about authoring a detective story, and Tony's polite intercession: Tony is deferring to Mark a little, showing some personal interest as a way of politely hosting this stranger from across the Big Pond; and also sucking out of the professional author any drop of helpful information about the way detectives work. The putative focus on Mark is a detailing for deflection. The subtle interest in detectives is strategically crucial, as Tony knows he will be confronting some of them.

[2] The "perfect murder." Again, a focus on Mark's professional intelligence since if someone like Mark does believe there is such a thing his belief could give Tony encouragement; and if Mark doesn't believe, Tony will have the spur to prove him uninformed. Either way, allowing Mark to show off any attitude at all is another little deference to his expertise and honor. Deference can be tactical.

[3] On the Maharajah: Tony would so like to own four Rolls-Royces and enough jewelry to sink a battleship.

[4] On Margot lending Tony her latchkey. It would have been sufficient for Tony to request a loan from Margot, point blank. Excessive and ornamental is his offering a reason, even this redundant reason since obviously he doesn't have his key or he wouldn't ask. This is a typical speech pattern for Tony, a statement of some kind, even a question, followed directly by filler. He's a word-spinner (much more than Mark is). There are also, here, two further cloaked intimations. First, Margot complaining she will be trapped at home hints to us how Tony is arranging for her to be trapped. Second, this "stay at home" is perfectly normal for them, as no fuss is raised. The wife should always be willing to stay at home. Or: Margot should always be willing to follow Tony's lead. Even if she did go out, she would have to await his return before she could return herself.

[5] Margot going out: Tony is betting that she won't be. Were he to say, "Yes, darling, do go," he would be counting on her rejecting the offer of freedom.

[6] Tony's concession to Margot, "Very well, we won't go," could have been phrased, if it meant only to indicate the possibility of Tony and Mark staying in, "We won't go." The prefatory "Very well" carries emotional tone, exasperation, irritation, pretend surrender (the pretense of which the longtime wife swiftly picks up, because she relents).

[7] Shears. On telling her she'll need shears, he adds effective "discourse" through mute action, fetching them for her when he knows quite well that she can fetch them for herself. "You'll need them, I'll go fetch them, I'm going to fetch them now, look at me fetching them, here they are." We know he wants a look inside that basket.

There is a much more replete *récit* to regale us when on the eve of the execution Hubbard pays a visit to the Wendice apartment and queries Tony about . . . another matter altogether. Two aspects of this conversation repay attention. Tony's characteristic persuasive fill-ins, and the continual verbal reference on both sides to something admittably interesting and intriguing but unavailable for direct observation; in short, invocations of magical keywords or phrases that carry the attention away, invoke imagination, bear the listener on a voyage, and cause distant, perhaps unknown, bells to sound. I will use *italic* to *highlight the persuasive deflections*, and BLOCK CAPITALS to indicate the enchanting allusions to WHAT IS NOT SEEN: in total all these present a domain of the abstract. Mark has been offering his salvation plan to Tony in strict confidence, and when the door buzzer sounds he swiftly retreats into the bedroom. Tony admits Hubbard, who, we know, is a sharp mind on the prowl.

> TONY (at door): Hello, Inspector. Is it about MY WIFE?
>
> HUBBARD: No, sir, I'm afraid not.
>
> TONY: Then what is it?
>
> HUBBARD: I'm making enquiries in connection with a ROBBERY that took place ... about THREE WEEKS AGO, sir.
>
> TONY (feigning irritation): Can't it wait *a few days?*
>
> HUBBARD (consoling): Of course, sir. I'm very conscious of your position. If I may, I'd like to say how deeply sorry I am—
>
> TONY (dismissive): Yes, Inspector, *all right. Now,* how can I help you?
>
> HUBBARD: The CASHIER of a FACTORY in LEDBURY STREET was attacked in HIS OFFICE ... and TWO MEN made off with SEVERAL HUNDRED POUNDS ... mostly in POUND NOTES.
>
> TONY (confounded): What is *all* this to do with me?
>
> HUBBARD: In these cases, all POLICE DIVISIONS are asked to keep a lookout ... for ANYONE SPENDING LARGE SUMS OF MONEY—
>
> TONY: I see.
>
> HUBBARD: —And I was wondering ... if you'd sold ANYTHING recently for CASH.
>
> TONY: Why?
>
> HUBBARD: MY SERGEANT happened to be making enquiries ... at

WALES'S GARAGE the other day, and it appears that you ... settled AN ACCOUNT there recently for ... just OVER SIXTY.

TONY: Yes, *I happened to have quite a bit on me. So* I settled for cash.

HUBBARD: I see. Had you just drawn this MONEY from your BANK?

TONY (sly smile): Have you been to my bank, *Inspector?*

HUBBARD (broad smile at being caught out): Yes, as a matter of fact, I have. But THEY wouldn't help me. BANK STATEMENTS are always jealously guarded.

TONY: *Yes, but* I'm *rather* surprised you didn't come to me *first. It was only a routine matter, after all.*

HUBBARD: I didn't want to disturb you. Where did you get IT, sir?

TONY: Is that *any of* your business?

HUBBARD: If it was STOLEN MONEY, yes, sir, it is my business. Do you mind if I SMOKE (*only then pulling out his pipe*)?

TONY: Go ahead. Do you *really* think I've been receiving stolen money?

HUBBARD: Until you tell me where you got IT, I shan't know what to think, shall I? You see, if you got this MONEY from someone you didn't know ... I mean, that might be THE VERY PERSON we're looking for. (*He has partially hidden himself behind a piece of furniture and now bends down.*) Hello! Is this yours?

TONY: What is it?

HUBBARD: Somebody's latchkey. It was lying on the floor just here.

TONY: No, *mine's here.*

HUBBARD (musing): No, no. It's not yours. It may be mine, then. (*checks Aquascutum pocket*) Yes. Yes, it is mine. It must have dropped out of the pocket. There's a SMALL HOLE there. That's the trouble with THESE LATCHKEYS, they're all alike. Sorry, sir, you were saying ...?

TONY: I don't think I was, *was I?*

HUBBARD: Yes. Yes, about that MONEY. I'd be grateful if you'd tell me where you got IT. A HUNDRED POUNDS is a lot to carry around.

TONY: You said sixty *a moment ago.*

HUBBARD: Did I? Oh, yes. Yes, MY SERGEANT decided to DIG a little deeper . . . before he put in HIS REPORT. He said that you also paid a BIT at YOUR TAILOR'S . . . and another for WINES AND SPIRITS.

TONY: *I'm sorry he went to that trouble. Had he come to me,* I could have explained it. I *simply* won *rather* a large sum at dog-racing.

HUBBARD: Over a hundred?

TONY: *Yes*, over a hundred. *It has been done before, you know.*

HUBBARD: Why didn't you tell me this straightaway?

TONY: I was ashamed *of being caught going to DOG-RACING . . . when my wife was UNDER SENTENCE OF DEATH.*

HUBBARD: Yes, I know how it is. It helps take your mind off THINGS.

From Tony we hear a kind of tiqueur's stammer, a nervous tendency to fill time with words. This may stem from anxiety, but it may also be a cerebral malfunction. Milland gives a kind of vacant stare, on and off, something that suggests Tony might be experiencing a fugue state himself.

As to allusions "foreign" to the business at hand—pointers outside the text itself, outside the space of the story, outside anything the viewer has been given to experience—an even richer compendium is to be found in Tony's First Act "confessional," when he reveals to Lesgate the scheme he has in mind. Note the divagations, explanations, detailed mapping in this long speech, in reproducing which, this time, I use <u>underlining</u> to indicate the nourishing cake that bears immediately, directly, irrevocably, and tightly on the plot line, everything else being Tony's frivolous icing:

TONY (to a raptly attentive Lesgate, seated comfortably on the sofa in front of him): After we were married, I played in championships, and took Margot with me. She didn't like it. And when we got back she tried to make me give up tennis and play husband instead. In the end, we compromised. I went alone to America for the grass-court season, and returned after the national championships. I soon realized a lot had happened while I was away. For one thing, <u>she wasn't in love with me anymore.</u> There were phone calls which would end abruptly if I happened to walk in. There was an old school friend who used to visit from time to time. One day, we had a row. I wanted to play in a covered-court tournament and, as usual, she didn't want me to go. I was in the bedroom. The phone rang. It all sounded pretty urgent. After that, she seemed rather keen that I play in the tournament. So I packed my kit into the car and drove off. I parked the car two streets away, walked back in my tracks. Ten minutes later, she came out of this house and took a taxi. I took another. Her old school friend lived in a studio in Chelsea. <u>I could see them through the studio window</u> as he cooked spaghetti over a gas range. They didn't say much. They just looked very natural together. You know, it's funny how you can tell when people are in love. I went for a walk. I began to wonder what would happen if she left me. I'd have to find some way of earning a living, to begin with. I suddenly realized how much I'd grown to depend on her. All these expensive tastes I'd acquired while I was at the top. Now, big tennis had finished with me and so, apparently, had my wife. I can't ever remember being so scared. I dropped into a pub and had a couple of drinks. As I sat in the corner, I thought of all sorts of things. I thought of three different ways of killing him. <u>I even thought of killing her.</u> That seemed a far more sensible idea. And just as I was working out how I could do it, I suddenly saw something which completely changed my mind. I didn't go to that tournament after all. When I got back, she was sitting exactly where you are now. I told her I decided to give up tennis and look after her instead.

In order to convey to Lesgate—in order to convey to anyone who might curiously be peeping in—that the marriage is broken, that there are recriminations on his part, that he would willingly do away with her, he spreads an elaborate table of wonders, including the meticulous dance steps by which he discovers her infidelity (and suggests that before the taxi scenario he had no clear idea of it at all). A tersely informative statement like "My wife is having an affair" is simply impossible for him militarily.

There is a lengthy follow-up in which he details his operational plan. Again, note the way Tony's mind seems to zoom into objects as he recounts a tale of actions we cannot see in any way except by imagining through his language. <u>Underlining</u> again:

> TONY (as though in recollection): There were long letters from [New York]. They usually arrived on Thursdays. She burned them all except one. That one she used to transfer from handbag to handbag. It was always with her. That letter became an obsession with me. I had to find out what was in it. Finally, I did. <u>That letter made very interesting reading.</u>
>
> LESGATE: Do you mean you stole it?
>
> TONY: Yes. I even wrote her two anonymous notes offering to sell it back.
>
> LESGATE: Why?
>
> TONY: I was hoping it would make her come and tell me all about him. But it didn't. So <u>I kept the letter.</u>

When she tells it, innocent Margot circumlocutes the bizarre story of the letter (something straight out of Wilkie Collins) to Hubbard as she trembles after the attack:

> TONY (faux helpfulness): Remember when your bag was stolen?
>
> MARGOT: Yes.
>
> TONY: Wasn't the key inside?
>
> MARGOT: Yes, but it was still there when I got it back.
>
> HUBBARD: Now, just a moment—I'd like to hear about this. What sort of bag?
>
> TONY (helpful again): A handbag, Inspector. My wife lost it at Victoria Station.
>
> MARGOT: But I got it back from the lost and found two weeks later.
>
> HUBBARD: Was anything missing?
>
> MARGOT: All the money was gone.
>
> HUBBARD: Anything else?

MARGOT: No.

HUBBARD: No papers or letters?

MARGOT: No.

HUBBARD: Are you quite sure about that?

MARGOT: Yes.

HUBBARD: And your latchkey was in your handbag when you lost it?

MARGOT: Yes, but it was still there when it was returned. But whoever stole the money could have copied the key.

HUBBARD: Where was the bag found eventually?

MARGOT: At Victoria Station.

A confusion as to what was going on with that theft, a vortical tale, but plenty of punchy indications of interesting things. Margot knows from Mark that the letter was found in the pocket of the dead man on the floor of her salon. Somewhat earlier, she spelled out the handbag tale to him. Here, my comments in square brackets detail what is to be understood behind her words:

MARGOT: One day Tony and I [invoking The Couple] were going to spend the weekend in the country with friends. [Friends, to be imagined, as well as the country seat, some kind of landed estate, no doubt.] While we were waiting on the platform [a tiny portrait of the grimy quay], I noticed my handbag was missing [Margot no doubt dropping her head, peeling her eyes, dropping a jaw, going white]. And the letter was inside [an image this time of the letter in its envelope, resting peaceably inside the handbag].

MARK: Where was this?

MARGOT: Victoria Station [For cognoscenti a picture of the arching iron beams of Victoria, the hubbub, the fancy delicatessens; for the uninformed, perhaps a Victorian tonality or spirit]. I thought I'd left it in the restaurant [Margot and Tony snacking at the station restaurant, perhaps tea, perhaps cakes], but when I went back to look for it, it had gone [distraught, Margot looks and looks and sees only other diners and empty tables and clear space on the floor].

MARK: You mean you never found it?

MARGOT: I recovered the handbag about two weeks later ... from the lost and found [Margot standing at a wicket, being handed her bag by a drab employee], but the letter wasn't there [she swiftly opens the bag and rummages inside]. Then about a week afterwards, I received a note [Margot opening the mail, becoming stunned]. It told me what I had to do to get the letter back.

MARK: Yes. Go ahead. Go on.

MARGOT: I was to draw fifty pounds from my bank [Margot at the teller's, decisive, formal] in five-pound notes [a wad of bills] and then change them for used one-pound notes [going to another teller? and the wad is magnified]. It said that if I went to the police or told anyone else he would show the letter to my husband [Margot standing with a Bobby; some nefarious dirty-handed cur unfolding the letter in front of Tony's incredulous eyes].

MARK: You still have the note? (*Margot fetches it.*) Printed, all capitals. Anyone could have done this.

MARGOT: And two days later I got this one (*hands over another*).

MARK: Both mailed in Brixton [the uninitiated picture a tiny village, perhaps quaint little brick buildings and pretty windowboxes; those in the know see curling streets, sooty architecture, a down-and-out part of London]. Throw half the money in a package [a thick, probably dun-colored envelope] and mail to John S. King, 23 Newport Street, Brixton SW9 [we see her addressing the thing, the large clear print]. You'll get your letter by return [She waits and waits and soon in the dream future the postman brings an envelope containing an envelope].

MARGOT: It's a little shop [perhaps a news agent's]. People use it as a forwarding address [letters coming and going all times of the day].

MARK: You didn't mail the money.

MARGOT: Yes.

MARK: Margot!

MARGOT: But the letter was never returned [Margot sitting by the window waiting for the postman day after day after day]. So, after waiting about two weeks I went there [Margot entering the little shop, perhaps a bell tinkling]. Said they had never heard of a man by that name [a little old lady or a little old man behind a worn, cheaply finished counter]. And the parcel was still there [her envelope]. It had never been opened.

One is struck by the back-and-forth quality here but then, on reflection, by all the carefully elaborated back-and-forths in the film, built each one from the same principles of construction. And from Margot just as much as from the others, a litany of intentions, observations, and buried thoughts, all of which can be sharply imaged in the listener's imagination yet do not directly appear: (1) friends in the country; (2) a British railway platform; (3) Margot's (Hermès) handbag and the utter absence of that bag;[19] (4) a letter stuffed inside it; (5) immense Victoria Station, London; (6) the restaurant there; (7) Margot's bank, wherever it is; (8) a wad of five-pound notes; (9) a bigger, more disheveled wad of used one-pound notes; (10) Margot hypothetically showing the letter to Tony (except that there can be no "hypothetical" images); (11) the blackmail note, unfolded, printed in all capitals; (12) Brixton; (13) Margot's envelope addressed John S. King, Brixton SW9; (14) the little shop; (15) Margot standing in the little shop; (16) Margot's package in the little shop, unopened. Objects, places, interiors, gestures, details, but no verbal reference to what we see: distraught and confused Margot moving around her salon with patient, attentive Mark scanning her. The eye picks up one scene, the imagination is led on a jiggling voyage from point to point conceiving of others. Even when the detail of the letter is mentioned—"Printed, all capitals"—Hitchcock forbears to insert a close-up that would show us what is being shown to Mark. Think of the entire conversation here as two contradictory things at once: rich information, and an airy roundabout.

Let me return us to another itinerary. We are seeing Tony seated in his easy chair, his prop cane by his side, then Lesgate in the sofa facing him, legs crossed, a look of fascination spread across his not-so-handsome face. There is warm lamplight from behind Lesgate. A fire burns behind Tony in the hearth. Two chums, a pleasant evening, a lush apartment, sweet quiet, time for reflection. Facial expressions: slightly contrived on Tony's part, eager on Lesgate's. This meeting could be any of a number of things, taken on its own value as a vision. Comfort and purposefulness from unobtrusively but rather decorously attired Tony, receptivity from informal Lesgate in sports coat, pipe in hand. The pacing of the talk is even and slow, almost lulling. But as we tune in, the imagination is taken off to distant ports of call: (1) Tony and Margot's wedding (wherever and whenever it was); (2) Tony on the tennis court, agile, championlike, grinning with victory; (3) Margot in the stands, not quite his fan, grinning and bearing it—she couldn't care less about tennis, perhaps sports altogether; (4) Margot arguing with Tony at home, probably just here in this room, telling him to stop playing tennis; (5) Tony heading off to America (Mark traveled by ship, does Tony go that way?); (6) Tony playing there on a grass court (we picture him in his whites), presumably meeting plenty of people; (7) Tony back in England at Wimbledon; (8) an "old school friend" in Margot's orbit; (9) Margot and Tony fighting again, not happy to be together, Margot not wanting him to play in a tournament; (10) the phone ringing outside while (11) Tony, in the bedroom, listens through the door; (12) Margot suddenly urging Tony to play in the tournament—is she coy?; (13) Tony packing his tennis things into his car; (14) Tony driving away from Charrington Gardens (perhaps with Margot watching through the window); (15) Tony parking nearby (we picture, somehow, a virtually empty street); (16) Tony walking back; (17) Tony lurking outside No 61A secretly; (18) Margot emerging (in a long coat?) and stepping into a taxi; (19) Tony getting into another taxi; (20) Tony arriving in Chelsea, of which we may well have no image but no matter, it is important only that we quickly jump to: (21) Tony peering through a studio window; (22) Margot and the friend (Mark) in the warm interior; (23) Mark cooking spaghetti on (24) his gas range; (25) Margot and Mark cuddling; (26) Tony pacing the streets of Chelsea, thinking about: (27) his own expensive tastes, possibly configured as clothing, champagne, good Scotch; then (28) a local pub; (29) Tony drinking there, in a (dark) corner; (30) three imagined scenarios of killing Mark—a cord, a knife, a gun?; (31) an image of killing Margot (hands on throat?). A chain of racing images, each one almost a film tableau, charged, urgent, cloudy, frightened, meticulous, urgent, more urgent, and so carefully narrated! Yet what we are seeing through the narration, actually, is two men in placid conversation, the face-to-face of a lively present serving against a scattered past stuffed with allusion.[20]

So much in this film hangs upon someone standing or sitting before our eyes, without agitation, rather easily recounting events that took place elsewhere and in another time, took place in some given order, took place with consequence, yet were not and are not seen by us taking place. Even the attempted murder itself, at first spelled out in rehearsal so that we can imagine every little detail of it, turns out when finally we watch not to conform to the picture in our heads. Over and over, the picture in our heads versus the picture on the screen. Indeed, the picture on the screen calculated purposefully to instill a picture in our heads, a teasing picture, a false picture, the sort of picture that lards travel brochures urging us to leave the comforts of home and rush off on an expensive jaunt to some exotic place photographed to look inviting.

The critical interlocution between Tony and Hubbard on execution eve is a voyage beyond voyages, tantalizing, mystifying, challenging our trust: (1) "My wife," that is, Margot in prison, dark, depressing, gray, terminal; (2) a lively robbery, three weeks back; (3) the gallows, impossibly looming, about which Hubbard kindly commiserates; (4) a cashier in a Ledbury Street factory (what kind of factory? What kind of cashier?)—Ledbury Street is in Peckham, South Bank, ultra-modest working class, and not so very far away from Brixton; (5) this cashier in his office—an old man with a visor and heavy spectacles, a quill pen?; (6) two men barging in (thugs? Athletic types?); (7) a huge wad of pound notes amounting to several hundred pounds; (8) police divisions across London, bobbies diligently checking up on expenditures in their area (assiduous policemen, vigorous policemen, telephoning, jotting notes); (9) Wales's Garage (located we know not where); (10) Tony present there, spending sixty pounds (pound notes going into a grease-stained palm?); (11) Tony's bank, wherever it is; (12) Hubbard begging the bank manager for help courteously, gravely; (13) the bank manager definitively shaking his head; (14) the inside of Hubbard's Aquascutum pocket and whatever he may have stuffed there (a character's characterological backstage, which could function, too, as the actor's backstage); (15) a small hole there (announced with dramatic irritation, but entirely invisible: a hole that is a dramatic hole); (16) Tony spending money at his tailor's (Jermyn Street?); (17) Tony spending money at the wine store (Scotch? Single malt? Caol Ila? Laphroaig?); (18) Tony at the dog races; (19) at the races, Tony thinking of Margot at the foot of the gallows (although we can never know what Tony, or any character, is thinking when they say they have been thinking).

All the talk, talk about talk, talk recounting talk, talk begging talk, talk countering talk, talk about facts, talk about inventions, talk outbidding or outwitting talk, talk revealing, talk concealing, talk detailing, talk complicating, talk promising and frustrating... all the saddening and elevating talk of *Dial M for Murder* offered by a woman who doesn't grasp the full implication of what she is saying; by a canny husband who talks to keep your mind away from what is happening; by an American chum who has a very great deal of skill with talk, even so much as to be convincing that he is only throwing out an airy hypothesis while actually mouthing what he secretly believes; by an Inspector whose terseness belies a meticulous strategy. The talk in general either (a) says what we are already seeing; or (b) says what we never see evidenced; or (c) plays for time; or (d) tells an unrecognized truth, but in all cases is offset from the events that play to our viewer sensibilities directly. It is as though we cannot quite see what, trapped in the movie theater, we are staring at and need guidance, and also as though we should watch out for guidance, since we can never be certain where it leads.

More troubling still, perhaps. That again and again here, and with the deftest skill, Hitchcock is revealing how the world we speak of and the world as it is, are not the same. Is *Dial M for Murder* in a very crucial respect a silent film?

Now we are borne forward to a strange destination.

A FEINTING SPELL

Playing tennis with a Maharajah... sitting to write a detective story... cooking spaghetti on a gas range... a note composed all in capitals... the restaurant at Victoria Station... friends in the country... a little shop in Brixton SW9... a factory in Ledbury Street... Mrs Wendice's handbag... Mrs Wendice's sewing basket... Mrs Wendice's nylon stockings... the green curtains (an arras) behind which Lesgate should hide... the public telephone at the club... getting into a taxi... trying a key in the door...

Not just a key, a latchkey.

The door is latched. The latchkey will undo the latch. First, this is plain ordinary "good English" as spoken in England, one of the Britishisms of the film (exemplified no end by Williams as Hubbard). The English are here, the English are there, the English are everywhere. Yet not quite. In locksmithing, a *latch* is a device, mechanical, that joins two surfaces *while also permitting their separation.* Think of marriage as a latch, think of the latchkey that could permit the separation of Tony and Margot. Tony has arranged Margot's conviction for murder as a latchkey. Hubbard is rearranging Tony's arrangement as a latchkey of superior quality, the *right* latchkey. Out of politesse or out of a final impotence, Mark has no latchkey that could work here. And Margot is innocently removed from all this business. But we have the keys to these characters. Margot, who is not *quite* English. She has learned to be in England, to be "English." She has learned the drawbacks of being married to an English tennis player, who wants one kind of court or another, one venue or another, one sort of life or another. She has picked up some aspects of a London drawl. But this young woman was not raised in England. She has all the veneer of the American parvenue, the girl returning to her cultural roots (as, discussing the fictional form he calls "The Eastern," Leslie Fiedler writes of Henry James's women, returned from America's East Coast to Europe [*Return*]). Mark is definitively American, putting himself out as having East Coast panache, East Coast cultural sophistication, but by his easy-going naturalness, his vigorous health, and his shining brightness he is clearly a denizen of California, one of *los angeles* from the future. In Tony one has the climber, a working-class boy with some athletic talent who wangled his way into the privacies of a visiting princess. Hubbard is the more proper, the more affectedly elegant, which might lead to the false surmise he is in truth above these others while really he has learned, as no Upper has to, and in the capacity of his work, how to mix in well with whatever folk are around: examine by joining. A. N. Wilson remarks on the utter falsity of the posh *English* accent we hear so often on screens: "not aristocratic in the least" (19).

As to those latchkeys, the final triumph in the film, the turn that swiftly brings the comic elements together in a reconciliation of identity, belongs to the Inspector, who finds—the only one to find, still alive—the latchkey that opens the latch. His task, in the polish, is to separate Margot from ugly Tony, and false Tony from both noble Margot and his own hopeless masquerade, by—we should observe—showing how to open a door. A Shakespearean finale. Tony cannot open a latch, and this is morally correct, since as a man who wished to kill Margot, unlatch himself from her, he should in the final results be incapable twice, incapable retrospectively in his instructions to pathetic Lesgate and incapable now, as, opening the door with the right (the wrong) key, he closes the door on himself, forever. All these latchkeys look alike, as the Inspector says, but *they all work differently*.

Yet, further on latching and unlatching, the film makes a statement on another level, something weirdly hinted at yet never, for all the speech, spoken aloud. There is a rather clanging, repeated murmur through all the many conversations, recountings, fabrications, inventions, spontaneous lies, and subtle truths we hear and observe, to the effect that Tony Wendice is a tennis player. Not only that we see him in the back-and-forth but that a Back-and-Forth is very generally claimed for him, a give-and-take that unlatches the door to success, that is, to the future. Beyond the row of gleamy trophies on the mantel, to which the eye is escorted many times, there is blunt statement:

- One of the first things we hear from Margot's pretty mouth: "Tony said he meant to give up tennis and get a job."

- Tony to Lesgate, after being asked whether the man hasn't seen him some place since they left Cambridge: "Ever been to Wimbledon?"

- Tony confiding to Lesgate, as part of his account of learning Margot is in love with someone else, that after an abrupt phone call, to which he was not fully privy, she changed her mind and told him to play in a tournament, so he packed his tennis kit into his car and drove away. Packed his tennis kit.

- Then, further, Tony's chagrin: "Now, big tennis had finished with me and so apparently had my wife."

- Then, Tony's numerous invocations of himself as tennis player whilst explaining things to Hubbard before the execution. He wanted to go to America to play on grass; he came back for the British championships.

- And, "Do you still play?" Lesgate asked. "No, I've given it up. Rather, tennis gave me up."

- At another point, Lesgate's curiosity:

LESGATE: Why do you think she married you?

TONY: Well, I was a tennis star.

All these keenly worded, pointed references to Tony and tennis, these indications of where he plays and on what sort of court and in what context, these comments about tennis contributing all this richness to his lifestyle (as the eye calmly roves around the pleasant room full of luxuries). Tennis tennis tennis talk without a single caught view of (a) Tony in tennis whites, (b) Tony clutching a racquet, (c) Tony at play on a court, (d) Tony celebrated as a champion (not even one of his clippings). It's all talk, yet repetitive talk and pointing... nowhere. In *Strangers on a Train* (1951), after all, Hitchcock had shown quite clearly (1) what tennis is (at the championship level) and (2) how in a motion picture to depict it. Tennis in *Dial M* is a different sort of game, not only a game of words but a game of lies and deflections and vacancies.

Tennis of the tongue.

And once we see the elaborate pointing to vacancy (think of it as the oddest tennis of the film) we may reflect yet again on all those long-winded tales, tales from Tony excusing himself secretly and in advance; tales from Margot trying to make sense of things; tales from Mark, trying to invent a living story; and tales solicited by the ever curious, insatiable, and wizard-like Hubbard, Hubbard the *hub bard*. What the tales do—what in this film, almost without relief the talking does and does and does and does—is: distract. Words point us away from the action. And what is the action of this film, the fourfold action, away from which the talk points?

[1] A dignified and mature woman with a healthy love life (and love of life) who is, for one reason or another, eager to have an affair *that her husband need never know about*. She is circumspect, or at least tries to be, amateur though she is. She wants fun, even pleasure, but not trouble, nor the guilt of inflicting pain or shame. Not even release, just a little tickle once in a while. At least for starters....

[2] A fundamentally unconfident husband, jealous all the time, fearful he will lose the luscious advantages of being married to a woman with more money than he has, perhaps sensing himself to be the bore he is

and smart enough to see that if she has not tired of him yet she soon will. A clinger, a clutcher, and a cad.

[3] A simple enough murder plan, spieled out in a tone that makes the planner seem like a genius (Tony primping again) but actually dependent on the services of a non-professional whose crimes thus far have been cheap and picayune, who has no particular thirst for the job and must be seduced by a promise of payoff, and who seems nervous and unaccomplished when he is at work (just as Tony's recollection of Swann's escapade with the treasury funds at Cambridge shows he always was).

[4] Thus, in sum, a plan for crime that cannot possibly succeed, set in the context of a visit to England by a man who writes crimes that inevitably do succeed (and who happens to be in love with Margot, bless him). It will turn out that only because of Tony's crime will any real liaison be possible for them.

A bad marriage, and thus a marriage that each partner envisions differently, one aiming at a murderous "latchkey" and the other planning to use performative guile, lies if necessary, but essentially to do no harm, since she doesn't intend her husband to become aware and only awareness could really hurt him.

That is what is boiling onscreen, in every scene from one angle or another, in every breath. But while it boils, we find ourselves participating in chat about a Maharajah on a tennis court, a little shop in Brixton SW9, the pilfering of a bag at Victoria Station (the station for traveling to Wimbledon), and tennis, tennis, tennis, tennis, tennis.

What, after all, is tennis, if we think in terms of the accomplishments it requires? It is two things. It is serving or hitting the ball to an exact point on the far court where the opponent is either least likely to be now or least able to arrive at in time for a rebound. Tricky forwarding. And it is exceptionally agile motion to field a ball coming at you from any angle, at any speed, so that you are never caught off guard. Slick parrying. Anybody who has won trophies playing this game—there are trophies on Tony's mantle; he claims they are his—will know how to make somebody else fall off balance; and how to retain balance against all tides. Tony Wendice, we are to believe.

With Lesgate, Tony playing a server.

With Hubbard (and with all the others), Tony playing a parrier.

And his personal style, as we both see and admire, is camouflage, calculated misdirection, the feint. The film is an excursion in feinting, something of a feint itself, this latter because in having his characters play tennis against one another and in playing with his audience this way, Hitchcock is something of a feinter, too. What happens in the film is served our way, not always straightforwardly, and we must be there to counter it when it arrives. But to help waylay our talents and thoughts, the serve is accompanied by a host of distractions, a kind of battle charge. There is only one creature introduced to us who is tranquil, informed, experienced, sober, uncommitted, delicate, sympathetic, and fully present, and that is Hubbard. Hubbard who knew all along. Hubbard who just (grimace) couldn't get that latchkey right, until...

Until he could.

Hubbard, who told us everything when he reflected off-handedly to Tony that a distraction "helps take your mind off things."

CHAPTER FIVE

RICH AND STRANGE

To the End of the World and Back Again

> Nothing of him that doth fade,
> But doth suffer a sea change
> Into something rich and strange
>
> *The Tempest*, I.ii.400–402

COMPASS

By the time the Very Great War (1914–1918) had ebbed, seeped into the sands of the brassy 1920s and metamorphosed into the Equivocal Peace of the early 1930s (a peace that promised more than it could possibly deliver),¹ and while emergent sharp consciousness of the class divide was not yet interrupting either daydreams of prosperity or the quest for pleasure in western Europe, it happened in England that a Ruskinian model of adventurous discovery wore somewhat thin. In the early 1930s, when film's sound revolution was well underway and Alfred Hitchcock was releasing his *Rich and Strange* (1931), it was no longer the mountainous and breathtaking Swiss Alps or Pyrénées of southern France, or the by-now familiar Riviera with its corporeal and intellectual shocks, or the precarious stony hill towns of

northern Italy that puissant travelers wanted to visit (as their ancestors had in the nineteenth and early in the twentieth centuries), notwithstanding that these places could offer views spectacular beyond spectacular of the geophysical sublime, and notwithstanding the ongoing commercial viability of travel (Karl Baedeker was still publishing his guides enthusiastically [the 15th edition of *Northern Italy*, the 16th edition of *Rome and Central Italy*, the 17th edition of *Southern Italy*, and, in 1931, a new edition of *The Riviera*]). To the middle classes—this film was a portrait of, a challenge to, and a riddle about the middle class—Gothic Europe, its mythic valleys, its ancient noble crags, its ruined cathedrals, its precipitous waterfalls (of the sort that bested Sherlock Holmes), and the glory and grandeur of the Continental past that had entranced such writers as Johann Wilhelm von Archenholz, Johann von Goethe, Ruskin, Henry James, and Arthur Conan Doyle, no longer beckoned. It had become time to discover—or, as privileged Westerners preferred to think, rediscover—the East.

And as always for the Occidental imagination, the East was reachable only by way of a voyage, seriously committed, expensive, perspective-altering. The voyage to the East would sharply raise cultural strangeness, latent racism not merely personal but structural, and the thrilling proximity to experience that one could have when, on the deck of a ship sailing eastward, one could taste the perfume of sunrise in the air.

INTO THE SUN

Not really new, the geographic and social wonders of the East had been revealed to the European imagination at the end of the thirteenth century with Marco Polo's *Travels*.[2] Having spent almost a quarter century in the retinue of Khubilai Khan, the book suggests, he visits many Asian venues on his journey homeward and finds himself astounded by the vistas and wonders to be found there. He notes that from Comorin, for one case, "you can go out thirty miles into the sea and catch a glimpse of the Pole Star rising out of the water for about one cubit" (*Travels* 288). And the islanders of Socotra "can make the wind blow from whatever quarter they may wish. They could calm the sea at will, or raise a raging storm and a howling gale"; but their greatest enchantments, in Polo's experience, were not to be committed to text, so esoteric was their form:

> They are masters of many other marvellous enchantments; but I think it better not to speak of these in this book, *because these enchantments produce effects which, were men to hear of them, might set them marvelling overmuch.* (298; my emphasis)

The wandering Polo thinks back to his compatriots at home, realizes how uncomprehending they would be at the sights that are so deeply affecting him. Nor anything more entrancing than the glitter of precious gems. In the Kingdom of Motupalli,

> in the summer, when there is not a drop of water to be found, then diamonds can be found in plenty among these mountains. But the heat is so great that it is almost intolerable. Moreover the mountains are so infested with serpents of immense size and girth that men cannot go there without grave danger. But all the same they go there as best they can and find big stones of fine quality. Let me tell you further that these serpents are exceedingly venomous and noxious, so that men dare not venture into the caves where the serpents live. So they get the diamonds by other means. You must know that there is a big deep valley so walled in by precipitous cliffs that no one can enter it. But I will tell you what men do. They take many lumps of flesh imbrued in blood and fling them down into the depths of the valley. And the lumps thus flung down pick up great numbers of diamonds, which become embedded in the flesh. Now it so happens that these mountains are inhabited by a great many white eagles, which prey on the serpents. When these eagles spy the flesh lying at the bottom of the valley, down they swoop and seize

the lumps and carry them off. The men observe attentively where the eagles go, and as soon as they see that a bird has alighted and is swallowing the flesh, they rush to the spot as fast as they can. Scared by their sudden approach, the eagles fly away, leaving the flesh behind. And when they get hold of it, they find diamonds in plenty embedded in it. (272–73)

Polo's texts richly report unsatisfied attraction to strange habits and customs, to notably "precipitous" terrain, to the wily, energetic aggressions of creatures entirely non-European, to the wealth of natural knowledge. In the quality of the writing, even through the veil of its translation, one can sense the way a cultivated Western personality would have been surprised, modified, infected, swept away by exposure to the traditions and flavors of the East. To participate in this reverie, one hardly needed to be infected by (as Edward Said lists)

the imagery of exotic places, the cultivation of sadomasochistic tastes..., a fascination with the macabre, with the notion of a Fatal Woman, with secrecy and occultism, all combined. (180)

Whilst Said finds the idea of the Orient a somewhat elaborate artificial construction—

Consider how the Orient, and in particular the Near Orient, became known in the West as its great complementary, opposite since antiquity. There were the Bible and the rise of Christianity; there were travelers like Marco Polo who charted the trade routes and patterned a regulated system of commercial exchange, and after him Lodovico di Varthema and Pietro della Valle; there were fabulists like Mandeville; there were the redoubtable conquering Eastern movements, principally Islam, of course; there were the militant pilgrims, chiefly the Crusaders. Altogether an internally structured archive is built up from the literature that belongs to these experiences. (58)

—still, as a dream force, a mythology, a way of leaving home for *something new*, the East served Europeans of the early twentieth century particularly well and can be examined as the energy source for a great experiment in movement.[3]

An experiment with side effects. We can surely detect, as Said does, in Western conceits of exoticism a curious blend of appropriation and adoration, and this was far from new. Richard Altick makes mention of the British Museum's "Otaheiti or South Sea Room" as of 1778, into which objects and souvenirs crowded over the ensuing decades, to such an overwhelming degree that a critic complained, "Never was such a disgraceful jumble of things seen" (297–98). The London Missionary Society had another museum, later the Museum of East India House, in which a singularly popular exhibit was a mechanical tiger devouring "a civilian Englishman with black shoes, round black hat, scarlet coat, green breeches, and yellow stockings":

> Turning a barrel-organ crank in the tiger's side—a duty assigned to a slave in the original setting [in Mysore], and later a privilege enjoyed by visitors to the museum, to the constant annoyance of students in the adjoining library—activated bellows, stops, and other equipment in the respective interiors, producing, on the part of the tiger, deep-throated roars and, on that of the man, heartfelt shrieks and groans. While the tiger moved his head, his prey writhed on the ground and eventually expired. (Altick 299)

Writing of the "male perspective in exotic geography," one that surely also "catalogued the poses, practices, and 'perversions' of exotic men" (179; 181), Benjamin Schmidt is careful to pay attention as well to the latent and surface sexual content, thoroughly misogynist, of images and actions carried out in the "exotic" East. Adultery, especially, roused punishments, even when only presumptive, as Schmidt shows:

> The most horrific such episode—a tale brimming with lurid descriptions of the exotic body and with appalling details of salaciousness, licentiousness, voyeurism, violence, and more—was the vivid account in Struys's *Reysen* (1676) of the flaying by a Central Asian "gentleman" of his putatively unfaithful wife. The story ... takes place in Shamakhy, in the eastern Caucasus (present-day Azerbaijan), although the dramatis personae had more vague and perhaps all-purpose affiliations. The principal "body" in question belonged to a so-called Polish woman, described also as a "slave"

and a "wife"—one of thirteen, thus part of an Oriental seraglio—who is tormented by her "husband," the latter classically identified generically as a "Persian" and thus implicitly as a Muslim. The woman's crime is never fully clarified: she is suspected of an unspecified misdeed, while a later reference to "chastity" may allude to a sexual impropriety. Yet her punishment is described in painfully precise detail: the victim is stripped naked, crucified on wooden stakes, and flayed alive. All of this was perpetrated by the husband himself and witnessed by the narrator ("I stood myself... and heard her cry out most bitterly"). (176)

If the classical "Grand Tour," with its excitement, renewal, surprise, and a general sense of wonder, an apotheosis, had characterized the experience of the wealthy European making the journey eastward into Europe yet not all the way to The East, in search of a hitherto unfamiliar, classical arena in his own culture, it also presaged certain eastern raptures to come, that both echo the experience of ancient voyagers eastward and look forward to the pure amazement of our heroes Fred and Emily Hill (Henry Kendall, Joan Barry) when they enter strange climes. We shall see how in the people the Hills meet on their special Journey to the East they find both unfamiliarity and rapture.

It can be difficult to imagine or grasp *rapture* in an age of fast-paced momentary thrills such as our own. Here is a rapture on light and color from Goethe's *Letters from Italy* (in the era of the Grand Tour):

> My tendency to look at the world through the eyes of the painter whose pictures I have seen last has given me an odd idea. Since our eyes are educated from childhood on by the objects we see around us, a Venetian painter is bound to see the world as a brighter and gayer place than most people see it. We northerners who spend our lives in a drab and, because of the dirt and the dust, an uglier country where even reflected light is subdued, and who have, most of us, to live in cramped rooms—we cannot instinctively develop an eye which looks like such delight at the world.
>
> As I glided over the lagoons in the brilliant sunshine and saw the gondoliers in their colourful costume, gracefully posed against the blue sky as they rowed with easy strokes across the light-green

surface of the water, I felt I was looking at the latest and best painting of the Venetian school. (47)

Experience as Art. And a report of geographical glory at Chamonix seen by Ruskin in 1833:

> There is not another scene like Chamouni throughout all Switzerland. In no other spot that I have seen is the rich luxuriance of the cultivated valley, the flashing splendour of the eternal snow, the impending magnificence of the bare, spiry crag, and the strange, cold rigidity of the surgy glaciers so dreadfully and beautifully combined. (*Life* 37)

Soon later his enthusiasm came to Schaffhausen:

> The Swiss tour of 1835 reinforced the experiences of the earlier tour. Already, the Ruskins displayed their tendency to visit the same places: Geneva, Chamonix, St. Martin, Vevey, Neuchâtel, Lucerne, Thun, Fribourg, and Baden. True, there was also a new mountain pass—the St. Gotthard—but they continued on this new route only as far as Airolo. Essentially, Ruskin seems to have experienced in 1835 the satisfaction that comes from familiarity. Again, he found delight in the approach to Switzerland—especially in the "Jura cottage" which he associated with "the sense of human industry and enjoyment" (qtd. in Hayman 2). Again, as in Schaffhausen in 1833, he had a vision—looking down from the Col de la Faucille on "the whole Lake of Geneva, and the chain of the Alps along a hundred miles of horizon" (qtd. in Hayman 2).

And von Goethe again, seeing the mountains of the Mittelwald on 7 September 1786: "Now a new world opened to me" (*Travels* 5).

The idea was—born for Englishmen in the mountainous aeries of Europe but then carried forward to the East—that a voyage can open a new world. That the world as one knows it can be vanquished, replaced, evaporated, and reborn in unrecognized, confusing form. More than selfies, more than trinkets snagged by barter, more than towels filched from the hotel in Shangri-la, a voyage involved confrontation, a jarring discontinuity with habit, a sense of the self in an unexplored, perhaps even untouched space where oddity presents itself directly and fully to the eye. (Noteworthy examples of British amazement in the far lands are to be found throughout the annals of Capt. Cook's voyages [see my *Cinema* 143ff].) Of all movements, the journey eastward—all the way eastward—has a special magic, addresses a special impulse. It brings the traveler, Hermann Hesse wrote, to the Home of Light, engages the traveler with "the eternal strivings of the human spirit towards the East, towards Home" (13).

L'INVITATION AU VOYAGE

Hesse published *Die Morgenlandfahrt (The Journey to the East)* in 1932, early in the year, one may surmise, since he finished it in April 1931. On 13 June Hitchcock released *Rich and Strange*, a representation of, but also in truth a journey to, the East in several ways, not only geographically but also experientially for the two main protagonists. In leaving their flat to embark on a voyage of adventure, they are as yet unaware of the profound way in which their voyage will bring them "Home," will cause them to "suffer a sea change."

Was Hesse prescient even about the cultural climate that, at the film's outset, brings Fred and Emily to a state of such complacent boredom, flatness of affect, and resignation that they are prepared to leave their established lives behind? After the World War, he writes, one found one's country "full of saviors, prophets and disciples, of presentiments about the end of the world, or hopes for the dawn of a Third Empire." It was a time of phenomena and shocks:

> Shattered by the war, in despair as a result of deprivation and hunger, greatly disillusioned by the seeming futility of all the sacrifices in blood and goods, our people at that time were lured by many phantoms.... There was also at that time a widespread leaning towards Indian, ancient Persian and other Eastern mysteries and religions. (10)

The rhapsody of the Hills' apparent "sea change" is also prophesied by Hesse, in a strand of poetry he cites as part of his narrator's recollections:

> He who travels far will often see things
> Far removed from what he believed was Truth. (7)

Yet it may be that in his broad spirit of romanticism, at once so unclear and so alluring, Hesse failed to fully grasp the elusive transformation of which Shakespeare hinted: *The Tempest* is a sea change for all its characters, after all, and for its audience, too. And it is the "sea change" we must invoke, since the Hills' voyage is expressly by sea, fraught with visions and vistas of the sea, dependent upon the characters' and the audience's capacity for seaworthiness (Fred instantaneously takes to bed, seasick, Emily thrives; which path do we follow?). The sea change is importantly metaphorical: a shifting of one's perspective on the world, a renewed and restored and re-purposed vision, and a kind of second life facing a new horizon. The body sunken "full fathom five" is transposed; or its constituent elements, broken up by the tides, are recomposed into a strange figuration: coral made of the bones, pearls dropping into the eye sockets, quite as Ariel sang. And what of that something rich and strange? For surely the reborn soul beneath the waves is not what in conventional language might be thought either rich or strange. Shakespeare knew the language in which he wrote. "Rich" in its origins meant powerful, controlling, dominant, and only much later comes to be associated with bounteous wealth. "Strange" means alien, unknown, unrecognized, and only later comes to mean odd or abnormal. That the drowned (besotted, swept away) body might be refashioned into "something rich and strange" suggests both the controlling force of mortality and the ever-presence of a mystery exceeding the boundary of knowledge. The weight of reformation and the uncanniness of experience.

A journey must have a launch, and there is no better launch than tedium. The dryness that makes men search for water. The flatness that makes them seek mountains. The hunger for spice that characterizes a too-well-understood, conventional, and perfunctory routine. The problem for a filmmaker, however—and Hitchcock of course masterfully grasps this—is that because a film is a voyage in itself still it will fail if it commences with the boredom from which it needs to be launched. *Rich and Strange* must find a way to show a state of affairs Fred and Emily will wish to leave behind, but depict it in such a way that the audience will be immediately delighted and engaged (having carefully left their own quotidian tedium on the sidewalk). While cinema moves on relentlessly, it never leaves anything behind. We begin with a ledger in which a hand is entering figures diligently but without devotion: very short shot. Then, longer, the workroom itself, in which a number of men sit at identical seats in orderly rows, their heads bent in identical postures at their sluggardly work.[4] In the extreme left foreground, f2, is the clock, now just registering 6.00.[5] The camera glides right as we see the half-figures of all these men darting away from their work and heading for the exit. Outside the room now the men enter a corridor, joined by a pack of women coming from another room (a division of labor by gender). The stairwell toward the exit, tramp tramp tramp. In the street it is teeming, and the camera waits patiently facing the door,[6] to see the workers emerging in pairs, male pair number one, female pair number two, and so on, each pair composed of two figurines opening twin black umbrellas in unison: birds taking flight; a military drill; boarding the Ark.[7] Suddenly one man is by himself, Fred, with an umbrella that won't open.[8] A comic moment, as a closer shot of him shows the weary and dejected face, somewhere between Stan Laurel and T. S. Eliot. The whole situation is marginally droll, slightly acerbic as well, definitely a critique of regimented labor in modernity yet also a portrait of a man who wishes to be outside all this. "I want to *LIVE!*" The entire sequence is hardly more than a minute of screen time, very tightly composed, very carefully timed, all to the point. And, it is worth noting expressly, entirely wrought of images, which is to say, framings, postures, rhythms, expressions, light patches, characterizations. We are informed without being told.

Now the tube, inordinately crammed with sleepy, daydreaming, withdrawn citizens minding their own business, except that Fred knocks against a woman's hat and a decorative pompom comes away in his hand, to her manifest irritation.[9] He muffles and jiggles, trying hard to replace it in a very good takeoff of a Charlie Chaplin routine. Delicate, sweet, hopelessly well intentioned in a threatening cacophony. A close-up insert of a young man wolfing down a sandwich shows how, even in the early 1930s, the poor worker cannot take time for a leisurely meal but must feed himself in motion.[10]

Now a signal moment:

Opening his paper—noteworthy choreographic difficulty—Fred comes across a box ad: "Are you satisfied with your present circumstances?"—that key word, *circumstances,* being a precise pointer to the social world that is built around him and the word *satisfied* an instant antiphrasis. And you, reader: are you satisfied with your present circumstances, trapped in these sentences?

At home, Fred is welcomed by Emily with her definitively cheery voice and glowing smile, a face she has possibly put on as accessory to her wifely duties or perhaps a signal that her day has been blither than his.[11] We are intended here to witness a private domestic scene, yet something realistic and informative rather than a stage setting for high melodrama. The routine, the casualness, the familiarity, the gentle curtness, the unconnected gestures, the careful stepping-through of the *pas de deux* in a comfortable if perforce limited space. Blasé, blasé, blasé. Emily is seated at her sewing machine, diligently working on a new dress. He flops into his chair, disgruntled that she doesn't have better clothing (not, I think we are to think, because he is worried about how to delight her as much as because he would like her to be a better status symbol for showing off). It does not appear yet that these two are tired of one another, or that either would entertain even the hint of a prospect of searching the horizon for an appealing paramour. Yet their routines are unquestionably stifling: the static camera shots enclose them but more importantly enclose us as we watch them being enclosed. Fred is chomping at the bit. Copying and copying and copying numbers into columns in the office,[12] the columns multiplying without end, what a prospect! A life ruled by glyphs. Every page of every ledger followed by still another page and still another ledger. And the sense that as one labors one makes no accomplishment. At home, the dusting and cleaning to prepare for the dust and dirt that will follow, so that every gesture of the arm, every torsion of the spine leads only to the tide of time, which leaves deposits. The silt of the everyday.

But now:

A letter has (magically) arrived for Fred, from his (unintroduced) uncle (delivered at the door by the obsequious char). Hitchcock allows us to peek over his shoulder—neat and unambiguous typewriting—and for a full twelve seconds (so that the viewer can actually read):

My dear Nephew,

I've thought a lot about our conversation of the other day.

You say you want to enjoy LIFE as a change from your existence—well, see my solicitors and they will fix you up with the money to experience all the life you want by travelling[13] everywhere.

> You may as well have the money now instead of waiting until I die.

The return address is given as 8, Gordon Place, E.C.4. E.C.4 is east of Blackfriars and St. Paul's, and it contains no Gordon Place; a perfectly ordinary Hitchcockian transposition of geographies in order to fictionalize. But there is a Gordon Place in Kensington, echoed here for British viewers, perhaps; and a Gordon Square in Bloomsbury (where Barrie set the Darling house for *Peter Pan*). A mythical, a dream location, the sort of place where might be composed and prepared a letter, brief and charged, that could change one's life. But also a clue, because although she does not know it yet, Emily is soon to meet a Commander Gordon (Percy Marmont), whose name, a musical strain, may be wafting across continents in order to embed itself on the top of this letter.

A little textual interpretation about a key phrase, "You say you want to enjoy LIFE." Hitchcock is always introducing provocations, and the lover of his work finds great pleasure in musing upon their implications and consequences. Here is offered the distinction between "life" and "existence." Consider the appearance of this particular missive in this particular flat at this particular time, its denigration of tedious domestic routines, pointedly the Hill routines (so tidily enunciated in preparation for this moment) into the condition pejoratively considered "mere existence," or "existence but nothing more." The existence of the lower class, say, much as the existence of the animals in the forest and the existence of the trees among which they wander. Being without character. For Heidegger, *Sein* but not *Dasein*. And then the spontaneous gift of "life," even Galvanically capitalized by the generous uncle. LIFE, meaning depth and fullness of opportunity, extensivity of reach, an allure in the air. Also, of course, although Fred and Emily do not immediately take this in, a way of being that is fully conscious of not being, perhaps even a sense of superiority, a way of experiencing and contemplating the stifling limits of experience that once appertained to the self and now belong exclusively to others. In Heidegger's *Sein*, contemplation is both forced and regulated, but in *Dasein* there need be no regulated break for contemplation, so richly fluent, so ongoing is experience. Will the Hills' treasure journey open the possibility of seeing things deeply, and also seeing oneself seeing?

Needless to say, Fred and Emily froth over with a mixture of joy and relief, quite as though released from bondage by a magical *vade mecum*. A close shot of the stovetop shows one of Emily's pots boiling over, lest we fail to catch the spirit.

THE SUN WILL COME OUT TOMORROW

It is signal that on learning a very great sum of money is to be made available to him Fred's first gesture is to sweep Emily's sewing onto the floor, barking peremptorily that she will have better to wear now. (Hypertextually: she has been cast in a kind of "movie" and will have a costume designer at her service.) This is a cry of triumphally receiving just desserts, an instantaneous posture of victory, showing Fred considering himself to be, finally and justly, above the man he was. He is now a man asserting his personality through what the wife may have—what she will indeed feel obliged to have. At the same time, however superior, he is a man in practice, as though after a lifetime's hopeful rehearsal he can finally imagine himself today as the person he always hoped to become tomorrow: anticipatory socialization.[14] The uncle's bequest is not so much a windfall for Fred as a sudden and unplanned for, yet at the same time wholly rational, fulfillment of expectations. He ought to be the sort of person who receives a boon like this, and this was always the case. Here, presto, he has become his own avatar! When Emily reads the letter in astonishment, Hitchcock uses a macro-close-up to show us the line that lifts her attention off the page, with the words lifted for us, too,[15] and scrolling leftward in simulation of the rightward movement of her reading eye: *Money to experience all the life you want by travelling*. We can see now that "life" means two things to these two people. For Fred, ascension. For Emily, revelation, because already in hopes of it her eyes are opened wide, as though to brilliances and subtleties, evanescences and apparitions.

Now Hitchcock inserts a title card with the last two lines of Ariel's song. That is, his touching upon *The Tempest* is no frivolity. Shall Fred be Prospero and Emily Miranda? Is the Uncle Ariel?

They are crossing to France with great excitement and with Fred's camera clicking away—"To get to Paris you have to cross *the Channel*"—and once they are there, following a few touristic snapshots, at once completely familiar and twinkling with exoticism—"To get to the Folies Bergere you have to cross Paris"—we find them at the music hall of the Moulin Rouge on the Boulevard de Clichy, beneath Sacre Coeur. The brazen spectacle of bodies and glitter, fast-paced music, jittery cancans. Paris the intoxicating. Paris the pleasurably mad. They join a huge audience, well prepared in advance to find entirely expected delights. Luc Sante is helpfully descriptive:

> It was primarily a music hall, a showcase for revues, rather than a dance hall proper (at least after 1900); it was explicitly intended for the slumming rich; and the cancan was already old news by the time it opened in 1889, for all that it has ever since claimed to be its birthplace. Still, the Moulin Rouge is worth noting for the quality of its terpsichoreans, many of them painted by Toulouse-Lautrec: Jane Avril, La Goulue (the Glutton), Grille d'Égout (Sewer Grate), La Môme Fromage (the Cheese Kid), Nini Pattes-en-l'Air (Feet in the Air), Rayon d'Or (Golden Ray), Sauterelle (Grasshopper), Claire-de-Lune, Cha-tu-Kon, Cléopatre, Cascadienne, Cri-Cri. La Goulue (Louise Weber; 1869–1929), whose most celebrated male dance partner was Valentin le Désossé (the Boneless), enjoyed and endured a career of extremes. From inhabiting the *hôtel* owned by La Païva, mistress of Napoléon III, on Avenue du Bois, she went to jail "after some lark," then became a lion tamer in a traveling zoo, then a laundress, "then nothing," and spent her last years drinking in the Zone. (170–71)

A haven of loucheness then, and a haven for slummers. The "slumming rich," who may have found a way to escape envy: "The greater the number of people we take to be our equals and compare ourselves to," writes Alain de Botton, "the more there will be for us to envy." Vertical hierarchy, which makes possible the act of dropping down, or at least pretending to drop and be low, maintains and emphasizes class difference and restricts similarities on high. As to similarities and differences, class theory prior to the reformations of the seventeenth and eighteenth centuries had insisted on a Christian society that

> took the form of a rigidly stratified monarchy, a design said to reflect the ordering of the celestial kingdom. Just as God wielded absolute power over all creation, from the angels down to the smallest toads,

> so, too, his appointed rulers on earth were understood to preside over a society where God had given everyone his and her place, from the nobleman down to the farm-hand. (de Botton 28)

A place for everyone, and now, in the thriving Capital of Modernity, also a place from which one could deliriously pretend to slide.

We must inquire about the true elevation of the audiences who frequented the Moulin, the degree to which any of these "slumming rich" approached the nobility, power, and social girth of the "appointed rulers on earth." This inquiry has value because in positing the Moulin Rouge as the locus of the Hills' "awakening" to their newfound "wealth"—the Moulin of all places—Hitchcock makes a subtle, even sly reference to the true social position of the ostensibly "rich uncle" and by association the degree of elevation now accorded the lucky beneficiaries. In this audience of high slummers Fred and Emily are higher than they had been once upon a time, to be sure, but possibly not so very high after all, and this may come to have relevance once the real journey has begun. The actual aristocrats of Paris would be in boxes at Garnier's opera, adoring Wagner conducted by Furtwängler. If Fred and Emily form a snobbery, it will be, like all aspects of character, derived from their class, "not a snobbery linked with nostalgia, but, on the contrary, with what is just one-step-ahead-of-the-very-latest-thing, which is to say that it is a snobbery based not on tradition but on fashion and fad" (Mills 337).

The Moulin Rouge, while not being more than ten or fifteen minutes distant from it, is not the same as the Folies Bergère on the Rue Richer, a name Hitchcock may have invoked in order to capture the general English imagination of exotic, lascivious Paris. The presumable moral outrage of the stolid Englishman and his wife faced with gay semi-nudity and dancing sexuality is nicely evoked as Fred modestly turns his eyes down and Emily, who has slid her shoes off for comfort, giggles nervously. Optical superimpositions make the dancers and hot lighting swirl in a stunning vortex.[16] After the show a loll through the restaurant where Emily claims a "bearded" stranger has pinched her bottom. A quick move through the nocturnal street ablaze with electric light.[17] And a concluding comedic phrase—"And to get to your room you have to cross the hotel lounge"—as in their hotel lobby Fred mistakes the circular elevator indicator for a clock and follows the dial to set his wristwatch without noticing that it is moving. In the room, tipsy Emily notices a package on the mantel and begs to see it. He has bought her a luscious peignoir, which she now holds up demurring that she couldn't wear it. This is an overt little nod to *Blackmail*, where Anny Ondra's Alice holds up a tutu with the same coyness.

The theater introduces the problem of appearance and performance, suggesting the delicate interplay between being or merely seeming (pretending) to be one of the Uppers, especially if one's ability to broadcast a new status is impaired some: at the station as they departed London, Fred was passed by a workmate who helpfully warned, "Hurry up, old man, you'll be late for the office." We are receiving a mini-essay on the status of the *parvenu*. Fred and Emily have never had *money* before, and now that they have it the substance is as strange, as remote, as unfamiliar to them as the East is going to be. If the journey eastward is a voyage to "Home," at this instant Home is financial ability coupled with innocence on one side, illusion on the other, all energized by the desire not to be who (and where) one used to be.

TO THE FAR AWAY

Michel Foucault writes of a familiar theme revivified by the mystics of the fifteenth century:

> the motif of the soul as a skiff, abandoned on the infinite sea of desires, in the sterile field of cares and ignorance, among the mirages of knowledge, amid the unreason of the world—a craft at the mercy of the sea's great madness, unless it throws out a solid anchor, faith, or raises its spiritual sails so that the breath of God may bring it to port. (10)

The skiff in our case, if not quite a *Narrenschiff* then at least a vessel filled with bored zanies and well-groomed strangers on the hunt, features, like all containers of its type, as a closed form in a dangerous field. Once it has sailed, the ship becomes one's province, one's society, one's hiding place, and one's Adventureland. The voyager does not "get away" for a breather, but takes a breather on deck, at the heavy railing, gazing out to the unbounded prospect of the sea. Very early on Emily is doing that by moonlight, when a tall, dignified-looking man strides up with a pipe smoking in his mouth. This is Commander Gordon. Debonair, certainly. Skilled at social moves, as we can see by watching him delicately pose himself in Emily's precinct but then gently shuttle in her direction. How is your husband feeling? he asks somewhat peremptorily, in this way signaling (a) that he is aware she has a husband; (b) that he is aware her husband is indisposed (unlikely to interrupt); (c) that he makes bold, openly, to stand in her husband's place. Fine, says Emily, who also muses she likes to see people enjoying themselves, but here Hitchcock gives a stunning cut to Fred tucked under the blankets, his face the greenest thing that has ever been photographed in black and white. Is she keeping to herself the extent of his indisposition, or is she blissfully unaware? A steward comes in to urge Fred to have a little something and flashes a menu card that we, too, are given opportunity to see—rustling some empathy, perhaps, for his utterly nauseated condition. The print lifts up from the card and flies into our sickened faces, dishes Fred's "good fortune" has made him entirely incapable of enjoying:

> Pea Soup   Clear Barley Broth
> Lobster Mayonnaise
> Boiled Leg of Pork
> Creamed Carrots
> French Fried Potatoes
> Cream Sherry Trifle
> Macaroni au Gratin
> Coffee (Turkish)
> Gorgonzola Cheese
> Biscuits

"Ask my wife to get me a grape."[18] But in a reprise edit we stand on deck at the empty railing to watch Emily and the Commander now striding away in the far glimmers, arm in arm.

The ship is on the Mediterranean, passengers frolicking, children racing on deck, bathers in the pool, sailors on the bridge, engines pumping energetically, the waves happily sloshing past, and Fred is still imprisoned in no-man's land. Emily perches in wicker with the Commander, sunlight dripping upon them. In a disturbing echo of *Blackmail*, when he shows her a snapshot of himself sitting on the veranda of his cottage in Indonesia she draws with his pen a crude cartoon of herself sitting beside him. With giggly smiles she has come to a realization: "You're just a man and not my husband. So if you get bored of me you can just get up and walk away." But she goes on. "I love Fred and he loves me.... But when I talk to him I'm always afraid of saying something foolish. He's terribly clever." Gordon protests. "And I'm not?"

He puts a hand to his face. "It's a very lucky thing we're not in love, isn't it."

"Love is a very difficult thing, Mr Gordon.... I don't think it makes people brave like it says in the books. I think it makes them timid."

She is still holding his pen. He narrows his eyes and begs for an honest answer, white duck trousers, navy blazer, the omnipresent pipe. "Are you trying to ... pull my leg?" But then, as he becomes apologetic, Hitchcock jumps back to a medium long shot in which, had we not noticed it when they coupled by the rail at night time we can hardly fail now to see that he is a person with very long legs.[19] Suddenly a chummy interruption from a bluff man emerging from the lounge, taking Emily for "Mrs Gordon." She becomes serious. So does Gordon. As the scene slowly fades to black they are looking into each other's faces not as the emotional surfaces of intimate others but as the masks each will wear in the ship's public parade. Not only performance in itself, then, but the acknowledgment that performance exists and then the recognition of that acknowledgment. Yes, there are masks and yes, we are wearing them.

Dinner over, and Fred still abed, they are sitting again but now in formal dress. Another interruption, this time by a somewhat flitty woman we have seen a few times racing about the boat. To a "comic" muted trumpet cue, this gossip takes a seat between them. "It's just struck me. I have the very thing for your poor dear husband," not that anyone has informed her about the husband in our sight. He's the talk of the "town"? This is a nervous, bespectacled, very richly dressed "waif" type not, we may guess, as old as she looks, full of unreflective enthusiasms and sudden half-thoughts. A Shakespearean Fool but also something of a beast: Caliban, perhaps. And for Emily, of course, a female companion to at least temporarily take Gordon's place yet also not a woman who is interested in Emily at all.

What sort of companion could this be? Bohemian, certainly, which might suggest at least a craving to be fond of the arts. One of those who make swift but careful observations of human behavior—appearance and manner, as Erving Goffman suggested (in *The Presentation of Self in Everyday Life*)—in order to predict, to relish, to be entertained. Here for instance is a beautiful young sylph who claims a husband sick in bed but consorts with the elegant Commander—what is she to be labeled? Does she substantiate on paper the riches she displays? She seems a little innocent for a seasoned traveler and if, traveling, she is not seasoned then how high can she possibly be (since elevation leads to seasoning)? The quirky visitor is more eccentric than noble, flirts somewhat too quickly, shuffles too quickly, comments too quickly to allow for serious inspection. If she is the Fool of this piece, should we listen very carefully to her every syllable? Fred, meanwhile, by his indisposition and moroseness is not only making possible but actually instigating the romantic escapade on which Emily is launched. A perfectly open contradiction here to the too-worn Victorian conceit of the libidinous husband venting himself in "houses of ill repute" while his demure *femme* lingers in domestic imprisonment. Peter Gay comments acerbically on Dr. Otto Adler,

> who in 1904 published *The Defective Sexual Feelings of Women*, trying to substantiate his thesis with case reports. They include patients he had brought to orgasm during an examination, and others whom every open-eyed observer would have qualified as beset by potent, if frustrated or somewhat specialized, erotic longings. It may be a platitude that those who will not see will remain blind, but it is true. (83)

And sagaciously on Freud, who

> took the neuroses of his female patients as representative of respectable Victorian sexuality; one reason I have written this book has been to refute, or at least to complicate, this all-encompassing judgment. We have seen plentiful and sound evidence that frigidity among middle-class women was not so prevalent as Freud believed; he was on more solid ground as a theorist and a clinician than as a critic of the bourgeoisie. (139)

Through Emily's flirtation, something she takes rather seriously, Hitchcock is revealing an astute regard for female sexuality as natural and real, a view he would not later compromise in his Freudian epic *Spellbound* (1945), in *North by Northwest* (1959), or elsewhere. Emily's tentative bond to the flibbertigibbet Fool and her spellbound bond to the elegant bachelor go hand in hand, since both constitute adventures in a domain very far removed from the cozy but entirely limited home life she and Fred had led together. We will see later that the Fool has eyes on the Commander, too.

ITINERARY

The unfolding of the story parallels the unfolding of the exploration as the voyage takes Fred and Emily from the Mediterranean, by way of Port Said and the Suez Canal to Ceylon (now Sri Lanka) and Singapore. The strangers who populate public modes of travel are invoked again and again: our Spinster / Old Maid / Fool (Elsie Randolph); a trio of athletic women who march up and down the deck, day and night, in army lockstep; and a fabulously wealthy Princess (Betty Amann) who catches Fred's eye once he is deckside again and soon becomes his precious treasure. Debonair and polished, the Commander has fully befriended Emily but is also discernably accustomed to meeting pleasant-looking and unfamiliar women in places like this. It becomes evident to her that he is falling in love (he is old enough to be her father) and she fears, in light of Fred's dallying with the Princess, that her affections are being turned as well. A sea change. Still, early in the twentieth century, proper London was prudent and cautious about the voyage to the East. The Victorian sentiment (the Queen sent the Prince of Wales out in 1862) still held: if one was "well surrounded and ... never allowed to go out alone, and [was] moreover constantly kept reminded of all that is right and good, the Queen does not see how it is possible ... to get into mischief" (Dennison).

At Singapore, not far from his country estate, the Commander begs Emily to join him for a wonderful future. Let go of Fred, he beckons; the man is an idiot, the laughing stock of the entire ship, because in reality (as, presumably, everyone but Fred and Emily know) the Princess isn't a princess, she's a destitute nobody preying on any victim she can find, a pathetic impostor. Emily, deeply torn, but finally seeing her duty to dear, sad, crestfallen, hoodwinked Fred, leaves this aging Casanova and returns, in a kind of limbo, to their hotel.

We see Fred in the deep background, cleaning himself up at a sink, and the Princess bent over her vanity primping. She hears a knock at the door. It must be the waiter with the bill, she announces. She is peering at herself in the glass, and we see that behind her, crystal clear, Emily has stepped timidly into the room. "Fred... ," she calls, and when he steps forward to "get the bill" he sees his wife. The Princess carefully makes to turn and discover Emily's presence for the first time. "Oh!" A strange and touching gracefulness. She offers to let them speak alone, and tells Fred she will await him downstairs. As he steps away to "put on a shirt" the two women are side by side, their faces almost touching but their eyes aligned away from each other's. "Thank you ... Princess," whispers Emily, and the Princess, first smiling a little, then sneering a little, then fixing an expression that is both a smile and a sneer and also neither, says with definition, "You did not *go* with him! Little fool! You *damned* little fool!"

Now, game time. The lethal game, "Truth or Dare":

FRED (fiddling with his shirt): I was just fixing up to go bathing with the Princess. You don't want to come, do you? I thought you'd be going somewhere with Gordon.

EMILY (empty): He's gone.

FRED: He's what?

EMILY: He's gone to his home, up country.

FRED (triumphant): Ah! Fancy that!

EMILY (plainly): He wanted to take me with him.

FRED (alarm raised): What's that?

EMILY: He loves me ...

Emotion flooding, she makes it clear, too clear for his taste, that she'd have gone with Gordon if it hadn't been for him ... that Gordon would have made her happy. Fred is incensed.

EMILY: He started to show me you as the outside world sees you, not as I see you, blinded by love and all this long time together.... He said that you were a sham. Of course I recognize your faults. Whereas before I'd always dressed you up in all kinds of silly virtues.

FRED (sarcastic, but stung): Very much obliged, I'm sure.

EMILY: I saw that I was a wife for you, that without me you'd be lost.

And now, sword withdrawn, she poises herself for the lunge.

EMILY: You've got to get all this straightened out and not wreck everything through this trip.... She's a sham.

FRED (spitting with defensiveness): You don't tell me! Is anybody or anything real, then? And in what way is the Princess a sham, if it's not troubling you too much?

Emily is loosening her strictures, possibly in confusion for her own feelings with the Commander and possibly because her commitment to Fred has become inflamed. But her composure does melt, and her gaze shifts wildly:

EMILY (forcefully): She's a common cheap adventuress. And she only threw her hat at you because you were the one man on board weak enough to—

FRED (in fury): Shut up! Shut up! (*He throws her onto the bed*) ... I go to the Princess. My things can be sent on. Goodbye. (*He leaves.*)

Her face is running with tears. A knock at the door. She dries her cheeks and turns to receive a letter from an attendant. As the handwritten page comes onscreen we hear the Commander's voice reading it, the page becoming blurry as she weeps:

GORDON (off):

Dear—

Knowing you—I accept your verdict.

You have made your choice and I see the way of it. I don't know much about love, how long it lasts or what the remedies are, but I love you,

Emily, so much that I can't write any more—only blessings and prayers for you.

Gordon

He has enclosed the photograph with her artwork.

But now Fred has returned, chastened as a schoolboy. "Don't you dare say I told you so!" The Princess, it seems, has caught the train for Rangoon:

> FRED (stunned): She's gone. She was a fraud. She thanks me for my company and says her father kept a cleaning shop in Berlin. The swine! ... What a fool she's made of me! What a fool!
>
> EMILY (his loyal friend): Poor Fred!
>
> FRED (vicious): And I tell you again, if you say I told you so I'll strangle you, I swear I will. Wish I could strangle her! And all the time she was just a rotten streetwalker.

Sound of a band. From the window we look down past Fred. A marching band is blaring out "Nearer My God to Thee," with a bevy of dancing girls in tow.

But the weather can always get worse. It turns out that beyond his nonsensical peccadilloes, Fred took the liberty of giving the "Princess" a thousand pounds of his and Emily's money, and she has fled with it. He and Emily have little alternative but to buy passage away from Singapore on a tramp steamer, hardly re-accommodated to one another but headed away from the maelstrom of their adventure. This boat goes into the mist—shades of *King Kong* (1933)—and, rather abruptly as it feels, swamps.

The wreck is quickly abandoned except for the two Hills, locked in their cabin. In the morning Emily discovers that the shining porthole will open and leads Fred through it onto the empty deck, mist crawling in, the massive mechanism of the ship now entirely disabled and silenced and listing, nothing but an object floating and slowly going under, the outside world entirely eradicated.

But here approaches a Chinese junk! While Fred and Emily eagerly take shelter on its deck, a horde of workers jump silently onto the crippled ship to ransack it. And now they are sailing away, amid a company they entirely fail to comprehend, true Others, silent Others, from the (until now silent) Other Side of the World. The voyage to the East has led them into entirely uncharted seas. Given the choice between racism and anthropology—as Leslie Fiedler presents it in *The Return of the Vanishing American*—they choose the former, huddling together in self-protection from these uncommunicative (thus malevolent?) strangers with their inexplicable habits and taciturn (might one dare to suggest, respectful?) manners:

> The White thinker ... finds himself becoming either (like de las Casas) a missionary or (like Montaigne) an anthropologist, falling prey either to the Spanish passion or to the French.... even in Montaigne (*"chacun appelle barbarie ce qui n'est pas de son usage..."*) the seeds of the *Encyclopédie* are already germinating. Reflecting on the Indians of "la France Antarctique," which is to say, present-day Brazil, he reacts like a true scientist confronted with a new subject for study; he recognizes, in fact, that the invention of America implies the invention of a new science: the systematic investigation of the *other* man, the *other* culture. (41)

Voyaging through a merciful fade-out and fade-in, white Fred and Emily soon find themselves alighting from a cab outside their residence in predominantly white London on a misty evening (as though the mist surrounding the junk has spread across the world to make even familiar London a zone of strange otherness). The char has their dinner ready on the table. It is easy enough now to fall into a picayune marital tiff as typical of conventional English middle-class life as anything could be, about whether Fred could find a way to fit a baby pram through the corridor outside or should commit himself to working harder, get a promotion, and find them a bigger flat. End of story.

Except that voyage stories do not really end.

As film works by moving on and moving on, it being the moving on that makes for the motion picture experience; and since a voyage—not to say the voyage of life—fills time in a similarly progressive way, the sort of escapade our heroes have embarked upon is perfectly appropriate for the medium and comes to a conclusion that is nothing but arbitrary. In effect, viewers have been traveling with the film as Fred and Emily have with their adventure; for all, travel and travail. That Fred and Emily should seem to have an itinerary is hardly illogical, it offers an order of service: a stop in the harbor to admire old architecture, buildings that suggest timelessness—

> EMILY (to Fred, pensively): To think that place has been there all these years. All those strange people having their babies, dying, cooking their funny meals. Strange ... It's been there all these years.

—a stop for shopping in a bazaar; journeys in horse-drawn carriages in old imperial outposts under the blazing sun and the waving palms. The shipboard experience as we are carried from point to point is a journey within a journey, offering so many hitherto untasted delights and always, since the sea is never constant, in a different but indeterminate place: the charge of the unfamiliar, the invocation of "friendly" manners among unknown, yet still recognizable strangers whom one blithely takes as unmet familiars, the extraordinary oceanic vistas, chance encounters with attractive figures who may lead one along whatever unmapped routes. Then, surrounding all these events and metamorphoses, forming a kind of skin, the marital journey itself, beginning in abject tedium and hopelessness (a present which is already its own future), then falling into unpredictability, thence to rapture, thence to complication, thence to peril. (That wavering arm in the hotel lobby clock indicated an elevator that was going up, coming down, going up, coming down.[20])If in the end there must come what seems an almost predictable return (yet a return we never actually predict) to homely safety, now bustling with energy and plans, now reenergized by distance, it still yields uncanniness, quite literally a sense of *vacation*.

Anyone could tell a story like this, straightforward, in a way conventional, elegant in its simplicity. Man and woman go off to see the world; lose each other; find each other again. Hitchcock of course goes far beyond—or better, far into—such simplicity. For one thing, by alternating carefully composed location setups in the East with close-framed shipboard encounters he jumps the viewer back and forth between two quite contradictory kinds of view. In the first, what might be called the *action*, as we see the turbulent wake of the ship or its busy smokestacks, or the city of Port Said gleaming in the sun, or a bustling marketplace, we have a sense of watching a detailed and accurate travelogue, of actually moving through time and space from an established location—the ship's decks—to exciting ports of call. Shots looking down from the deck as the ferries are filled with passengers going ashore; distant establishing shots of the tiny ship upon the vast sea. In the second perspective, we are caught up with personality, intrigue, possibility, eventfulness: in short, social drama. The collision in space of bodies as yet objective and unknown to each other. We thus roll back and forth through a repeated contradiction: the person-ality of individual characters, their histories known or speculated upon, their unfolding futures, counterpoised against a global and confusing geography busy with uncanny cultural traffic. There is a world bigger than what is outside the window; multitudes are living in ways we cannot imagine. Have been living that way "all these years." Stunning visions of place coupled with ambiguous visions of people.

A HITCHCOCKIAN PASSPORT

Hitchcock "docks" at two "ports" worth special notice: social class and its conundrums, and the particular difficulties and dangers posed by mystery. Although *Rich and Strange* is not plotted out as a screen mystery story (a whodunit, a ghost tale), under its surface, through and through, lingers the unknown or the only superficially known, a darkness covered by a questionable surface. And although social class, being omnipresent, can hardly be missing from a complex tale of personalities and placements, still, class identities, conflicts, and implications are always potently charging the atmosphere and the action here.

Class

There is a meticulous shipboard presentation of stratified labor. We see not only languid travelers, affectedly bored, seeking a toy to fiddle with in the rather enormous and empty (functional) space of the ship; but also paid workers, the captain and his uniformed crew on the bridge, a first officer spying the waters near the hull through his binoculars, a seaman using the Chadburn to communicate with the engine room, and the sweating navvies among the pistons of the engines, slaving in heat and relative darkness.[21] As they stroll the deck one evening, building up the tickles of their romance, the Commander and Emily pass an open doorway through which we see a quartet of workers gambling in their off-time, shirtless, raucous, entirely without the decorum they would be forced to show when on duty. The pleasure seekers themselves (the *clientele*) are very *dressed*. It does not do in this context to bring one's sloppy clothing, if one even has such material. Long gowns, jewelry, silks, and satins. The Princess has an outlandishly large chapeau, straight out of Toulouse-Lautrec (a clue Fred is unequipped to pick up). The men are in nappy blazers with white ducks, all country club, all built to show off status but also to cleanly retire from affront so that the magnetic personal features can shine through.

Hitchcock, who always prepares his cadences, introduced the theme of class differentiation at several points early in the film, quite beyond the introductory passage in which Fred's demeaning job is explicitly spelled out and the Hills' home life crisply shown in its limitations. In Paris, the contrast between the Folies Bergère with its posh habituées and the Moulin Rouge with its collection of sights bordering on the world of Dada and surrealism, charging and stunning a broader and lower, if still monied audience eager for splash and twinkle, for the tease of the uplifted leg rather than the scathing play with artful nudity one could have seen, only a few years earlier, with Josephine Baker:

> The show was no challenge for her; in fact, in a scene called "Plantation," she was dressed in overalls and white socks almost entirely copied from a *Revue Nègre* costume. In another sketch, she went bare-breasted, draped in a few ropes of pearls, a bunch of red feathers plastered to her backside. (Baker and Chase 146)

In the Hitchcock design one is given only hope and promise, not taste, of the very esoteric and very high, the aromatic rumor, receiving something that may look very much like a paradise but is in truth a reflection of climbers' dreams. Consider the vertical pressures of class:

[1] Fred Hill, a man at least four times presented in relation to social inferiors, each time occupying what he believes to be a status higher than the servant's:

> In London he is polite if aloof with his char but increasingly abrasive and demeaning to other servers as time goes by and he has begun to acclimatize himself to "being rich." Since the film has established him as (only) a lowly clerk subservient to the whims of his

employers, it might easily seem to an unreflective audience that for Hitchcock the social world is simplistically binary, a haven of Uppers resting on the laborious shoulders of Lowers hardly ever seen in sunlight (H. G. Wells's caricature of Eloi and Morlocks in *The Time Machine* [1895]). But things are more complex. In the world of *Rich and Strange*, everyone we meet is conceivably above someone else and below still others; that is, go as low as you dare but someone will be lower. The vertical ladder of British social organization is never fully shown, surely never soundly implied, but this ostensibly "solid" arrangement is revealed in all its precariousness on the tramp steamer—an explicitly "cheap" passage, much "lower" than what the Marseilles-to-Singapore ship afforded—when the water takes over (a splendid long effects shot where the junk cruises toward the camera while in the distance, to a diabolical whistle, the steamer goes under) and all persons are rendered equal in their fear, equally challenged upon the (true) surface of the sea. Stranded with Fred and Emily on the junk, we find social relations entirely indiscernible. Fred is the arbitrary figure standing in for the fundamental confusion of social class in an age of mobility. He presumes to superiority, being in fact nothing but a worker himself: from Hitchcock's point of view we are all of us nothing but workers, but our projects differ in scope and range and reward.

In the lobby of the Paris hotel, stupefied on liquor, he is comically waylaid by that elevator indicator, but when the car arrives and the doors open he leads Emily off in another direction without so much as a nod of affirmation to the erstwhile young operator. Not a quick smile, not even an admission the young worker is standing there, alive, in front of him.

In bed on the ship, he is peremptory, even impolite with the steward whose entrance to his cabin is for one purpose only: to bring some good cheer, and hopefully a lovely meal, that will rouse this poor man from his unhappy stupor. The steward is a kind, helpful, devoted, and quite efficient worker, hiding no resentment, speaking with curt (effective) warmth. But Fred dismisses him with the surly (if nauseated) comment about the grape. This is a very clear demonstration of disdain for those whose labor keeps one's own "ship" afloat yet who are not to be seen or acknowledged laboring.

In the Singapore hotel room, he more than once barks scathingly at a Chinese cleaner who tries to enter the room with his mop. Here is not only a disregard for the vital presence of another person but a wholesale denigration of this young man to subhuman status, because of his race. The anthropological attitude, as Fiedler calls it, demands accepting the other as equally human but living according to cultural rules as yet unrecognized; a single God stands above all, while racism actually pushes the Other into an identity one's singular God would not recognize as human, an identity that is beyond saving. Saving or condemning, the two paths. And Fred has become a condemner.

[2] Then our Fool, Miss Emory, wearing a coherent surface of social discomfort—she is profoundly nearsighted—and displaying the insatiable curiosity of the gossip. Again and again, without warning or invitation, she intrudes on other people's privacies without apparent awareness, offering little more than apology and excuse for a sloppiness she is unable to stanch. But is she not, in this, something of the archetypical *parvenu,* the figure not *of* the society but one who has fallen into it, always giving off the wrong signals, if signals at all, and, extremely unsure, articulating a self too boisterously, too loudly, too repetitively, too emphatically, and all without actual relation? The social signaling trouble is significant since in a situation like this ship, with its assembled company, social signaling is imperative and central. This one chirps a constant refrain, directed here, there, and everywhere: "Good EEEEVening!" just as though others eagerly recognize and appreciate her and welcome her presence (as they do not), as though her wishes are received with good nature. She has no real friends on board, yet has "befriended" everyone. At a rug dealer's in the Port Said bazaar she gives two key signs of blithe ignorance: she tests (that is, examines) a prospective rug by standing on it and bouncing up and down on her toes, as though some Persian rugs have more "give" than others and this feature is the cognoscenti's way of distinguishing between them. (The cognoscenti want information, not feel.) And nosing a hanging rug she demonstrably finds the odor abysmal (Persian rugs are very

often cleaned with urine), in this way distancing herself sensually from the flavors of the Far East she has paid so much to explore. This person is not without funds but she is desperate for society, desperate, especially, to connect with an available male, as we see from her exaggerated and embarrassing attentions to the Commander pressed without letup even in the face of his disattention. Fred seems not to notice her most of the time. Yet she plays significantly into the film's marital disruption subtheme, contrasting against beautiful Emily now gone dreamy-eyed with the Commander and the sultry, intoxicating Princess who is a marriage killer if ever was.

[3] The shipboard crowd is a shifting congregation where no real society may form *but where real society may be imitated every day*. Shipboard companions are temporary friends, after all. When Toffler writes in *Future Shock*, "Relationships that once endured for long spans of time now have shorter life expectancies. It is this abbreviation, this compression, that gives rise to the almost tangible feeling that we live, rootless and uncertain, among shifting dunes" (45–46), he is reflecting a passage away from more deeply rooted pre- and early-capitalist relationships toward a frenetic social form in which organization is temporary and flexible, in which every moment is a voyage from a now vanished port to an invisible future (see, too, Bennis and Slater). In England by the early 1930s the movement to a temporary society was underway, at least in planning offices, where in the mid-1950s action was generated. Given shifting and fluctuation, the unrelenting social mobility aboard ship, our Fool is hopelessly old-fashioned in believing that if only she projects the correct etiquette that etiquette will place and save her coherently. Seeing that her etiquette is failing she raises her voice, becomes a kind of carnival barker in a shuffling crowd. We find her most at home, indeed, in the Carnival sequence, where she dresses as Little Bo Peep (who has lost her sheep). But her constant attempt to fit where she doesn't fit is primarily a reflection of the Hills, who are only less obtrusively doing the same (and Fred more than Emily); because of that unobtrusiveness—which is entirely realistic in the context of the Hills' uninitiated status—one needs the exaggerations of the flirt for the contrast that makes for visibility.

Miss Emory acts with high amplitude so that we will inevitably take her as a reflection of what has come to be a commonplace feeling of hopelessness about class in England: hopelessness because the hopes of the bourgeoisie are confounded and blocked. She calls up, by sharply contradicting it, a centuries-old attitude, far outmoded now, when everyone "knew his place," place was fixed, and there were no unsatisfied hopes to be frustrated. The rich already had treasures. The poor weren't going to get any.

[4] The hapless clumsiness and ineffectual posturing of Fred Hill trying to "climb the hill" of class would swiftly have turned the film into farce were it not for Henry Kendall's majestically delicate mime and Hitchcock's devious and brilliant architecture. If cinema in its very early days was a working-class entertainment (see Gomery), by the advent of the sound era, with increased exhibition expense and increased ticket prices the audience was increasingly dominated by those who were neither so poor they had to use up their lives in labor nor so wealthy they could have concerts given in the salons of their country estates. This new middle class was itching to climb, just like Fred dragging Emily in tow. The two of them are their viewers, in short. And knowing of his audience's penchant for looking up, to more golden futures if not only to the screen's shine, Hitchcock presents a bumbling hero and his put-upon wife situated in such a way as to mobilize audience sympathy. We want the Hills to succeed on their voyage, although one would be hard pressed to determine either what success could be for them, an actual change of class being out of the question, or how enthused one might become about their infidelities. When Emily has a chance with the man we take to be a highly placed dignitary, and when Fred finds himself pursuing a Princess, we are hoping for them a little—pulled in two contradictory directions at once—even as we fear for the breakup of their marriage, that bastion of bourgeois virtue. We rest upon a wish that if they must be disappointed they will at least not fall on their faces. It is only because we are rooting for Fred—if not for his romance then at least for his ability to convince people of his importance—that we can be drawn into his intriguing problem of being confounded in desire, the fate of forgetting oneself as one travels.

Mystery

But, as we might have anticipated (indeed, as we were warned) in the Théâtre du Moulin Rouge, where far more of the stage entertainment was shown than necessary to confirm Fred and Emily's presence, performance, masquerade, staginess, and deception are incessantly standing in the limelight in this film. We are put in a position to notice, for example, when, boarding the ship from the gangway, the Commander is greeted with comradely effusion by a group of uniformed ship's officers, who recognize him as a "regular," someone with whom they have had chummy encounters many times before. Much later, if we remember this, we can look back and wonder whether his entire dance with Emily is a semi-professional routine. Although he meets her without giving any sign of the local knowledge he must have, presenting himself as "just" a fellow passenger here for adventure in its purest sense, we must ask whether this man always befriends a "going" young beauty when he comes aboard, whether in his discourse with Emily about friendship and love and her pulling his leg he is rehearsing a scene played many times before with a new partner who is an ingenue. When the two of them pass by the card-playing crew at that open doorway, is the Commander remembering having joined their card game on several previous voyages?

Given that she constantly sounds an undertone of the ingenue's innocent trepidation—until the steamer sinking—Emily won't notice, and won't be looking to notice, an act. In the Singapore carriage, when she dismisses him and the prospects he has offered, the Commander gives two blunt signals that are both camouflaged: first, he has not *discovered somehow* that the Princess is an impostor, *he knows it*. Notwithstanding that we have never seen him with her privately, that he can have had no special access to her away from our sight, still he knows about this charlatan from outside the action yet inside the world of the story, presumably from other voyages. Just as he has been on board before so has that woman, "princessing" a squadron of vulnerable blokes eager to climb a ladder that wasn't really there. She can smell them coming, as the Commander knows (perhaps all too well, because he has a trained nose, too). Bumbling and unprotected as he is, Fred cannot be improved upon as a perfect mark, exactly as Emily finally tells him.

Next, as in that carriage Emily protests that she is worried about what will happen now to poor humiliated and defrauded Fred, the Commander drops his cheery mask, becomes as cold-faced as an executioner: "I don't know *and I don't care.*" A mark of surprising incivility, odd if not out of place for a man keeping the stance to which he has been pretending. That letter he writes Emily: tenderly handwritten, and presented through his voice-over, offering her his prayer, and also enclosing that telltale photograph in which she placed herself at his side, a kind of chiding reminder. We may fall into a swoon at the touching pathos of this letter; but such an item is easy to produce and having been produced be produced again. One can recollect how very general its comments are. Toffler points to "the era of the temporary product, made by temporary methods, to serve temporary needs" (73). The typewriter the uncle used for his letter offered a temporary method of communication, keys that could say anything anywhere; but the formality and cliché of the Commander's written note, though it suggests private intimacy, may work in the same mechanical way.

The Princess is the character fingered, accused, thrown into flight. But who, among those we meet, is not an impostor?

DESTINATIONS

Can we say this voyage, or this Voyage, ever ends, at least before the screen goes dark?

The formal destination of Fred and Emily's journey *East of Shanghai* (as in the United States this film was billed, public familiarity with Shakespeare not presumed) is, finally, not really a destination at all, nor is it, truthfully speaking east of Shanghai even though on the magical junk a point east of Shanghai may very well be our destination (for the strange duration of a cinematic ellipsis). We are given a view of land approaching, but no hint of what it is. None of the sailors on the junk speak English, even if they do speak *human*, even if they recognize two living people in desperation and give rescue without comment or question. Where can we say we find ourselves as viewers, when this is all done?

Where, indeed, is the place in which all of this journey and all its parts are set? The place through which motion happens ... the place to which one finds direction. This will be a logical construct, a formalization and a bounding, a site and set of pressures that help privilege some outcomes over others. "All art partakes of the Spirit of Place in which it is produced," writes D. H. Lawrence in his *Studies in Classic American Literature* (167), but can we not say, more than only art, "All experience"? It is place, finally, that characterizes an event, gives it proportion and depth and atmosphere. When Hitchcock's title card, prefacing the final stop on the journey, informs us that Emily prefers people to places, and in this way gives a hint that we may drop aside the various ports of call to which this journey has brought us and concentrate instead on the idiosyncratic characters and the figurative place they inhabit with each other, we must remember not only the import of the comment but also how those words are filling a cinema screen and how, here and in all films, the vision consistently frames people in their territories, established or temporary. A more pressing way to say this: always the vision frames a flicker of emotion set upon and transforming the stage of the embodied face.

The ship is Fred and Emily's territory, their stage, for the duration of the journey, just as their tiny flat was in the film's beginning and will be again at the film's end; every migration landward is a straining upon the leash pinioned to the ship, a tug upon the anchor, and every disembarkation is followed by a re-boarding, until the end, when another journey commences. The ship that beckons, the ship that bears. The deck upon the sea. The island. With broad flaring funnels, pristine lifeboats dangling, and carefully swept decks on which one may sicken into a *chaise*, the ship is all one's world. Ropes coiled, sky lush, motion incessant. Motion incessant both seaward and filmic. And also a refuge for all those whose lives were unbearable on land:

> For they did exist, these boats that conveyed their insane cargo from town to town. Madmen then led an easy wandering existence. The towns drove them outside their limits; they were allowed to wander.... In 1399, seamen were instructed to rid the city of a madman who walked about the streets naked. (Foucault 6)

Lives unbearable to civilized others, who expelled them? Or lives unbearably suffering the routine exigencies of civilized life?

Is it not a voyage *away from civilization* that we experience on board with our heroes? They leave behind the lacings of conventional union, the marriage vows undertaken in the name of a secular (if not also a religious) authority well institutionalized, and the obligations to fit themselves into the economy, not to say the deft maneuvers by which they do so, Emily with her sewing machine and application of talent by room light and Fred with his noxious position, over leaving which he can gloat to himself at the railway station because he knows that now, being late for work is out of the question. They can leave behind time, as in regulated time, the "fixing of our experience of time which constitutes the dominant ideological form of time in commoditized society," ... consistent with Kracauer's understanding of mass culture in the 1920s as, at least in part, the negation of unorganized, unstructured time. In this context, boredom becomes the "only proper occupation" if not a radical resistance to the media's incessant production of images and sounds (Doane 162, quoting Chanan 41 and Kracauer 334). Kracauer goes further, famously, in an essay that could have been a pretext for the shipboard sequences of the Hill voyage. "People today who still have time for boredom and yet are not bored are certainly just as boring as those who never get around to being bored" (331). When he was at labor, Fred surely never got around to being bored; nor did Emily with her constant arranging of the flat for the tidiness we cannot help seeing. But now, *voilà*, they have journeyed into boredom, yet also a particular boredom, to which they have not fully adapted since it is not a customary state of affairs in their class. They flit around mentally, searching with desperate eyes for people to meet, since their placement now is so provisional, with so many waystations forbidding and incomprehensible.

But Hitchcock brings *placement* to a crisis.

Where can any of his viewers find a viewing self? Walking into the theater where *Rich and Strange* is showing, from the rain-pelted street, they notice the raindrops on their sleeves, then settle into seats smelling of yesterday's patrons, nibble their chocolate, stare with all expectation and with no expectation at that white daunting rectangle. How to become the being it is necessary to become, floating in the air above the ledger where the hand writes and having written, pauses?

On the junk there is a startling, very disconcerting moment. One of the Chinese (crewmen, passengers?—we do not know), scurrying away from the sinking steamer, became entangled by foot in a guyline and is slowly, as the ship goes under, being dropped upside-down into the sea. Fred and

Emily stare helplessly at this ghastly apparition, but then in a sharp jump to a profile side view Hitchcock shows the whole gang on this junk looking off left at the sight, preternaturally silent, without gesture. Whoever this victim is, friend or foe, esteemed or degraded, the survivors have cut themselves off so as to observe in stunned neutrality. In the truth of the fiction, they are separated from this poor man by only a few yards of sea and could move to rescue him, but seem also to be separated by a different *kind* of distance, as are we watching in the darkness. Here the drowning is to be suffered but the viewer's sensibilities are neatly rescued by the sight of Emily tucked into Fred's neck and Fred watching in a shock sufficient for both of them. It is as though he is pronouncing that watching is all one can do, a solid truth for us, to be sure, but not, we would wish to believe, for him.

Watching is all we can do. In his *Frame Analysis* Goffman tells us, "Watching is doing" (381).

Back in the middle-class apartment from which we thought to emerge and see the world. Back in the everyday, which is the pattern of life, after all. Back in England, back on the island "famous beyond all other islands in the world" (Blaeu 59). Back, too, in a rhythm of supposition: possible futures, a new flat or not a new flat, this pathway or that one, yet always a path within the boundaries of the system, a path that if it accords with our desire (as Michel Mourlet said of cinema) also accords with the world as it can be envisioned if we envision it by the rules. You can travel, even travel far, but you are not going anywhere.

God made him, and therefore let him pass for a man.
—*The Merchant of Venice*, I.ii.56–57

A voluntary deliberation is always a deception.
—Sartre

An unfortunate commonplace of contemporary thought about Hitchcock is that his Grand Cinematic Experiment was *Rope* (1948) (the film that gives the appearance of having been photographed in one eighty-minute shot).[1] In truth he was an experimental spirit all the time, this in many different ways, and perhaps no case is more exemplary, or more stunning, than *Suspicion* (1941), a film he boldly opens as though it were a radio program. The screen is in pitch darkness (a *camera obscura*), so that it is not possible to make out forms or spatial arrangement. We hear a familiar, charming, extremely courteous male voice making excuse: "I beg your pardon. Was that your leg? I had no idea we were going into a tunnel. I thought the compartment was empty. I'm so sorry, I hope I didn't hurt you." The Cary

Grant twang, soft, mannered, never anything but to the point. The gentle flame of considerate politesse, our first exposure here in a cavern where no exposure is possible.

When after a few seconds of apologetic scrumbling the tunnel is left behind (but in this film is the dark tunnel ever left behind?), the window light reveals a cozy compartment already occupied by a young woman who sits reading while the young gentleman who was speaking finds his way into a seat facing her. Already by the mid-1860s, travel reading was "the general and sole activity of [railway] travelers" (Schivelbusch 68). As we watch these two fitting their bodies into this package, we may discern something that was a truism in late 1930s England, but that readers today might overlook or miscomprehend: both are dressed *for the country*. He is distinctively tweedy. She is in layers of tweed and wool. They may be coming from the city—they are in fact coming from London, as in a few seconds we will see on their tickets—but they are not city folk at heart. For them the city is a regrettable necessity, anything but the paradise Robert Browning's "Italian Person of Quality" espies:

> But the city, oh the city—the square with the houses! Why?
> They are stone-faced, white as a curd, there's something to take
>   the eye!
> Houses in four straight lines, not a single front awry;
> You watch who crosses and gossips, who saunters, who hurries by;
> Green blinds, as a matter of course, to draw when the sun gets high;
> And the shops with fanciful signs which are painted properly.
> ("Up at a Villa—Down in the City")

Oh, nothing at all like that.

The city and the country, then (and the train voyage to join them). Darkness and light. Raymond Williams writes that a key to understanding the problem of innocence "is the contrast of the country with the city and the court: here nature, there worldliness" (46). Urban etiquette is employed for the cramping train compartment, the antithesis of rambling fields under a cupola of sky that inspire an underpinning penchant to be among the shrubs and trees, where the rivulets flow (and where, Williams reminds us, it is through property relations that labor is organized). To bring matters to a dramatic head with pleasing swiftness: this is a first-class compartment on a British train (that is, a setting in which travelers are classed, one of the transportational mainstays in a nation bedrocked on social class). In all of Hitchcock's films, it is imperative to see social class in action in order to grasp the full weight of the work (for those who grow up in England class is not a landmark, it is an atmosphere), but when the subject is England, even, as here, seen from a base in Hollywood, one had better not neglect class indicators. It will turn out that we never wonder at all about the class of this young woman, and that we never stop wondering about the class of the new friend.

As we are to learn almost immediately, questions will be posed as to whether this man's ticket gives him proper access to this compartment—Tania Modleski, somewhat peremptorily in my view, labels him "lawless and irresponsible" (57)—but Hitchcock wishes to pose a much more profound puzzle. The ticket, its price, and its entitlements entirely to the side, does this man *belong* here? Is he proper, as he presents himself in the world, outside of the stub of paper he holds in his hand? Is there, in fact, a connection between propriety and paperwork, some genuine logic behind judging character and merit on the basis of systemic tokens like railway tickets (judging books by their covers)? Instantly as the light comes in, Hitchcock's camera makes unquestionably evident, unquestionably and gloriously, that these two are made for each other. If any man were to stumble in here in the dark, this is the one who should do it. One is immediately comforted, stabilized by the picture of them together, just to the point where the comfort and the stability are made questionable. From this encounter onward we will see the uncoiling of a "chain of evidence," "fact" following "fact" following "fact," that pulls against the support beams of our certainty. Pulls against a certainty prompted by a vision that could not be clearer. Can it be said we will be invited to voyage away from the clarity of a vision to a doubt about "realities"? Surely we will wonder how, if it is so very palpable and so very lambent, the picture of this man and this woman together can raise suspicion.

ON THE RAILS

It is not hard to suffer doubts at the beginning of our story (and our voyage), notwithstanding the chain of facts delivered our way in a (secure) railway compartment. Shall we call it a cast iron chain? A train of thoughts?

(a) We are on the Southern Railway: printed on ticket.

(b) The ticket permits travel from London Waterloo to Hazledene, which we will soon discover is in Sussex.

(c) There is a hunt, we will soon discover, at, or very nearby, Hazledene, since a hunt scene is the destination to which the train brings us.

(d) Like all trains, this one runs a route. If a horse-drawn carriage could move more or less anywhere in the early years of the nineteenth century, a train uses only its right-of-way. From his earliest childhood (as reported by Donald Spoto)[2] Hitchcock was obsessively devoted to the routes and schedules of the British train system. When he films trains in England, he is expressing knowledge about both geography and class and motivation, and more generally and excitingly about a kind of refined mechanism, like clockwork.

(e) In England the difference between a third-class carriage, to which Johnnie's ticket entitles him, and a first-class one is more than coin—in this case, coin that he doesn't happen to have. The first-class passenger has more quiet, more leisure, more privacy, and more upholstery.[3] And significant to first-class travelers (thus, of interest to us) is the sharply reduced likelihood of meeting anybody one doesn't already know.[4] Lina's ticket has probably been bought for her by a father who zealously guards his daughter's social encounters. The train guard's responsibility is to maintain the class boundary here, to at least behave, on behalf of the railway and of British high principle in general, as though he wouldn't dream of permitting that the happily ensconced Lina McLaidlaw might have to share her space with someone "who doesn't belong." But the structure here calls up more than a trainman's personal attitude: the company offers assurances to purchasers of first-class tickets that no one but another purchaser of a first-class ticket will be sharing their carriage. That is, the trainman's first reaction is that Johnnie must move.

In England it is not enough to occupy a spot. One must belong there.

But: this apparently simple little compartment scene is chockful of strange twists and revelations, answers, as it were, to doubts—doubts about appropriateness and social bonding, and doubts about realism:

[1] *Doubt as to belonging.* The needling issue that brings disturbance to the scene immediately, but that also prods the typical viewer all the way through this film: does Johnnie Aysgarth (Cary Grant) have *any rightful place*, specifically here in the compartment and generally at the side of someone like Lina McLaidlaw (Joan Fontaine)? Is he an interloper (that is, is the deep theme of the film the stranger's entrance to a civilized gathering)? If Johnnie doesn't belong, there is something louche about his presence in this little space, even by accident. And there is something rudely impertinent about his manner and behavior. Lina, who doesn't normally interact *at all* with people who are not in her class, is on the cusp here of not interacting with Johnnie, as we see when she signally turns her eyes back to her book, but there is something indeterminate about him, decidedly and ticklingly indeterminate.

Permit an address to this worry without delay: Johnnie actually *doesn't not* belong. He has not sneaked into a voyage that is unsuited to, incorrect or improper for, and rigorously blocked from (people like) him. There are quite a few clues on offer for putting this assessment together:

- Although at the moment he surely doesn't have the right ticket, he did know how to find the first-class carriage: not only a point of standing at the right part of the platform, as guided by staff, but doing so with the casual nonchalance of someone who never questions his rights and has never traveled any other way.[5]

- He doesn't have enough money on him, true, but he does not regard this paltry fact as a problem that merits his attention. What's money, after all, that anyone should care about it? (Is he a Mr Darcy?) He feels no compunction in asking a member of his own class to help him out for good nature's sake, and when, putting forward the most casual glance into her bag, he spies some postage stamps he has no compunction, either, about reaching for one. "There you are. That'll do. That stamp." She is only very slightly taken aback by the abruptness of his movement, neither offended nor presumed upon. The upper class is unified in the single respect that all its members possess a great deal more than they can estimate—land, title, history, (perhaps but not necessarily) money; they need pay no heed to wealth, their own or their interlocutors', when interacting with each other: what any one has they all have, to some recognizable degree—not only have, but have in spades, in fact, so that handing over a trifle here or there literally does not signify. She knows this, but so does he. It is to a middle-class audience, especially an American one fond of, but irremediably removed from, the British aristocracy that Johnnie's taking the postage stamp signifies. More than anyone in Britain watching with an understanding of class, American viewers find him outrageous, presumptuous, scheming, and generally untrustworthy. He is a purloiner, a prick in the side, a gate crasher. In fact he is merely doing *what one does*, acting as though the gate one has crashed isn't really there. Hitchcock, the Englishman, had come to America and seen its curious charms. He knew what social class was to the American mind: that is, what it *wasn't*.

- Yet Johnnie also knows how to affect an entirely amicable superiority over inferiors, even uniformed, authoritative, stern ones. As the conductor begrudgingly accepts the postage stamp and makes to exit, Johnnie offers up a trifle of sage advice: "It's legal tender, old boy. Write to your mother." Flip as it may sound, this suggestion has the merit of indicating an authentic use for postage stamps, thereby lending the conductor a feeling of security that he's really getting an object of value. But "write to your mother" goes further. "We are both grown men," it whispers, "and we are always guilty of neglecting our dear mothers; drop her a note." And even more, the snip indicates a reality Johnnie knows as well as the conductor does: that to the Railway the price difference of 5.04, just now exacted from him, is in truth a trivium. This entire little ceremony was about nothing but decorum, status, and power. Write to your mother, who taught you decorum. Lina can see that Johnnie is not the non-U fool she may, even for a split second, have taken him to be.

[2] *Doubt as to realism.* The Southern Railway is one of the real subtenders of the travel fiction set out in this film, not an invention out of the air circulating in the studio research department. It had been formed in 1923, from an amalgamation of four smaller lines, and now serviced Sussex and the wider south, much as the Southeastern Railway does today. During the War—Britain was on the cusp of being drawn into the War when this film came out—the Southern delivered servicemen and women to ports of departure in Hampshire and elsewhere. Hazledene is a fictionalization, but very likely based on a spot like Haslemere, in Sussex, or even Southease, near Rodmell, where a hunt and hunt ball were hosted famously in 1938. The hunt—something which interested Hitchcock ongoingly[6]—was, far more than a mere decorative sport, a strict and elaborate social arrangement, even a ceremony of bonding, designed for the affirmation of vertical placement and standing in a power structure of big landholders going back to feudal times and beyond. England's shires are very often wide and lush, rich with estate farming and controlled through a coterie who make up the membership of the House of Lords. This is notably true in the south (Pryor 463ff.). It is to such an environment that Johnnie is headed (in the wrong carriage), and we will see clearly, in the very next scene, that when he arrives he is greeted enthusiastically *and familiarly* by upper-class young women who expected his presence (because he is already known). He is no middle-class tourist scouting a foreign territory (like the viewer in the theater). Johnnie will not join the hunt, but he will dress properly for it (he schleps—somehow—proper dress) and in his handsome garb he will be the subject of a telling photograph, the making of which is the event that actually, in the visual narrative, gives him *entrée* to Lina since it is while he poses that he catches sight of her rearing up on her steed. Hitchcock arranges for us to *see* the actual instant of equine overwhelming as a conjunction between a rider and a poser (poseur).

[3] *Doubt as to bona fides.* Johnnie's bona fides can be picked up over Lina's shoulder on the train as, putting down her book on child psychology (that is, her manual on how to ascertain the psychological quirks and foibles of children), she picks up the *Illustrated London News* and finds inside a declarative photograph of this same Johnnie with Mrs Newsham, a grinning doyenne if ever was. The matching chummy smiles and casual poses these two give can be taken as evidence of their social proximity[7] (for much more on reading photographed poses, see Goffman *Advertisements*). Susan White sees Lina "respond[ing] with sexual arousal to [a] recognizable Cary Grant character" (184). Johnnie is a member of Mrs Newsham's set, he belongs "out here" just as much as Lina does. Even if he presumed his way into Mrs Newsham's intimacy, it was not a presumption from without the cabal.[8] Briefly about Lina's placement: Newsham, the girls who flock around Johnnie, and numerous other folk we meet at the ball are parvenus in a way that Lina and family are not. These others are continually absorbed with making shows of their status and gravity in life, whereas Lina is natural, merely living in class rather than bonding to it. As she had been in *Rebecca* (1940), Fontaine was perfection itself embodying Lina as a young woman with vitality and feeling, in this case her august class entirely aside.

[4] *Doubt as to confusion.* Johnnie somehow did not know the train was going into a tunnel: Hitchcock's opening sally and one to be disattended at peril. "I beg your pardon. Was that your leg?" If his arrivals at Hazledene station are somewhat routine, if he is a typical passenger on this route from Waterloo Station on the Southern Railway, how can it be that he does not know about the tunnel upcoming? (Emerging from Waterloo trains encounter no tunnels nearby; he has been hunting for a compartment as "inviting" as this one for several minutes.) We will return to this train problem. What happens for the viewer is a chance to catch the acoustic to-do of him stumbling, and then see the visual indelicacy of Lina's privacy being disturbed, even as he gracefully apologizes. An awkward social moment, the knife edge of drama. She is doubtlessly confused; he gives all the appearance (and sound) of being confused; and we begin in confusion. Not the stable order and pattern

of class and class relations, but the jumble of indeterminacy. Should our voyage manage to end with the indeterminate again, it will have been a strange voyage indeed: curiouser and curiouser.

[5] *Doubt as to garments.* At work in the city, Johnnie would wear a suit, very possibly for a man of this class a suit made expressly to fit his body, perhaps at Turnbull and Asser on Jermyn Street (they have his measurements in a book; they have his patterns at the ready). Lina would wear a skirt from Hardy Amies with a cashmere twin set from a very reputable dealer in Scottish woollens, such as Knockando. Here, however, they are both in tweed variations, casual dress but, for this class around 1938, casual only to a point. Nothing lazy or underdone. All the proper layers and accoutrements making up a costume that gives off just as many signals in its relaxedness as a formal one would in its formality, albeit signals of effortless leisure. We must remember of Johnnie that one can send a signal by intent as well as by habit; and of Lina that one can send a signal by habit as well as by intent. Nor is it the leisure that signifies social placement; it is the effortlessness. And their capacity for articulate signaling is given away by their mutual changes of garment once they are at Hazledene, and the country business of riding, chasing, drinking, and standing next to the right folk is on.

[6] *Doubt as to rails.* Of all the possible articulations of travel and movement Hitchcock could have used, he summons the railway, partly—but only partly—in order that two people can be locked together in a single carriage.[9] One has to take into consideration all the aspects of the forms Hitchcock uses in composition, not merely their received values. If we think of the railway proper, its structure and history, its way of operating, we find much to consider:

- The engine draws its carriages along that track artfully carved by the conversion of what was once hilly terrain into a uniform plateau, so that instead of the bumps and rattles of horse-and-carriage transportation prior to, say, 1840 the railway could afford a "smooth" ride.[10] Everything of the film moves like a train on rails, in one direction only, without reversing, and toward a station that is already fixed near the tracks. We are not being entertained here by modernist Brownian motion. There is an underpinning regularity, singularity, and efficiency of operation—on the train *and in the film*. And the ride will be so smooth as to be virtually unnoticeable. This last is, of course, a Hitchcockian trademark.

- The smoothness felt by the customer—the railway passenger or the cinemagoer—depends hugely on the springs and padding that support the seat, that smoothly grace the ride. Hence the concern for a well-upholstered setting, on the train, at Lina's parents', in the Aysgarth house, at Isobel's, everywhere in the film—and the more upholstery the better. Whilst, as Wolfgang Schivelbusch shows, upholstery began on the railway—"The provision of a sufficient intervention of elastic materials reduces the movement, which in a springless railway waggon is inconceivably distressing" (a *Lancet* pamphlet qtd. in Schivelbusch 122)—it quickly found itself in the bourgeois home:

> Such upholstery ceased to be functional when it appeared in realms such as the living room, where there were no mechanical-industrial jolts or jerks to be counteracted. Thus the jolt to be softened was no longer physical but mental: the memory of the industrial origin of objects, from railway stations or exhibition halls constructed out of steel to chairs constructed out of wood. (123)

The jolt was mental. We can see in the compartment that Lina sits contentedly, even complacently—jolt-free—reading as the train moves forward. Her eye presumably glides across the printed lines of the page just as the train is gliding upon its (to the rider, invisible) tracks.[11]

- Train travel offers the rider a new gaze, what Schivelbusch calls "panoramic perception": the rider sees, as it were, by a glimpse from the corner of the eye (the *coup d'oeil* for Ortega); sees in motion, sees without fixed perspective, and all this while the point of departure and the point of arrival are entirely hidden from view. You are going but you don't see where. When the compartment scene begins in darkness, the acoustic quality is beautifully managed so that we get a crystal-clear sense of the actions taking place seriatim, but when the world passes by the window of a train in motion the traveler has a much less definitive, more provocative sense, akin to what as a youngster Hitchcock might have seen in silent cinema.

Finally,
- A train on the railway doesn't—cannot—leap off its rails. It is locked on a track, always. Metaphorically speaking, one train doesn't become another one; it is what, and where it is, and that is what and where it stays. In the sense that the train is a metaphor in *Suspicion*, it suggests that whatever our Johnnie is, he will remain. And the same with Lina. If there is a gap or conflict between them, will it—can it—be bridged?

BLITHE SPIRIT

Johnnie Aysgarth, one can see fairly straightforwardly if one overcomes one's suspicions, is a blithe spirit, alive in the feeling of the moment and with no perspective on his future, or anyone else's. He prefers a way of moving forward that does not implicate him in arrangements, cautions, or expressiveness of a signal kind, so that he can merely breathe enjoyments as time goes by. Lina will come upon this to her horror, since she is anything but a child of the moment though she can will herself to surrender to a momentary call. She is privileged, but not blithe. She comes from staid parentage, solid blue-chip wisdom, trust-in-this-and-don't-trust-in-that. Her father needs only his pipe and his paper, and a beating heart to which he can mutter. Her mother needs her needlepoint. Period. In effect the McLaidlaws don't give themselves up to the winds of change because they don't give themselves up; they don't move; the family is entirely stagnant, if also cozy as cozy can be. "Nothing *ever* happens to a family that traditionally marries at least one heiress every other generation," as Hitchcock's Mark Rutland (an American, but of European heritage) will say in *Marnie* years later.

But Johnnie: he can be a friend to one person today, another tomorrow. (Beaky [Nigel Bruce], his dear old chum, is "in his embrace" the moment he shows up out of the blue, but entirely uninvoked before that.) His promises are entirely sincere, *when he makes them*. What he loves he loves passionately, fully, and devotedly, *while he loves*, but can one count on that love? Indeed, the issue is, what does "count on" mean with Johnnie? Can one frame an investment on his trust? No. Can one rely that he is true? But absolutely yes: *yes now*. Johnnie has never worried about the future, another signal of his class: he needn't concern himself because his future is his present. All through the film we have the sense—disturbing for some middle-class viewers whose assumptions of bearing, propriety, time, and permanence are quite at variance with his—of how very completely, even haphazardly (because for him hazard is nothing) this man exists on the cusp of the moment. He comes into a windfall and he spends it, almost a reflex action. Whereas General McLaidlaw would have cautioned him with a strategy: put it into savings:

> For him jam is not jam unless it is a case of jam to-morrow and never jam to-day. Thus by pushing his jam always forward into the future, he strives to secure for his act of boiling it an immortality. (Keynes 370 qtd. in Brown, *Life* 108)

Johnnie sees Lina for the first time—*really sees*—while she rides a rearing black stallion, magnificent creature, aflame with animal vigor and she upright and wholly dexterous in the saddle. Is Johnnie not, somehow, that stallion? Or certainly a creature enflamed by experience and sensation. Yet obviously, too, at least from her perspective at critical moments, he is wounded. Think of him, perhaps, as a young creature so conscious of his own movement the world spins past the corner of his eye. Like the train rider or even the victim of a train accident, he has been somewhat jolted and dislocated:

> At the time of the occurrence of the injury the sufferer is usually quite unconscious that any serious accident has happened to him. He feels that he has been violently jolted and shaken, he is perhaps somewhat giddy and confused.... He congratulates himself upon his escape from the imminent peril to which he has been exposed. He becomes unusually calm and self-possessed. (Erichsen 95–96 qtd. in Schivelbusch 140)

One can very easily imagine that a person such as this—*not*, I must emphasize, a proper, rule-conscious, middle-class bourgeois such as the viewer is most likely to be but a spirit like Johnnie, the subject of the story—might casually, effortlessly, saunter up to a wicket, his mind on anything but the business at hand—because he doesn't do business, he merely experiences and he merely plays the odds—and simply ask for a "one-way to Hazledene." Such a person could easily be seen by any ticket seller as meriting a first-class ticket, as he behaves and looks just like all those myriad others who come to get first-class passage to places like Hazledene and expect everyone to recognize this. Yet at the same time having plunked down three-and-six—perhaps even without looking—our Johnnie is administered a third-class ticket, perhaps with comment withheld. (Lina is surely holding a monthly return; she goes back and forth to London routinely and unpredictably.) The worker at the wicket knows the rules: Do not question your superiors, do not guess as to their secret motives. Johnnie scoops up the ticket and boards the train and in fact does not learn *until we do* that he's in the wrong compartment. "Wrong," that is, from the system's point of view, because since it offers perspective on a lovely, charming, attractive, and interesting young woman this could hardly be a righter place. How does Johnnie have that wrong ticket, then? He has it because he wasn't paying attention to the small ditties of social organization whilst he swam around them. Interested in adventure, pleasure, ease, not ticket prices, he likely doesn't even see the money he lays down, but simply pulls out coins and gives them over, one, two, three. The ticket seller was a blur, too. Johnnie's in a living daydream.

It is true that we are not shown the scene of Johnnie buying his ticket. We must speculate upon what is offscreen on the basis of all that is on, all that in our presence is said about it; and even then, we can never be sure. Yet speculating about what we cannot and do not see is something every viewer does all the time. How easy to misread this way; to misread people altogether, certainly this curious male. To conceive of him cadging a ticket, to think him a sneak. Hitchcock has made explicit arrangements, through what he offers and what he invites us to speculate upon, whereby we are led to doubt Johnnie Aysgarth, and to doubt him, if with energy still without cause. But doubting is always a reading beyond what is given to be read; a voyage.

In his extended daydream Johnnie has been putting himself out a bit in the neighborhood, one young woman after another, and the season has come, he appears to feel, for marriage and settling down. The joys of marriage to Lina, in fact, are so natural as to require no hints: huge smiles, then travel stickers from all the major points of call being pasted on luggage. Sooner than presto they are returning in wedded bliss to a new home, pre-arranged by him (but arranged, she will learn, upon her bank account). The place is bright, clean, ethereal. It is almost possible to hear the sunlit air singing. There are to be seen (and catalogued) art on the walls, plush matching furniture, sun-filled windows, a garden, and ... Ethel, an innocent maid. Servants: Johnnie has never been without them. Even if he doesn't want this sunny retreat for himself he wants it for Lina, and she is deeply thrilled. He wants her to be happy and this is no con game.

CHANCE

It need not be emphasized that Johnnie Aysgarth is a gambler, and that he owes money and exists on the edge of fate: a more than perfect role for the acrobatic, enigmatic, equivocal Cary Grant. As to gamblers, writes Roger Caillois,

> Games of chance determine the beliefs, knowledge, habits, and ambitions of these nonchalant addicts, who no longer govern themselves and yet find it extremely difficult to adapt themselves to another culture, so that they are left to vegetate on its periphery, eternal children. (147)

Is Lina, reading *Child Psychology*, prescient, then? Did she "see" him coming? The gambler is the iconic figure of momentary chance. He has gambled and sometimes won; he has gambled and often lost. Lina is no gambler, but at the beginning of the film she has not learned this about herself yet. She thinks that running off with Johnnie she is taking a brave flyer, but Lina cannot fly. She will come, only later, to understand, as her wondering comes to a head.

The underlying foundation of the film, however, is not a pair of fascinating characters but the inherent difference between them, the one effervescent and variable as the wind, the other constant and committed and principled and calm. Each is something of a train upon a single track. Those crossings on railroad tracks, where a train can shunt over to a new track (on which it will still be locked). As we see so powerfully both in *Shadow of a Doubt* (1943) and *Strangers on a Train* (1951) these crossings form an obtrusive, a challenging, a provocative "X," but two trains do not and cannot join, merge, unify, and transmogrify at such a crossing point any more than one train can jump up and hop to a track it isn't on. Marriage does not turn two trains into one, or two people into one, or two philosophies into one. Lina's romantic conceit about marriage promised her otherwise, but it was a romantic conceit. What she must determine at the moment of the film's startling conclusion is whether, in life, and for better or for worse, and as long as they both shall live, she can be with Johnnie Aysgarth, the companion of her heart. And he must make the same decision as regards her, because it had appeared that she loved him boundlessly but now he knows differently. And though they have been husband and wife for some time, in the very last two seconds of the film we can see that now they are preparing themselves for marriage. But we will come to that.

THE KNOT

Johnnie may be ready to tie the knot—to bid his extended adolescence farewell—but it is Lina who makes the proposal. A proposal of sorts, at any rate. Outside her parents' house, standing by the mullioned window, and hearing her father inside grumbling to her mother about how their daughter will very likely be a spinster for the rest of her life, she turns and plants an unreserved kiss on his mouth. The deal is proposed and sealed in a single gesture, then, notwithstanding that she does not, will not ever really approve of it, as far as we will see. The General does know of this man "John Aysgarth" *and his debts*, and thinks him a bad find. A presumptuous monkey as well, jumping into the hunt ball without an invitation, on the General's "ticket." This chappy is simply beneath one's station, yet Lina is of age and cannot be dictated to. Or can be dictated to only by way of the Last Will and Testament, a scathing rebuke that will not permit a riposte and a sour gesture at that.

There is nothing for Lina and Johnnie but to elope. She hints at her intention by dragging him to the McLaidlaw house in the middle of the hunt ball and escorting him into the study for drinks. There on the wall, shepherding their presence, overseeing, surveilling, indeed spying on them, and bearing an expression of silent contempt, the General gazes out from a large painted oil. If the man himself won't bless the union, his image is being used by the lovers as a make-do. But this substitution raises to the fore the issue of originals and copies, which is to say feelings and appearances, states of mind and performances. The image in the portrait is crisper, less ambiguous, and more "plainspoken" than any image we can find of the General himself as, for one example, he sits at the head of the table muttering or sits muttering in his reading chair. He's a mutterer, a truly authentic Upper: just let the vowels out, and anyone intimate enough to merit being in one's vicinity will know enough to make the interpretation. McLaidlaw, his pleasantly doddering wife, and their pleasant but utterly stifling home are to be escaped at all costs. Lina walks out with her little bag, tears falling on her cheeks but determination stiffening her stride. It could be argued that the General of the portrait, nothing but paint on canvas, speaks more forcibly than the man does in real life, more forcibly than anyone seems to speak inside this house.

Marriage for Lina involves fabulous imaginations of gilded joy and silvered hopes: that she can escape her childhood by taking protection under the wing of a handsome Prince Charming met, as seems perfect, only by chance. Here, as in so many other films, Grant has every earmark of this Royal: sparkle in his gaze, sparkle in his intelligence, and the perfect comeback for every critique and every query. A walking charm school. Dignity in his bearing, very good posture, elegance of movement, a dancer. But there is a kind of security Lina needs that all this (superficial) glory cannot donate. She needs to know that she is the Prima Ballerina in his imagination and concern, and whilst he surely adores her and dotes on her pleasure there are obviously many other interests blooming in his field, many other horses to bet upon. She needs money, and her father's disapproval of the marriage will more or less block her inheritance (at the Reading of his Will we discover, along with the suddenly chastened Johnnie, just how firm the block can be). And she needs safety and security, a difficult challenge if one is living on thin ice.

The knot with Johnnie is complicated by qualities and circumstances. As seems, he truly wants to make good, and recognizes that until now in life he has not done so. Yet his every scheme is thwarted, his every promise to repay loans vitiated by Fortune. He is being drawn into a whirlpool but he wants that Lina should love him and that he should be the kind of person who would merit that love. Worst of all, he wants—he needs—to believe that she believes in him; it is one of the characteristics of childhood, or the late childhood we call adolescence that she would find discussed in her book, that the self requires openly declared support. His sense of self rests on her sense of him, since still, at this point in his life, Johnnie *is* what significant other people call him. If the disparagement of the General is not so very hard for him to bear it is only because the General is not one of his significant others.[12] Lina surely is, but she clings to her father in an obedient and respectful way; recognizes that such obedience and respect are part of her duty. (In the context of this story it is her ability to recognize a filial duty that shows Lina is not a child.) Johnnie is particularly happy with Beaky, perhaps not quite a significant other but his long-time chum and a man of warmth and simplicity, likeable to all, who has for him nothing but affection (although an affection tempered by resigned acceptance of Johnnie's obvious faults). Beaky loves him and so he stays with Beaky. Beaky loves him and so Lina takes to Beaky. They are a happy and untrammeled triad. But trouble is coming.

TANGMERE TANGLES

Johnnie and Lina are on parallel voyages toward a state of accord, perhaps or perhaps not possible to find, and there are complications. Perhaps the conjunction of "Beaky" and "death" came up earlier when, on the terrace, to celebrate Johnnie's having won 2,000 pounds at the track by "putting two hundred on a ten-to-one shot," the trio were having drinks happily together:

> LINA: Where did you get the 200?
>
> BEAKIE (charming): I say, old girl, that's not a very tactful question.
>
> LINA: Where did you get it?
>
> JOHNNIE: You know very well there was no American. I got it for the chairs, of course.
>
> LINA: You sold the chairs to gamble all your money on a horse.

JOHNNIE: Not exactly. I owed the bookies some money. It's an ancient story, but you know how bookies are. I got the 200 to pay them off. But then, along came this hot tip and ... Darling, come on, give us a smile.

BEAKY: Come on, old girl. I know: you tickle her chin, and I'll make faces.

JOHNNIE: Think that will work? Come on, smile. Come on, dear.

BEAKY (*making a face*): Do you see ... see the glimmer of a smile, old boy?

JOHNNIE: No, not a thing, Beaky. You know any other tricks?

BEAKY: Yeah. I got something that never fails.

JOHNNIE: Well, c'mon, let's see it.

BEAKY: I'll make a noise like a duck.

JOHNNIE: Uh huh. (*Beaky makes duck noise.*) No, no, that's not doing it. Shall I do this at the same time? (*Reaches out to tickle Lina's chin.*)

BEAKY: Yeah, try that.

JOHNNIE: Come on, dear. Uh uh. Oh! I forgot something! Darling, look, look. Look. It's a receipt from a certain shop for a certain pair of chairs. Paid in full, and they deliver within the hour. (*Lina weeps with joy.*) Oh, look, she's smiling!

BEAKY: By Jove, so she is!

When drinks are delivered Beaky quickly insists on brandy, "maybe just this once": to greet the return of the chairs which were Lina's father's wedding present, celebration, but brandy is apparently poison to him. He takes a few gulps and instantly drops into a kind of semi-catatonic fit, eyes opened wide and unseeing. "I've seen it happen before. There's nothing much you can do about it. That's no use, darling. It will either kill him or it will go away by itself." And presto, Beaky does come out of it just fine. But we now know that he and a beaker of brandy ("Beaky" as in "with a beak" but also as in "user of a beaker") are incompatible lovers. Brandy could k-i-l-l ... B-e-a-k-y. Lina could not help but see then, and cannot help but realize now, that for all his charm and warmth Beaky is a fragile bird. That life is fragile. *But also that Johnnie knew this already and knows it still.*

In the street, Lina comes across the fabled Mrs Newsham (Isabel Jeans), who cattily informs her that Johnnie has not won but in fact lost money at the track. Lina steps into the offices of Johnnie's new employer, Capt. Melbeck (Leo G. Carroll), where a worse shock awaits: Johnnie was dismissed weeks ago, for having pilfered 2,000 pounds. She goes home, sits at her vanity, and beside a crystal candelabrum (light pouring with ultimate clarity through it) inks a letter telling him that she is leaving him, that she is sure he will be able to explain. (We wince a little at her snideness.) But on second thought—

Why ever does a second thought come into life?

—on second thought she tears it up, at which instant Johnnie steps into the room behind her and says quietly, "Then you've heard." Catastrophe, the marriage in shambles, the sun gone to light some other sky. But what he means to refer to, and the telegram in his hand horribly confirms, is not the Melbeck story at all. Her father has died. "I'm so sorry, darling. I'm terribly sorry!"

When the Last Will is read out it happens that the General has left to his daughter and her husband the portrait of himself by the esteemed Sir Jonathan Nettleworth. Oh, my!

Johnnie takes Lina for a drive by the sea. Melbeck, he explains calmly, didn't like his (too daring) ideas. "Look at all this land, for instance!"—the surf is pounding far below, the cliffs are majestic unto the far horizon, the land is virginal. "If I had 10,000, or better still, 20,000 . . . I could start a development here."

"All you need is 20,000?" she asks, her tone very plainly indicating she might be able to give it to him, and that she is thinking about it. The courage of devotion, the commitment to being of help whenever and wherever, a light that occasionally fades now come on again.

"Or 30,000. An extra 10,000 wouldn't hurt a bit."

Johnnie proceeds with Beaky to form a corporation that will build estates on the Devon cliffs: Tangmere-by-sea, 1,600 acres. They will certainly make a fortune. Beaky has thrown in 30,000 pounds of his own and has registered the corporation in Johnnie's name. But soon, having come to see in her husband a man who would do anything to save himself from disaster, she fabulates a scenario in which he has murdered Beaky. The three of them are playing a nice little "family" game of Scrabble one evening and suddenly there is superimposed over her entirely doubtful face a vision of one man pushing another off the cliff edge, then a close shot of Beaky screaming as he drops into an abyss. Soon she drives out alone to the cliffs and sees a set of tire tracks leading off into nowhere. Johnnie must somehow have killed him! But home again she sees that there is Beaky, healthy as a plum, and heavens, what an adventure!, he drove out there—was backing up my car and almost went off the cliff but Johnnie saved my life! Johnnie standing passive, not smiling, not expressing anything. Not. Expressing. Anything. He is apathetic? Or: this is not a matter worth bringing into civil conversation.

That Scrabble game, in which one puts together words that inspire the imagination. (What else are words for?) Having begun with "D-O-U-B-T," Lina forms the word "M-U-D-D-E-R." We see her finger drop into frame in a close-up and shift an "R" into the position of the first "D." Murder born of *mudder* (*mutter:* mother), which is to say, of Lina, mother of this invention. Is murder afoot? And if it is, if it were to be, who a better perpetrator to imagine as "murderer," even as "mudderer," than the only person nearby who has been consistently opaque?

CARY GRANT'S GRANT

Consistently the opaque figure at the center of the ceremony (and never to forget that every ceremony is a voyage from the obvious, from the mundane).

It is no effort to have the irking sense that Cary Grant not only *plays* Johnnie Aysgarth but in some way *actually is* him. That is, his star persona is a much-repeated indication of some slick, duplicitous, shining but controversial deeper self. If onscreen there is always something charming about Cary Grant's character there is always something suspect, too. And something suspect about charm altogether if judged by a rational person like Lina, with both feet on the ground. (Early in the film we see that the gay young women Johnnie is meeting in Hazledene are swept away deliriously by his every charming wink, and these types Lina labels despicably shallow.) Charm cannot be natural for the legalist, it must be an agency of manipulation, and manipulation to what end? After all, who but a charmer, a paragon, could have so burnished a physique as to shine like a kind of monument![13]

Who but an inveterate charmer, Lina must secretly wonder, could be so eloquent while at the same time maintaining such a foggy air of ambiguity? Constantly she must voyage away from her assumptions and finds herself in a no-woman's-land of uncertainty and doubt (the land Hitchcock intends for his viewer's "home" in this film). Does this Johnnie(/Cary) have a magical power that transcends all screen visions of him (see *Bringing Up Baby* or *Holiday* [both 1938]), or is he an ongoing victim of circumstance (see him in *Arsenic and Old Lace* [1943] or *None But the Lonely Heart* [1944])?

More ineffably, perhaps: why is it that we love him so much?—because surely we do. We love and reach out—to save him, to help him succeed, to assist him to convince (see him in *Charade* [1963]), to catch him before he falls off the mountain. And that pelt he carries—it is polished and decorous but at the same time wild enough to withstand the friction of the environment, hygienic but able to be dirtied without, somehow, actually gaining a macula (his charm is immaculate all through *North by Northwest* [1959]). In *Suspicion*, the first of four films he made for Hitchcock, he is caricatured already as a figure conceivably, yet not demonstrably, duplicitous, a figure who dances on the high wire where sincerity rests on one side and guile on the other. Is it the puckish smile, the glittery skill at social, vocal, gestural acrobatics? Is he the Fool?

From seeds plantations grow—the voyage from origins. The seed implanted in Lina originated with her father, her dignified, her self-possessed father (Cedric Hardwicke), notably in his decidedly distinct (if thoroughly mumbled) dubiousness about John Aysgarth's soundness as a partner. But dubiousness about his soundness is precisely the attitude Grant repeatedly inspires (his early dialogues with Henry Kolker in *Holiday* spell this out literally). In every scene he plays, every scene his character gracefully inhabits, he utters not one syllable more than is necessary (hence his ambiguity, at least conversationally) and he moves according to a plan that seems contained in secrecy. Lina summons the gumption to escape her parents' home; but no means has been found whereby a child may escape the implantations of the father. If at first she goes so far as to doubt Johnnie she soon finds him off-puttingly amazing, extreme, inexplicably strange, even alien. By the way he squints "up" to the portrait of the General he makes it plain how little patience he can find for this Colonel Blimp type to whose shining epaulettes she is so attached: the "blimpish" Brit, "so convinced that neither England nor the Conservative Party can do wrong" (Kynaston, *Family* 682). Then he naughtily pilfers the pair of estate chairs sent over as wedding gift (sent only once the mother has let the General know how radiant Lina seems after her honeymoon), this abuse a blatant mark of disrespect for not only the General but also Lina, who treasures them as she treasures the giver. She will find them on display in a cold shop window. Then there is the chain of unnerving surprises: the Melbeck story, the Tangmere involvement, the dark visit of the police to report Beaky's death in Paris, the club porter in London denying that he has seen Mr Aysgarth followed up much too soon by Johnnie's subsequent claim that he was there . . .

And for each dip there is a matching elevation. See-saw. Johnnie has brought presents for everyone, a nice new stick for Beaky, a fur stole for little Ethel, show it to your young man, an adorable little West Highland who sits up eagerly at Lina's feet, and, as a grand finale, the Royal thrones, now returned to Lina with all his love. The real estate project went and collapsed, he confesses later, but only because of the chalkiness of the soil (that is, not because it was a faulted idea in the first place). Yes, yes, Beaky was over in Paris but Johnnie was in Liverpool trying unsuccessfully to realize funds on the basis of an insurance policy. Every cloud has a silver lining, on which the sun's keen reflection peeks but always, it seems, too briefly.

Then a most horrible dip:

While he bathes, Lina steals a quick peek at a letter to Johnnie from an insurance company only to find clearly affirmed that his policy can be paid only upon the death of his wife. When one voyages in a vehicle on sea or in space, it takes only a pinprick to bring disaster. And what goes up must come down. What springs into the sky must go into the earth.

Seen from Lina's point of view, in an inimitably frigid and methodical way Johnnie Aysgarth has proceeded from catching her eye to captivating her emotion to making her his wife to . . . setting her up for murder. What a voyage that is! She packs a bag to go back to mother's, and on his insistence allows him to drive her there. Two of them in the car, speeding along.

Wind in the hair. The awesome cliffs.

The road creeps to the precipice (a not inaccurate representation of such conditions in England).

He turns and sees something, reaches swiftly over. Her door flies open. He grabs at the handle and drags it shut. She is in hysterics, pulled away from him in such terror that he may as well be the Heroic Villain chummy Isobel boasted of putting in her novels. He brakes the car, irate.

> JOHNNIE: Lina! Stop it, you little fool! Stop it! I've had enough! How much do you think a man can bear? Listen to me! You throw me out of your room, you go running off to your mother's and now you shrink away from me as though you hated me. You're my wife, Lina! ["Please, no!" she cries, pulling back.] You almost killed us both back there. Because you had to pull away even when I was reaching over to save you from falling out of the car. Well, you don't have to put up with me anymore.

Far too evidently, Lina's secret—Lina's secret passion of suspicion—has been given away. He sees that he is repulsive to her morally, entirely unfit to be by her side, *as she would estimate.*

Or is he "smoothly" recouping after a failed murder attempt, preparing for another one soon to come? What do you believe, dear reader? What do you *choose* to believe?

Always for Hitchcock: always: *What do you believe?* Or: *What trip are you on?*

This scenic dualism, not only her world and his, not only her reading of him and his of her (notwithstanding that he reads much less fluently than she does, lives a much more introspective life), not only that he is on one side of a chasm and she on the other, but that you, reader (*mon semblable*, writes T. S. Eliot), still at this moment cannot decide with surety which way to interpret what you see and hear of him, that still with some sense of propriety you may find it so very difficult to accept Johnnie's blithe eagerness as *proper.* Yet also not deny it. In the Scrabble game, Beaky's tiles spelled D-O-U-B-T-F-U-L: shall we take this as our mantra? This twinning of contradictory hypotheses brings the film to a startling climax.

A voyage to that clifftop again:

At one and the same instant as the car screeches to a halt, we see Lina's desperate fear coupled in marriage with one or the other of two eventualities: Johnnie has suddenly, and for the first time, awakened: he sees that he frightens her now and has frightened her all along, he sees the quality and depth of her fear, he sees how she has been tortured by him and that for Lina attaching herself to him was an act of courageous daring. Or he has deftly picked up that she recognizes what his plan was and knows that now there is no chance, at least no chance now. The upshot will be freedom for her, divorce and prison for him. Or else, the upshot will be reconciliation and the beginning of a true marriage. A Cavellian epiphany.

Dear judgmental reader: Which do you hope it will be?

ECCENTRICITIES

[1] *Art.* In all the film there are two—only two—bluntly neutral forces, a pair of police agents (Lumsden Hare, Vernon Downing) who are making a polite enquiry, nothing more. They have no axe to grind, they have no inkling of the suspicion they raise. Both as they enter and as they depart the Aysgarth home they courteously pause in the atrium. Whilst the older man addresses Lina, the younger stares bewildered at a small framed canvas he can't seem to make out. Perhaps all through the interview he can't get this thing out of his mind. We are given a portrait shot of this canvas both when the detectives enter and when they exit, because when they exit he stops and looks again, still dumbfounded. Both times it is at once "merely a work" hanging on a wall and also a puzzle that is driving this young observer mad. In fact the canvas is an example of cubism, a form of painting from the very early twentieth century that was popularized by Miró and Picasso, among others.[14] The idea behind cubism is that a favored object or group of objects is painted from many points of view, as though simultaneously (painting as film): the painter's formative action proceeds in a linear fashion, as it must, but looking at the canvas the viewer is presented with multiple perspectives, multiple identities, in one *coup d'oeil*. Might *Suspicion* be Alfred Hitchcock's cubist portrait of Johnnie, and might this young police officer be a stand-in for Lina, the appraiser who gazes at Johnnie with the same kind of baffled (but smitten) incomprehension? Both performers exude "youth." In her

case, the perspectives can be reduced to two, that the subject is noble and that he is venal. She cannot resolve this equivocation. She cannot make out who he is outside of this "cube," the hero or the villain. A love story passes through the valley of decision.

[2] *Green wool.* As Lina secretly prepares to flee from the McLaidlaw home, she dutifully comes into the sitting room to ask Papa if she can get him anything and he responds that no, there's nothing he needs. Pipe in mouth. Newspaper raised up as an arras to shield him from the world it reports. A quiet man. A comfortable man. Undoubtedly a man who has put aside his desire for adventure in this life. And Mama (May Whitty) quietly hands over a piece of green wool and asks if she could stop at the shop in town and pick up some more of the same color; this is for a needlepoint that is in progress—we may well imagine, and perhaps even profit by imagining, that the needlepoints are endless in this house but not until, confronted with the black and white image, we have managed to imagine the peculiar green. A tiny pang of regret is produced by Hitchcock in the viewer's heart here, because as Lina goes into the hallway, gathers up her little suitcase, and exits through the door, we know she is not going to bring back that green wool. Deny mother a small request. Although clearly she loves her mother, and means no harm. But coming back is out of the question.

It is a tiny but utterly brilliant step of Hitchcock's, this invocation of the green thread. Through it, he completely, if very briefly, captures the pang of leaving home. Making that decision. Packing that little suitcase. Leaving it to stand in the hallway. Coming in to say a warm and gentle goodbye, quite as though one will see everyone later for tea. The quiet slip through the door. The project with the green wool will remain incomplete, for now at least, just in the way that Lina's going away will leave the project of her childhood, a devotion to, and also of her parents, incomplete and broken off. We need this little green piece of wool, because there are no other plain evidences of the deep affection the parents feel for their only child, but this green wool is in her hand now, the hand of her mind. Ariadne's wool . . .

[3] *An overlooked clue.* In order to spend a little more time with this new and alluring stranger, Johnnie Aysgarth, Lina agrees to go to church with some other young girls attracted to him, go to church although usually she never does this. But as the four of them step up to the quaint little gray stone building, Johnnie seizes Lina by the arm and takes her the other way, up a tiny hillock where the wind is blowing. We cut into a shot of him wrestling with her hair and her pulling away in fright. "Now, what did you think, I was trying to kill you? Nothing less than murder could justify such violent self-defense." It is Johnnie and no one else who introduces the word "murder" to this story, and attaches it to a projection of himself. What, do you think me a murderer? If Johnnie is no innocent, here is all the evidence one could want. Yet every piece of evidence has two sides, like a coin of the realm. If he is using this invocation as a blanket to cover over a truly malicious intent—he has found a victim, he has followed her, he has set her up for proximity—he is a perfect personification of evil. And if he is not that type, he is making light, having fun, showing spirit.

Another tiny observation we can make here: she is pulling away, but not hitting at him. He calls her motion "violent." Is he using language to mirror the very contrasting hyper-pacific nature of the McLaidlaw home in which she learned the world? Is he mocking what he takes to be her received sensibility that violence can inhere even in slight, delicate, reflex actions? Or is he speaking entirely for himself (as, from here on, we will discover Johnnie tends to do)? Is he telling her—and us—that he himself withdraws from even so slight a "violence"? That, quite against what anyone might think, he is frail himself, delicate, easily bent this way or that by the wind of life?

[4] *Monkeyface.* From that moment on the hillock onward, Johnnie adopts the moniker "Monkeyface" for Lina. Why, of all things, Monkeyface? He is playing (the screenwriters Samson Raphaelson, Alma Reville, and Joan Harrison show) with our deeply embedded conceit that there is an expressive relation between apes and humans, that, as so many people like to say, and notwithstanding their position on the evolutionary scale, monkeys actually do seem to be like us in so many ways. The

foremost way, of course, is that their faces seem expressive, that is, seem to give off presentations of inner feeling. We can take the monkey to the mirror—"You look more like a monkey with a bit of mirror"—because it senses a self just as we do. And yet I think there is no reason to think monkeys are consciously expressive in a self-generative way. They are masters at imitation, which is why we call precise imitation aping. The monkeyface is an expressive array, using the musculature of the face, created by imitation of a similar array seen in the surround. We smile at the monkey, the monkey swiftly smiles back at us (a quick learner). Johnnie is suggesting politely to Lina that her expression of emotion, here and elsewhere, originates far from genuine feeling. She is aping what she sees all around. Speaking broadly, he is suggesting that she is a child of her class, that she takes as individual and sincere only a mode of relation and expression that is copied from social form.

And he is suggesting, too, by implication, that he does not do this. That his emotion has found a direct pathway onto his face.

[5] *Generations.* General McLaidlaw disparages Johnnie to Lina in a notably indirect way:

> McLAIDLAW (with his mind turned elsewhere): John Aysgarth? Is that Tom Aysgarth's boy? How'd you meet him? Pity he's turned out so wild. Rough luck on Tom. What's this, horseradish?

- He has as much concern for Johnnie as for horseradish.
- He has no interest in Lina's being interested in Johnnie, recognizing only that she has named him.
- He has no recognition of Johnnie as a person in his own right, only as the son of a chum, Tom Aysgarth. (A chum we never meet or hear of again.)
- If he has what might be called concern it is only that this poor Tom we never see has, unfortunately it seems, been saddled with a "wild" son. But:
- There is not even genuine concern for Tom, only a logical mutter, a news report, the "right" thing to say if one is to trouble one's lungs to say anything. Saying is work, after all, and members of this class neither work nor believe in work as something appertaining

- to them, nor give it the least thought unless someone working for them makes a mess they must be "asked" to "clean up."
- And the General is displaying a willingness to accept as bold truth mere rumors he has heard bandied about, to the effect that Johnnie is a "wild" one, since we can see quite plainly that Johnnie is anything but wild. Lina's no fool: "Why did you say that John Aysgarth was wild, Father?"—And, since he who makes pronouncements must always be ready to pronounce: "He was turned out of some club for cheating at cards, wasn't he?" *Some* club, note; not *my* club. The General wasn't there.
- We will see plenty of reason to surmise that Johnnie is an adept at "cheating," yet would such a talented man be likely to regard cheating at cards in a gentleman's club as a serious infraction? Isn't a card game in such a place, for Johnnie, a perfect simulacrum of the blimpishness he utterly rejects (in a spirited generational revolution)?
- Further, if rumors have been bandied about in such a fashion that the General can hear them, they are local rumors, since the General never goes anywhere. (Why go, if you can have things brought to you here?) If there are local rumors about him, Johnnie is local, too.

English life at the time, in the landowning class, was expressly sheltered. The clustering of the McLaidlaws in their home, the way the General stands drawn into himself at the Hunt Ball, all suggest a culture in which people generally don't go out visiting. Lina's visit to Isobel Sedbusk is atypical, but they have some undefined special friendship that predates the story. People in general might meet in the street, or in an office for business, but at home they are walled off. Thus, Johnnie Aysgarth might have a family home not so far away from Lina's yet never have met her. Or he might be a frequent visitor to these parts:

MCLAIDLAW: What's he doing down here?

LINA: Staying at Penshaze.[15]

MCLAIDLAW: Lord Middleham wouldn't have him there . . . if he had been turned out of a club for cheating. Maybe it wasn't cards. Maybe a woman. He was co-respondent or something, I believe.

Or ought to have been co-respondent. You can't expect me to remember every detail about everybody.

In short, I don't really know, I don't remember, I haven't the details, why hound me for them, since I have the privilege to bad-mouth this boy whatever it was he did. Or might have done. Or should be thought to have done, anyway. I don't know at all but why would you question what I say? I am a man of my tastes, have always been, Pukka Pukka, I like my horseradish, I like my wife to be quiet, card game or woman all the same, all the same.

- The old General is more closely connected to his friend Tom than to Tom's progeny, a hint that he is likely more closely connected to his friend Tom than to his own progeny. A generational divide.

[6] *At the ball.* A generational divide that is given express display at the Hunt Ball, where McLaidlaw and a young man dancing hopefully with Lina and several other men standing about are wearing military jackets with pinned-on decorations. This little country society is populated by men who fought in the Great War, and survived. They look to one another as lifelong comrades. The children must make their own way. We have nothing to do with the children.

"I say, old boy, isn't that going a bit too far?" (Johnnie to the portrait, as he romances Lina in her favorite room). *Old boy,* as you would have yourself addressed, General.

ALL THE NEWS THAT FITS

Let us rehearse the film from another angle, working to discover a structure subtly vibrating in it. The issue is text, less its presentation in front of characters than its display in front of us watching those characters. Text as news for them, as information, as a bolster of status, even as truth, but always delivered onscreen in such a way that there are no secrets from us, who struggle to peek. Photographs in the newspaper, for example, creatures snapped to net their reality, the camera being well known to have supplanted the limner's hand with a quickness about which we can recall Balzac's comment [in *Séraphita*] about artistic talent being tied to the "quick grasp" [qtd. in Benjamin 41]). Words in a telegram, the marriage of print (the Renaissance) and electricity (the modern age). Handwritten notes, epitomes of grace. Typewritten letters, epitomes of capitalism.

[a] *The book.* Safe on her lap, that young woman in the railway carriage had CHILD PSYCHOLOGY by Henrietta Wright M.D., M.A., an author who gave the world a thick tome. We can presume this reader interested in children, in their psychology; or in herself, a creature not quite adult yet (in her view). Or perhaps—since nowhere else in the film does she show any academic interest in this subject—she is merely passing time with a volume it was convenient to get one's hands on. The apparent textual "clue" may be nothing at all. But Hitchcock makes sure we see it, so that we can use it for beginning our collection: so that we can be decoders. Later in the film we will be positioned, should we look back, to find it ironic that with a child such as Johnnie in tow—"I'm just beginning to understand you. You're a baby"—Lina should have been prepping with this of all possible guides, since as the film opened Lina didn't know what would come and we didn't either.

[b] *The ticket.* It's a first-class compartment these two are in, and we know because when the conductor stops by for tickets she easily hands over a Southern Railway first-class ticket Waterloo to Hazledene, and ... *close-up on it*. Trains from Waterloo typically head toward the West Country. Hazledene is in Sussex, south. Trains heading that way typically leave from Victoria. If it is merely that Hitchcock has made a fictional adaptation (as he is always doing), the invention of "Hazledene" would suffice. Perhaps this ticket is a clue to some kind of special train, a rare once-a-day departure, what might normally be used by a traveler very accustomed to the London-to-Hazledene voyage and wanting privacy, quiet, and seclusion, and also one who knew there would be a stop at Grinstead, quite close by. A tiny matter, surely. Yet the shot in which we are informed about the ticket is intended to be revealing, the form of the shot even augmenting the information it contains. We are to *read this ticket*. Trains, travel, class, and Sussex life are now on the table. And once again, we believe what we read, even though we are *watching* all this, and watching is not reading.

[c] *The other ticket.* But Johnnie's ticket is (only) a third-class ticket. Therefore, as he is now gruffly informed, he must either move carriages or pay the difference. Move: head away from this attractive woman. Pay: impossible, since he carries no cash. (What sort of person would carry no cash—in the late 1930s, much before the age of credit cards?) Begging her for help, Little Jack Horner reaches into the lady's purse and pulls out that plum postage stamp for the conductor: "Legal tender!" To understand the fizzling chemistry between these two, need we really pay attention to what is printed on those tickets? Another close-up is showing us Johnnie's.

[d] *The News.* Lina has now put down her book—Text Version A—and has picked up the *Illustrated London News*—Text Version B—in a full-page spread of which she discovers a large photograph of this same person. The representation and the thing represented; the picture *of* Man and his Image. Image to be taken seriously even if Man is not. "MR. JOHN (JOHNNIE) AYSGARTH AND MRS. HELEN NEWSHAM, SEEN AT MERCHESTER." In the background, respectable members of an upper-class set in an open-air country setting. The consort is in a long, draping, bleached fur coat with a stylish feathered cap, just too much for words, and she wears a movie-star (which is to say, at once warm and distant) smile. The swank companion is all Tweedledum and Tweedledee, hand casually in pocket, overcoat slumped over one arm, hat jauntily tilted, his mouth offering an identical, arcane, try-to-penetrate-me-if-you-will smile. What could MR. Aysgarth be doing with MRS. Newsham, one might wonder (speculation going amok, especially if one has the sort of mind to conceive of adulteries in the first place). More importantly, if this is actually the *Illustrated LONDON News*— an English paper—and Hitchcock is using it to loop in his audience, why have the "editors" of the thing placed periods after Mr and Mrs? How distinctly transatlantic! Was it Hitchcock, newly resident in America? Yet no matter, can we really *trust* the newspaper presentation here? As to the photograph itself, what journeying amateur snapped it and turned it in? What were the actual circumstances, and did these two icons make a sudden up-turn to the camera, pasting these equivocal smiles, or were they artfully posing?

One could pose a deeper question: In Hitchcock's work, does Cary Grant *always* have a pasted look on his face? Pasted: insincere but utterly punctual. Wherever he stands or sits, no matter with which woman? Moments afterward, at the Hazledene hunt, Johnnie, who doesn't go with the pack, is posed between two strange women by yet one more photographer avid for a snap (that he can sell to the press, no doubt, and featuring a man whose name this stringer already knows). We see, in medium shot, postures (or impostures) that seem to reveal old friends. The *News* photograph from the train is reprised at Lina's home, torn out now and saved as a souvenir. Johnnie discovers it on her window seat, having been dragged along by some mutual friends and now formally introduced to her. He has picked up the book Lina was reading. Is he thinking to find himself in there? Watch out, at any rate, for the "news" that newspapers print and also for the "true" wisdom in a textbook about child psychology.

[e] *The directory.* As she scouts the London Directory Lina's fingertip lands on L. L. Ayscough.[16] But then finds John D. Aysgarth, A11 Albany, W.1. Well there he is, in official print. A decent address (in a good part of Camden Town), a middle initial to indicate a "true" social identity. No will-o'-the-wisp, this one. He's actual. Though, if we stood back—if she were to stand back—it would become evident that a phone listing isn't all that informative.

[f] *The invitation.* Lina has now received and is perusing (so that the image of it shows up in full-screen close-up) a printed invitation to the Beauchamp Hunt Ball ("to be held at Hazledene"). Printed invitations are costly and emerge directly from the intention and arrangement of bona fide purveyors of sociability, in the case of a hunt ball from authentically wealthy patrons of a country set. The invitation is for Lina's parents and herself, "Miss McLaidlaw." If this invitation is as unimpeachably real and true as seems, so will be the hunt ball itself. Those who skirt, sashay, and swirl around there will be doing so in formal patterns long established, and in indication of genuine social statuses to be taken seriously. If a young man dances with a young lady at the Hunt Ball, *there more than anywhere else in the neighborhood*, their coupling will be given weight, not only by the parents but by all

observers present. A gate-crasher would get the same attention as an invitee, only because of the setting. Lina is not looking forward to the event; she has a headache.

[g] *The telegram.*

> MARCH 8 1938
> MISS LINA MCLAIDLAW
> HILLSIDE=HAZELDEAN SUSSEX=
> SEE YOU AT THE HUNT BALL. DON'T
> FORGET TO BRING YOUR UCIPITAL
> MAPILARY=
> JOHNNY.

Presto! a smile eradicates her headache, she races for a change of clothes. "Beware of all enterprises that require new clothes" (Thoreau, *Walden* 21). This telegram, like the other documents, is presented *to us* in full-screen close-up and is, we could note, a strange item, indeed. Begin by understanding that in England in the late 1930s, just prior to the War, the telephone was not an instrument in frequent use, certainly in aristocratic rural enclaves and generally in the big cities, so that rather than sending a telegram by phoning it in one walked into a telegraph operator's station (usually at a post office) and filled the message into a form. How, then, did the "Johnnie" whose name appeared for us more than once in print, J-o-h-n-n-i-e, suddenly become "Johnny"? Would a fellow have a lapse writing his own name? But what are *we* being told? We are being told that even telegraphs are not to be trusted—the same sermon again. Or else the newspaper had it wrong. Either way, now there is and earlier there was *print on the screen* and it is fraught. More: how does Hazledene, the village whose name was printed on the third-class railway ticket he held, held for this odd train from Waterloo because presumably he goes down there a wee bit, suddenly become Hazledean, except that Johnnie doesn't really read. He spelled it for the telegram as he heard it pronounced; he apprehended it only through hearing. More on this to follow, but it's interesting here to think that Johnnie doesn't read: he is literate, but he doesn't pay attention to what is in print, he doesn't detect and collect. Therefore—jump back—when he was holding Lina's book on her window seat he wasn't really reading, he was only posing as the kind of devoted book reader he already recognized her to be. Later in the film we will learn that he's borrowed another book, but we never see him read, or even touch, it. He didn't receive an invitation to the Hunt Ball that would require reading; he invited himself, since the film makes it plain that it is the McLaidlaws who have an invitation, not he.

The little code ending the telegram is a private joke Johnnie has been sharing with Lina since they stood together on the village hillock and he dubbed her "Monkeyface." Again, he not only arranges the world as he hears it, he invents it at will (and spontaneously), since he calls her suprasternal notch an "ucipital mapilary." A musician in his way, Johnnie speaks to make life euphonious.

[h] *The letter.* Johnnie courts Lina, they elope. A brief visual ballet shows that they are in Monte Carlo, Venice, then Paris. Now a closely shot label marked MR. & MRS. John Aysgarth, WICKSTEAD ENGLAND (periods again, but the label was probably not made in England). The trunk onto which this is slapped has labels from Nice, from Rome, and from some indeterminate spot in Germany. Culture. They arrive home. A lovely house, worked up by a professional decorator (who will send a bill). Light, upholstery, space! Smiles of domestic contentment. But how does Johnnie plan to keep all this up? A letter comes from his cousin George Melbeck apparently offering a job. Again a full-screen close-up, so close to the page some words are cut off: "will give the idea your fullest consideration and let me know if you would like to take the job." Marital accord. Tranquility. And reader: don't believe for a second that this Johnnie isn't genuinely out there looking for a job; it's in print.

Of course, if the story is to go on (with our hopes and beliefs suspended before our eyes) there can be no real tranquility. Our tranquility requires disturbance. Beaky Thwaite must show up, charming if goofy, life of the party even when there's no party, and a man who speaks before he calculates: so easy to fault him, so easy to find him immature, and so difficult instead to regard him as blessed. Lina settles into a new, precarious life.

[i] *The printed presence.* But one day she is standing in front of the village bookshop with her old chum Isobel Sedbusk (Auriol Lee), much-published author of crime fiction. The two women are on the pavement just outside the large picture window, and on the other side of the glass, a notorious case of print announcing itself as such, sits a large publicity photograph of Isobel, advertising her new book copies of which fill the display. Clothed in black, hand to face, her long angular cheeks in beautifully lit view, the photographic Isobel looks precisely like a *character*: not, that is, a movie character—what the gazing Isobel is—but a fictional creation made to sell books. An authorial face for a dust jacket. An AUTHORIAL PRESENCE. Talking with Lina beside the photograph, Isobel in the flesh is all different: in light clothing, a scarf hanging jauntily from her neck, a pally smile on her lips. Clearly this is the same body that was used for making the photograph but it is not the same person as the one we see pictured. If we are to take the direct presentation of everyday business (Lina and Isobel looking in the window) as *real*, then the photograph is unreal, and the persona inside it is (nothing but) a fake. The two women walk away chatting happily, past a newsagent with a CRICKET RESULTS poster in the window: a cheaper entertainment than crime fiction, far less ornate and sophisticated, aimed at the people who labor to support and serve the educated elite; not gaudy artifice but plain facts. Is it a plain fact that Johnnie is from *below*, only masquerading as a country gentleman? Is his foray with Lina his private little game, his nicely authored fiction?

[j] *The murder mystery.* Outside the selfsame bookshop, and this time clasping a trio of purchases including Sedbusk's MANSION MURDER MYSTERY, Lina later runs into Mrs Newsham. Two things to note about Lina holding these books: (1) She is not only a voracious reader—more than one book at a time—she is a voracious reader of murder mysteries, and the title of the one book we are given to notice offers a familiar clue to others of its type: the country mansion, the notably dramatic slaying, the quirky family who live there, each member being a possible suspect and one of them, usually very wealthy, the unfortunate victim. Lina's head is filled with the sort of

conceits and patterns that derive from these compositional conventions, entirely set off from the everyday world, the world of the street with passing automobiles, one of which contains Newsham. (2) This book title, for Lina and conceivably also for us, associates three delicate words in synchronous alignment: a *mansion* (Lina's home before marriage, and now her lovely house with Johnnie; in short, a comfortable—too comfortable?—abode); *murder*; and the idea of *mystery*, a state of affairs entirely unclear in rational terms. Is *Suspicion* a kind of mansion murder mystery, in the end? Does Lina have a certain susceptibility to seeing ordinary arrangements as instances of this grotesque form?

[k] *The dismissal.* Stopping in to visit Capt. Melbeck, the man who offered Johnnie a job, Lina learns that her new husband owes him a substantial debt, having been dismissed weeks earlier because 2,000 pounds suddenly went missing. She is aghast. *My money has been flying away to pay for this rake?* She returns home and in her bedroom begins to pen a letter flashed full-screen: "Johnnie—I am leaving y—" ... A portrait shot of Lina's troubled, beautiful, borderline teary face. Back to the letter, full-screen. "It is very important that we never see each other again. I am sure you will be able to explain everything very smoothly to yourself as well as to others. Lina": an oddly provoking, even chilling acoustic echo somehow attaching itself to the phrase *very smoothly*. Now we can see what Lina has seen, that is, we can believe ourselves seeing what she believes herself to have seen, by noting the interpretation that she has lent to events: Johnnie is a *smooth operator*, someone who greases the gears of the machinery inside his constructions. Johnnie the fake, but the clever, elegant, efficient, and altogether *professional* fake. She is about to fold her epistle into its container but she stands, reflects an instant, hesitates, and rips it up, the soft, luxurious furnishings of her bedroom dropping out of focus in the background. But silently he has entered from behind, dressed in a dark suit and holding his own folded paper in his two coupled hands.

[l] *The announcement.* "So you've heard." He's terribly sorry—a voice as meek and sincere as has ever been heard on the screen—but: and again a telegram, again full-frame:

JULY 2, 1938.
MRS. JOHN AYSGARTH
THE GROVE   WICKSTEAD   SUSSEX
DEEPLY REGRET YOUR FATHER DIED EARLY
THIS MORNING FROM HEART FAILURE. YOUR
MOTHER WISHES YOU TO COME AT ONCE.
WILSON.

Who Wilson is we don't know and couldn't possibly care. But here is Lina overthrown by grief, Lina who truly cared about her father, and whose father was the needle on her compass, the beacon of her life, a light source that could have dimmed the world and made this John D. Aysgarth crystal clear in his emptiness once and for all.

Yet can we say the General really did try to help? She is lost in high seas chained to a deceiver. After the reading of the will Johnnie stands before the portrait, reduced if not chastened. He gazes up at that empty face, his back to the camera, and gives a (mock?) salute. "You win, old man." Her letter to Johnnie and the telegram in Johnnie's hand synchronous. Criss-cross.

[m] *The map.* Johnnie has taken Lina on a drive by the cliffs to see the property he intends to collaborate with Beaky in developing as a resort site. Waves pummeling the rocky shore, steep picturesque cliffs, but in the photograph he gives her to see, the map of his future, only stillness, nor a single human breath. If in the bookshop window a photograph doubled for a person here a photograph doubles for a landscape. And Johnnie's words double for facts.

[n] *The game.* Scrabble with Johnnie, Lina, and Beaky. D-O-U-B-T is fingered out on the tabletop. O reader, do not make the mistake of taking that word as Hitchcock's summary of Lina's condition. Hitchcock needs make no such summary, he has given us the condition and he knows that you doubt already, that doubt is your watchword. You have voyaged from comfy certainty into doubt, perhaps without noticing the motion. But in doubt you have made your bed.

[o] *The message.* Now on the table is P-O-N-S-O-R. Then, marked by being upside-down, G-U-S-H-R-Y-K-R-M-W. Then Lina's directorial

finger making M-U-D-D-E-R. Wait: having made, make change: the finger slides the first D out and replaces it with an R. The dirty word. Especially when it is close to home, and she is home now. (With an extra E and R, as Beaky notes offscreen, she could make M-U-R-D-E-R-E-R.) There comes up in vivid imagination the photograph of the cliff property, now with a superimposition of two little men standing at the precipice and her eyes pried open in shock. One of the figurines has gone over! In close-up we see Beaky's astonished face filling the screen, because it is he. Formula as invocation, the journey from garble into intelligibility being also a journey from presence into prediction. She has made a mantra, and she believes it to be coming real—as in making a curse.

[p] *The note in the flowers.* Unable to sleep, Lina awakes troubled and walks down the stairs. Handwritten on a slip of paper (and, yet again, presented full-screen in close-up):

> Tangmere-by-the-sea
> 1,600 acres
> apply
> Eustace Dodd & Co
> High Street
> Nearhaven.

Tangmere the tangy, Tangmere the *étang*, Tangmere the future, into which she now drives, alone. At the cliff head she is challenged by the physical force of the place. But worse, there are tire tracks leading off the edge. Lina has come to a station where visions of death are all around. Back home are becalming Johnnie and heartwarming Beaky, however. Not long later Johnnie has gone off. She finds a note tucked into a bouquet of flowers:

> Will be back
> soon darling
> All my love
> J.

Full-screen portrait of this note, with one flower leaning over it, a flower of love. Another notation (proposition) for us to see in print through Hitchcock's supremely directive photography: *pay attention— read this—take note of what it says.*

[q] *The obituary.* With Johnnie gone, Lina is visited by a pair of police inspectors, who show her a newspaper announcement:

STOP PRESS

ENGLISHMAN
FOUND DEAD

An Englishman met with
a mysterious end in a house
in Paris. He is believed to
be a Mr. Gordon Cochrane
Thwaite of Penshaze Cou [*cut off onscreen*]
Yorkshire.

(Penshaze, where Johnnie used to stay when he came down.) She drops into grief, into a shroud with room for only one because Johnnie is still ... where? Is he in France? Did he kill Beaky, was he the "Englishman," last to see the deceased alive? Another newspaper lies nearby with a bold headline:

MYSTERY

When Johnnie comes home he sadly recounts that he was in Yorkshire, not France. Poor Beaky, he drank too much brandy, we know he can't handle that. As Hitchcock gives no dramatic follow-up to the pieces of "fact" in the newspaper account, he leaves it to Lina (and her partner, the viewer) to speculate. Speculation is travel.

[r] *The consultation.* At Isobel's cozy cottage. Making an "expert" response to a question about poisoning, she is standing beside a shelf of bound

trial summaries. Really, her brother would know, he's the expert because he works in the coroner's office. Full-screen framed portrait of the brother, a bland-faced fellow in dark-framed spectacles staring at the viewer as though diagnostically. I will return to this photograph before saying good-bye. But oh, my!—one book is missing from the set, George Houghton's *Trial of Richard Palmer* . . .

But oh, yes!, Johnnie has it!

At home, Lina finds the volume hidden away and we have yet another full-screen close-up: *Trial of Richard Palmer*. George Houghton. Near it an envelope addressed by hand to

> Geo Melbeck Esq.
> 22 High Street
> Wickstead

of which, once again, a full-screen close-up.

All these full-screen close-ups of texts and partial texts. Again and again, handwriting, typing, printing, full words, broken words, the Scrabble tiles.

She pulls out the letter to Melbeck and reads what we, too, can see, in . . . yes, still another full-screen close-up: "___ the scheme I had in mind did not come off. If you could be patient a little while longer I'm sure I can find some other way to pay back the money I owe you. It has been very difficult for me to secure ___." Polite, submissive, imploring with etiquette, and offering confidence. A sweet enough note. Or, we must have begun finally to wonder, is it only piquant sauce to cover rotten meat?

[s] *The business communication.* A tea tray in bed for Lina. Many pillows, fluffed coverlets and sheets, the feeling of placid satin. Two letters have come . . . for her husband. Private and Confidential. Life Insurance Company 510 Old Broad Street and also Confidential The Guarantors Assurance Co., Ltd. 981 High Holborn London WC1. As Johnnie is in the bath she takes a liberty, sneaks on her eyeglasses and reads (what else but another full-screen close-up!):

> The Grove,
> Wickstead, Sussex

Dear Sir:

Replying to your inquiry regarding a loan of five hundred pounds against insurance policy number 163958 TR, we regret to state that under the conditions of this policy, such a loan cannot be granted. According to the terms of the policy, payment can only be made in the event of your wife's death.

If you recall, under the recent ____

He is emerging in his robe, presumably refreshed. The two of them smile into each others' faces. At such an instant, what else can one do? "In the event of your wife's death," a mantra now, resounding, swelling. Event. Wife. Death.

[t] *The dinner.* At Isobel's, a little dinner party. Among company, in a little social "game," a "murderer" is hunted around the table. Johnnie is given Isobel's formal imprimatur as *not* being one. This label—INNOCENT—is printed upon his character, a stamping and an enclosure, an enlightening and a brand. If anyone else in the film tried to place this label (upon Johnnie's trunk!) we might be far more suspicious but, of course, *Isobel would know.* She writes murder mysteries (old copies of which will surely compete for sales with murder mysteries by Mark Halliday). Isobel's label is a text that supersedes text. An identification that, Lina must believe, leans very close to truth.

[u] *The speedometer.* Driving out on the clifftop, speedometer in full-screen at 50 mph, then 62 mph. When one is anxious or distraught the foot can easily weigh on the accelerator. Is Johnnie simply unconscious of what he is doing? Or else, is he anything but unconscious, is he in fact devious, pressing down intentionally to gain a speed far too fast for this road? A suicide/catastrophe? How are we to interpret the speedometer as text, conveyance of an appalling premonition of disaster? The speedometer also *suggests itself*: indicates a speeding that "says" *speeding indicated.* Withdrawing a little, one can think about the various *speedy*, even on-the-spot diagnoses and conclusions that have been formed inside this story, and formed by us as the story travels, even if we have been observing ourselves forming them.

DIFFIDENT

As to Lina, the word "diffident" doesn't quite fit her. There is a certain withdrawal, a too-observant self-preservation. She has the caution of the very elevated, conscious without let-up that the masses may encroach at any moment, that the masses are gathering on the perimeter, a caution bred by others, to be sure, but now accepted by her in the most intimate way. What others will want, she seems to presume, is to edge their way in for a taste, for a direct exposure to what has always been denied. We see the guardedness in her freeze as Johnnie spies what's in her purse in the train compartment. We see it in her hesitation to walk out with him, her recalcitrance on the hillock, the desperation that throws her into kissing him only to pave a route away from her overprotective parents. We see her guarding herself when she is brought into her specially designed new house, her wonder, her fear to accept it outright. We see her hesitation with Beaky until she relaxes into friendship. We see her dismayed withdrawal when Johnnie fails to brighten at the paternal gift of the chairs. We see her open doubt when he arrives with the gifts. We see her pulling away even from the horrible Mrs Newsham on the street, not only a female's withdrawal from a competitive female but also a bona fide Upper's withdrawal from anyone who isn't *quite* on the inside. We see the self-guarding etiquette she uses in social situations, with Melbeck, for instance, and with Isobel. We see her regard for Johnnie in scene after scene, wavering between yielding admiration and terrified alienation: is he *in*, this man? has he long been there? or is he an outsider in masquerade? What does he truly want, after all? What, and what manner of thing?

She not only accepts with interest but also imbibes with devastating effect (as he does brandy) the simple observations Beaky offers up about Johnnie's scathing flippancy:

> LINA: He's given up betting.
>
> BEAKY: He has, has he? Don't you believe it, not Johnnie. He's a great lad, he is. You mustn't mind Johnnie cutting up. That's what makes him Johnnie.

Two zooms for us: (1) "He's a great lad," a direct indication from someone who knows Johnnie longer and better than Lina does: a great *lad*, that is, a boy dressed up in a man's body. And (2) "That's what makes him Johnnie": which is to say, the cutting up, the gambling, the charm—these are all intrinsic to the personality, not strategies in temporary employ. They are part of the distinctive and complex array that make up the individuality of this person, that make him incomparable. Incomparable Beaky should be trusted when he makes this comment. And part of Johnnie's character, too, is his insouciance, his bluntly visible failure to see the precipice on which he moves. Erving Goffman writes,

> When we look closely at the adaptation to life made by persons whose situation is constantly fateful, say that of professional gamblers or front-line soldiers, we find that aliveness to the consequences involved comes to be blunted in a special way. The world that is gambled is, after all, only a world, and the chance-taker can learn to let go of it. (*Ritual* 181)

A person whose adaptation is *constantly* fateful, as though Johnnie actually lives on the edge of the knife blade. And as we watch him, we do see that it is not events but the consequence of events to which his sensitivity is blunted, repeatedly, always. *Always.*

But Lina, who does not understand what is intrinsic to her own, will not grasp what is intrinsic to anyone else's personality. The very conceit of doing so is too esoteric, psychology textbook be damned. She accepts partial information from others, Melbeck quite especially, and formulates elaborate scenarios from it, as though some single fact, appropriately illuminated, could give away a whole scene. The picture of her father in the portrait seems to float with her, a guardian, everywhere she goes; a guardian and a ghost, and always to be judging, weighing, diagnosing. Have you got your wall up? But at the same time, even more crucially, whilst putting up one's guard one must be certain to cover it with one's front. Have you got your front up? Goffman writes of how a person "will often present initially a front of diffidence and composure, suppressing any show of feeling until [she] has found out what kind of line the others will be ready to support for [her]" (*Ritual* 16). A *front* of diffidence, not actual diffidence. Diffidence as a mask, to cover an active strategy of self-protection, long ago learned, unremittingly in use.

INNOCENT MEN

Hitchcock's "innocent man" theme, as it is often called, works smoothly and evenly to produce spectatorial pleasure even in the nodal moments when the protagonist's identity comes under question, say, with Manny Balestrero (Henry Fonda) in *The Wrong Man* (1956) or with Roger Thornhill (Grant) in the Townsend study, bullied by Vandamm (James Mason) and Leonard (Martin Landau), where he is—as he himself would put it—misidentified as George Kaplan, to his peril. Another quite fascinating retroactively tagged "innocent person" is Bernice Edgar (Louise Latham) in *Marnie* (1964). Another is the "defecting" Michael Armstrong (Paul Newman), derogated by his fiancée Sarah Sherman (Julie Andrews) in *Torn Curtain* (1966). Often thought archetypical is Richard Hannay (Robert Donat) in *The 39 Steps* (1935), accused of a London murder and chased across the United Kingdom before his innocence can be declared. Another landmark case is the visiting stranger in *The Lodger* (1927), presumed guilty of mass murders until he is found—almost too late—to be innocent. A more charming and picaresque example is John Robie (Grant) in *To Catch a Thief* (1955), widely thought a prince of cat burglars, even by the girl who falls in love with him.[17]

A variant is the case of the "false innocent," as we find with Mrs. Paradine (Alida Valli) in *The Paradine Case* (1947), a woman whose lawyer works intensively to free her in a murder trial only to discover that she is, in fact, guilty. Another is Lars Thorwald (Raymond Burr) in *Rear Window* (1954): about him our heroes have suspicions but without good reason except that things don't smell right. As it turns out the man is in fact a brutal butcherer who has chopped up his wife and deposited parts of her around New York.

In all these cases, however, the innocence of the "innocent figure," whether (a) claimed strenuously by that person and denied by others or else (b) presumed by others who discover their error, is a matter of moral definition between characters. Both the person caught in the "innocence trap" and the hunters who catch him or her are characters in the film. This means not only that there are very good diegetic reasons presented, *at some point*, for how and why a person as clean and noble as this should fall under such a negative approbation, but also that there are very good diegetic reasons presented for how and why the identity that accusatory others erect is a mistaken one. In *The Wrong Man*, for example, when the detectives come to Manny's house to take him away, we have already learned enough about him to have a fairly keen sense that he is innocent; but we also learn enough about police procedure to deduce painfully why he has been picked up. Hitchcock elaborates the cunning inaccuracy of systemic perception until it reaches a stunning apotheosis near the ending, since the problem with Manny is that he fits a witness description and what we will learn is that with any such description there are many people who could fit it; indeed, that "fitting" is a problem in itself.

What concerns me here, however, is a different version of the "innocent" theme altogether, one in which the audience is expressly implicated. Rather than sitting back in the shades to watch the threads of false accusation fall out, we participate in it directly, and the direction of orientation of the filmic statement, rather than being *lateral*, from one character (or set) to another in our field of view, is *presentational*, between a character and the viewer. If there are characters onscreen who either agree with the viewer's assessment or, in abject fear of the character labeled, lead the viewer to make that assessment in their stead, all the better, since in any event it is the viewer, not the assisting characters, finally producing and affixing the label. I might call these "dirty innocent" films for the simple reason that their mechanism depends on the central character being signally beneath praise, even louche, the sort of person who can attract the antipathy of the audience, with ease and with visible reason. One very perplexing case is Uncle Charlie (Joseph Cotten) in *Shadow of a Doubt* (1943), whose violent capability is made visible—and then only tentatively so—in the film's finale, a point when he has been hounded by many other people for crimes, of his participation in which *absolutely no* evidence is presented onscreen. There are plenty of reasons given for suspecting this duplicitous, craven, ugly, antisocial, even misogynist man, but the two principal cases of action—his young niece Charlie (Teresa Wright) almost falling to her death on a sabotaged staircase outside her house and Uncle Charlie himself grappling with her near the door of a moving train—come precariously close to tagging the man definitively ... but finally stop short. What is not stopped short in this film is the accusation of him by others, strong enough to make us wonder, make us worry, and finally make us crusade. The viewers' crusade.

But *Suspicion* is the Hitchcockian masterwork of "dirty innocence." I have argued here for consideration of the class similarity yet psychological differences between Johnnie and Lina with one express purpose only, to make clear how every single one of his undertakings and peccadilloes, every gesture, whilst undergoing fluctuating interpretation from anxious Lina, can render Johnnie a thoroughgoing riddle if not a roué *for us*. He may well have motive for violent action; he may come into the means; and there is surely some dispute about whether or not he has the character: but motive, means, and character are fundaments of speculation, and speculation only. A telling example: at the Sedbusk dinner table that odd little game, "Who Might Have the *Look* of a Possible Murderer?" Lina is quickly dismissed, and it falls to Isobel, the reigning expert, to pass judgment on Johnnie. She is unequivocal and explicit, even emphatic. There is no chance on earth that he is a murderer. He doesn't have it in him. A cut to Johnnie reveals a typically unexpressive moment, yet his face seems to have relaxed a little into amenity. Or has it relaxed because The Expert has given him cover? Or because finally, once and for all, and from the lips of this hostess, he is anointed the Innocent he would believe himself to be were he to step away from the track of his feeling and pick up a self-judgmental eye? To read past the surface of this dilemma—or to attempt such a reading, since generally speaking there is no reading past the surface of dilemmas—we could look at the pronouncer. Isobel is a woman of advancing age, thus no fool. She has created dozens upon dozens of fictional murderers and from other bits of her conversation we can gather that she has a penchant for realism (never shying away from consultation with her medical-expert brother, for example). What she says is probably based in some practical wisdom and insight, if we could say there is such a thing as insight. She seems wise, at any rate—one could argue, the only character in *Suspicion* who seems wise. Yet at the same time her métier is fiction, not science, and she resides therefore in the domain of the artful, even, it could be argued, the *merely* artful. Yet, too:

The domain of the artful is Alfred Hitchcock's domain. Not only is Isobel our closest signpost to wisdom, she is the closest relation to the filmmaker we find here, the woman who is making whole "worlds" up, just like, right now, right here, Hitchcock. Given the general state of doubt into which the story casts us, I do not think it unreasonable to think of Isobel's diagnosis of Johnnie as wholly correct. We must at least try to work our way through the film by adopting her point of view.

At the same time (Isobel would know), a false moral diagnosis is a fabulous theme for a work of fiction, and as she may be making one here so may Hitchcock.

If Johnnie is deeply innocent or, at least, imaginably so, something else now gains forelight as the centerpiece of this drama, something that until we stand back and see the film this way passes entirely unnoticed because it appears—like a fox on the run—to fit so artfully into its surround. And that is Lina McLaidlaw's suspicion in the first place. The suspicion she never hesitates to show, that she shows with her hesitant self-protective face from the moment light comes onto the screen; and that, because (along with Johnnie) we find her so attractive, we pick up and share with her as though no other position could be reasonable in the face of this man. He arouses suspicion, he has always aroused suspicion. Johnnie Aysgarth is the living altar of suspicion. And so is Cary Grant.

What, then, is suspicion? More crucially, what can be its ultimate value? Jean-Paul Sartre asks,

> How can I evaluate causes and motives on which I myself confer their value before all deliberation and by the very choice which I make of myself? The illusion here stems from the fact that we endeavor to take causes and motives for entirely transcendent things which I balance in my hands like weights and which possess a weight as a permanent property. Yet on the other hand we try to view them as contents of consciousness, and this is self-contradictory. Actually causes and motives have only the weight which my project—*i.e.,* the free production of the end and of the known act to be realized—confers upon them. When I deliberate, the chips are down. And if I am brought to the point of deliberating, this is simply because it is a part of my original project to realize motives by means of *deliberation* rather than by some other form of discovery (by passion, for example, or simply by action, which reveals to me the organized ensemble of causes and of ends as my language informs me of my thought). (*Being* 581)

Thinking his way through feeling, Sartre sees that thinking itself may be problematic, and if thinking then surely the knowledge that seems to blossom from it. Hitchcock will often take up the theme of knowledge in its capacity to block or eviscerate feeling, nowhere more explicitly or more powerfully than here and in *The Man Who Knew Too Much* (1956), where the metrical and notational aspect of music is pitted directly against the harmonic and emotive element. Before plunging too far down the rabbit hole with Lina, let us note that she is surely a calculating person. We can see her eyeing Johnnie with an estimating gaze even on the railway, and later when he tugs her hair and calls her "Monkeyface," and when she is introduced to their sparkling new home. Her eyes are always wondering, "How? From where?" She is always assembling the facts of her present and her past into some logical arrangement, and the hyper-rational Isobel, her creative chum, does nothing to inhibit this kind of thought. Lina wants knowledge, and when she seems distraught it is because she hasn't come into it.

Isobel and her protégée are both committed Cartesians. They draw away from inspirations, they back off from what Stanley Cavell calls the "mystery of the unfamiliar" (*World* 182). They are concerned with what is legal, not what is tender. They are, strictly speaking, as Descartes has it in his Fourth Meditation, careful, not in the sense of *having care* but as in *taking caution*:

> I have become accustomed to withdrawing my mind from the senses, and I have carefully taken note of the fact that very few things are truly perceived regarding corporeal things, although a great many more things are known regarding the human mind, and still many more things regarding God. The upshot is that I now have no difficulty in directing my thought away from things that can be imagined to things that can be grasped only by the understanding and are wholly separate from matter. (81)

The "whole separation" from matter is invoked powerfully in the film: each time Lina "relapses" into a secure, loving submission to Johnnie's bountiful protectiveness she is in his arms, fallen from the peak of her critical promontory into the confusing, aromatic, pulsing field of his embodied self. Every time she enters a sphere of blackening and terrifying doubt she has withdrawn her mind from her senses, since what she senses of Johnnie, entirely insufficient to appease her dominating curiosity, is as painfully inscrutable as what we may sense of anyone. She wants to theorize his position, his intention, his identity, his project rather than moving into accompaniment with him. What Lina's hyper-cautious father and silent mother have failed to teach her, somehow, is that though we cannot live with perduring doubt, the belief in the supremacy of certainty that gives doubt rise is problematic.

Doubt about others, that is. Doubt about our human family. Because there is a Greater, more illuminating, more enthralling Doubt, of which Cavell has raised the specter. That is something far beyond what wounded Lina experiences as we watch. Cavell can move to his consideration, to his wonder, because what holds his attention and his love as he writes, more even than the world itself, that vague construct, is film and its touch upon a world. *Touch*. In reading him, one is drawn to an always more enchanting and more stupefying view of Johnnie and Lina as creatures of the screen, to the story as a filmed story, to the events as pictures: "I speak of film's growing doubt of its ability to allow the world to exhibit itself, and instead its taking over the task of exhibition, against its nature" (*World* 132). Not only that film shows and can show, but that it "takes over the task" of showing, it modifies, according to composition and balance, light and depth, articulation and silence, not only the face but the heightened gesture of the face. Not only the event but the moment.

What of film's "doubt," however? Does film, attached as it is to the surface of things, recognize this attachment, deeply acknowledge its impotence to see what cannot be seen and at the same time devote itself to the project of showing what cannot be seen by way of what can? Lina has not come quite to this special stance: she is keenly aware that in Johnnie some purposes and features are not visible, but instead of working her way toward him through a passion she backs off in suspicion of what she cannot possibly know. He has become for her, as she has very much not become for him, something objective. Eric Rohmer and Claude Chabrol write of the Hitchcockian symbol that through it "we not only clearly discover the Idea, but—if it can be put that way—we feel it"; and of this complex Idea one element is foremost, "the fundamental *abjectness* of a human being, who once deprived of his freedom is no more than an object among other objects" (147). Lina's suspicion robs Johnnie of his freedom, makes him, in her judgmental phase at least, an abject thing. And, Rohmer and Chabrol indicate, the innocent is distanced from the accusations he is undergoing but also feels them more intensely for that.

In his *À rebours* (*Against Nature*), Joris-Karl Huysmans argues that even dropping away the pretentious labels of epicureanism and false artifice, say by reflection alone, a person can reach the very heights of a life-giving imagination—to leave facts and information behind, then, and proceed on a special kind of voyage, even, as Cavell has hinted, a voyage against nature, by way of film. Film takes up the demonstrative world and makes of it a new, a newly illuminated, demonstration. Huysmans writes of how a man

> could procure himself, without ever stirring from home, in a moment, almost instantaneously, all the sensations of a long voyage; the pleasure of moving from place to place, a pleasure which indeed hardly exists save as a matter of after recollection, almost never as a present enjoyment at the moment of the actual journey, this he could savour to the full at his ease, without fatigue or worry, in this improvised cabin, whose ordered disorder, whose transitional look and temporary arrangement, corresponded closely enough with the nature of the flying visits he paid it ... A man can undertake long voyages of exploration sitting in his armchair by the fireside, helping out, if needful, his recalcitrant or sluggish imagination by the perusal of some work descriptive of travels in distant lands. (19)

In *Suspicion*, ironically, the catharses of encounter, trust, and love are possible only after, *and because*, our two heroes have abandoned their "improvised cabins" and gone into the world for an exploratory hike, she having come to the end of a tether in her parents' home as the cozy walls keep her isolated from the world and he bent on scouting possibilities in a frenzy of disconnection. Each of them undertakes a "long voyage of exploration" while we watch. For one the voyage leads away from suspicion and toward reconciliation; for the other the point of departure was narcissism of a sort and the destination is growth. The voyage brings each of them from place to place, always without satisfaction, always in hope of some calming resolution that seems never to come but the absence of which is the more painful the more keenly it is sensed.

Even more painful sensed by us than by them. In this Hitchcockian masterpiece, as we must come to see, Lina's suspicion is but a convenient and aesthetically appealing simulacrum of the viewer's. We find reflected onscreen our own fulsome capacity to doubt Johnnie, entirely without evidence, to fear him without reason and hold back from him without a plan, this even from the first syllables in his voice. As, at film's end, Johnnie and Lina drive off from the clifftop and into the far horizon, we are left open to escaping our own suspicions, to either laying aside our own protective fabric of doubt or wrapping ourselves inside it for entrenchment. At the end of exploration might or might not life's reward be waiting in some innermost sanctum, beside some innermost hearth?

RIDDLE

The Hitchcockian work typically contains at least one element that cannot be explained in line with the well-received theories that fans, scholars, and researchers have put forward as a canon. Element: a scene, perhaps a camera angle, a phrase of dialogue that rings right but doesn't meaningfully harmonize. Perhaps even a single shot. My own experience thinking about Hitchcock's films has been that giving the anomaly particular, even special attention and musing it through as deeply as seems possible in the flow of life—which for any of us is a great current containing much that has nothing to do with film or this filmmaker—seem to lead to the discovery of a kind of new light, or new point of view, from which the entire film shifts and clarifies in value, shifts and clarifies like a mother's face looming forward toward a baby and resting at one special distance. As example: one could argue that in *Vertigo* (1958) the little passage in which Midge stops her Karmann Ghia in the middle of Lombard Street near Scottie's house and observes him with Madeleine is such an odd moment, a piece of grit, as it were, around which the oyster can fashion its pearl: not that she sees the two of them together; but that she is in her car, rolling down that street, when she sees. In *Saboteur* (1942), the moment when Philip Martin sits to piano and plays Delius's "Summer Night on the River." In *Psycho* (1960), the sheriff's wife being careful to remember how she helped Norman pick out the dress his mother was buried in, it was periwinkle blue. *Periwinkle blue*, in a black and white film.

In *Suspicion* the anomaly, as I would term it, is one single shot, inserted in a context to which it is tangentially, but only tangentially, related and at a moment that has nothing to do with what came before and what will come after:

A camera's portrait close-up of a portrait, a framed photograph of a dignified looking man in thick spectacles, glaring forward at the camera. We will meet this man at dinner, the brother of Isobel Sedbusk (Gavin Gordon) and forensic analyst for the Home Office (the government agency responsible for undertakings *within* the United Kingdom). It is certainly easy enough to at least superficially explain the presence of this shot, given that as we meet him the man is sitting at table with Johnnie, Lina, Isobel, and an intelligent but somewhat silent woman, Phyllis Swinghurst (Nondas Metcalf). The brother sits dutifully devouring his squab: he slices into it like a coroner doing an autopsy, and indeed does gaze down at the bird's interior as he slices it open (*autopsy* means "seeing with one's own eyes"). We could, as I say, position the photograph of this man as a detail regarding his identity, especially in this close-knit circle.

The discussion at the table involves killing and morality, and ultimately whether anyone sitting there has the physiognomy of a murderer. A specific issue raised by Johnnie, once the talk gets around to poison as a method of killing, is whether or not anyone has discovered a poison traces of which cannot be detected. The brother jerks his action to a halt and turns his eyes askance at Isobel, a gesture picked up by Johnnie. This brother, then, is the scientific expert—as opposed to his eagerly fictionalizing sister—who can attest to the existence of such a chemical. If this poison is, so to speak, the MacGuffin of the film, something Johnnie could—and, Lina fears, will—use to kill for her money, the gawking face of the governmentally sanctioned brother is its telltale icon: there must be *some* kind of observable icon for reference, especially since, in this case, the MacGuffin itself is invisible and undetectable. We might see the photograph as a giveaway that there is factual, organic truth to the undetectable-poison theory.

However:

It is not in the dinner scene that Bertram Sedbusk, M.D. is invoked this way. It is earlier. Lina has been considerably perturbed: by Johnnie's absence when poor Beaky died in Paris; then by the intrusion and inferences of the local police, who suggest that an unknown Englishman bet Beaky he couldn't drink brandy. She has already been entertaining fantasies about Beaky's special vulnerability: her daydream. So now, is she living with a rank murderer? She makes a visit to her good friend Isobel on the pretext of being wholly caught up with the author's new book. The conversation, intimate, cozy, sunlit, calm, turns to killing by the administration of brandy to someone who cannot tolerate it, and Isobel invokes that celebrated case of Richard Palmer—

> ISOBEL: The fool got bored with the brandy method and went on to real poison.
>
> LINA: He was a fool, wasn't he.
>
> ISOBEL (continuing to search): Maybe I put it under the "T's."
>
> LINA: If he'd stuck to brandy, he might have . . .
>
> ISOBEL: That's an interesting idea. Suppose I ask my brother about it. He's the Home Office Analyst. Conducts post-mortems and all that sort of thing. I get some of my neatest ideas from him,

—the trial record of which is mysteriously missing from her bookshelf. Then she has that chilling recollection: "Johnnie borrowed it a couple of weeks ago."

It is here that we meet the clear-eyed brother.

And yet this encounter Hitchcock arranges for us with the expert Dr Sedbusk actually does not have roots in the scene:

- Isobel is a person devoted to verbal description, not imagery. Everything of her practice is verbal. She is invoking an important brother, but is not a person who would feel the need to illustrate, and so the photograph is not a hint of, or reference to, her own intention at the moment. *She is not showing it*, though she has placed it quite generally on show.

- Isobel may well be thinking of her brother, especially thinking of him as a man who conducts post-mortems and from whom she gets some of her neatest ideas (note the scripted link between the word "neat" and the word "post-mortem," a process that is neat in some ways, its establishment of facts and voyage to conclusions, and distinctively not neat in others, its undoing of the order of the body). She may have him in mind, yet we are nowhere in the film brought so close to Isobel as a character, as a personality, that we would care to have an inside view of her mind. We are brought that close to Lina, so when Lina imagines Beaky being pushed off the cliff we are shown images of that imagination. Isobel's fraternal reference is casual and doesn't call for a photograph or any other sort of imaging. She has a brother, fine. He needn't have presence now just because he has been invoked. And at any rate, we shall be meeting him by and by. As happens, when we do meet him we can be charged by his resemblance to this photograph: that is, he is a man who looks like a photograph of a man. But when we see the photograph we do not know that we will be meeting the man.

- Bertram's so-claimed optical acuity is questioned by the image, too. What it is impossible to neglect in seeing this fast-fleeting shot is the thickness of the eyeglass lenses. They suggest bluntly that this is an extremely near-sighted person who can see only what is physically close to him, thus possibly a man whose "learning" and "information" are questionable in this respect. Even if an object were almost touching him, he would probably see it better with his glasses on (think of Miriam Haines [Laura Elliott] in *Strangers on a Train* [1951]). Metaphorically, as he gazes out at us spectating, he cannot see what he is looking at, not only because we are in another moment in space and time but also because even if without his glasses the character had been standing before it the camera would have been undetectable for him at that distance.[18]

- The conversation at the moment we are shown this photograph is highlighting the hypothetical progress of a murdering mind, from using brandy to using real poison, brandy being only a poison-like substance and one that would affect only some bodies. We will come to attend to Dr Sedbusk in light of a suggestion that there is an untraceable poison but that suggestion isn't being made now, won't in fact be made for some little time; and when it is made it will be made by Johnnie himself and the extreme expressivity of the doctor will make him look different than he does in the portrait.

- Indeed, when the photograph of the doctor is placed before us it seems to come out of the blue in terms of the flow and content of Isobel's talk. It is like a jump away, an incoherent hint. And it could, one must notice, be taken at this moment—given that Isobel doesn't point to it when she mentions her brother—as the author's treasured photograph of some particularly fascinating killer. If we look at the blank stare behind the lenses, the cold stolidity of the face altogether, it is not difficult to imagine malice, albeit well groomed.

The question that seems provocative here is: why is the shot of this photograph in the film? Not long before, Lina looks up for inspiration to the portrait of her father and that portrait fills the frame, eyes looking out at us. Is the portrait of the brother iconic for Isobel in the same kind of way? Does she look up to the brother, who gives her not only some of her "neatest" ideas but some supreme elevation of confidence as well? Possibly so, but even if she does regard him with adoration, we don't have reason to care because Isobel is by no means central to the action here. Central to the action is Lina's querulousness as the conversation winds on, her starting up by raving about the new novel and then progressively becoming more and more fearful, more and more disturbed at the simple verbal intimation of things.

As it is conventionally understood—opportunity for arcane information to come Lina's way—the scene would play perfectly well without this photograph. In the same way the police visit scene plays quite well with only a verbal indication of an Englishman in Paris.

In the later dinner-table scene Isobel never for a moment seems so attached to her brother that she can't get him out of her mind. He is a kind of dull, bureaucratic, self-involved cipher, self-involved perhaps because the world is so hard to get at for him. He can't quite "get the picture."

But in a way there are Dr Sedbusks all over the place, surely all over this film. The world, whatever we may think it, is hard to get at for everybody, if not optically then sensually, philosophically, psychologically, historically. It is hard to get at things, hard to see them, yet Lina, in her bravery, thinks herself perceptive; thinks Dr Sedbusk is very much not like her. Viewers of the film would like to think the same of themselves.

Once more, that image: those thick, those glaring lenses! The lenses sitting upon a face staring out coldly *and neutrally*; neutral because of the coldness, cold because of the neutrality. The direct suggestion, one that we *see* much before we think about it—indeed, a suggestion we may well see instead of thinking about—is: *sight*. Sight ... looking ... detecting ...

inspecting ... the picture itself and, as we look at the screen, *this* picture itself. The compromised ability to "get the picture." I have been positing Johnnie as a man whose sight is afflicted—far more, actually, than Dr Sedbusk's, because Johnnie *can* see but he doesn't; isn't looking; doesn't labor to put the pieces of the world puzzle together in order to make structure, motive, exigency, and outcome clear. *That's what makes him Johnnie.* He throws himself into situations and rides them out. And the Home Office Analyst is a metaphor for ... not murder, not poison, not detection but: Lina. Lina the fact collector, the assembler—and fashioner—of codes ("M-U-D-D-E-R" > "M-U-R-D-E-R"). Lina, who wants more than anything to love Johnnie except that her trepidation gets in the way. Lina, who means well, but who is blocked from seeing by her uninterrupted vision. Johnnie doesn't see; Lina doesn't see. Does the audience see?

For us—Hitchcock is here, now, always concerned with us—the riddle is that Johnnie's true character, his inner child always mistaken for being in the wrong because it is clothed in the body of an adult, is something we are given to see. We are given to see it, just as Lina's persistent not seeing is given to us to see. There is only one element of this story not given to us to see, and that is the faces of Johnnie and Lina in the final moment as they drive away from the cliff toward ... toward their future. Are they settling into friendship with one another again? Are they more distanced than ever? Is Lina now, and will Lina ever permit herself to be, even somewhat less repletely filled with suspicion? And what will happen to Johnnie, if he keeps loving her?

THREE PATHS TO HAPPENSTANCE

Left Behind

The reading of the General's will being done—as to "will," we must remember always that look of complacent willfulness on his face in the portrait, and in life—Johnnie is taking Lina for a drive by the edge of the sea. He is in a dark pin-stripe and dark fedora, she in lace-trimmed black, with a black veil. They are musing about futures and possibilities, expressing their twin loves. "Marrying you is the one thing I've never changed my mind about," says he. "I want nothing but to spend the rest of my life with you." She only stopped loving him once, says Lina, when she found out he had been dismissed by Capt. Melbeck. Very tight shot of his darkened face under the dark brim, but then, relaxed into a smile, he dismisses Melbeck: "My ideas are too daring for him." They stop in front of the truly majestic, wild, deeply promising environment, a stunning evocation of inscrutable Natural Force with, just behind the car, a little rise of ground on which a few fat sheep are grazing: perfect bucolic simplicity, as in Boucher. Somebody should do something with this land. He could make a start with 10,000 pounds; better with twenty. In fact, another ten wouldn't hurt on top of that. Landscape + capital investment = tomorrow.

Then on the Aysgarth dining table Johnnie and Beaky are plotting out a plan, the first man in a light suit with swank wide lapels, his friend in an immodest checked blazer. Lina is still in black, but at her ucipital mapilary she has an artful flounce of gay white muslin. Beaky will sell some shares in Paris to form the company, Johnnie explains, but the thing will be in his name. They will "buy up" the land and then sell part of it, realizing a hundred percent profit immediately, and then "build something" on the rest. Here and always, Lina does not know any reaction but prudence and protective retreat: "But from whom do you buy the land? How much do you pay for it? To whom do you sell it?" It will be Beaky's money, says Johnnie, "my idea." He leaves the room to take a telephone call leaving Beaky alone with Lina, who gently questions the probity and sense of handing all the control over to Johnnie. But suddenly Johnnie is at the door, overhearing. He amicably sends Beaky up to his room and takes Lina aside.

A new Lina.

A new Johnnie.

A Lina who has dared to venture outside the tiny, pretty picket fence of her own pretty self-enclosure. A Johnnie who has felt an invasion:

> JOHNNIE (with brusk, staccato tone): Look here. What right have you to interfere in my affairs?
>
> LINA (stumblingly): Well, I wasn't really, I—. Well, I was only—
>
> JOHNNIE (glaring): You were only what?!
>
> LINA: Well, I was only trying to tell Beaky that he shouldn't leave everything to you because if something went wrong he should take a

little responsibility, too. It's not as though you were both experienced businessmen. (*She is understandably being protective of Johnnie, trying to think out a way to prevent him being caught off-guard with a nightmare. They walk toward the camera. He is boiling.*)

JOHNNIE (cutting): What the devil do you know about business? . . . Suppose Beaky had taken you seriously. You'd have ruined the whole scheme, do you realize that?

LINA (still trying): Yes, but if it weren't any good.

JOHNNIE: (*They have come to the foot of the staircase.*) That's my business, not yours. (*She steps ahead of him. Shadows on the wall in the background.*) If I say it's good, it's good. I'm going through with this deal . . . (*The enshadowed stairs, the two bodies climbing side by side, faces encountering each other.*) I don't want any interference from you or anyone else. Is that clear?!

LINA (*near the top of the stairs*): Yes, that's clear.

What is surely clear is that Johnnie had a "whole scheme" up his sleeve, and we are given no clue about it. At the same time, why should Lina, or the viewer, be given a clue about Johnnie's private scheme? Why should she, or we, expect clues, according negative moral value to his secretiveness?

As they move with identical speed up the stairs, in a magnificent example of performers' muscular control, the two faces do not turn away from each other as shadows creep across. He turns and walks ahead of her as the scene fades to black. He is leaving her behind, no doubt. She is *de la baggage inutile*.

Doubt

The next morning. Lina is in her garden attentively "manicuring" a shrub. She faces the camera space at screen left, the shrub in front of her, some patio stones and steps and flowers and trees spreading behind. Comfortable, decorous, almost enchanting space, the kind of space that leads to dreaming. She is in her cashmere twin set (her class-defining cashmere twin set) and might well be daydreaming as she uses the shears (that Hitchcockian tool *par excellence*). But a figure creeps in from the right. Male, in a dark coat, back to camera taking up the whole right side of the image. Gazing at her.[19]

"Hello, Monkeyface!"

She looks up wide-eyed, eyebrows pulled up. Instant fear and defensiveness after a half-beat, with the importation of a smile that is swiveled toward surprise. "You frightened me, I didn't see you coming."

He walks around the bush to stand, smiling warmly, at her side. "I thought you might like to know, I'm going off the real estate plan."

"Why? What happened?" (Curiosity, but also manifest dubiousness.)

"Nothing..."

"Beaky know about this?" (Beaky, ready to put in—perhaps already having put in—30,000 pounds.)

(Lifting a cigarette to mouth): "No, not yet." ("Not yet": I am keeping it secret from him, I am going to snag his money. Or, I haven't got around to telling him yet. Or, I just haven't seen him this morning.)

"Why are you doing it?"

"Oh, I don't know," looking down pensively, self-doubting, "Perhaps the land isn't any good. Who knows? Or, uh, perhaps I don't like the idea of risking Beaky's money. Or, uh," turning his head to the side, "Perhaps it's a stiff job and I'm too lazy." A well-timed slightly self-mocking smile. He has an ascot around his neck, and a matching kerchief tucked into his breast pocket: all the essence of respectability. Lazy respectability? Or is the application of the epithet "lazy" to him meant to be our mocking of what he thinks she is thinking now?

Her face opens, in supplication. "Are you still angry about last night?"

JOHNNIE: No, I'm not angry.

LINA: Are you sure, because I... I couldn't sleep all night. Because you've never spoken so sharply to me before and I... I was afraid t—

JOHNNIE: Afraid of what?

LINA (quietly): I was afraid you'd stopped loving me.

JOHNNIE (gently, with sincerity): No, Monkeyface, I'm not angry. (*He touches her head.*) And I love you very much. *Pausing, then retaining the skeleton of his smile, he turns and walks away puffing the cigarette, his dark back receding as he heads for the steps to the house.*

The camera dollies into LINA's reflecting face as the next shot comes up in a lap dissolve: D-O-U-B in the Scrabble game. Does all doubt begin with doubt about being loved? More terrifying: does all doubt begin with the word "doubt"? Or is that word the best we can do to point at a complex and condition that elude understanding?

Milk

Home after the Sedbusk dinner party, Lina admits that she feels she would like to be alone tonight. Johnnie becomes quietly snide: she used to have trouble sleeping when he wasn't there, now she has trouble when he is. When he walks out of the bedroom she trembles and collapses to the carpet. We find her next recuperating in a glowing white-satined bed, white satin sheets over her, white satin headboard behind.[20] Warm bedside light. Johnnie is tenderly on one side of her and Isobel on the other, present, apparently, all day long since he called for her. "He's one in a million, that Johnnie of yours!":

> ISOBEL: And I warn you, you'd better get well. If you leave me alone much longer with this husband of yours, my career will soon be over ...
>
> LINA (feebly): He flirted with you, I suppose.
>
> ISOBEL: Flirted? Worse than that. He's worming all my secrets out of me. I should think he were writing a detective story on the side. (*The kind of supposition a self-centered author like this would harbor.*)
>
> LINA (fearfully, but with a pleasant half-smile): (*As light glows on the satin sheet and headboard.*) What secrets?
>
> ISOBEL: He's always pestering me. I always swear I won't tell you and I always do.
>
> LINA (fingering her sheet nervously, dropping her gaze): Did you tell him anything today?
>
> ISOBEL: Did I! Bertram was furious! Said he'd never confide in me again. (*Lina's eyes stretch open in curiosity.*) But honestly, have *you* ever been able to deny Johnnie anything?

LINA (looking aside): Never. It . . . It was about that poison, wasn't it.

ISOBEL: Don't remind me of it. I'm ashamed and mortified and disgraced. I'm just a fool, that's all. If he writes a story on that one before I do . . . I suppose I'll deserve it. Imagine. A substance in daily use everywhere. Anyone can lay his hands on it. And within a minute after taking, the victim's beautifully out of the way. (*Lina's eyes have been opening wider and wider. Her head falls back into the pillow.*) Mind you: it's undetectable after death.

LINA (with eyes lifted up, as though to Heaven, and as though taking a final breath): Is whatever it is . . . painful?

Isobel's answer indicates not only that Lina might well fall into awestruck wonder about this magic, but that she herself, who uses words about such things so fluently, has fallen, too. "Not in the least. In fact, I should think it would be a most pleasant death."

What has Lina faced, so far, this vulnerable young person conscious of the world as threat? That this man Johnnie Aysgarth is somewhat forward, if charming. That he thinks it proper to play with her—reach out on the hillock to undo her top button—rather than moving slowly ahead, nineteenth-century fashion, in modest steps. That he is boisterous enough to crash the Hunt Ball. That, married, he is eager to spend money, even if the money is hers. That he makes plans, as it were, "on a ledge," for example, betting on horses when he hasn't a farthing in his pocket. And then he breathes the same atmosphere, the village of Wickstead, the corners at Hazledene, in which her dear chum Isobel not only pens stories of murder but even brings the subject up in amicable conversation. Murder in the air. She is prepared through all of this for these scenes I describe, and what does she take away from them?

- That he not only drives (quickly) by the very ledge of the cliffs but is in fact planning to take himself, and her with him, onto a financial "ledge" by getting into a massive real estate project (in which, she knows, he has no expertise; or does one require expertise?) that could bring utter ruin.

- That he is seducing his chum Beaky into the project, and into funding it, so that her participation conversationally is powerfully resented, even bitten at. He is an ambitious cad, perhaps, willing to walk away from her if she gets in the way of what he believes he wants.

- That he still calmly protests that he loves her, implying that she can count on him. Though he seemed angry, he is not angry. Or makes that claim. (That is: he is not what he seemed.)

- That there exists a lethal, phenomenal substance, utterly mortal yet also utterly commonplace—we are never given more clues than that—*and that Johnnie has been learning about it.*

We have come all the way now from a pleasant railway carriage in the dark to the darkest copse in the Forest of Suspicion. It is night, play time of spirits. Lina is abed, unable to sleep, frightened, disoriented, acquiescent facing terror. A high overhead shot looking down from the upper level to the atrium below, where the staircase rounds off to the floor. From the right some opening of a door and a long exceedingly brilliant triangle of light rushing across the space to counterpoint the array of shapely shadows. A dark male figure emerging with a tray containing a white glass, moving leftward with a steady pace, gaining the stairs, easily mounting. We are before Johnnie now, tracking upward and backward as he climbs, and we see the glass of milk radiating like the pallid face of the crucified Savior. A perfectly—exquisitely—unexpressive face. The staid hands of a butler. The milk coming forward, spreading light, not—as we all know, because this is one of the iconic moments in all of Hitchcock—because it reflects some light (there is no light to reflect) but because it has its own incandescence, its own cold blaze. Forward. Forward. Forward directly into the camera.

Suspicion is Hitchcock's perfect masterpiece of what he calls *suspense*. The preparing of the audience for a thrilling moment but the holding off of that moment, suspending it (like the Cumaean Sibyl). When she drinks this, is Lina to know that she is meeting her death? When she drinks this, is Lina to trust that Johnnie is bringing her a glass of milk to help her sleep? We can imagine her in the bed as she reaches out to take what he offers, rapidly rushing through a calculation of his ambiguities one after another, his train of ambiguities rushing into a tunnel, and asking herself how many ambiguities one can tolerate before dropping into the thing we call *certainty*. Because there is no action of Johnnie Aysgarth's in this film that does not support multiple explanations. And there is no action that does not hint at something malevolent, yet only hint. How many hints can pile up? How much before we need to know?

Before not only Lina but also the viewer needs to know. Not guess, imagine, speculate, wonder, but *know*.

Because as Hitchcock has framed his film, we are never given to know.

Suspecting and suspecting (watching Lina suspect and suspect), we must come to ask whether the "substance in daily use everywhere," that after death leaves no trace, is suspicion itself. Suspicion not only the motive, not only the mechanism of interaction, but in fact the poison. DOUBT ... SUSPICION ... MUDDER ... MURDER. Hints piling up until we know; drops ingested until we drop.

How many nuances make a fact? How many coincidences make a happening? How many potentialities make a truth? How much suspicion does it take to make for a very pleasant death?

Julio Cortázar writes of a "confidential memo" from the "Secretary of OCLUSIOM" to the "Secretary of VERPERTUIT": how at an emergency meeting of the "Executive Committee," elections are held "to replace the six office holders who fell under tragic circumstances, i.e., they fell into the water with the helicopter that was taking them on a survey of the desert area, all of them perishing miserably in the regional hospital through a nurse mistakenly administering them sulfanilamide in doses clearly unacceptable to the human organism." Votes are counted, and we discover that one by one, gentlemen are elected who bear the name Felix. One, then two. Then three. Then four Felixes. Then five. Then, yes, six. "The composition of the Committee is read and ends up organized in the following order: reading from the left, President and oldest surviving member, Mr. Felix Smith. Members: Felix Voll, Felix Romero, Felix Lupescu, Felix Paparemologos, Felix Abib, and Felix Camusso." They all quickly offer resignations, citing reasons of health (Cortázar 69).

Perhaps, to read a fiction like this Johnnie would roll in laughter and Lina would tumble into a fever of consternation. How many happenstances can one live through, after all, challenging both agility and sufferance?

A CINEMATIC GESTURE

It is true that I have been citing moments over and over, repeating phrases, repeating shafts of light, in order to gain access to the mental state we may imagine is Lina's as she endures her marriage and the action of the story. Catching something, not being sure about it, reflecting on it later, having second thoughts, having third thoughts, never leaving the provoking shards of the sculpture to fall away into obscurity. Her father has died, Johnnie is so very sorry. He could use 20,000 pounds, maybe even thirty. Beaky will put up the money, but the investment will be in Johnnie's name. He's gambled away her sacred chairs, but then has bought them back for her. The father in the portrait. "You win, old boy." In cinema we see and move on, on to more sights and on to memories of what we saw, recalculations, repositionings, second sight.

That shining glass! What is in it?

Well, any fool will tell you it is milk, specifically cow's milk, a nice cold glass brimming with health and offering a good night's sleep. Perhaps warmed up for dear Lina, and even with a little dab of honey if she'd like that. A spoonful of sugar helps the medicine go down. If you're interested in being academic and proper, it's easy enough to follow Marvin Harris's description of this as "chilled bovine mammary secretions," something people in Western culture are coddled to love. She's being carried a glass of nighttime milk by dutiful Johnnie, and if he has poisoned the milk perhaps the ritual slowness of his progress up the stairs will convey.

Perhaps.

It does seem apparent that Hitchcock's composition here is designed to open quite another door to our musing, however. Let us dwell upon, and even taste, the design by which Johnnie brings Lina her treat:

- That shot from the air, hovering in space. We are not standing on the balcony, or attached to the ceiling, looking down. We are in suspension, a thrumming hummingbird. Below is a cavern of darkness, darkness without form.

- And suddenly with a portal opening a sharply etched form, triangular, brilliant, yawning forward, counterposing numerous arcing shadowy threads, the limbs of a forest gazebo, the vaults of a cathedral.

- The small body marching across with its load, a servant body, a messenger and deliverer, purposeful and forward-looking but also unidentifiable in itself. That we realize it is Johnnie is only a fruit of logical thinking; the eye does not catch this.

- Mounting the stairs, and not just any stairs. The gently curving staircase that is all organic, part of some gigantic digestive system by which this whole tale is assimilated into the body of consciousness. At first the most noteworthy aspect of this figure is its steady ascension. Climbing up and up, coming our way. We watch, having already arrived at the destination, magically.

- And then he is clearly shown, the relaxed and unexpressive face of the living sculpture. Immaculately garbed, even now, late at night. The little tray easily carried in one hand. The eyes never dropping to check on the parcel. The tray might well be attached to the hand, a part of the heroic body.

The glass itself: no one has failed to notice that it is radiant, and many have even sought to resolve the holy mystery by delving into the production practice in order to find that yes, Hitchcock arranged for a tiny light bulb powered through a wire that ran through Grant's clothing to a battery pack. The glowing milk.

But this is rational. And the way this bleachy presence strikes the eye is far less rational. It *looks like* milk, but it is not milk. It shines in the darkness like a beacon—that is, it might well emanate from a position very, very far away. It belongs to a domain that is itself certainly far away, a non-rational, non-quotidian domain, in which substances have powers borrowed from the trees, from the rocks, from the celestial bodies. To say that as we see this, especially as we see it coming very close and looming into the lens we do not know what it is, do not know its qualities and potentialities, do not know how to name it or what files of memory to call up in recognition, to say that this is a mystery, is only the beginning of a wholesome reception. This glow, this *light*, is from *I know not what you are*, from *I cannot feel you as good or bad, only as light in the darkness*. The glass radiates with Johnnie light, or with an everlasting light from otherwhere, and in doing this becomes the absolute symbol of indeterminacy.

Indeterminacy, which can lead in many directions including suspicion, the true poison. A glass of suspicion, or a glass of tomorrow. To signal this indeterminacy, unmistakably, Hitchcock brings us at the very culminating moment of this film to the middle of a voyage, where Johnnie and Lina are speeding away on the cliff road, with us resting behind. Away, away, and whither they go nobody will know.

The radiant glass does not sing as it glides up the stairs, nor does Johnnie sing as he brings it, but if there were singing we would hear, I suspect, Rilke:[21]

> To you is left (unspeakably confused) your life,
> Gigantic, ripening, full of fears,
> So that it, now hemmed in, now grasping all
> Is changed in you by turns to stone and stars.

NOTES

INTRODUCTION

1. *The Man Who Knew Too Much* is absent from these pages for a unique reason, namely, that I have addressed it substantially elsewhere, most recently in the BFI Film Classics series in 2016.

CHAPTER ONE

1. Michael Powell's *Peeping Tom* was released in London in May 1960, only months before *Psycho*. Originally the British Board of Film Censorship gave Powell a hard time, catching him, as it were, in the role of a Peeping Tom peeping at his murderous Peeping Tom; the British Film Institute now accords the film high praise.

2. "There has been much debate," writes Ruth Harwood Cline, "about whether the Fisher King's castle is situated outside of conventional time and space and whether it disappears and reappears" (Troyes 83n).

3. I thank Peter Treherne for offering this observation.

4. A tiny nod to the moment in *Leave Her to Heaven* (1946) when Cornel Wilde ingratiates himself to Gene Tierney late at night with exactly the same catering.

5. In his *Slaughterhouse-Five, or The Children's Crusade: A Duty-Dance with Death* (1969), Kurt Vonnegut Jr. borrows this thematic, with Montana Wildhack and Billy Pilgrim caught inside a cage on Tralfamadore, so that their mating can be viewed as pleasurable entertainment. The *chivarée* turned to science fiction.

6. No stageline except the cuts themselves, hiding a now-invisible off-camera space or "wings" in which action can be prepared and reflected

upon. But to entertain an experience of such a stageline is to obstruct the continuing pleasure we can obtain by delicate avoidance.

7. See chapter 2, "Beaux Gestes," in my *Moment of Action* (2016).

8. A commonplace epithet of the 1950s and 1960s, based on a popular household cleaning product of the same name from Procter & Gamble. How does Procter & Gamble come up with the name? *Span-new* dates from the early fourteenth century and refers to a piece of unstained wood suitable for spoon making. In the sixteenth century a *spic* (spike, nail) was thought neat, tidy, and clean. Samuel Pepys uses "spick and span." Procter & Gamble registered the product in 1926. As to Hitchcock's use of bathroom settings, there is an extended discussion in *An Eye for Hitchcock* (141–50).

9. T. S. Eliot, "Burnt Norton" (1935), in *The Four Quartets*.

10. Although a faulty deposit machine was tried in New York briefly in 1961, the ATM as we know it premiered on 27 June 1967, in Enfield, north London. At the time, banks did have special outside slots so that people could make after-hour or weekend deposits. Perhaps Marion's failure to use one suggests there was no such slot at Lowery's bank; that she had other plans for the money; that she wasn't thinking straight; or that his bank's slot was damaged and wouldn't open. We aren't told.

11. Gus Van Sant did not in his 1998 remake.

12. Still at the time a major moral conundrum for young people. The first birth control pills were not available through the US Food and Drug Administration until the 1960s.

13. "*Psycho* was supposed to begin," notes Bill Krohn, "with a helicopter shot going up to the window of Marion and Sam's hotel room, which Hitchcock told a reporter would top the opening of *Touch of Evil* (1958). Even though that shot, filmed by the second unit, was discarded and replaced with three shots (one of a miniature) made after filming ended, the illusion works. The film seems to begin with a continuous shot where Hitchcock's camera asserts its power" (234). Eric Schramm graciously reminds me that *Touch of Evil* also features a motel room attack on Janet Leigh.

14. Janet Leigh recounted to TCM how a great deal of preparatory research was undertaken to determine the lighting and shower curtain required to permit an exact body representation to be visible at a distance, then up close.

15. On which see John Belton, "Technology and Aesthetics of Film Sound," in Belton and Weis 63–72; and Eyman.

16. Assistant Director Hilton Green explained: "We built a hydraulic device into the ground very much like an automatic garage door opener. We pushed the car in and the car clamped on as it hit. The device turned and pivoted a little bit, then pulled the car down steadily at a certain tempo, then stopped cold—all mechanically done. You could only do it once, or else you'd have to clean up the whole car and set it up for reshooting the following day. It was done in one take" (qtd. in Rebello 126).

17. As, for analysis of scenes in Hitchcock, including some in *Psycho*, Rebecca Barton has done.

18. In a purely graphic way, the draped fingers are a foretelling of the draped body over the tub that will be Marion's fate.

19. For a discussion of Lila's choreographic entry to the Bates house, see my "A Modern Gesture."

20. In all of Hitchcock, there are a small number of positive mysteries, that is, graphically arranged objects the details and/or meanings of which are never, ever, ever opened to the viewer's intelligence. This bound volume is one of them.

21. While screenings were scheduled, usually four or five a day, prior to *Psycho*, viewers could pay and enter at any point they wished, remaining seated until the entire program had cycled back to where they came in; or, indeed, as long as they wanted to stay in the dark.

22. By which, in writing, theater managers were enjoined from permitting any spectator to enter the theater for any reason after projection had begun. This was the beginning of audiences lining up for scheduled projections; prior to *Psycho*, a viewer went into the theater whenever it seemed desirable, day or night.

23. My suspicion is that this little comment, memorable because cute, is much less about Arbogast knowing something about kitchen techniques than about Arbogast as a familiar to the advertising world, because what he is doing here is aping a tag line for Kraft Foods's Jell-O. The cuteness comes from the comment's existence as advertisement, not from Arbogast's personality, which is far from cute. Aspic, however, is used to glaze, but also to preserve, cooked meats and fishes.

24. "One finds it difficult to believe that there *are pains*, but no smell," Father André tells Father Logan in *I Confess* (1953). See *Eye for Hitchcock* 201ff.

25. So many deeply touched viewers have seen that the eye/drain superimposition at the center of the dissolve (that was effected at the optical printer [see Rebello 115]) resembles the lens of a [of Hitchcock's] camera but in fact any eye at all, living or dead, will show such a resemblance, and invocation of the camera in that context serves very little to take us more deeply into the scene. What is profound is the blackness of the pupil, which is the space out of which the colored geometrical forms emerge in the title sequence of *Vertigo* (1958).

26. In "Two Bits for Hitch," I discuss the meticulous performative work of two actors, Richard Wattis and Alan Mowbray, but a serious study of character performance in Hitchcockian film is in order; often very professional actors with large resumés, often doing very small parts with the most revealing and careful detailing.

27. In personal conversation, 1969.

28. Rainer Maria Rilke, "Archaic Torso of Apollo" (c. 1908).

29. A remarkable answer to this question, yet in a different context of sorts, is offered by Jack Clayton in *Our Mother's House* (1967).

30. Because I follow a different path, I find myself a little at odds with William Rothman's reading of the psychiatrist, who, he writes, "seizes the limelight, chews up the scenery, and plays his role to the hilt. He is an unappealing character, smug and self-satisfied, who appears completely unmoved by the fates of Marion and Norman" (*Gaze* 338). I would agree he plays his role to the hilt, but so do all the actors in this film. As to being unmoved about Marion, Hitchcock has arranged that we never did have opportunity to "befriend" her; Arbogast, too; and Norman's fate is left to our fascination.

31. I am grateful to Christopher Husted for letting me in on the secret of this Herrmann chord. It is a tritone in A-flat with a D in the basses.

CHAPTER TWO

1. Hannay, according to *Beyond the Thirty-Nine Steps* by Buchan's granddaughter Ursula Buchan as reviewed by John Lloyd, was "a Scots-born mining engineer" (Lloyd 23). James Chapman, who has studied the novel,

reports him as a "South African mining engineer returning to London in 1914 who is shaken from his metropolitan *ennui*" (50).

2. In 1935, Canada was the largest and in some ways most proximal of the many nations in the British Commonwealth, of which the king was head. Four years before, the Act of Westminster had formalized the Commonwealth. Hannay is portrayed as a typical but in many ways shining citizen.

3. The Buchan novel has him as an engineer, the kind of person who would know something about bridges like this and thus be able to "engineer" his escape there, except that in the novel the bridge does not appear.

4. "To the proud native's ear," wrote John Wilson, "every stream murmurs a music not its own ... and the lark more lyrical than ever, seems singing his songs at the gates of heaven" (302).

5. "The opening up of Northern Scotland by the railways in the second half of the nineteenth century led to a growing popular interest in the enjoyment of Highland scenery, which the railway companies were keen to exploit" (Pryor 503–4).

6. Among Buchan's Scottish habits was "vigorous walking, including mountain climbing" (Lloyd 23).

7. A notably primitive building style, very old in the United Kingdom. Thatches or slender boards are mounted vertically in parallel seams, and the space between them is filled in with a plaster daub. Sometimes the daub is made to cover the wattles as well. It is proof against weather, but also inexpensive to build. Thatching for the roof would be locally found, but the thatching of a house or cottage roof is a trade job if it is to be done well. On thatching and stone walls see Fearn and Garner, respectively.

8. T. S. Eliot, "The Waste Land" (1922).

9. To this sad but luscious recollection of hers there is a splendid homage paid by Frank Perry in his *Diary of a Mad Housewife* (1970) when Jonathan (Richard Benjamin) tells Tina (Carrie Snodgress) in their softly lit kitchen, "I used to wake up at three o'clock in the morning crying because it wasn't there anymore. (*Chuckles*) It's three o'clock in the morning now!"

10. I heard once about a pair of young Glaswegians who were driving their car on a bridge over the Clyde. At the very other side was a traffic light, and the girl turned to the boy and said, "Listen, if that light is green when we get there, let's get married." It was, and they did.

CHAPTER THREE

1. Charles Baudelaire, "L'invitation au voyage," from *Les fleurs du mal* (1857).
2. T. S. Eliot, "The Hollow Men" (1925).
3. Something that analogizes the mushroom cloud at Bikini, or that presages the fireball spectacles of 1980s action cinema and its progeny.
4. He knew the material of the story. Daphne du Maurier was the daughter of the actor/manager Gerald du Maurier (the original Captain Hook) and a longtime friend of Hitchcock.
5. See Ezra Pound, Canto CVI: "God's eye art 'ou, do not surrender perception"; and Perret.
6. A process that required a special lens over which, reported Peggy Robertson, there was some consternation, since the Disney man who owned it had retired from filmmaking and wanted nothing to do with the picture. There being only one such lens in the world, the decision was made to gamble on safety and send it to Tokyo for duplication (Hall 253). In-camera mattes had some advantages: no photographic "duping" was required, and so the final composite was not a photograph of a photograph, thus crisper and cleaner. The sodium yellow process gave "extremely fine detail" (Memo 2). The contract with Disney for the sodium vapor process was struck 21 March 1962.
7. The developmental, or evolutionary, link between humans and avians is explored in reverse, and with powerful effect, in Olaf Stapledon's *Last and First Men: A Story of the Near and Far Future* (1930), where several hundred millennia into the future the human beings of the mid-twentieth century morph into flying creatures. I am deeply grateful to the late Kenneth Boulding for introducing me to this book.
8. William Butler Yeats, "The Second Coming" (1919).
9. A research note from 8 November 1961: "Have Peggy [Robertson] check: can we find out whether lovebirds make much noise ... Little songs in morning ... chirping" (Research memo).
10. Yeats, "The Circus Animals' Desertion" (1933).
11. In the Eichmann trial in Jerusalem, beginning 11 April 1961, the defendant was encased in a glass case, bulletproof but transparent to vision. Shooting on *The Birds* began eleven months later, 5 March 1962.

12. In this shot the camera has a 35-mm (slight wide-angle) lens, which helps emphasize the facial distortion.

13. The garment, a two-piece, is modeled in some way on the 1920s Chanel suit, but Chanel's was made in grays and blues, to simulate masculine suiting of the time, and Head's is in a mysterious, rarified green.

14. Curiosity that "killed the cat" that could have killed the birds?

15. *Macbeth*, V.v. 19–20.

16. A variation of the theme struck with the crofter's wife and her eagerness to know the sophisticated Hannay, in *The 39 Steps*.

17. "Mrs. Brenner has been living [in Bodega Bay] since her husband died 4 or 5 years ago," a set dressing memorandum of January 1962 read. "At present, the script does not provide for the nature of the late Mr. Brenner's profession or economic status. I think it is fair to assume, however, that whatever their business was, the elder Brenners were well off enough to have an apartment in San Francisco and the farm at Bodega Bay as a weekend retreat. We can obviously infer that, after Mr. Brenner's death, the two places were more than sufficient for Mrs. Brenner's needs so she gave up the apartment and came to live permanently at the small farm at Bodega Bay" (Set Dressing Memorandum).

18. "Her furnishings would be quite modest but very tasteful, perhaps a little chintzy.... Some thought should be given to music in Annie's house. This should consist of a player and piles of records" (Set Dressing Memorandum).

19. I am grateful to William Rothman for bringing this instant to my attention again. Melanie rejects her mother's care:

> MELANIE: She ditched us when I was eleven and ran off with some hotel man in the East. *You* know what a mother's love is.
>
> MITCH: Yes, I do.
>
> MELANIE: You mean it's better to be ditched?
>
> MITCH: No, I think it's better to be loved.

20. Stanley Kubrick will make joking reference to this analogy in the titles of *Dr. Strangelove or: How I Learned to Stop Worrying and Love the Bomb*, released nine months after *The Birds*, to the day.

21. A concluding shot Hitchcock will reprise in *Marnie* (1964), his next film, in a different key.

22. "For the father's portrait it will be necessary to research who is the best portrait painter in San Francisco. I think also, we should look for some water colors done by such an artist as Don Kingman (who is a well known San Francisco water colorist" [Set Dressing Memorandum]). The chapter here on *Suspicion* (1941) offers light upon another portrait of a father.

23. "We will require, on location, a dummy piano with *full length* keyboard, and also a tape recorder ... for Tippi Hedren to practice the Debussy Arabesque ... Vic Aller mentioned that Columbia has such a dummy piano" (Robertson to Deming).

24. The children who were filmed in this scene and the ensuing chase were all residents of Bodega Bay.

25. This rhyme has numerous variations, one in the Max Hunter Folk Song Collection at Missouri State University beginning, "I married a wife in the month of June / Nickey-nackety-now-now-now / O I took her home by th light of th moon / Nickety-nackety-nighty-jim-dackety / Rickety-rackety-riptun-quin-quality / Nickey-nackety-now-now-now."

26. Regarding denucleation see Paul.

27. See for a full treatment of circumlocution Henry James's *What Maisie Knew* (1897).

28. A reprise of the Ambrose Chappell taxidermy shop scene in *The Man Who Knew Too Much* (1956).

29. The location was the Gaffney farm, owned by Rose Gaffney, two and a half miles from Bodega Bay, including 432 acres and associated buildings. Alfred Hitchcock Productions made agreement with Mrs. Gaffney on 12 October 1961.

30. I am grateful to the staff at the McElroy Octagon House in San Francisco.

31. "Island on the land" is Carey McWilliams's epithet for Southern California.

CHAPTER FOUR

1. In Kensington. Not near Maida Vale at all.

2. Among the many novelties on show for consumers during the 1951 Festival of Britain were numerous new wall coverings and upholstery fabrics in the *moderne* design. See further Kynaston, *Family* 5-12; Brittain-Catlin.

3. This painting has more than once been attributed, by writers about the film, to the French painter Rosa Bonheur (1822–1899), since, as is claimed, Hitchcock would have known as an art collector about her work and might well have cherished the idea of placing such a canvas in the film (she died the year he was born). There are problems with this attribution, among which are the fact that Bonheur used a palette notably darker than we find here; and that her canvases invariably contain animals, such as sheep and cattle. My search in the Warner Bros. Property Warehouse has turned up nothing about the painting. (See further Jacobs 107.)

4. At the 1974 Lincoln Center tribute to Hitchcock, the murder scene in *Dial M* was shown and he commented, "As you have seen on the screen, scissors are the best way," referencing both the materiel in the scene and the editing that assembled the pieces. See Truffaut 346.

5. Hitchcock is in there, doing his cameo, but there are entirely different reasons by which Margot doesn't recognize him. Yet even that is complicated, since Margot is intended to be real as of 1954, by which time, in the UK, he was plenty well known even, we may surmise, to such socialites as she.

6. Krohn writes of the attempted murder sequence. "C'est dans cette sequence qu'il trouve enfin les couleurs pour filmer le sexe et la mort fusionnés." I am grateful to Bill Krohn for sharing the English version.

7. Chosen by Kelly herself, writes Bill Krohn (*Work* 130).

8. Something of a tribute to English efficiency. By stark contrast, in *The King of Comedy* (1982) Martin Scorsese has Robert DeNiro play a scene where in Times Square he wants to receive a call on a pay phone; six or so are lined up, but all but one of them has broken, so he is holding up the only available phone by waiting at it.

9. Jorge Luis Borges, "The Garden of Forking Paths" ("El jardín de senderos que se bifurcan," 1941).

10. A cursory Internet search will show legion claims that Kelly had a mammoth sexual appetite and very typically had affairs with her co-stars. One such item, by Veronica Walsingham, quotes the purportedly lascivious Zsa Zsa Gabor, who had nine husbands: "She had more boyfriends in a month than I had in a lifetime. She went to bed with anyone she fancied at the time." See www.ranker.com/list/grace-kelly-scandals/veronica-walsingham.

334 NOTES TO CHAPTER FIVE

11. The reader who is struck by the idea of tentative (neither fully explored nor unequivocally affirmed) meaning in Hitchcock more generally might find enjoyment in Schantz, who explores the filmmaker's production of intellectual uncertainty.

12. Composed 1931, popularized intensively by Pat Boone in the summer of 1957.

13. Le Corbusier quoted in Lelouch's *A Man and a Woman* (1966): "If from a fire you could save a cat or a Rembrandt which would you choose?"

14. *Fellah*: a native laborer in the Middle East.

15. This idea receives full and gripping development in Michelangelo Antonioni's *The Passenger* (*Professione: Reporter* [1975]), especially the remembered balcony conversation between Locke and Robertson.

16. The double blue is a creamy white, heavy, knit V-neck sweater with a darker and lighter border of blue around the neck opening: symbol of identification for Cambridge rowers and other athletes.

17. In his discussion with François Truffaut, Hitchcock makes very clear why he opted for this dominating set and eschewed the popular tactic of filming stage plays by "opening up" the action.

18. For an early, and most telling, example of this kind of elucidation by mouth (and one with which Hitchcock would have been familiar), see the doctor's lecture to his students in *Das Testament des Dr. Mabuse* (1933).

19. As seen in this film several times, the Hermès *sac à dépêches* (renamed the Kelly Bag in 1977) was used by Hitchcock for Kelly in *To Catch a Thief* (1955) because the costumer, Edith Head, was entranced by it. Kelly continued to use it afterward.

20. For a later homage to this technique of not showing what we hear talked about, see Louis Malle's *My Dinner with Andre* (1981).

CHAPTER FIVE

1. "Weimar was synonymous with movement and evanescence," Modris Eksteins writes. "Weimar was transition, interlude, interregnum. It dislodged, broke up, and disappeared, with surprise as the counterpart to breakdown" (79).

2. Written from prison, after his return.

3. Only a few of legion examples being music infected by the craze for Chinoiserie in the first decades of the twentieth century: Ravel's *Shéhérazade* (1903), Debussy's *Poissons d'or* (1907), Puccini's *Turandot* (completed by Alfano, 1926); Diaghilev's production of *Les Orientales* (1910) for the Ballets Russes; or in literature Lafcadio Hearn's *Kwaidan* (1904).

4. Short but telling, indicating a working space also referenced in King Vidor's *The Crowd* (1928), with a more dramatic abstractness than is used by Hitchcock, who wishes that we should consider the situation in its physical terms. There is some reference made in Jacques Tati's *Play Time* (1968).

5. Jerry Lewis will make reference to the dominating presence of this clock in the typing pool scene of *The Errand Boy* (1961), where, still decades later, a regimented workforce (only apparently divided by differences) slaves to the beat of time.

6. A point of view to which Hitchcock will return, movingly, in *Frenzy* (1972).

7. The Lumières' seminal *Ouvriers sortant de l'usine* (1895) showed a chaotic flight.

8. The obvious parallel is to be found in *Foreign Correspondent* (1940).

9. See Hitchcock's reprise in the opening bus sequence of *The Man Who Knew Too Much* (1956). For Hitchcock the vehicle of public transit is inherently a site of danger, and particularly a danger emanating from the difficulty of controlling bodies in relation to one another inside a very constrained space. Lewis reprises this moment in *The Errand Boy,* too, inside an elevator in the Paramutual Executive Office Building, with a man chewing bubble gum and another smoking a cigar.

10. Something of an homage, I suspect, to the factory sequences in René Clair's *À nous la liberté* (1924) and, like that film, an anticipation of the conveyor belt and feeding sequences in Chaplin's *Modern Times* (1936).

11. Now that we have sound, we can note that here, and throughout the film henceforward, there is a very subtle undertone of *Blackmail* (1929)—the first English sound film—because the Joan Barry playing Emily is the same Joan Barry who dubbed the vocals for the Czech Anny Ondra in that film.

12. An echo of the beginning of Vidor's *The Crowd* and, even more remotely, of Bob Cratchit slaving in Dickens's *A Christmas Carol* (1843).

13. Hitchcock brings the phrase "money to experience all the life you want by travelling" onto the screen in macro-close-up, a few words at a

time, as though the camera-eye and the character-eye and the viewer-eye are all, together, sliding rightward across it. This touch is picked up by Orson Welles, near the beginning of *Citizen Kane* (1941), and then again by François Truffaut as Montag begins to discover *David Copperfield* in *Fahrenheit 451* (1966).

14. A discussion about anticipatory socialization with John Long in the fall of 1967 has been most helpful to me.

15. A purely visual analogue to onomatopoeia.

16. A device Hitchcock will use again in Manny's prison cell, in *The Wrong Man* (1956).

17. A seductive high-contrast image reprised more than once by Raoul Coutard for Godard's *À bout de souffle* (*Breathless*, 1960).

18. Even mortified this way, the good-humored and certainly egotistical Fred imagines himself the tantalized youth in Boucher's Rococo masterpiece *Pensent-ils au raisin?* (1747).

19. A motif Jimmy Stewart will recapitulate in a different key in the Moroccan restaurant scene of *The Man Who Knew Too Much* (1956).

20. Like poor Scottie Ferguson on Midge's stepladder.

21. In a more operatic way, this stratification will be employed by Federico Fellini in his *E la nave va . . .* (*And the Ship Sails On . . .* [1983]), especially in a Verdian sequence with the sweating slaves in the engine room.

CHAPTER SIX

1. For enlightened discussion of *Rope*, see Miller; Badmington.

2. Spoto notes how as a boy he "continued to study timetables, and astonished his family by reciting from memory the schedules of most of England's train lines" (19). Patrick McGilligan, observing that "Railway-mania is a phenomenon among the English," notes that by the time Hitchcock was eight "he fondly recalled the 'Phantom Rides,' a spectacle [from Hales Tours] featuring footage snapped from the cowcatcher of a train speeding through scenic locales" (11; 15).

3. On upholstering trains see below, and Schivelbusch 122–23.

4. There may be propriety here in my sharing a little tale only a few dear friends have heard from me. In 1972, when first I visited London, I telephoned Buckingham Palace (the number for which was in the telephone

directory) and asked whether I could speak with the Queen to give her my best wishes. (This was a genuine, if stupid, gesture, not an attempt at wit.) This is what the man at the other end of the line said to me: "But the Queen doesn't meet anyone she doesn't already know, does she."

5. A man faking this nonchalance, perhaps? Well, all signs can be faked, but the critical point for making judgment when one is potentially always in doubt is the number of coherent signs on offer. Lina here offers fewer signs of her own proper belonging, in fact.

6. It had been referenced in *The Farmer's Wife* (1928), with a huge pack of eager beagles following the horses away, and would be referenced again in *Marnie* (1964), with spectacular effect. *Marnie* has a double reference, in effect, since, starting in the late eighteenth century, the "finest fox-hunting country" in England was at, of all places, Rutland (Pryor 499).

7. The principal text on social proximity and topological placement is Edward T. Hall's *The Hidden Dimension*. See esp. 10ff.

8. This woman (Isabel Jeans) gets almost no further treatment beyond a very short scene on the street when, driving by, she meets Lina; there we are given a portrait in motion that replicates the still portrait in the newspaper.

9. A borrowing from Ernst Lubitsch's *Design for Living* (1933).

10. Wolfgang Schivelbusch notes that the landscape travelers saw from the train window appeared to be "another world" (24). On the variable terrain and leveled track see his *Railway Journey* 20ff.

11. As to Lina's reading, many early travelers learned reading in motion as a form of pleasure. And relaxed pleasure was a frequent outcome of railway travel. Schivelbusch quotes Hippolyte Taine:

> The wheels rolled on indefatigably, with a uniform noise like that of a prolonged roaring note played on an organ. All mundane and social ideas faded from my mind. No longer did I see anything but the sun and the countryside, in bloom, smiling, all green and with a greenness so various and illuminated by that gentle rain of warm beams that caressed it" (152 qtd. in Schivelbusch 77).

But, too, "The train compartment became a scene of crime—a crime that could take place unheard and unseen by the travelers in adjoining compartments" (79). Plenty of films have depicted railway crime, none more brutally than Fritz Lang's *Dr. Mabuse der Spieler* (1922).

12. On the earliest use of the term "significant other" see Sullivan 9ff.

13. On the distinctive monumentality of Cary Grant see Cavell, "North."

14. On Hitchcock's fondness for, and collecting of, art see Bill Krohn, "Musée." For further discussion of Hitchcock and art see Païni and Cogeval; Gunning.

15. The name "Penshaze" suggests that "down here" is Cornwall, but we are in Sussex. It is doubtless intended to seem the country home of folk whose ancestors, at least, were Cornish, people who are fond of the Cornish seacoast.

16. To be repeated with the diligent Val Parnell (Alan Mowbray) in *The Man Who Knew Too Much* (1956).

17. For an analysis of this film, including attention to Robie's presumed guilt, see "Catching *To Catch a Thief*" in my book *A Dream of Hitchcock*.

18. I am grateful to Ariel Pomerance for a professional reading of Dr Sedbusk's lenses.

19. For a fascinating comparison see the moment in which Grant's character is introduced in *Notorious* (1946).

20. A remarkably similar arrangement to Jean Harlow's in George Cukor's *Dinner at Eight* (1933).

21. *Abend* (c. 1904).

WORKS CITED

HER = Margaret Herrick Library, Academy of Motion Picture Arts and Sciences, Beverly Hills

Albee, Edward. *The Zoo Story and Other Plays*. New York: Penguin, 1995.

Altick, Richard D. *The Shows of London*. Cambridge, MA: Harvard University Press, 1978.

Anonymous. "Memo. Travelling Matte Systems in General Use." Alfred Hitchcock Collection, HER, n.d.

———. Memorandum indicating set dressing requirements for *The Birds*. 24 January 1962, *The Birds* folder 111, Alfred Hitchcock Collection, HER.

———. Research Memo, 8 November 1961, re love birds, *The Birds* folder 104, Alfred Hitchcock Collection, HER.

Bachelard, Gaston. *The Psychoanalysis of Fire*. 1938. Boston: Beacon Press, 1964.

Badmington, Neil. *Perpetual Movement: Alfred Hitchcock's Rope*. Albany: State University Press of New York Press, 2021.

Baker, Jean-Claude, and Chris Chase. *Josephine: The Hungry Heart*. New York: Random House, 1993.

Barton, Sabrina. "Hitchcock's Hands." *Hitchcock Annual* 9 (2000): 47–72.

Barton, Sabrina. "Hitchcock's Hands." Hitchcock Annual 9 (2000): 47–72.

Bataille, Georges. *Erotism: Death and Sensuality*. Trans. Mary Dalwood. 1957. San Francisco: City Lights, 1986.

Baudelaire, Charles. *The Flowers of Evil (Les fleurs du mal)*. Trans. James N. McGowan and Jonathan Culler. New York: Oxford University Press, 2008.

Benjamin, Walter. *Charles Baudelaire: A Lyric Poet in the Era of High Capitalism*. Trans. Harry Zohn. London: Verso, 1997.

———. "Franz Kafka: On the Tenth Anniversary of His Death." In *Walter Benjamin: Selected Writings*, Vol. 2, 1927–1934, ed. Michael W. Jennings, Howard Eiland, and Gary Smith, 794–818. Trans. Rodney Livingstone et al. Cambridge, MA: Harvard University Press, 1999.

Bennis, Warren G., and Philip E. Slater. *The Temporary Society: What Is Happening to Business and Family Life in American under the Impact of Accelerating Change*. San Francisco: Jossey-Bass, 1998.

Blaeu, Joan. "England." In *Joan Blaeu Atlas Maior of 1665: Anglia*, ed. Peter Van Der Krogt, 59. Los Angeles: Taschen, n.d.

Blanchfield, Brian. "Coming Up with Guy Davenport (March 31, 2017)." *Oxford American* 96 (Spring 2017), www.oxfordamerican.org/magazine/item/1144-coming-up-with-guy-davenport.

Borges, Jorge Luis. *Dreamtigers*. Trans. Mildred Boyer and Harold Morland. 1964. Austin: University of Texas Press, 2004.

Boswell, James, and Samuel Johnson. *Boswell's Life of Johnson: Tour to the Hebrides (1773) and Journey into North Wales (1774)*. Vol. 5. Ed. George Birkbeck Hill. 1786. New York: Macmillan and Co., 1887.

Bottomore, Stephen. "I Want to See This Annie Mattygraph: A Cartoon History of the Coming of the Movies." Pordenone/Londres: Le Giornate del Cinema Muto/BFI Publishing, 1996.

Brittain-Catlin, Timothy. "Picking Up the Thread." *World of Interiors* (March 2017): 94–103.

Brown, Norman O. *Apocalypse and/or Metamorphosis*. Berkeley: University of California Press, 1991.

———. *Life Against Death: The Psychoanalytical Meaning of History*. Middletown, CT: Wesleyan University Press, 1959.

Browning, Robert. *The Poems and Plays of Robert Browning*. New York: Modern Library, 1934.

Burke, Kenneth. *Permanence and Change: An Anatomy of Purpose*. 1935. 3rd ed., Berkeley: University of California Press, 1984.

Cage, John. "Lecture on Nothing." In *Silence*, 109–27. Middletown, CT: Wesleyan University Press, 1973.

Caillois, Roger. *Man, Play and Games*. Trans. Meyer Barash. 1958. Urbana: University of Illinois Press, 2001.

Cavell, Stanley. "North by Northwest." In *Themes Out of School: Effects and Causes*, 152–72. Berkeley: University of California Press, 1984.

———. *The World Viewed: Reflections on the Ontology of Film.* Cambridge, MA: Harvard University Press, 1979.

Chanan, Michael. *The Dream That Kicks: The Prehistory and Early Years of Cinema in Britain.* London: Routledge and Kegan Paul, 1980.

Chapman, James. *Hitchcock and the Spy Film.* London: I. B. Tauris, 2018.

Chion, Michel. *The Voice in Cinema.* Trans. Claudia Gorbman. New York: Columbia University Press, 1999.

Clunn, Harold P. *The Face of London: The Record of a Century's Changes and Development.* London: Simpkin Marshall, Ltd, 1932.

Coleridge, Samuel Taylor. *The Poetical and Dramatic Works of Samuel Taylor Coleridge.* Vol. 2. London: Basil Montagu Pickering, 1877.

Conley, Tom. "*The 39 Steps* and the Mental Map of Classical Cinema." In *Rethinking Maps: New Frontiers in Cartographic Theory*, ed. Martin Dodge, Rob Kitchin, and Chris Perkins, 131–48. New York: Routledge, 2009.

Conrad, Joseph. *Heart of Darkness and Selections from The Congo Diary.* New York: Modern Library, 1999.

Corbin, Alain. *A History of Silence: From the Renaissance to the Present Day.* Trans. Jean Birrell. Malden, MA: Wiley, 2018.

Cortázar, Julio. "A Small Story Tending to Illustrate the Uncertainty of the Stability Within Which We Like to Believe We Exist, or Laws Could Give Ground to the Exceptions, Unforeseen Disasters, or Improbabilities, and I Want to See You There." In *Cronopios and Famas*, 68–70. New York: Pantheon, 1969.

Davenport, Guy. *The Geography of the Imagination.* San Francisco: North Point Press, 1981.

———. *Objects on a Table: Harmonious Disarray in Art and Literature.* Washington, DC: Counterpoint, 1998.

De Botton, Alain. *Status Anxiety.* New York: Vintage, 2005.

Deleuze, Gilles. *Francis Bacon: The Logic of Sensation.* Trans. Daniel W. Smith. London: Continuum, 2003.

Deming, Norman. Inter-Office Communication to Paul Donnelly, 9 February 1962, re Technicolor, *The Birds* folder 122, Alfred Hitchcock Collection, HER.

———. Inter-Office Communication to James Weinberg, 4 April 1962, re Technicolor, *The Birds* folder 122, Alfred Hitchcock Collection, HER.

———. Note to Alfred Milotte, 1 January 1962, regarding photography of skyborne birds, *The Birds* folder 59, Alfred Hitchcock Collection, HER.

———. Note to Alfred Milotte, 7 March 1962, re cease of bird photography, *The Birds* folder 59, Alfred Hitchcock Collection, HER.

De Montaigne, Michel. "On the Cannibals." In *The Essays: A Selection*, ed. and trans. M. A. Screech, 79–92. London: Penguin, 2004.

Dennison, Matthew. "Sights of Wonder." *World of Interiors* 39: no. 7/8 (July/August 2020): 157.

Descartes, René. *Discourse on Method and Meditations on First Philosophy*. Trans. Donald A. Cress. Cambridge, MA: Hackett, 1999.

De Troyes, Chrétien. *Perceval or The Story of the Grail*. Trans. Ruth Harwood Cline. Athens: University of Georgia Press, 1985.

Doane, Mary Ann. *The Emergence of Cinematic Time: Modernity, Contingency, the Archive*. Cambridge, MA: Harvard University Press, 2002.

Dolby, Katherine, comp. *My Dearest, Dearest Albert: Queen Victoria's Life through Her Letters and Journals*. London: Michael O'Mara, 2018.

Du Maurier, Daphne. "The Birds." In *The Birds and Other Stories*, 1–39. London: Virago, 2004.

Durgnat, Raymond. *A Long Hard Look at* Psycho. London: BFI, 2002.

Eksteins, Modris. *Solar Dance: Van Gogh, Forgery, and the Eclipse of Certainty*. Cambridge, MA: Harvard University Press, 2012.

Eliot, T[homas] S[tearns]. *The Four Quartets*. London: Faber & Faber, 1944.

———. *Selected Poems*. London: Faber & Faber, 1930.

Erichsen, John Eric. *On Railway and Other Injuries of the Nervous System*. Philadelphia: Henry C. Lea, 1867.

Eyman, Scott. *The Speed of Sound: Hollywood and the Talkie Revolution, 1926–1930*. New York: Simon & Schuster, 2015.

Fearn, Jacqueline. *Thatch and Thatching*. Princes Risborough, Buckinghamshire: Shire, 1976.

Feeney, Paul. *A 1950s Childhood: From Tin Baths to Bread and Dripping*. Stroud, Gloucestershire: History Press, 2009.

Fiedler, Leslie A. *The Return of the Vanishing American*. New York: Stein and Day, 1969.

Forster, E[dward] M[organ]. *A Room with a View*. London: Edward Arnold, 1908.

Foucault, Michel. *Madness and Civilization: A History of Insanity in the Age of Reason*. Trans. Richard Howard. New York: Routledge, 1989.
Friedan, Betty. *The Feminine Mystique*. New York: W. W. Norton, 1963.
Garner, Lawrence. *Dry Stone Walls*. Princes Risborough, Buckinghamshire: Shire, 1984.
Gay, Peter. *Schnitzler's Century: The Making of Middle-Class Culture 1815–1914*. New York: W. W. Norton, 2002.
Godwin, Joscelyn. *Athanasius Kircher's Theatre of the World: The Life and Work of the Last Man to Search for Universal Knowledge*. Rochester, NY: Inner Traditions, 2009.
Goethe, Johann Wolfgang von. *Goethe's Travels in Italy Together with His Second Residence in Rome*. Trans. A. J. W. Morrison and Charles Nisbet. London: George Bell and Sons, 1885.
———. *Letters from Italy*. 1786–88. Trans. W. H. Auden and Elizabeth Mayer. London: Penguin Classics, 1995.
Goffman, Erving. *Frame Analysis: An Essay on the Organization of Experience*. Cambridge, MA: Harvard University Press, 1974.
———. *Forms of Talk*. Philadelphia: University of Pennsylvania Press, 1981.
———. *Gender Advertisements*. New York: Harper & Row, 1979.
———. *Interaction Ritual: Essays in Face-to-Face Behavior*. Chicago: Aldine, 1967.
Golding, William. *Lord of the Flies*. 1954. London: Penguin, 1988.
Gomery, Douglas. *Shared Pleasures: A History of Movie Presentation in the United States*. Madison: University of Wisconsin Press, 1992.
Goodman, Paul. *Speaking and Language: Defence of Poetry*. New York: Vintage, 1971.
———. *The Structure of Literature*. Chicago: University of Chicago Press, 1954.
Gunning, Tom. *The Films of Fritz Lang: Allegories of Vision and Modernity*. London: BFI, 2000.
———. "In and Out of the Frame: Paintings in Hitchcock." In *Casting a Shadow: Creating the Alfred Hitchcock Film*, ed. Will Schmenner and Corinne Granof, 29–47. Evanston, IL: Northwestern University Press, 2007.
Halberstam, David. *The Fifties*. New York: Fawcett, 1993.
Hall, Barbara. Oral History with Peggy Robertson. HER.

Hall, Edward T. *The Hidden Dimension*. Garden City, NY: Doubleday Anchor, 1969.

Harris, Marvin. *Cows, Pigs, Wars, and Witches: The Riddles of Culture*. New York: Vintage, 1974.

Hayman, John. *John Ruskin and Switzerland*. Waterloo, ON: Wilfred Laurier University Press, 1990.

Hesse, Hermann. *Journey to the East*. Trans. Hilda Rosner. New York: Noonday Press, 1957.

Hitchcock, Alfred. Letter to Evan Hunter, 21 December 1961, re personality types in the Bodega Bay restaurant, *The Birds* folder 19, Alfred Hitchcock Collection, HER.

Huysmans, Joris K. *Against Nature*. Mineola, NY: Dover, 2018.

Jacobs, Steven. *The Wrong House: The Architecture of Alfred Hitchcock*. Rotterdam: 010, 2007.

James, Henry. *What Maisie Knew*. New York: Penguin, 2010.

Jay, Martin. *Downcast Eyes: The Denigration of Vision in Twentieth-Century French Thought*. Berkeley: University of California Press, 1994.

Keynes, John Maynard. *Essays in Persuasion*. New York: Harcourt, Brace, 1932.

Kracauer, Siegfried. *The Mass Ornament: Weimar Essays*. Ed. and trans. Thomas Y. Levin. Cambridge, MA: Harvard University Press, 1995.

Krohn, Bill. *Hitchcock at Work*. London: Phaidon, 2000.

———. "Le musée secret de Monsieur Hitchcock." *Cahiers du cinéma* 559 (July-August 2001): 66–71.

———. *Alfred Hitchcock*. Paris: Cahiers du Cinéma/Le Monde, 2007.

Kurlansky, Mark. *Salt: A World History*. New York: Penguin, 2003.

Kynaston, David. *Austerity Britain: 1945–51*. New York: Walker & Co., 2008.

———. *Family Britain: 1951–57*. New York: Bloomsbury, 2009.

Lawrence, D. H. *Studies in Classic American Literature*. Ed. Ezra Greenspan, Lindeth Vasey, and John Worthen. Cambridge: Cambridge University Press, 2003.

Le Carré, John. *The Night Manager*. London: Penguin, 2016.

Lem, Stanislaw. *The Chain of Chance*. New York: Harcourt Brace Jovanovich, 1978.

Lloyd, John. "Mr Standfast: A Redoubtable Scotsman of His Time." *Times Literary Supplement* 6068 (19 July 2019): 23–24.

May, Elaine Tyler. *Homeward Bound: American Families in the Cold War Era.* Rev. ed. New York: Basic Books, 2008.
McGilligan, Patrick. *Alfred Hitchcock: A Life in Darkness and Light.* New York: Regan, 2003.
McWilliams, Carey. *Southern California Country: An Island on the Land.* New York: Duell, Sloan & Pearce, 1946.
Miller, D. A. "Anal *Rope.*" *Representations* 32 (Fall 1990): 114–33.
Mills, C. Wright. *The Power Elite.* New York: Oxford University Press, 1956.
Modleski, Tania. *The Women Who Knew Too Much: Hitchcock and Feminist Theory.* Second edition. New York: Routledge, 2005.
Morton, H. V. *In Search of Scotland.* London: Methuen & Co., 1929.
Ortega y Gasset, José. "On Point of View in the Arts." In *The Dehumanization of Art and Other Essays on Art, Culture, and Literature,* 105–30. Princeton, NJ: Princeton University Press, 1968.
Païni, Dominique, and Guy Cogeval. *Hitchcock and Art: Fatal Coincidences.* Montreal: Musée des Beaux Arts, 2000.
Panter-Downes, Mollie. *London War Notes.* London: Persephone, 2014.
Paul, Robert A. "The Eyes Outnumber the Nose Two to One." *Psychoanalytic Review* 64, no. 3 (1977): 381–90.
Perret, Nellie M. "'God's Eye Art 'Ou': Eleusis as a Paradigm for Enlightenment in Canto CVI." *Paideuma* 13, no. 3 (Winter 1984): 419–32.
Poe, Edgar Allan. "The Philosophy of Furniture." *Burton's Gentleman's Magazine* 6, no. 5 (May 1840): 243–45.
Polo, Marco. *The Travels.* Trans. Ronald Latham. Harmondsworth: Penguin, 1958.
Pomerance, Murray. *Cinema, If You Please: The Memory of Taste, the Taste of Memory.* Edinburgh: Edinburgh University Press, 2018.
———. *A Dream of Hitchcock.* Albany: State University of New York Press, 2019.
———. *An Eye for Hitchcock.* New Brunswick, NJ: Rutgers University Press, 2004.
———. "A Modern Gesture: Perpetual Motion and Screen Suspense." *Film International* 5, no. 5, issue 29 (Fall 2007): 42–53.
———. "Two Bits for Hitch: Small Performance and Gross Structure in *The Man Who Knew Too Much* (1956)." In *Hitchcock Annual* 9 (2000): 127–45.

Pryor, Francis. *The Making of the British Landscape: How We Have Transformed the Land from Prehistory to Today*. London: Penguin, 2011.
Queen Victoria. *Leaves from the Journal of Our Life in the Highlands: From 1848 to 1861*. 1868. Cambridge: Cambridge University Press, 2010.
Rebello, Stephen. *Alfred Hitchcock and the Making of Psycho*. New York: St. Martin's Press, 1998.
Rilke, Rainer Maria. *Ahead of All Parting: The Selected Poetry and Prose of Rainer Maria Rilke*. New York: Modern Library, 1995.
Robertson, Peggy. Inter-Office Communication to Norman Deming, 8 February 1962, re dummy piano, *The Birds* folder 71, Alfred Hitchcock Collection, HER.
Rohmer, Eric, and Claude Chabrol. *Hitchcock: The First Forty-Four Films*. Trans. Stanley Hochman. New York: Frederick Ungar, 1979.
Rothman, William. *Hitchcock—The Murderous Gaze*. 1982. 2nd ed., Albany: State University of New York Press, 2012.
Rothman, William, and Marian Keane. *Reading Cavell's* The World Viewed: *A Philosophical Perspective on Film*. Detroit: Wayne State University Press, 2000.
Ruskin, John. *Travels in the Land of Serpents and Pearls*. Trans. Nigel Cliff. London: Penguin Classics, 2015.
———. *The Works of John Ruskin*. Ed. Edward Tyas Cook and Alexander Wedderburn. London: G. Allen, 1903–12.
———. *The Life of John Ruskin*. Ed. Edward Tyas Cook. New York: Haskell House, 1968 © 1911.
Sadoul, Georges. *L'art muet (L'Après guerre en Europe 1919–1929)*. Paris: Denoël, 1975.
Said, Edward. *Orientalism*. New York: Vintage, 1979.
Sante, Luc. *The Other Paris*. New York: Farrar, Straus and Giroux, 2015.
Sartre, Jean-Paul. *Baudelaire*. Trans. Martin Turnell. New York: New Directions, 1967.
———. *Being and Nothingness: A Phenomenological Essay on Ontology*. 1943. Trans. Hazel E. Barnes. New York: Washington Square Press, 1956.
———. *Saint Genet: Actor and Martyr*. Trans. Bernard Frechtman. Minneapolis: University of Minnesota Press, 2012.
Schafer, R. Murray. *The Tuning of the World*. New York: Random House, 1977.

Schantz, Ned. "Hospitality and the Unsettled Viewer: Hitchcock's Shadow Scenes." *Camera Obscura* 25, no. 1 (2010): 1–27.

Schivelbusch, Wolfgang. *The Railway Journey: The Industrialization of Time and Space in the 19th Century.* Berkeley: University of California Press, 1986.

Schmidt, Benjamin. *Inventing Exoticism: Geography, Globalism, and Europe's Early Modern World.* Philadelphia: University of Pennsylvania Press, 2015.

Schreiner, Olive. "*The Buddhist Priest's Wife* (1892)." In *Daughters of Decadence: Women Writers of the Fin-de-Siècle,* ed. Elaine Showalter, 84–97. New Brunswick, NJ: Rutgers University Press, 1993.

Scott, Marvin B., and Sanford M. Lyman. "Accounts." *American Sociological Review* 33, no. 1 (February 1968): 46–62.

Simmel, Georg. *The Sociology of Georg Simmel.* Trans. and ed. Kurt H. Wolff. New York: Free Press of Glencoe, 1950.

Slater, Philip E. *The Glory of Hera: Greek Mythology and the Greek Family.* Princeton, NJ: Princeton University Press, 1968.

Solzhenitsyn, Alexander. *One Day in the Life of Ivan Denisovich.* New York: E. P. Dutton, 1963.

Spoto, Donald. *The Dark Side of Genius: The Life of Alfred Hitchcock.* New York: Ballantine, 1984.

Stapledon, Olaf. *Last and First Men: A Tale of the Near and Far Future.* New York: J. Cape and H. Smith, 1931.

Starobinski, Jean. *The Living Eye.* Trans. Arthur Goldhammer. Cambridge, MA: Harvard University Press, 1989.

Sullivan, Harry Stack. *The Interpersonal Theory of Psychiatry.* London: Tavistock, 1955.

Taine, Hippolyte. *Carnet de voyage; notes sur la province, 1863–1865.* Paris: Hachette, 1897.

Thoreau, Henry David. *Walden: Or, Life in the Woods.* Boston: Ticknor and Fields, 1854.

Toffler, Alvin. *Future Shock.* New York: Bantam, 1971.

Truffaut, François. *Hitchcock.* Trans. Helen Scott. New York: Simon & Schuster, 1983.

Tsivian, Yuri. *Early Cinema in Russia and Its Cultural Reception.* London: Routledge, 1994.

Vidich, Arthur J., and Joseph Bensman. *Small Town in Mass Society: Class, Power, and Religion in a Rural Community.* 1958. Rev. ed., Urbana: University of Illinois Press, 2000.

Weis, Elisabeth. *The Silent Scream: Alfred Hitchcock's Sound Track.* Rutherford, NJ: Fairleigh Dickinson University Press, 1982.

Weis, Elisabeth, and John Belton, eds. *Film Sound: Theory and Practice.* New York: Columbia University Press, 1985.

Wells, H[erbert] G[eorge]. *The Time Machine.* New York: Henry Holt & Co., 1895.

———. *The War of the Worlds.* Mineola, NY: Dover, 1997.

White, Susan. "A Surface Collaboration: Hitchcock and Performance." In *A Companion to Alfred Hitchcock*, ed. in Thomas Leitch and Leland Poague, 181–97. Malden, MA: Wiley-Blackwell, 2011.

Williams, Raymond. *The Country and the City.* Oxford: Oxford University Press, 1973.

Williams, Rowan. *The Edge of Words: God and the Habits of Language.* London: Bloomsbury, 2014.

Williams, Tennessee. *Camino Real.* New York: New Directions, 1953.

Wilson, A. N. "An Archipelago of Parvenus: Class, Aristocracy, Family and Fantasy." *Times Literary Supplement* 6078 (27 September 2019): 19–20.

Wilson, John. "On the Genius and Character of Burns." In Samuel Austin Allibone, *Critical Dictionary of English Literature*, 1: 302. Philadelphia: Lippincott, 1874.

Wittgenstein, Ludwig. *Tractatus Logico-Philosophicus.* Trans. C. K. Ogden. London: Routledge & Kegan Paul, 1922.

Yeats, W[illiam] B[utler]. *The Collected Poems of W. B. Yeats.* Ed. Richard J. Finneran. New York: Collier, 2008.

Žižek, Slavoj. *Enjoy Your Symptom! Jacques Lacan in Hollywood and Out.* London: Routledge, 1992.

———. *Looking Awry: An Introduction to Jacques Lacan through Popular Culture.* Cambridge, MA: MIT Press, 1992.

INDEX

Page numbers in italics denote images.

À bout de souffle [*Breathless*] (Jean-Luc Godard, 1960), 336n17
Abraham and the angels, Biblical story, 85
Adler, Dr. Otto (b. 1929). *See* Gay, Peter
Albee, Edward (1928–2016), 174. *See* "Sandbox"
Albertson, Frank, 20
Aldrich, Robert, 66
Allegory with Venus and Cupid (Bronzino, c. 1545), 158
Aller, Vic, 332n23
Allyson, June, 45
Altick, Richard [Daniel] (1915–2008), 226; and British Museum "South Sea Room," 226; and London Missionary Society, 226; and Museum of East India House, 226
Amann, Betty, 222–23, 241
America: aristocracy in, 57; 1950s, 14, 154, 156; 1960s (and sexuality), 19; small-town consciousness in, 14, 17; American girls in Europe, 158, 166, 217
Amies, [Sir Edwin] Hardy (1909–2003), clothing, 182, 266
Anderson, John, 19
Andrews, Julie, 301
À nous la liberté (René Clair, 1924), 335n10

Aquascutum, Royal Warrant for, 189–90, 195, 196, 215
Arabesque No. 1 in E (c. 1888) (Claude Debussy), 131, 332n23
Arcadia, 159
À rebours [*Against Nature* (Joris-Karl Huysmans)], 307
Arsenic and Old Lace (Frank Capra, 1943), 278
Ashcroft, Peggy, 74
Attlee, Clement [Richard, 1st Earl Attlee] (1883–1967), 156. *See also* Britain
ATV (Associated Television, 1955–81), 77

Bach, Johann Sebastian (1685–1750), 160
Bacon, Francis (1909–1992), 31
Baedeker, Karl [Ludwig Johannes] (1801–1859), 223; Baedeker blitz (*see* Britain, England; Baedeker Guides; Europe)
Baisers volés ([*Stolen Kisses*], François Truffaut, 1968), 172
Baker, Josephine [Joséphine] (1906–1975), 248
Ballets Russes de Monte Carlo, 335n3
Balsam, Martin, 46
Barry, Joan, 227, 335n11
Barton, Rebecca, 327n17
Barton, Sabrina, 42

349

Bataille, Georges [Albert Maurice Victor] (1897–1962), 48, 135. See also *Story of the Eye*
Baudelaire, Charles (1821–1867), 110
Beckett, Samuel [Barclay] (1906–1989), 32
Benjamin, Richard, 329n9
Benjamin, Walter [Bendix Schönflies] (1892–1940), 58, 124
Beyond the Thirty-Nine Steps (Ursula Buchan), 328n1
Bikini Island, 330n3
"Birds, The" (Daphne du Maurier), 117, 131. See also Hitchcock, Alfred, Films
Bogart, Humphrey, 190
Bonham-Carter, Helena, 159
Bonheur, Rosa (1822–1899), 323n3
Boone, Pat[rick] Charles Eugene (b. 1934), 334n12
Borges [Acevedo], Jorge [Francisco Isidoro] Luis (1899–1986), 172
Boswell, James (1740–1795), 78–79
Bottomore, Stephen, looming response, 32
Boucher, François (1703–1770), 314
Boulding, Kenneth, 330n7
Bringing Up Baby (Howard Hawks, 1938), 278
Britain: Act of Westminster, 329n2; aristocracy, 98; Attlee government and nationalization schemes, 156; British Board of Film Censorship (BBFC), 325n1; British Commonwealth, 329n2; British Film Institute (BFI), 325n1; British Ordnance Survey (Ordnance Survey Limited), maps, 73; British Railways, 213; British Union of Fascists, 98; and Canada, 329n2; Colonel Blimp type in, 279; electric hearth in, 190–91; Eton College (since 1440), 157; Festival of Britain (1951), 157, 332n2; Foreign Office, 99, 157; Hampshire, 264; Haslemere (Sussex), 264; Hertfordshire, 71; Home Office, 309, 313; House of Lords, 264; and the hunt, 261, 264, 272, 285, 286, 289, 291, 318, 337n6; image of the British man, 190; language and dialect, 216ff; N[ational] H[ealth] S[ervice], 156; 1950s telephone use in, 154ff, 169–70, 171, 172, 290; Rodmell (Sussex), 264; Southampton (docks), Southease (Sussex), 264, 174; Southeastern Railway, 264; Southern Railway, 261, 264, 265, 287; as temporary society, 151; train system: 260–68, reading in, 259; social class in, 156ff, 182, 184–85; wattle and daub (construction), 329n7; Winchester College (since 1382), 157
England, 69, 70, 71: archetype of the "Londoner," 71, 72; automobiles in, 86 (*see also* Vauxhall); Belgravia, 184; Blackfriars, 233; Cornwall, 338n15; and German bombing campaign, World War II, 117–18, 127 (*see also* Baedeker); and German fascism in the 1930s, 98; Enfield (North London), and ATM, 326n10; Georgian reign, 103; MI6, 99, 100; Gordon Place (Kensington), 233; Gordon Square (Bloomsbury), 233; Hall Road (London), 155; Harrington Gardens (London), 155; Heal's [furniture and design] (since 1810), 157; Hertfordshire, 71; Home counties, 71; Jermyn Street (London), 215, 266; Kensington (London), 233; Kilburn (London), 155; National Gallery (Trafalgar Square, London, since 1824), 158; Peckham

(London), 215; Piccadilly Circus, 77, 86; postwar meat rationing in, 156; public schools (Winchester and Eton Colleges), 157; Regent's Canal (London), 155, 180; Shaftesbury Avenue, 77; St. John's Wood Road (London), 155; St. Paul's Cathedral, 233; Sussex, 71, 261, 287, 338n15; telegraph in, 290; telephone system of the early 1950s, 154, 169–70; Turnbull & Asser (shirtmakers, London, since 1885), 266; War Office, 99; in wartime, 71; Waterloo Station (London), 174, 261, 265, 287; West End, 77; and yearning for Ruskinian adventure, 222ff. *See also* Hitchcock, Alfred, Settings

Scotland, 71, 73: Clyde, River, 329n10; far from London, 86; for the English, 77; Glasgow, 329n10; Jacobite Rebellion, 78, 90; Killin, 73, 91; Loch Tay, 73; opened to tourism, 329n5; Perthshire, 73, 80. *See also* Hitchcock, Alfred, Settings

Wales, 166. *See also* Milland, Ray

Brown, Norman O[liver] (1913–2002), 60, 108

Brownian motion (named for Robert Brown [1773–1858]), 267

Bruce, Nigel, 268

Buchan, John (First Baron [Lord] Tweedsmuir, 1875–1940): 70, 329n6: and Canada, 70; and King George V, 70; and Québec, 70–71; and Scotland, 77

Buckinghamshire, 166. *See also* Williams, John

Bullitt (Peter Yates, 1968), 62

"Burnt Norton" (T. S. Eliot), 326n9

Burr, Raymond, 301

Cage, John [Milton Jr.] (1912–1992), 32

Caillois, Roger, gamblers, 271, 300

Canada, 69, 70. *See also* Buchan, John

Caol Ila (Scottish distillery, since 1846), 215

Carroll, Leo G[ratten], 276

Carroll, Madeleine (1906–1987), 74

Cartwright, Veronica, 119

Casanova, Giacomo Girolamo (1725–1798), 242

Cavell, Stanley [Louis] (1926–2018), 6, 24, 32, 33, 281, 305, 306, 307

Chabrol, Claude [Henri Jean] (1930–2010), 306–7

Chadburn (shipboard communication device), 247

Chanel, [Gabrielle Bonheur] "Coco" (1883–1971), 330n13

Chaplin, Charlie, 93, 231; Tramp, 93

Chapman, James, 328n1

Chapman, Lonnie, 141

Charade (Stanley Donen, 1963), 278

Chinoiserie, early twentieth-century craze for, 335n3

Chion, Michel (b. 1947), *acousmêtre*, 172–73

Christmas Carol, A (Charles Dickens), 335n12

"Circus Animals' Desertion, The" (William Butler Yeats), 121, 330n10

Citizen Kane (Orson Welles, 1941), 336n13

Cline, Ruth Harwood, 325n2

Clunn, Harold [Philip] (1879–1956), 155–56

Coleridge, Samuel Taylor (1772–1834), 11–12

Collins, [William] Wilkie (1824–1889), 210

Conley, Tom, 107

Constable, John (1776–1837), 159

Cook, Capt. James (1728–1779), 229

Cortázar, Julio (1914–1984), 320

Cotten, Joseph, 302

Coutard, Raoul, 336n17

Coventry, 10
Crowd, The (King Vidor, 1928), 335n4, 335n12
Cubism, 281
Cummings, Robert, *154–55*, 155, 166, 178, 199

Dada, 248
Das Testament des Dr. Mabuse [*The Testament of Dr. Mabuse*] (Fritz Lang, 1933), 334n18
Davenport, Guy [Mattison] (1927–2005), 8, 56, 57, 58
David Copperfield (Charles Dickens), 336n13
Dawson, Anthony, 155, 166, 199
Day, Doris, 45
Deacon, Richard, 139
De Botton, Alain (b. 1969), 235–36
Debussy, [Achille] Claude (1862–1918). *See* Arabesque No. 1
Deleuze, Gilles (1925–1995), 31
De Montaigne, Michel [Eyquem] (1533–1592), 66
De Niro, Robert, 333n8
Descartes, René (1596–1650): Cartesianism, 305; Fourth Meditation, 305
Design for Living (Ernst Lubitsch, 1933), 337n9
"Dial M for Murder" (Frederick Knott, BBC Radio, 23 March 1952), 155, 160. *See also* Hitchcock, Alfred, Films
Diary of a Mad Housewife (Frank Perry, 1970), 329n9
Didion, Joan, 149
Dinner at Eight (George Cukor, 1933), 338n20
Donat, Robert, 69, 301
Donath, Ludwig, 120
Downing, Vernon, 281
Doyle, Sir Arthur [Ignatius] Conan (1859–1930), 58

Dream of Hitchcock, A (Murray Pomerance), 6, 338n17
Dr. Mabuse, der Spieler [*Dr. Mabuse the Gambler*] (Fritz Lang, 1922), 171, 337n11
Dr. Strangelove or: How I Learned to Stop Worrying and Love the Bomb (Stanley Kubrick, 1964), 331n20
Du Maurier, [Dame] Daphne [Lady Browning] (1907–1989), 117–18, 330n4
Du Maurier, Gerald, 330n4
Durgnat, Raymond (1932–2002), 45, 54

Edinburgh, 166. *See also* Dawson, Anthony; Britain, Scotland
Edward VII (1841–1910), 189; as Prince of Wales, 241
Edward VIII (1894–1972), as Nazi sympathizer, 98
Eichmann, Adolf, trial in Jerusalem, 330n11
Eksteins, Modris, 334n1
E la nave va . . . [*And the Ship Sails On . . .*] (Federico Fellini, 1983), 336n21
Eliot, T[homas] S[tearns] (1888–1965), 3, 39, 71, 231, 280
Elliott, Denholm, 159
Elliott, Laura [Kasey Rogers], 311
Errand Boy, The (Jerry Lewis, 1961), 335n5, 335n9
Europe: Baedeker Guides to (Northern Italy, 15th ed.; The Riviera, new edn.; Rome and Central Italy, 16th edn.; Southern Italy, 17th edn.), 223; Doyle, Arthur Conan, 223; French Pyrénées, 222ff; German bombing of Britain in World War II, 117; Gothic, 223; "Grand Tour," 227; James, Henry, 223; Northern Italy, hill towns of, 223; Riviera, the, 222ff; Ruskin, John, 222, 223: and Chamonix, 228; and Schaffhausen, 228; Swiss Alps, 222ff; von

Archenholz, Johann Wilhelm, 223; von Goethe, Johann Wolfgang, 223, 227; and Mittelwald, 228; Weimar Germany, 334n1; the voyage to the East, 229ff
Eye for Hitchcock, An (Murray Pomerance), 6, 326n8, 328n24

Fahrenheit 451 (François Truffaut, 1966), 336n13
Feeney, Paul, 170
Fiedler, Leslie A., the Eastern, 217
Fonda, Henry, 301
Fontaine, Joan [Joan de Beauvoir de Havilland], *258–59*, 262
Forms of Talk (Erving Goffman), 187
Forster, E[dward] M[organ] (1879–1970), 159
Fortune magazine, 5
Foucault, [Paul-]Michel (1926–1984), *Narrenschiff*, 237
Four Quartets (T. S. Eliot), 326n9
Frame Analysis: An Essay on the Organization of Experience (Erving Goffman), 257
Freaks (Tod Browning), 147
French New Wave, 172
French Revolution (1789–1799), 170
Friedan, Betty (1921–2006), 163
Furtwängler, Wilhelm (1886–1954), 236
Future Shock (Alvin Toffler), 251, 254

Gabor, Zsa Zsa, 333n10
Gaffney, Rose, farm used for *The Birds*, 332n29
Gainsborough Pictures (Shoreditch), 79
"Garden of Forking Paths, The" ["El jardín de senderos que se bifurcan"] (Jorge Luis Borges), 333n9
Gassmann, Remi, 109
Gavin, John, 22
Gay, Peter [Joachim] (1923–2015), on Dr. Otto Adler and on Freud, 240

George V (1865–1936), 70
Globe Theater (South Bank, London), 69
Goffman, Erving (1922–1982), 187, 240, 300; appearance and manner, 240; on diffidence, 300
Goodman, Paul (1911–1972), 13, 199
Gordon, Gavin, 309
Graham, Martha (1894–1991), 188
Grant, Cary, 157, *258–59*, *258–59*, 262, 271, 273, 277–79, 289, 301, 322, 338n13
Great War, The. *See* World War I
Greece, and the classical age, 23
Green, Hilton, 327n16
Griffies, Ethel, 113
Gulliver's Travels (Jonathan Swift), 3

Hales Tours, 336n2; "phantom rides," 336n2
Hardwicke, [Sir] Cedric [Webster], 278
Hare, Lumsden, 281
Harlow, Jean, 338n20
Harris, Marvin, 321
Harrison, Joan, 283
Hartnell, [Sir] Norman (1901–1979), 182
Hasse, O[tto] E[duard], 120
Head, Edith, 121–22, 331n13, 334n19
Heal's [furniture and design] (since 1810), 157. *See also* Britain, England
Heart of Darkness (Joseph Conrad), 188
Hedren, [Nathalie Kay] "Tippi," 114, 332n23
Heidegger, Martin (1889–1976), *Sein* and *Dasein*, 233
Hermès (Paris, since 1837), 213, *sac à dépêches*, 334n19
Herrmann, Bernard (1911–1975), 50, 67, 328n31
Hesse, Hermann [Karl] (1877–1962), 229, 230
Hidden Dimension, The (Edward T. Hall), 337n7

Hitchcock, Alfred: and actors, 18; Alfred Hitchcock Productions, 332n29; and art, 333n3, 338n13; and the artful domain, 303; as author of dialogue, 128; and bathrooms, 15; and the Blitz, 117–18; cameo, 333n5; casting, 166, 328n26; and casting *The Birds*, 116, 332n24; Catholicism, 33–4; and dogs, 121; as familiar in London, 76; and familiarization and de-familiarization of characters, 28; Lincoln Center Tribute to (1974), 333n4; and location agreements, 332n29; MacGuffin, 76, 87, 309; and moral balance, 33–34; parents, 67, 155; and performance, 168ff, 180; research memo, 330n9; set dressing for, 331n17, 331n18, 332n22; and social class issues, 247, 263, 266, 269–70, 285, 286; and special processes, 330n6; and tea on set, 143; and trains, 74, 78, 104, 261, 268–71, 272, 336n2; and Truffaut, 334n17; in the United States, 117, 263; and Victorianism, 34, 57, 240
- Celebrated scenes: *Birds* aerial shot, 110–14; *Birds* Fawcett farm, 135–39, 142–43; *Birds* jungle gym scene, 129, 134–35; milk scene from *Suspicion*, 317–23; *Psycho* shower scene, 9–16, 23, 24–33, 34–35, 37, 44, 61, 125; *39 Steps* crofter scene, 79–92, 101, 105–6
- Films: *Birds, The* (Universal, 1963), 4, 18, 55, *108–9*, 108–53, shooting commences, 330n11 (*see also* "Birds, The"); *Blackmail* (British International Pictures [BIP], 1929), 73, 153, 237, 238, 335n11; *Dial M for Murder* (Warner Bros., 1954), 4, 108, 153, *154–55*, 154–221, 298, 333n4; 3-D version, 187 (*see also* "Dial M for Murder"); *East of Shanghai*, 254 (see *Rich and Strange*); *Family Plot* (Alfred J. Hitchcock Productions, 1976), 6, 120, 165; *Farmer's Wife, The* (BIP, 1928), 337n6; *Foreign Correspondent* (Walter Wanger Productions, 1940), 80, 335n8f; *Frenzy* (Alfred J. Hitchcock Productions, 1972), 335n6; *I Confess* (Warner Bros., 1953), 6, 47, 120, 153, 328n24; *Lady Vanishes, The* (Gainsborough, 1938), 5, 93, 153; *Lifeboat* (Twentieth Century Fox, 1944), 153; *Lodger: A Story of the London Fog, The* (Gainsborough, 1927), 81, 153, 301; *Man Who Knew Too Much, The* (Gaumont British, 1934), 76; *Man Who Knew Too Much* (Paramount, 1956), 5, 76, 77, 96, 118, 120, 153, 305, 325nIntro1, 332n28, 335n9, 336n19, 338n16; *Marnie* (Alfred J. Hitchcock Productions, 1964), 6, 55, 57, 141, 153, 268, 301, 331n21, 337n6; *North by Northwest* (MGM, 1959), 6, 55, 74, 108, 118, 157, 241, 278; *Notorious* (RKO, 1946), 120, 153, 338n19; *Number 13* (Gainsborough, 1922), 79; *Paradine Case, The* (Selznick International, 1947), 301; *Psycho* (Shamley, 1960), 4, 5, *8–9*, 8–67, 120, 125, 153, 308, 325n1, 326n13, 327n17, 327n21, exhibition contract for and screening of, 9, 45, 327n21, 327n22; *Rear Window* (Paramount, 1954), 6, 139, 157, 158, 301; *Rebecca* (Selznick International, 1940), 6, 40, 57, 153, 265 (*see also* "Rebecca"); *Rich and Strange* (BIP, 1931), 4, *222–23*, 222–57; *Rope* (Warner Bros., 1948), 118, 153, 258; *Sabotage* (Gaumont British, 1936), 153; *Saboteur* (Frank Lloyd Productions, 1942), 6, 81, 153, 308; *Secret Agent* (Gaumont British, 1936), 153; *Shadow of a Doubt* (Universal, 1943), 153, 272,

302; *Skin Game, The* (BIP, 1931), 153; *Spellbound* (Selznick International, 1945), 6, 82, 118, 153, as Freudian epic, 241; *Stage Fright* (Warner Bros., 1950), 120, 153; *Strangers on a Train* (Warner Bros., 1951), 6, 153, 219, 272, 311; *Suspicion* (RKO, 1941), 4, 118, 153, 258–59, 258–323; *39 Steps, The* (Gaumont British, 1935), 4, 68–69, 68–107, 118, 301, 331n16; Puritanism in, 92; shooting dates, 98; *To Catch a Thief* (Paramount, 1955), 6, 75, 153, 157, 164, 301, 334n19; *Torn Curtain* (Alfred J. Hitchcock Productions, 1966), 4, 6, 55, 73, 80, 82, 98, 118, 120, 153, 301; *Trouble with Harry, The* (Paramount, 1955), 5, 153; *Vertigo* (Paramount, 1958), 6, 18, 55, 57, 58, 136, 143, 153, 165, 308, 328n25, 336n20; *Wrong Man, The* (Warner Bros., 1956), 153, 301, 302, 336n16

- Settings:

Africa: Port Said, 241, 246, 250; Suez Canal, 241

America: the "Bates Motel," 12, 14, 17, 18, 20, 35, 44, 45, 46, 48; Bodega Bay (California), 113ff, 120, 122, 123, 124, 125, 127, 128, 130, 139ff, 146–52, 331n17; Chicago, 74; Lombard Street (San Francisco), 308; Millerton (California), 123; New York, 185, 195, 301; Nob Hill (San Francisco), 123; Olema (California), 123; Phoenix, Arizona, 19, 22, 24; San Francisco, 124, 149; San Francisco Bay, 18; Union Square (San Francisco), 139

Asia: Ceylon [Sri Lanka], 241; Rangoon, 244; Shanghai, 254; Singapore, 241, 244, 249, 250, 253

England: Argyll Street (London), 76; Bank of England, 80; British Foreign Office (London), 99; British Museum, 11, 68, 140, 226; Brixton, 179, 213, 215, 216, 220; Cambridge University, 162, 180, 181, 182, 198, 218, 220; Camden Town, 180, 289; Chelsea, 184, 214; as famous island, 257; Harrington Gardens (London), 155; Ledbury Street (London), 195, 215, 216; Leytonstone, 67; London, 176, 177, 195; London Palladium (Argyll Street), 75, 76, 77, 93, 99; London Stock Exchange, 80; Maida Vale, 154, 155, 180, 184, 191; Marylebone Road, 155; the Old Bailey, 189; Oxford University, 157, 181; Piccadilly Circus, 77; Regent's Canal, 180; Royal Albert Hall (South Kensington), 76; Shaftesbury Avenue, 77; Victoria Station, 179, 213, 216, 220; West End, 77; (The Championships, tennis, since 1877), 158, 182, 203, 214, 218, 158, 182, 203, 214, 218; Yorkshire, 296

Scotland: Argyle Street (Glasgow), 81, 87, 89, 92; Edinburgh, 74; for the English, 78–79; Fifeshire, 70; Firth of Forth, 70; Forth Railway Bridge (Edinburgh), 70, 74, 78, 79, 80, 81, 1000; Glasgow, 81, 87, 88; Grampian Hills, 79, 80; the Highlands, 79; Jacobite Rebellion, 78, 90; Killin, 73, 91; Loch Tay, 73; the Lowlands, 79; Perth, 70; Perthshire, 70, 73, 80; poverty in, 90; Royal Scotsman (train), 74, 78, 104; Sauchiehall Street (Glasgow), 81, 87, 92

Europe: France, 296; Holland, 80; Marseilles, 249; Mediterranean Sea, 238, 241; Newhaven (Nyhavn) (Copenhagen), 80;

Hitchcock: Setting: Europe *(cont'd)* Paris: Folies Bergère (Rue Richer), 234–35, 236, 248; Moulin Rouge (Boulevard de Clichy), 23, 236, 248, 253
Hitchcock, Patricia, 21
Holiday (George Cukor, 1938), 278
Holiday Inn, 17
"Hollow Men, The" (T. S. Eliot), 110, 330n2
Hollywood: culture as basis for films about Britain, 260; sound technology in the 1930s, 32, 222; stars, 9, 45; Studios: Columbia Pictures, 332n23; Universal Studios, 113; Walt Disney Studio, 113, 330n6; Warner Bros., 333n3
Hotel Berlin (Peter Godfrey, 1945), 66
Hound of the Baskervilles, The (Gareth Gundrey, 1931), 79
Howard Johnson's, 17
Hurricane, The (John Ford, 1937), 108
Husted, Christopher, 328n31

Illustrated London News, The (from 1842), 265, 288, 289. See also Britain, London
Instagram, 192
Isbell, Marion [William] (1905–1988), 17
Istanbul (Turkey), 112
It Happened One Night (Frank Capra, 1934), 123

Jacobs, Steven, 166–67
Jaeger-LeCoultre self-winding watch (1953–56), 165
Jeans, Isabel, 276, 337n8
James, Henry (1843–1916), 144, 179
Jay, Martin, 135
Jell-O (Kraft Foods), 327n23
Johnson, Samuel [Dr] (1709–1784), 78–79
Journey to the East. See *Morgenlandfahrt*

Kaplan, Abraham (1918–1993), 6

Keats, John (1795–1821), "Ode on a Grecian Urn," 116
Kedrova, Lila, 82
Kelly, Grace, *154–55*, 155, 156, 164, 166, 178, 192, 199, 333n7, 333n10, 334n19; Kelly bag (*see* Hermès)
Kendall, Henry, 227, 252
Karmann Ghia, 308
Kidnapped (Robert Louis Stevenson), 90
King, William Lyon Mackenzie (1874–1950), 70
King Kong (Merian C. Cooper and Ernest B. Schoedsack, 1933), 244
Kingman, Don, 332n22
King of Comedy, The (Martin Scorsese, 1982), 333n8
Kiss Me Deadly (Robert Aldrich, 1955), 66
Knockando (mills, since 1784), 266
Knott, Frederick [Major Paull] (1916–2002), 155, 160
Knowles, Bernard, 79
Kolker, Henry, 278
Kracauer, Siegfried (1889–1966), 256
Krohn, Bill, 6, 164, 326n13, 333n6, 333n7, 338n14
Kwaidan (Lafcadio Hearn), 335n3

La Dolce Vita (Federico Fellini, 1960), 122
Landau, Martin, 301
Lang, Doreen, 114
Lang, [Friedrich Christian Anton] "Fritz," 171
Laphroaig (Scottish distillery, since 1815), 215
Last and First Men: A Story of the Near and Far Future (Olaf Stapledon), 330n7
Latham, Louise, 301
Laurel, Stan, 231
Laurie, John, 74
Leave Her to Heaven (John M. Stahl, 1945), 325n4

Le Carré, John [David (John Moore) Cornwell] (1931–2020), 115
Le Corbusier [Charles-Édouard Jeanneret] (1887–1965), 334n13
Lee, Auriol, 292
Leigh, Janet, 9, 18, 22, 23, 45, 326n13
Lem, Stanislaw [Herman] (1921–2006), 16
Le Sentier, Switzerland, 165
Les fleurs du mal (Charles Baudelaire), "L'invitation au voyage," 330n1
Les Orientales (Michel Fokine), 335n3
Lessing, Doris [May] (1919–2013), 149
Le Trou ([The Hole], Jacques Becker, 1960), 172
Letters from Italy (Johann Wolfgang Von Goethe), 227–28. See also Europe
Levi Strauss & Co. (San Francisco, since 1853), 192
Liberty of London, 76–77
Lifar, Serge, 154
Life magazine, 139
"Little Gidding" (T. S. Eliot), 71
Lloyd, John, 328n1
Lock, Max (1908–1988), 118
Long, John, 336n14
Lorre, Peter, 66
Los Angeles Times (in *Psycho*), 40
Lost Weekend, The (Billy Wilder, 1945), 166
"Love Letters in the Sand" (J. Fred Coots, Nick Kenny, Charles Kenny), 334n12
Luftwaffe, 127
Luria, A[lexander] R[omanovich] (1902–1977), 68

Mannheim, Lucie, 73
Mantell, Joe, 112
Marmont, Percy, 233
Mason, James, 301
Mastroianni, Marcello, 122. See also *La Dolce Vita*
Max Hunter Folk Song Collection (Missouri State University), 332n25

McCarthy, Mary (1912–1989), 149
McDevitt, Ruth, 130
McDonald's, 17
McElroy Octagon House (San Francisco), 332n30
McGilligan, Patrick, 336n2
McGovern, John, 140, 150
McIntire, John, 50
McQueen, Steve, 62
McWilliams, Carey (1905–1980), 49, "island on the land," 332n31
Metcalf, Nondas, 309
Miles, Vera, 46
Milland, Ray, *154–55*, 155, 166, 189–90, 199, 208
Mills, Mort, 19
Miró [I Ferrà], Juan (1893–1983), 281
Missouri, 166. See also Cummings, Robert
Modern Times (Charles Chaplin, 1936), 335n10
Modleski, Tania, 45, 260
Moment of Action (Murray Pomerance), 326n7
Monroe, Marilyn, 45
Montreal, 69, 95
Morgenlandfahrt, Die ([Journey to the East], Hermann Hesse), 229
Mosley, [Sir] Oswald [Ernald, 6th Baronet] (1896–1980), 98
Mourlet, Michel (b. 1935), 257
Mowbray, Alan, 77, 328n26, 338n16
My Dinner with Andre (Louis Malle, 1981), 334n20

Narcissistic personality, 184
"Nearer, My God, to Thee" (Sarah Flower Adams), 244
New Jersey, 17
Newman, Paul, 301
New Yorker, The, 127
Night and the City (Jules Dassin, 1950), 193
Nightingale, Florence (1820–1910), 95

358   INDEX

Noli Me Tangere (Titian, c. 1525), 158
None But the Lonely Heart (Clifford Odets, 1944), 278

Oakland, Simon (1915–1983), 8–9, 62, 66
"Ode on a Grecian Urn" (John Keats), 116
Oldenburg, Claes, 154
Ondra, Anny, 237, 335n11
One Day in the Life of Ivan Denisovich (Alexander Solzhenitsyn), 110
Ortega y Gasset, José (1883–1955), *coup d'oeil*, 267–68; and "reality," 21
Our Mother's House (Jack Clayton, 1967), 328n29
Ouvriers sortant de l'usine [Workers Leaving a Factory] (Louis Lumière, 1895), 335n7

Page, Anita, 147
Panter-Downes, [Mary Patricia] "Mollie" (1906–1997), 127
Paris: Eiffel Tower (Paris), 79; Folies Bergère (Rue Richer), 234–35, 236, 248 (*see also* Hitchcock, Alfred, Settings); Garnier, [Jean-Louis] Charles (1825–1898), 236; Moulin Rouge, music hall, 235, 236, 248, 253 (*see also* Hitchcock, Alfred, Settings); Opera (Opéra de Paris), 236; Rue du Faubourg Saint-Honoré (Paris), 182; Sacre Coeur, 235; sewer system, 172
Parnell, Val, 77, 338n16
Parsons, Talcott (1902–1979), 56
Passenger, The [Professione: Reporter] (Michelangelo Antonioni, 1975), 334n15
Peeping Tom, 10
Peeping Tom (Michael Powell, 1960), 325n1
Pensent-ils au raisin? (François Boucher), 336n18

Pepys, Samuel, 326n8
Perceval, le Conte du Graal (Chrétien de Troyes), land of the Fisher King, 10
Perkins, Anthony, 15
Perkins, V[ictor] F[rancis] (1936–2016), 5
Perret, Nellie, 330n5
Peter Pan. See "Peter Pan"
"Peter Pan, or The Boy Who Wouldn't Grow Up" (James. M. Barrie, Duke of York's Theatre, London, 25 December 1904), 233, 330n4
Philadelphia, 166. *See also* Kelly, Grace
Picasso, Pablo [Ruiz] (1881–1973), 281
Play Time (Jacques Tati, 1968), 335n4
Pleshette, Suzanne, 117, 125
Poe, Edgar Allan (1809–1849), 56, 57
Poissons d'or (Claude Debussy), 335n3
Polo, Marco (1254–1324), in Cormorin, 224; discussed by Edward Said, 225; and Kingdom of Motupalli, 224–25; and Khubilai Khan, 224; about Socotra, 224
Pomerance, Ariel, 338n18
Pound, Ezra, Canto CVI, 330n5
Presentation of Self in Everyday Life, The (Erving Goffman), 240
Pride and Prejudice (Jane Austen), 262
Procession of the Trojan Horse into Troy (Giovanni Domenico Tiepolo, c. 1760), 158
Procter & Gamble, Spic and Span, 326n8
Prometheus complex (Gaston Bachelard), 112
Psycho (Gus Van Sant, 1998), 326n11

Ramada Inns, 17
Randolph, Elsie, 241
Raphaelson, Samson, 283
Rashomon (Akira Kurosawa, 1950), 202
"Rebecca" (Queen's Theatre, London, April 5, 1940), 117
Rebello, Stephen, 15–16

Renaissance, the, 287
Return of the Vanishing American, The (Leslie Fiedler), racism and anthropology, 245, 250
Reville, Alma, 283
Reynolds, Debbie, 45
Richardson, Mahalath, 149
Rilke, Rainer [René Karl Wilhelm Johann Josef] Maria (1875–1926), 323, 328n28, 338n21
"Risselty Rosselty" (building rhyme), 133–34, 332n25. See also Hitchcock, Alfred, Films, *Birds, The*
Robertson, Peggy, 330n6, 330n9
Rohmer, Éric [Jean Marie Maurice Schérer] (1920–2010), 306–7
Rolls-Royce, 203, 205
Room with a View, A (E. M. Forster), 159
Room with a View, A (James Ivory, 1985), 159
Rothman, William, 6, 328n30, 331n19
Royal Variety Performance, 77
Ruskin, John (1819–1900). See Europe
Russell, John L. (1905–1967), 15

Said, Edward [Wadie] (1935–2003), 225, 226. See also Polo, Marco
"Sandbox, The" (Edward Albee, 15 April 1960, Jazz Gallery, New York), 174
Sala, Oskar, 109
Salvation Army, 75
Sands, Julian, 159
Santa Cruz Island (California), 113
Sante, Luc (b. 1954), 235
Sartre, Jean-Paul [Charles Aymard] (1905–1980), 8–9, 258, 304–5
Schafer, R. Murray, 31
Schantz, Ned, 334n11
Shéhérazade (Maurice Ravel), 335n3
Schivelbusch, Wolfgang: new technologies, 191; panoramic perception, 267–68, 337n10; train voyages, 269; travel reading, 259, 337n11; upholstery, 157, 267

Schmidt, Benjamin, and misogyny, 226–27
Schramm, Eric, 326n13
Schreiner, Olive, 34
Scrabble (since 1938), 277, 294–95, 297, 313, 317
"Second Coming, The" (William Butler Yeats), 119, 148
Séraphita (Honoré de Balzac), artistry, 286–87
Shakespeare, William (1564–1616), 230, 239: *Hamlet* (c. 1601), 16, 85, 121, 148; *King Lear* (1606), 32; *Macbeth* (1606), 14–15, 123, 331n15; *Merchant of Venice, The* (1596–1599), 258; *Tempest, The* (1611), 91, 152, 222, 230, 234, 239
Sheraton Hotels, 17
Sidewalks of New York (Zion Myers, Jules White, 1931), 147
Silence from Hitchcock, A (Murray Pomerance), 7
Simon, Paul, 24
Simmel, Georg (1858–1918), 84
Slaughterhouse-Five, or The Children's Crusade: A Duty-Dance with Death (Kurt Vonnegut, Jr.), 325n5
Smith, [Dame] Maggie, 159
Snodgress, Carrie, 329n9
Spoto, Donald, 15, 261, 336n2
Starobinski, Jean (1920–2019), 199
Stewart, Jimmy, 336n19
Still Life with Onions (Guy Davenport), 56, 58
Story of the Eye (Georges Bataille), 48, 135
Studies in Classic American Literature (D. H. Lawrence), 255
"Summer Night on the River" (Frederick Delius), 308
surrealism, 135, 248
Susannah and the Elders, 36
Swift, Jonathan (1667–1745), 3
Switzerland, 165, 182, 228

360 INDEX

Symphony No. 3 Op. 55 ("Eroica") (Ludwig van Beethoven), 60

Taine, Hippolyte [Adolphe] (1828–1893), 337n11
Tandy, Jessica, 119
Taylor, Elizabeth, 45
Taylor, Rod, 119
Taylor, Vaughn, 20
T[urner] C[lassic] M[ovies], 326n14
Tearle, Godfrey, 74
Third Reich, 118
Thirty-Nine Steps, The (John Buchan), 70, 97, 329n3
Tierney, Gene, 325n4
Time Machine, The (H. G. Wells), Eloi and Morlocks, 249
Touch of Evil (Orson Welles, 1958), 326n13
Toulouse-Lautrec[-Monfa], [Henri Marie Raymond] (1864–1901), 248
Travels (Marco Polo), 223–24. *See also* Polo, Marco
Treherne, Peter, 325n3
Trevi fountain (Rome), 122, 124
Trouville (France), 112
Truffaut, François (1932–1984), 80, 164, and Hitchcock, 334n17
Turandot (Giacomo Puccini [compl. Franco Alfano], 335n3
Tuttle, Lurene, 50

Un homme et une femme [A Man and a Woman] (Claude Lelouch, 1966), 334n13
"Up at a Villa--Down in the City" (Robert Browning), 72, 259
U. S. Food and Drug Administration, 326n12
U. S. State Department, 99

Valli, Alida [Baroness Alida Maria Laura Altenburger von Marckenstein-Frauenberg], 301

Vancouver, 69
Van Gogh, Vincent [Willem] (1853–1890), 56, 179
Vauxhall Motors Limited, 86
Veblen, Thorstein [Bunde] (1857–1929), 57
Victoria Regina, 78: and Balmoral castle, 78; post-Victorian sentiment, 79, 241; and Scotland, 78–79; Victorian age, 34, 49, 57, 78, 240
Vogue magazine, 139
Von Archenholz, Johann Wilhelm (1741–1812). *See* Europe
Von Goethe, Johann [Wolfgang] (1749–1832). *See* Europe
Von Humboldt, [Friedrich Wilhelm Heinrich] Alexander (1769–1859), 139

Wagner, [Wilhelm] Richard (1813–1883), 11, 236
Walsingham, Victoria, 333n10
War of the Worlds (H. G. Wells), 118
"Waste Lane, The" (T. E. Eliot), 329n8
Watson, Wylie, 68
Watteau, Jean-Antoine (1684–1721), 131
Wattis, Richard, 328n26
Weaver, [Winston Sheffield Glenndenning Dixon] "Doodles," 140
Weis, Elisabeth, 31, 135
Well-Tempered Clavier, The (J. S. Bach), 160
West Side Story (Robert Wise and Norman Jewison, 1961), 62
What Maisie Knew (Henry James), 144, 179, 332n27
White, Susan, 265
Whitlock, Albert (1915–1999), 113
Whitty, Dame [Dame Mary Louise Webster] May, 281
Wilde, Cornel, 325n4
Williams, John, 164, 166, 199, 21
Williams, Raymond, 260

Williams, Rowan, 24–5
Wilson, A[ndrew] N[orman] (b. 1950), 217
Wilson, [Charles] Kemmons (1913–2003), 17
Wilson, Elizabeth, 114
Wilson, John, 329n4
Winnipeg, 69, 95
Wittgenstein, Ludwig [Josef Johann] (1889–1951), 118–19

Woman of the Year (George Stevens, 1942), 123
World Viewed, The (Stanley Cavell), 32
World War I, 189, 222, 286
World War II, 70, 189, 264, 290: and Canada, 70; Hitler, 93
Wright, [Muriel] Teresa, 302

Žižek, Slavoj, 130, 135

www.ingramcontent.com/pod-product-compliance
Lightning Source LLC
Chambersburg PA
CBHW030126240426
43672CB00005B/41